D0810253

THE
WILHELMS'
GUIDE TO
ALL MEXICO

Books by the Author

GUIDE TO ALL MEXICO
Fifth Edition

GUIDE TO MEXICO CITY
Seventeenth Edition

GUIDE TO THE CARIBBEAN

THE WILHELMS' GUIDE TO ALL MEXICO

FIFTH EDITION, REVISED AND ENLARGED

by John, Lawrence, and
Charles Wilhelm

McGRAW-HILL BOOK COMPANY

New York   Toronto   London   Sydney

FIFTH EDITION

2 3 4 5 6 7 8 9 0 B P B P 7 8 3 2 1 0 9

Library of Congress Cataloging in Publication Data

Wilhelm, John.
The Wilhelms' Guide to all Mexico.
Fourth ed. published in 1973 under title: Guide to Mexico.
Includes index.
1. Mexico—Description and travel—1951-   —Guide-books. I. Title.
II. Title: Guide to all Mexico.
F1209.W74   1978   917.2'04'82   78-7815
ISBN 0-07-070289-6

To Mother
who was a good traveler

Preface

As a foreign correspondent, I lived in Mexico for six years while gathering material for this book and traveled every highway and visited every major city and resort, and a plethora of small villages, personally. For subsequent editions my family and I have retraced all of these routes, and have completed visits from Baja California to Cancún, and from Laredo to Tuxtla Gutiérrez near the Guatemalan border.

This edition marks the participation in a major way of my two grown sons, Lawrence and Charles, who—in a house van called, appropriately, "El Orb"—traveled much of Mexico doing research and writing for this edition. Particularly, the enlarged new section on Baja California could only have been achieved by this mode of travel, and the results are a greatly expanded account of the new roads and many new hotels and resorts in this fabulous part of Mexico. Lawrence and Charles also traveled and reported on the entire west coast of Mexico. Laurie Hall was business manager for this research trip.

My wife, Margaret, traveled with me throughout the balance of the Republic for this edition, and her patience, and note-taking, were of immeasurable help. Our son Richard, now in the hotel business, and our daughter, Martha, helped on other occasions. So it is a family project.

Friends in Mexico are of assistance, and I particularly must mention Harry and Ruth Wright, who not only gave freely of their own vast fund of knowledge about Mexico, but continued to send us update material while the book was in preparation. Sally and Bob Benjamin are other sources of authentic information. Both couples know Mexico as only those who spend a lifetime there can.

In Acapulco the expertise of Gayle Dorantes, editor of the Acapulco section of *The Mexico City News*, was a great help, while Sully and Nancy Sullivan in Taxco provided invaluable assistance. Marcy Stanley also assisted.

In the chapter on traveling by car in Mexico—and this now includes a 10,000-mile trip we made down the west coast of Mexico over to Yucatán, and up the Gulf coast by Winnebago motor home—we were guided by that knight of the road, Dan Sanborn, who supplies mile-by-mile road guides from his McAllen, Texas, office.

On the west coast, from Guadalajara through Mazatlán, many people made contributions, including Gerry and Ann Maulsby, Jim and Gerda Kelly, and Mrs. Lawrence Williams.

In central Mexico, Riva and Leonard Brooks, famous for her photographic work and his internationally acclaimed watercolors, were of invaluable help. Mrs. Roy B. Dean and Mrs. David Donavan, true authorities, wrote detailed letters bringing up to date numerous statements in my earlier editions, and I am most grateful.

The newspaper people who aided me included Pepe Romero, Jaime and Virginia Plenn, and Joe Nash, all of *The Mexico City News*.

The staff of Fonatur, the tourist development organization in Mexico—especially Lic. Guillermo Grimm, marketing manager—were most helpful in getting to new developments such as Ixtapa and Cancún and advising of future plans.

To all of these people I am most grateful, and I hope you will be, too, as you use this book to travel about Mexico.

J.R.W.

Contents

MAPS

RACING?
TIJUANA
(SEE CHAP. 8)

FISHING?

San Diego

Tijuana · Mexicali
Yuma

Tucson

Ensañada

GUAYMAS
(SEE CHAP. 14)

El Paso

San Felipe

Nogales

San Quintín

El Rosario

Hermosillo

Chihuahua

Guaymas

Scammons Lagoon
Guerrero Negro · Santa Rosalia
Mulege

FISHING?

Los Mochis

Parral

Torr

Loreto

Topolo Bampo

LA PAZ
(SEE CHAP. 8)

La Paz · FERRY

Durango

CARNIVAL?

Cabo San Lucas

Mazatlán

MAZATLAN
(SEE CHAP. 14)

FERRY

Tepic

San Blas

Puerto Vallarta

Tep

QUIET BEACH?

Manzanillo

Ixtap Zihuatan

MANZANILLO
(SEE CHAP. 15)

PUERTO VALLARTA
(SEE CHAP. 21)

IXTAPA
(SEE CHAP. 13)

MEXICO

0   MILES   400

a. arias

PLAYPORT?

ACAPULCO
(SEE CHAP. 7)

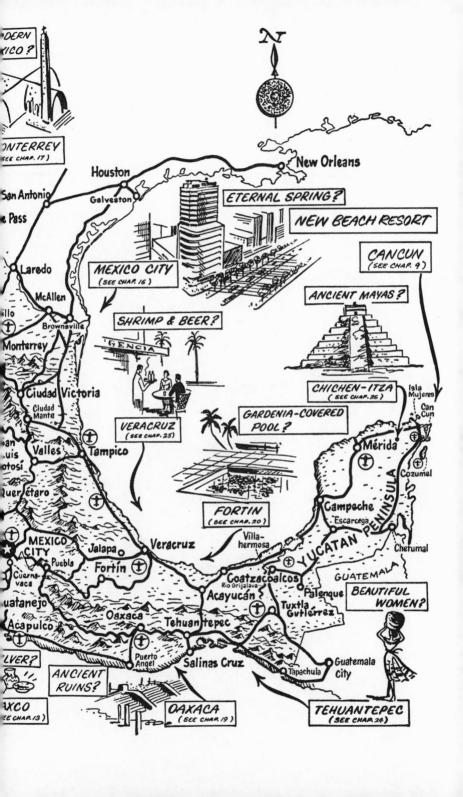

_____PART **1**

*GETTING
READY TO GO*

Making the Most of Your Mexican Trip

My first real view of Mexico came on an automobile trip down the old Pan-American Highway from Laredo through the flat plains and then the dramatic mountains, a thrilling, twisting, and winding roadway, often above clouds. Nothing closer to flying could be imagined as the car seemed to swoop and swerve around the heavily banked turns.

This route, now known as the Valles road, is still open, and for my taste is still the best way to drive to Mexico—at least one way. Today there is an alternate superhighway through Saltillo and San Luis Potosí, but it is dull compared with the exciting Valles route through tropics with banana trees and bright purple and orange flowering vines, then up into the panoramic mountains.

It is interesting to remember that as recently as 1937 you couldn't drive from the United States to Mexico City at all!

A friend of mine, Bob Benjamin, then a Rutgers student, and a friend of his drove to the end of the road in 1937 and found an American drifter, Sam Browne, had set up a small cantina and had a few hammocks to rent for overnight stays. He let the two boys live there, in return for which they painted a sign giving the distance to various points, as well as advertising his cantina and hammocks.

Years later Bob and I were driving between Tamazunchale and Chapulhuacán and we stopped to inquire if Sam Browne were still about. The local people said that he had passed away, but that his widow was still there. We found her, and out back, behind her house, was the big sign, still legible, which read,

SAM BROWNE'S CANTINA
DRINKS, ROOMS WITH HAMMOCKS

YOU CAN SEE some of the world's most dramatic scenery in Mexico—towering snow-covered volcanoes, exotic tropical flowers and green jungles, as well as ancient stone cities of pre-Hispanic times.

You can dance to soft music on cliffside balconies in Acapulco, with the palms swaying in the background and the waves roaring below. In other nightclubs there is hot tropical music, and sunbathing and surfing at the beaches.

You can visit the fine continental restaurants, with excellent French cuisine, in Mexico City, and you can shop for sterling silver, as modern as Georg Jensen, or for the lovely blue-green bubble glass blown in the local factories. And find the world's greatest bargains!

All of this will help to make you realize you can have a good time in Mexico. Hardly on $5 a day, but it is still among the least expensive of the major travel areas. We do not recommend places where you may be risking your good disposition and your health.

Upon stepping from your aircraft or car, you suddenly realize you are in a foreign country. On all sides Spanish is being spoken. But you couldn't be in a more delightful place.

This is the Mexico of towering volcanoes, palms and orchids, and very charming people. It is a land where the conquistador, Hernando Cortés, and his few men clambered up the Sierra Madre Oriental Mountains from Veracruz in 1519 and found a miraculous city of several hundred thousand Aztecs living in splendor. Here the Mexican capital is located today.

More than all this, when I think of Mexico, there come to mind the pre-Columbian Mayans, building their handsome stone temples deep in the jungles, the sweating naked bodies of copper-toned slaves erecting huge pyramids, rivaling those of Egypt, at Teotihuacán outside Mexico City, and the mystic Zapotecs, who sealed up their dead priests with fabulous jewels at Monte Albán.

I see Maximilian and Carlota stepping from their ship at Veracruz en route to become Emperor and Empress of Mexico at the behest of Napoleon III. Beautiful, fragile Carlota, who was to end her days in a madhouse; handsome, idealistic, but weak Maximilian, who was to die before a firing squad in Querétaro on June 19, 1867.

There comes to mind the great palace in Chapultepec Park, from where Carlota's bedroom windows opened to the balcony and a view of the city, from which she saw Maximilian's carriage below passing down what is now the Paseo de la Reforma en route to the National Palace.

Up the steep sides of the same castlelike Chapultepec stormed American troops in 1847, while Mexican boy heroes from the nearby military academy fought to their death in resistance. Some twenty years later, the ragged troops of Benito Juárez fought over the same ground, driving out the French-supported Emperor. This is rich history indeed.

This is a land with tales of violent revolutions, one of which rocked the country as recently as 1910. But the country rid itself of an iron-fisted dictator in the process, and slowly, by the 1930s, peace returned, and with it came stable government.

Mexico is a land of great artists—probably some of the greatest the world has ever known. Three twentieth-century masters created murals of a force and dimension rarely equaled—strong, massive paintings of overpowering violence. The lash of whips upon peons, the harsh priests of the colonial church, revulsion against war and death, the desperate struggle of the downtrodden against their oppressors—these were the themes of Mexican muralists, and their works can be seen today.

Diego Rivera was the best known of the trio. His murals, taken from Rockefeller Center to be re-created in the Palace of Fine Arts (the Bellas Artes) in Mexico City, had the intensity of his time. However, he was probably better in his whimsical, often pointedly sharp paintings of Mexican history in allegory, showing children in the park or peons carrying baskets of white calla lilies.

José Clemente Orozco, bitter, intense, despising his fellowmen, was in some respects the greater muralist. He did monumentally huge murals against war and destruction, also displayed in the Bellas Artes, and it was he who brushed onto canvas the rebellious spirit of the downtrodden peon.

David Siqueiros, labor leader as well as muralist, was the third of the trio. Though his paintings are not as highly regarded as those of Rivera and Orozco, his influence nevertheless has been strong, and his works are presented in the Siqueiros Polyforum Museum adjoining the Hotel Mexico in Mexico City.

Another great Mexican artist is Juan O'Gorman, who decorated all four sides of the twelve-story library building on the ultramodern University of Mexico campus with one of the handsomest natural-stone mosaics the world has ever seen.

And a more sophisticated trend in Mexican art is now being led by Rufino Tamayo, who employs delicate colors in obscure patterns.

Speaking of the University of Mexico, with some 200,000 students, brings up modern Mexico itself, with its supermarkets, its handsome, broad boulevards often lined with miles of flowers all year round, its superb new subway, and its towering glass skyscrapers which are architecturally admired throughout the world.

But be not misled by this modern veneer. There is a saying that *"afuera de México, todo es Ixmiquilpán"* ("outside of Mexico City, all is a small village"). This may be interpreted to mean that beneath the modernity—a kind of modernity as peculiar to Mexico as its history—there is a deep charm among the people that modern ways will not change.

It is still a country of women patting corn flour into tortillas, of hot chili pepper and fiery tequila; but more than this, it is a country of charming old customs whose history is lost in antiquity.

It is the country of famed Lake Pátzcuaro, where the Tarascans still observe a belief that a bride must be stolen, and where it is the custom to hold an all-night picnic by the dead once a year, and where fish are caught in picturesque butterfly nets.

It is the country of Mitla, where a professional go-between not only arranges marriages but also has a lifelong obligation to pacify both mothers-in-law. It is the country of the best-behaved babies in the world—tiny things with huge black eyes who patiently recline in shoulder-hung rebozos while their mothers go about the day's work.

Mexico today is also a country of many huge dams, some superhighways, and a score of metropolises which have power, lights, and schools for all. Much has been accomplished, but there is still much to do—and you will see Mexico in transition. Both the old and the new are there.

But the modernization of Mexico has not in the least diluted its colorful national character and culture. These are as strong, as vibrant, and as awe-inspiring as the day Cortés landed. We hope this book will help you to appreciate these facets as well as the tourist sights.

This and more is Mexico!

2

Introduction to Mexico

When we first came to Mexico to live, friends suggested we look for a home in the old cobblestoned village of San Angel.

The little town, now a suburb of Mexico City and not far from the University of Mexico campus, was a charming place with tall ahuehuete and eucalyptus trees towering over low Spanish-style homes set behind gates dripping in purple bougainvillea.

A colony of artists and writers had made it a favored residential area, and one of them was Diego Rivera, who built an unusual modern studio there. He often lived there while he was working, and at other times with his wife, Freda Kahlo, in Coyoacán. We often saw him in the neighborhood. Another neighbor, who still lives there, was the distinguished artist Juan O'Gorman.

The house we rented was also modern in style, having been recently built by a well-known Mexican doctor, Dr. Luis Sánchez Renero. Behind its walls, our children got to know the fascinating games and parties Mexican children enjoy. Often a piñata, a gaily decorated papier-mâché animal almost life-size, would be hung from our balcony, while blindfolded birthday guests would swing wildly and eventually crack it open, disgorging its contents of candy and party favors to a wild scramble below.

We learned the Mexican customs there. My wife went to the open market at Plaza del Carmen for our daily purchase of frijoles, papaya, or jitomates, and to the panadería for oven-fresh rolls. On gala nights we would invite friends in for a Noche Mexicana, often with fireworks in the form of a torito, and every night we would hear the whistle of the sereno as he patrolled the block.

We often recall those pleasant days in San Angel.

MEXICO, as our immediate southern neighbor, is close to the United States physically, but in history, customs, language, scenery, people, and way of life, it is as foreign to us as if it were half a world away.

Mexico is now a nation with a large number of professional people such as engineers, doctors, scientists, and businessmen as well as artists, writers, advertising experts, communication specialists, and leaders of industry. Many Mexican executives are more highly paid than their U.S. counterparts.

Aside from some professional beggars, extreme poverty is not visible on the streets anymore. The extensive Mexican Social Security system, as evidenced by the handsome clinics and hospitals throughout the country, is taking adequate care of a good part of the population.

Politically, Mexico has its differences with its neighbor to the north, and sensitive issues should be discussed with moderation. Mexico has become a leader in Latin America and in many international meetings, and at times has been a spokesman for the Third World. But the United States remains its major trading partner and Mexico's greatest dollar-producing industry is its tourist business, so leaders of both nations have worked to temper difficult issues.

Mexico has over 70 million inhabitants. A large proportion of them live in the temperate zone on the plateau running down the center of the country; situated here are the four major cities (Mexico City, Monterrey, Guadalajara, and Puebla) as well as such other important urban centers as Torreón, San Luis Potosí, Querétaro, and Oaxaca. Another major population group is located in the principal seacoast and port cities, which are invariably tropical in nature; they include Veracruz, Tampico, Acapulco, and Campeche.

Mexico City

The country's capital, Mexico City, including the suburbs, has some 12 million residents and is the second largest city in the Western Hemisphere and the fifth largest city in the world—larger than Paris. It is a cosmopolitan city with opera, ballet, art galleries, and other marks of a sophisticated populace. Chapter 16 is wholly devoted to Mexico City.

It is most interesting to note that Mexico City is located on the same site as the Aztec capital which existed before the white man arrived from Spain. It was then an Indian political and religious center of some 60,000 dwellings, with elaborate buildings, running water, and highly developed commerce.

The Aztecs who held the area which we now know as Mexico City were the dominant tribe in all Mexico when Cortés arrived. Their kings had great palaces, elaborate gardens, and even private zoos. Much of this gala note still persists in modern Mexico City.

Mexico's 1968 Olympics

Mexico was the host nation for the 1968 Olympic Games, and more than 100 nations had teams participating in this Olympiad. Most of the events were scheduled for Mexico City sites, and you can see the main Olympic stadium at University City, the Aztec Stadium (seating 100,000), and the huge Sports Palace at Magdalena Mixhuca near the airport.

Language

The Mexicans speak Spanish, except for remote areas where Indian dialects are spoken. In the Yucatán peninsula it is not uncommon to hear ancient Mayan still spoken as a living language, or Zapotec in Oaxaca. In the remote Sierra Madre Mountains of the north, the Tarahumaras still use the Raramuri language.

In the main tourist centers you can find someone who speaks English in almost any hotel or resort and even in most businesses. Still, there will be occasions when taxi drivers or others may not speak English. A phrase book is useful. Best idea of all is to learn a few words of Spanish. It is one of the easiest languages in the world, each word being pronounced exactly as it looks. Just start with the word Mexicans use for taxi, which is *libre* (LEE-bray), and you are in business. Mexicans love to see visitors trying to learn their language, and are most considerate and helpful.

The Food

Mexico's people have their own distinct diet, and the popularity of their food has extended to the United States, even though the widely held belief that our style of chili con carne is Mexican is absolutely false. (It is, rather, a dish that originated in Texas.)

The Mexicans have for years grown corn as their staple food, which they make into flat pancakes called tortillas. These are eaten from one end of the country to the other. They roll bits of meat in them and serve with a red-hot sauce, which makes them enchiladas, or they fry them in deep fat, which makes them tacos. Tiny green chilis called *chilis verdes* are eaten as condiments, and mashed beans, frijoles, are served much as we serve potatoes. A professor studying the Mexican diet was surprised to find it perfectly balanced and among the world's most nutritious, containing all elements necessary for good health.

Much of the world—in fact, nearly all—is afflicted with an amoebic condition which makes fresh vegetables and drinking water troublesome unless treated by washing in chlorine, and Mexico, too, has this problem. You can eat everything in first-class hotels and restaurants in Mexico, and drink their water, but away from these oases it is best to eat and drink only cooked or purified food and drink. This is no problem, as all good hotels and restaurants watch this for you.

If by any chance you do experience any stomach distress, local pharmacies carry quick-acting remedies such as Lomotil, the current medicine of choice; or Sulfasuxadina; or, if you are allergic to sulfa, another remedy, Neotracina. Mexico has excellent doctors whom you may consult.

Money

The Mexican monetary unit is the peso. Like the dollar, it is equivalent to 100 cents, or centavos as they are called in Spanish. The peso is a paper bill or a silver coin, and it is worth roughly 5 cents at this writing, or 20 pesos to one U.S. dollar. However, it is "floating," so the exchange rate varies. You can freely trade pesos and dollars back and forth at banks and hotels.

The Mexicans use what we consider our dollar sign, $, for their pesos, but it always has only one upright line. In this book we quote prices in both dollars and pesos, indicating pesos in words. The dollar sign is the dollar sign. It is always possible that the dollar–peso exchange rate will change as economic conditions demand. For this reason, and because of inflation, all actual prices are listed in Chapter 29 at the end of the book.

The Government

Mexico has had a stable government for the past forty years, and the same political party has been in power throughout this period. Major goals of the government have included construction of schools, highways, and power and hydraulic projects, as well as farm development and creation of new industry.

The country elects a new president every six years (the president is not eligible to run for reelection). A Senate and House of Deputies are also elected.

Recent administrations have injected public funding into all areas of business, industry, and mining in a program called "mixed economy." It is estimated that there is government participation in industry which contributes approximately 45 percent of the gross national product. Foreigners are now limited to no more than 49-percent control of businesses, but foreign investment nevertheless has grown to over $5 billion.

Highways have been extended to all parts of the country, and important new arteries include the famed Highway 200 along the Pacific coast, as well as the Pan-American Highway, which runs in three branches from various points on the U.S. border to Mexico City and on to Guatemala. Highways also run along the Gulf coast, then on to Yucatán and Quintana Roo on the Caribbean and to Chetumal on the border of Belize.

The government maintains a monopoly in the petroleum industry, which is a giant conglomerate of producing wells, refineries, chemical plants, and distribution networks called Petróleos Mexicanos or Pemex. All service stations belong to Pemex or are Pemex franchises.

COMMERCE AND INDUSTRY

Mexico is the world's largest producer of silver, extracting over one-half of the world's supply. It is also the world's third-largest producer of coffee and a leading producer of cotton. Its own special products, quantity aside, are chicle for chewing gum, sisal for twine, vanilla for flavoring, yam roots for synthesizing female hormones, bananas, oranges, winter vegetables, and what some people call the world's best beer.

You will notice many modern buses running on the streets of most cities, particularly in Mexico City, and it is worth knowing that all of these are now manufactured in Mexico. A consortium of eleven companies called Sahagum, financed by the government, has companies which manufacture from Mexican steel such products as trucks, buses, diesel engines, rail and subway cars, and tractors.

Mexico has substantial oil reserves and produces a million barrels a day and is able to export some oil. It also makes most of its own petrochemicals from oil and from its extensive sulfur domes. Oil fields and sulfur deposits are largely in the narrow Isthmus of Tehuantepec area in the south, and along the Gulf coast.

In the north, iron ore is made into steel in mills in Monterrey and Monclova in the state of Coahuila; this steel not only supplies the metalworking industry but is the source of pipe for the oil industry.

Mexico has doubled its power production in six years, but more increases are necessary to keep up with the growth of industry and the rise in population in some 10,000 cities and villages. Power is nationalized under a Federal Electricity Commission, and Mexico leads Latin American nations in power production. Power sources are huge hydroelectric projects utilizing the rivers running from the mountains to the sea on both coasts, and thermal power plants fueled by either oil, gas, or coal. Underground thermal heat exists in Mexico and is being developed as an experiment at one nuclear plant at Laguna Verde on the shores of the Gulf.

Landless peasants protest failure of the government to redistribute large landholdings, although some property has been distributed. However, those farmers with small acreage, called *ejidos*, have proven to be inefficient producers. In the meantime, chronic unemployment exists in rural areas.

GEOGRAPHY

Mexico has one of the most fascinating geographical displays on the face of the earth. It has great cactus-dotted deserts to the north, rugged mountain ranges running down each side, mile-high plateaus in the central area, snow-capped peaks spiring up among the highest on the continent, tropical beaches on both coasts, and, to the south, tropical forests and jungles.

Four Days—Border to Border. Mexico is a very large country; if it were superimposed on the United States, it would stretch from high up in Canada down to the southern border of Texas. Normally it takes four days to drive the length of Mexico from the Rio Grande to the Guatemalan border, at the shortest point, which is from Brownsville, Texas. At the farthest point, which is from Tijuana, it is 3,000 miles and a five- or six-day drive.

But Four Hours—Coast to Coast! On the other hand, at the narrowest point across Mexico's waist, the Isthmus of Tehuantepec, it is only four hours from the Pacific shoreline to the Atlantic (actually, the Gulf of Mexico). There was talk once of cutting a canal across the Isthmus, but the Panama project proved easier and faster. However, a rail line, a pipeline, and now a highway have been built to connect the two oceans at the Mexican Isthmus.

In the central and southern parts of the country, you can choose a variety of both climate and foliage by driving an hour or so in one direction or another. Sea level offers tropical heat, banana trees, and palms. Up on the plateaus there is balmy subtropical weather with brilliant flowers. In the temperate higher areas, perhaps only thirty minutes beyond, the air suddenly becomes crisp and the landscape is characterized by waving, long-needled pines and leafy oaks.

Mexico, of course, is known for the fantastic array of flowers it grows the year round, and notable among them is the poinsettia, which grows easily on the subtropical plateau. It was discovered near Cuernavaca in 1836 by Joel Robert Poinsett, an American diplomat, and introduced into the United States.

Mexico's jungle areas are full of orchids, which often sell for 20 cents a dozen where they are grown, and there are so many gardenias in some areas that many hotels have swimming pools covered with thousands of fresh gardenias each morning.

Mountains and Volcanoes. The two mountain ranges which give Mexico its distinctive cornucopia shape are known simply as the *Sierra Madre Oriental,* or Eastern Mother Range, and the much longer, broader, and more rugged *Sierra Madre Occidental,* its western counterpart. Wide apart at the north, they meet in a junction at La Junta, near Mexico City, part again to form the *Valley of Mexico,* in which the capital is located, and finally join again north of Oaxaca to form the *Sierra Madre del Sur.*

The heart of all Mexico is the relatively small, fertile valley 7,000 feet high in the mountains in the center of the country.

Measuring some 40 miles long and 30 miles wide, this green valley with several shallow lakes is blessed with a year-round springlike climate, free of excesses of heat or cold. This is the Valley of Mexico, once called *Anáhuac;* traditionally its conquerors have dominated all the country. To one side are the volcanoes of Popocatepetl and Iztaccihuatl, while in its center is the great capital of the country, Mexico City.

The highest peak in Mexico, and the third highest on the North American continent, is *Orizaba* (18,696 feet), which rises between Veracruz and Puebla. It is one of Mexico's many extinct volcanoes, and is some 4,000 feet higher than any U.S. mountain except McKinley.

Orizaba is said, by geographic authorities, to be one of the most perfect and beautiful of all volcanoes, comparable to the Japanese Fujiyama and the Peruvian El Misti. Its slender, graceful slope rising to its snow-capped peak is a sight easily visible on clear days from Puebla or Veracruz, and the road to Mexico City from Veracruz, via Jalapa, passes very close to it.

Mexico also has the fifth and eighth highest peaks on the continent. These are the famed volcanoes just 30 miles outside Mexico City—*Popocatepetl* (17,883 feet) and *Iztaccihuatl* (17,338 feet). Both are snow-capped the year round. Climbers regularly ascend both, and some even descend into the sulfuric crater of Popo, from which smoke and steam occasionally rise. Popo is known in legend as the warrior kneeling at the feet of his prone sweetheart, whose figure is the profile of the adjoining volcano, Iztaccihuatl, which does resemble a sleeping woman.

Mexico had a live volcano not too long ago, *Paricutín,* which erupted from a farmer's field in the western state of Michoacán in 1943, blasting fire into the air and pouring out molten lava that rose 2,000 feet, forcing 4,000 people to leave their homes, but it subsided ten years later. It is now dormant, and there are no live volcanoes in Mexico at this writing.

Earthquakes. Mild earthquakes occur each fall, due to a major fault running parallel to the west coast, and light tremors are felt nearly every year. Usually, the only effect of these earthquakes noticeable to those in the area is window blinds being jarred against the wall or chandeliers swinging. However, in 1474 the Aztecs recorded a terrible earthquake; in 1909 the capital of the western state of Guerrero, Chilpancingo, was reduced to a mass of ruins; and again in 1937 a heavy earthquake did considerable damage. In August 1957, an earthquake measuring a near maximum of eight on the Mercalli scale destroyed many large buildings in Mexico City, although most of the well-constructed ones escaped ruin. Fortunately, the chance that a tourist will experience such an earthquake is practically nil.

The Coastlines. Mexico's *Gulf coast,* similar to that of Louisiana and Texas, has the ports of Tampico, Veracruz (the country's busiest), Coatzacoalcos or Puerto México, and, in the Yucatán peninsula, Campeche and Progreso. The Gulf coast, 1,080 miles long, has many marshes, and its beaches, with some notable exceptions—including the hundreds of miles of powdery white beaches found in the Yucatán state of Quintana Roo and the resorts of Cancún and Isla Mujeres off Yucatán—are gray-hued and less expansive than those found on the Pacific coast. The port of Veracruz, important as it is, is man-made.

Mexico's *Pacific coast* has the difficult-to-imagine length of 2,860 miles, almost enough to stretch from New York to Los Angeles in the United States. This coastline has wide, intensely white sandy beaches for almost its entire length, with many interesting inlets and bays surrounded by palm trees and tropical vegetation. The natural port of Acapulco, now the Riviera of the West, is magnificent and is said to be one of the best harbors in the world.

Acapulco, however, is cut off from the rest of the country by the spectacular mountain range which comes down to the sea to form the bay and gives the town its majestic location. At this writing, there is no railroad connecting Acapulco with the rest of the country. So, as in the days of clippers and the China trade, cargo has to be hauled up the mountain road, although today it is a superhighway.

The artificial geographical line of the *Tropic of Cancer,* which divides the temperate and torrid zones, runs across Mexico about halfway between Monterrey and Mexico City, and can be noted by markers as one drives north or south across this location.

Lakes and Rivers. Over 60 percent of Mexico is desert or nonarable land, including tropical areas which cannot be cultivated, but it has some huge rivers and a number of sizable lakes.

Lake Chapala, near Guadalajara, is a beautiful blue lake 80 miles long and full of fine whitefish. *Lake Pátzcuaro*, near Morelia, is another beauty. *Lake Catemaco* south of Veracruz is another enchanting, fairly large lake set among scenic hills; it too has fine fishing. And there are scores of smaller lakes, many of them high in the mountains.

The most famous river in Mexico is undoubtedly the *Rio Grande*, stretching 1,800 miles long and forming most of the border between the United States and Mexico.

The huge *Papaloapan* (River of the Butterflies), near Veracruz, is the scene of a Mexican TVA-type program. The *Grijalva* and the *Usumacinta*, also flowing into the Gulf but from the base of the Yucatán peninsula, are other powerful and very wide tropical rivers. On the Pacific side, the waters of the *Fuerte, Yaquí*, and *Sonora* rivers are all being harnessed for irrigation and power.

Speaking of butterflies, millions upon millions of monarchs assemble each November on a pine slope in the Sierra Madres northeast of Mexico City at an altitude of 9,000 feet. They come from all over the northern continent and stay until spring. The August 1976 issue of *National Geographic* has excellent photos of these giant swarms of dormant butterflies that turn pine trees into orange and yellow pillars.

CLIMATE

The temperate zone of Mexico is the high central plateau, including Mexico City, and it is the land of eternal spring.

The tropical zone in Mexico is comprised of the lowlands along the Pacific and Gulf coasts and the land of the Isthmus in the south. The dry plains of the north get hot in the summer, but they can hardly be called tropical.

The popular tourist spots such as Cuernavaca, Taxco, and Oaxaca all have very pleasant weather, being located between the temperate and tropical zones.

3

Travel Preparations

Having decided upon a Mexican trip, you will find you have a choice of getting there by plane, train, bus, your own car, or even ship.

Plane travel is most frequently used. There are flights by a number of major United States carriers and two Mexican lines, from New York, Chicago, Los Angeles, New Orleans, Miami, Houston, San Antonio, and a growing number of other U.S. cities. Flights are relatively fast, inexpensive, and comfortable. Flying is an easy answer for those with a time limit on their vacation.

If you gave us our choice, without a time limit, we would elect to go to Mexico by car. It is a wonderful place for those who like touring by automobile. The roads are good, the scenery is dramatic and ever-changing, and a car is always handy to have at any resort. Cars can be rented in Mexico, too.

Our family once made a 10,000-mile trip through Mexico by a new form of transportation, a motor home. The 27-foot Winnebago self-powered unit provided us with beds for six, hot shower and tub (even while moving), air conditioning, and amazing speed and range. While we parked often on some of the lovely wilderness beaches, we also found trailer courts almost everywhere in Mexico with all the usual connections—and often pools and restaurants.

A ticket from your local Greyhound office will give you bus transportation to Mexico, or you can buy a train ticket from Amtrak, which will take you there by rail. Ships from New York dock at Veracruz and Tampico frequently. There are luxury cruise ships making seven- or eleven-day trips from Los Angeles to Puerto Vallarta, Mazatlán, Cabo San Lucas, and Manzanillo or Acapulco.

GETTING THERE

The most popular plan, and probably the best in most cases,

is to fly to Mexico City and stay there for a few days. Then take a bus or limousine on the popular Cuernavaca, Taxco, and Acapulco route, enjoy a few days by the seaside, fly back to Mexico City for a day or so, and continue home on the airline you came down on. We heartily recommend this itinerary for a first visit to Mexico.

Airplane. Flying will appeal to you if you have only two or three weeks of vacation, as it permits you to spend more time in Mexico sight-seeing or resting rather than in transit. Flying time is five or six hours from New York or Chicago to Mexico City. Airlines flying nonstop to Mexico from New York are *Eastern, Air France,* and the Mexican airline *Aeromexico. American Airlines* and *Mexicana* fly nonstop from Chicago, *Western Airlines* and *Compañía Mexicana de Aviación* (CMA) from Los Angeles, and *Eastern* from New Orleans. *Braniff,* serving Denver and Minneapolis, flies one-stop to Mexico City and nonstop from San Antonio to Acapulco. Connecting flights are available from all other cities in the United States. *Pan-American* flies from Miami and New Orleans to Mérida, Yucatán, with *Mexicana* connecting flights to all points in Mexico. *Hughes Air West* flies from Las Vegas, Tucson, and other western points. Cancún at the moment is served only by *Aeromexico* from Houston and Miami, but a new bilateral air agreement with the United States may in time change this and permit U.S. and probably other foreign lines to fly there.

Bus. You can buy a *Greyhound* ticket to Mexico City, but actually you will be transferred to a Mexican line at the border. Equipment on the Mexican side is just as modern as that used in the United States, as the major Mexican bus lines offer first-class service, but you will not find bus travel so comfortable as in this country.

For one thing, there are Pullman, first-, second-, and third-class buses, and we recommend only Pullman or first-class. You must specify this, as it usually means you will have to reserve a seat.

Mexican bus tours make only infrequent rest stops, and when they do stop, facilities are apt to be primitive. Restaurants especially are not very good.

At the same time, modern, often air-conditioned buses are in service, drivers are courteous, and buses will take you anywhere in Mexico. Stopovers are complicated, so make certain your ticket is correct and that a space is reserved for you at the time you resume your trip. Rates are usually much cheaper than in the United States.

Rail. The new U.S. federal passenger rail agency, *Amtrak*, reports it has made some connections with the Mexican rail lines at San Antonio and El Paso, but this can be determined only as the system develops. If there are connections to San Antonio or El Paso, you will be able to change to Mexican trains which are still regularly scheduled for passengers. It is a twenty-eight-hour train trip from Laredo to Mexico City.

While the railroad equipment is standard gauge and new, and service is provided daily, many passengers find Mexican rail travel disappointing, in that service is not too good, food is quite ordinary, and the trip can be wearing. At the same time, roomettes and compartments are available, and there is a lounge car in which service is dependable.

The *Pacific Line of Mexico* from Nogales goes down the west coast, and in recent years many college students have employed it to get to the west coast resort of Mazatlán. It also goes on to Guadalajara and Mexico City; be warned that this is a long and often tedious trip, but there are many who enjoy it.

Ship. There is no regular steamship route to Mexico at this writing, although there has been in the past. But inquiry at travel agencies in New York or New Orleans will usually disclose that freighters carrying passengers make stops at Tampico or Veracruz. Cruise ships leave frequently from Los Angeles. Princess Cruises (2020 Avenue of the Stars, Los Angeles, California) or Sitmar Cruises (P.O. Box 92359, Los Angeles, California 90009) to both Mexico and the Caribbean are available from travel agents.

Auto. There is a fine network of paved highways to Mexico City and on to other cities, with both hotels and motels along the way. This is undoubtedly a wonderful way to see Mexico's dramatic scenery, although it is wise to note that distances can be long between cities and that many of the highways go through mountains. But the mountain roads are paved, well banked, and usually have guard rails. There are several car rental agencies that are very helpful to tourists. These are listed in Chapter 6.

Trailers. Great caravans of trailers have gone to the farthest parts of Mexico, so you need have no fear about such travel. Permits are issued at the border much as for cars without any great delay, but you must bring your trailer out when you leave. Mexico is mountainous, so your car should have sufficient weight and power to haul your trailer up steep inclines.

There are over 160 trailer parks in Mexico listed in *Woodall's Guide to Trailering* (Woodall Publishing, 500 Hyacinth Place, Highland Park, Illinois, $6). Dan Sanborn, Sanborn Insurance, McAllen, Texas, provides a free list of about 200 parks and campgrounds in Mexico. Not all have complete facilities but a surprisingly large number do, and new ones are appearing each day, including some of the Kampground of America (KOA) group. Pure water can be purchased in large bottles in every Mexican city, or usually can be secured free from any soft drink bottler if you drive in and ask. Don't mix drinking and bath water (the latter from any filling station tap).

Principal Routes of Entry into Mexico by Automobile. *Laredo,* Texas, is the most popular. It is roughly 760 miles from Laredo to Mexico City: either two days of steady driving or three days in a more leisurely fashion. You have a choice of two routes from this entrance: one colorful, often tropical, and mountainous—but fascinating; the other cooler, straighter, faster, and less interesting.

The colorful route runs from Laredo at the border (or Brownsville or McAllen) to Monterrey, then to Ciudad Victoria and Valles and to tropical Tamazunchale, then up the looming mountains over spectacular scenery to the high Mexican plateau, and thus to Mexico City.

The cool and fast route is from Laredo to Monterrey, then over to Saltillo, then south on the new Central Superhighway to Matehuala, San Luis Potosí, Querétaro, and thus to Mexico City. This is by far the best for trailers or mobile homes.

We advise the auto tourist to enter Mexico on the first route, via Valles, and leave via the Central Superhighway.

The shortest route is to enter at *Brownsville*, Texas, which cuts out much driving in Texas as you hug the Gulf, and then go down a new paved road to Tampico and Tuxpan, then up a brief mountain drive to Mexico City. Out of Tampico you have a ten-minute ferry trip.

El Paso, farther west in Texas, is an entrance to the main highway going down the backbone of Mexico via Chihuahua, Durango, and Lagos to Mexico City. This is a long route of some 1,300 miles (a good three-day drive), but it is the best one for tourists coming from the Rocky Mountain States. Initially, this route is over flat, sun-baked desert, but as it approaches Mexico City it does pass through interesting cities.

Nogales, on the Arizona border, is by far the best route from the Far West; it leads down the famed Pacific Coast Highway, which is well worth the trip by itself. Here, one can stop at four wonderful seaside resort points—Guaymas, Mazatlán, Puerto Vallarta, and Manzanillo—and visit such other interesting places as Hermosillo, capital of the northwestern state of Sonora; the boom town Navajoa; the long-isolated Indian town of Tepic; and the big city of Guadalajara—all en route to Mexico City. This is a good route for trailers also, though you do hit some mountain grades approaching Guadalajara and on into Mexico City.

The new Pacific coast route 200 can be picked up at Tepic. It goes along the coast to Chamela, a new resort development, and on to Manzanillo. Eventually you will be able to drive to Acapulco this way, via Ixtapa and Zihuatanejo, but now you must jog inland and back.

Preparations

Reservations. You should call a travel agent, or the line (if you're going by air) by which you intend to travel, and make your reservations for both your trip down to Mexico and your return. Often tourists neglect to make return reservations and have difficulty coming back on the desired date.

One thing we do not recommend is a prearranged tour plan. We like to see a tourist left free to make variations in his route and generally adapt his trip to what he likes. Hotel reservations, of course, should be made in advance.

Tourist Card. You will have to get a *tourist card*. This can be obtained through any of the Mexican tourist offices in the United States (listed at the end of this chapter) or from any Mexican consulate. Usually an airline or travel agent will assist you in obtaining a tourist card, which is free. No passport is necessary, but usually you must submit proof of citizenship, which can be shown by a passport, a birth certificate, citizenship papers, or the equivalent. Tourist cards are good for a six-month stay and can be picked up at the border at the Mexican immigration office without charge. Proof of citizenship is required and should be carried with you.

A valid *vaccination certificate* is no longer required by the Mexican authorities upon entrance and by the United States upon return.

Insurance. Your *car insurance* is not valid in Mexico, so the custom is to buy insurance at the border for the exact period of time you will be in Mexico. It costs about $4–$5 a day and up for all risks. Dan Sanborn, the leading insurance man, has a main office in McAllen, Texas (P.O. Box 1210, McAllen, Texas 78501, tel: (512) 682-3401), where you can write or phone him in advance, and offices at every border crossing point. He prepares an individual trip portfolio for you of incredible detail, listing practically every mile-by-mile point on your trip with comments on roads, restaurants, hotels, trailer courts, and even shops. We have found his reports very sound and have come to live by them on the road.

Your car is admitted for six months and must be taken out before that time. Be sure to bring *title* to your car or other proof of ownership, or permission of the owner to bring it in if you do not own it. (See Driver's License and Insurance, page 53).

Clothes. You will need two complete sets. One will be for the fall-day type of weather in Mexico City. This means a woolen suit or sports jacket and a raincoat (from May until October), but nothing heavier, although a sweater is always good to have along. For outside of Mexico City, you will need summer sports clothes (sport shirts, summer dresses, etc.) and bathing suits the year round. For women, a scarf for church is suggested. Men and women should plan to dress rather well in Mexico City, meaning a suit and tie for men, but elsewhere sports clothes are worn at all times.

Don't load yourself down, however. Everything you might need can be purchased in Mexico. Clothing, film, cameras, and all types of drugs and sundries are available, so don't feel you have to remember every little thing. If you forget something, you can get it there. So set off relaxed.

MEXICAN GOVERNMENT TOURIST OFFICES

Here is a list of Mexican Government Tourist Offices in the United States, Canada, and Mexico City. You can write or visit them for travel information or tourist cards.

Chicago, Ill. 625 N. Michigan, Suite 1220, tel: 664-5779

Denver,Col. 701 W. Hampden, Cind. City, Englewood

Dallas, Tex. 1800 Main St., tel: 747-3479

Houston, Tex. 805 Walker Ave., tel: CA5-5935

Los Angeles, Calif. 3106 Wilshire Blvd. 90010, tel: DU5-6438

Miami, Fla. 100 Biscayne Tower Bldg. 33132, tel: 371-8037

New Orleans, La. One Shell Square Bldg. 70130, tel: 525-2783

New York, N.Y. 630 Fifth Ave. 10020, tel: CO5-4696

Phoenix, Ariz. 3443 N. Central Ave. Suite 101 85012, tel: 264-3819

San Antonio, Tex. 420 N. St. Mary's St. 78205, tel: CA3-6612

San Diego, Calif. 245 Westgate Plaza Mall 92101, tel: 232-6757

San Francisco, Calif. 219 Sutter St. 94108, tel: 986-0992

Tucson, Ariz. 25 East Broadway 85701, tel: 623-5721

Washington, D.C. 914 17th St., N.W., Suite 104 20006, tel: 296-4045

Montréal, Québec Place Ville Marie, Esso Bldg. 20, tel: 866-4070

Toronto, Ontario 85 Richmond St. West, tel: 364-2455

Mexico City, Mexico Juárez 92, tel: 521-4502

4

Inside Mexico—
Which Trips

Always, as the roads twist through the steep mountains of Mexico, one comes to little patches of corn, or maize, as it is called there. Often the fields seem to be tipped on end, and the poor peon, one feels, must have to hang from a rope while he cultivates the field, or milpa.

Such is the desperate need to make every inch of arable ground count, and to grow the corn that will be soaked in lime water, then ground into a paste in a stone metate and made into the thin unleavened pancakelike bread, the tortilla, which is the staple of the family diet all year long.

The patting of the paste into tortillas by the housewives' hands can be heard every morning, while in the cities little girls will come to the door each day with a basket of hot freshly baked tortillas. They cost a few pennies a dozen.

Tortillas are rolled with a meat filling, and fried to make tacos. They are cooked into soup, which now can be found canned in Mexico. Other corn is cooked in banana leaves and becomes tamales. Or cheese and chilis are ground over rolled tortillas, and reheated, to become enchiladas—red or green, depending upon the chili peppers used.

Corn is sometimes made into gruel and sweetened with chocolate, called atole or, in other forms, pozole.

The ancient god of corn in Mexico was Mok Santu, and one can easily understand why he was especially venerated.

So FAR, we have just talked about getting to Mexico. Now we will discuss what to see once you are there.

What you will want to see will naturally depend upon time, money, personal interests, and other factors. If you have only two weeks, perhaps a stay of three or four days in Mexico City, including a weekend for the bullfights, and one major trip outside the capital will be enough. Some people manage two or even three side trips during a two-week vacation, however.

MEXICO CITY

The Mexican capital has grown to be a huge city, with some terrible traffic jams in early evening, and its once bright and beautiful parks are now overcast with smog a good part of the time. Still, just as the visitor to the United States wants to see New York City, the visitor to Mexico usually wishes to see the Mexican capital.

There are some things you just can't see anywhere else in Mexico. For example, the Ballet Folklórico, the famed Museo de Anthropologia, the Pyramids of the Sun and Moon, and the University of Mexico are only in Mexico City. It also has the most shops and the best restaurants.

So we recommend a weekend in Mexico City coming or going. Traffic is not quite so bad on weekends, when many Mexicans leave the city, and the bullfights and floating gardens can be seen on Sundays. Markets and shops are usually open on Sundays, too.

You can outwit the traffic with astute use of the new subway (called the Metro), and the new fleets of buses going every which way every few minutes also help.

Walking tours are an excellent way to see the city, and a companion guide to this book, *John Wilhelm's Guide to Mexico City* (available at hotel newsstands or from Dimsa, Apartado 1767, México, D. F., México) has maps that enable you to manage by yourself.

See Chapter 16 for a complete description of Mexico City.

SIDE TRIPS

Acapulco, by way of Cuernavaca and Taxco, is the old standby for tourists in Mexico, and we heartily recommend it. The trip is just the right length, taking a leisurely four or five days, and you will see a variety of villages, tropical scenery, and seascapes not found in any other single excursion. You can also be sure of encountering some of the best hotels and dining rooms in Mexico (see Chapters 7, 10, and 23).

It is possible to get to Cuernavaca in about an hour by

limousine, bus, or your own car on the new superhighway. You might stop in Cuernavaca for lunch, then go another hour or so farther on to Taxco for the night, and the next day complete the drive down to Acapulco, an additional four or five hours. You can return by plane direct from Acapulco to the Mexico City airport in one hour.

Cuernavaca is a charming overgrown village filled with colorful flowers and tiled-roof houses. Located about 2,500 feet lower than Mexico City, it has a year-round balmy climate that many Americans find just right. It has a permanent colony of American residents, some retired and some just resting. It is a good place for either. Details on Cuernavaca are given in Chapter 10.

Taxco is one of the most picturesque towns in all Mexico; its pastel-colored houses tumbling up and down the hillside along the cobblestoned streets are a joy to behold. It is an old colonial mining town which has been preserved by law as it was in colonial days. Silver mining is still carried on, and this is a fine place to buy silver (see Chapter 23).

Ixtapa, a new Pacific resort area, is a destination all by itself, and tourists can travel there directly and spend their entire vacation ensconced in one of the numerous luxury hotels. Tennis, golf, fishing, and snorkeling are available. Rates are high but in line with what one would pay at top-flight resorts in the United States or the Caribbean. At this writing, flights to Ixtapa are from Mexico City or Guadalajara, but one should check with a travel agent about direct flights from the United States. Special charters taking all comers are frequently available and very good. See Chapter 13 for details on Ixtapa.

Acapulco by Direct Flight. Braniff, Eastern, Aeromexico, and Western have flights from many parts of the United States directly into Acapulco, while other flights touch down in Mexico City but continue on to Acapulco with the same plane. Package tours, often with children free, for a two-night stay in Acapulco can be purchased at travel desks in Mexico City.

Acapulco is still the largest resort city in Mexico, with the largest number of first-class hotels. Most have large swimming pools, practically beach clubs by themselves, and the spectacular scenery is everywhere. All hotels have good restaurants, and there is much gaiety and dancing. Golf, tennis, and surfing are popular sports. See Chapter 7 for details.

Puerto Vallarta has become very popular recently. It is north of Acapulco on the Pacific coast. There is a good road in from Tepic, and air service. A number of fairly sizable hotels have been built, but check your reservations before going.

Puerto Vallarta has a bigger bay, and perhaps even a nicer climate, than Acapulco. It does not have Acapulco's exciting night life, although it is getting some. The little town is picturesque and you can make a side trip to Mismaloya, where Richard Burton and Ava Gardner made the movie *The Night of the Iguana*, and on to Yelapa, a very primitive tropical colony. The trip, by boat, is scenic and costs only about $8 per person. See Chapter 21 for details.

Mazatlán and Manzanillo. Mazatlán is a bigger port, even farther north. It has some large hotels, and has long been noted for good fishing as well as for its beaches. Manzanillo, south of Puerto Vallarta, is wild and rustic; it has some charming beaches in small coves, but the port town is quite ordinary. (See Chapters 14 and 15.) All of these west coast resorts now have modern hotels, and a nice vacation can be had going from one to the other.

Fortín de las Flores involves a trip through the scenic mountains past the dormant volcanoes Popocatepetl and Iztaccihuatl, through Puebla (where you can lunch), and then on to a tropical garden area on the Veracruz road to the town of Fortín de las Flores, where the Hotel Ruíz Galindo has the famed pool with gardenias floating on it. You can also go to Peñafiel, with its medicinal waters, where there is a resort hotel, or a little farther on to the town of Córdoba. Two hours beyond lies Veracruz (see Chapter 25).

Pátzcuaro is part of an easy day's drive on the westward road toward Guadalajara. Along the way you can stop for lunch or overnight at the famed spa, San José Purúa, but the main object of this trip is to see beautiful Lake Pátzcuaro, with its Indian fishermen and their butterfly fishing nets. The hotel at Pátzcuaro is the Posada Don Vasco. Here you can buy handsome lacquered wooden trays. You can also go on to Morelia, an old state capital, for the night, or even to Guadalajara, which is a twelve-hour drive from Mexico City. (See Chapter 18 on Morelia and Pátzcuaro and Chapter 11 on Guadalajara.)

Guanajuato, Querétaro, and San Miguel de Allende. Guanajuato and Querétaro, lying about five or six hours to the north of

Mexico City, are interesting historical points, and you can stop overnight in the pretty little town of San Miguel de Allende, near Querétaro, where there are good hotels. San Miguel is quaint, and many artists stay there year round. It has an excellent climate. (See Chapter 12 on Guanajuato and Chapter 22 on San Miguel de Allende and Querétaro.)

Oaxaca, which is about an eight-hour drive to the south of Mexico City, can be reached by going through the mountains to Puebla but without much time to stop. You can also fly directly to Oaxaca. In Oaxaca you can see some of the outstanding archeological ruins on the North American continent, such as Monte Albán and Mitla. Oaxaca has a fine climate and some good hotels (see Chapter 19). From Oaxaca you can also visit the intriguing regions of southern Mexico such as the Isthmus of Tehuantepec (Chapter 24).

Yucatán and the Island of Cozumel. While we still consider a trip to Yucatán rather a major undertaking, the ease of flight these days, with jet planes going daily from Mexico City to Mérida, the capital of Yucatán, and other planes stopping at Cozumel en route to Jamaica, it obviously is possible to include these points in your Mexican trip. In fact, you can return home this way by having your ticket routed Mexico City–Mérida–Miami or New Orleans, and there is no extra cost. There is a direct flight by Mexicana from Miami to Cozumel.

Yucatán has the fabulous ruins of Chichén-Itzá, Uxmal, and others, and both of these famed Mayan archeological zones have comfortable hotels with pools. Mérida itself is worth a day, and there are good hotels there, too.

Cozumel, an island off the coast of Yucatán, is still quite primitive even though it now has, I would say, one exceptionally good hotel, two very good hotels, and several that will spoil your trip if you get caught in them. The major attractions are crystal-clear water, some coral reefs for skin diving, an unending supply of lobster, and plenty of quiet, as there isn't a phone on the island. It is at its best in the winter, but be sure your plane and hotel reservations are in order. (See Chapter 26 for details.)

You can take a bus trip from Mexico City to Mérida (but not Cozumel), via Veracruz, Coatzacoalcos, Isla del Carmen (the famed shrimp grounds), and Campeche, which is noted for its fish and seafood. The total trip takes thirty hours, although we would recommend breaking it into parts. First-class fare is under $12, but the leg room isn't quite adequate for Americans and the ride can be tiring for an older person. But it is manageable, and quite safe and scenic. A bus trip from Tijuana to Mérida, traversing the entire country at its longest dimension, costs only $60.

Cancún is a new luxury resort area built on a spit of land alongside the shore of the Yucatán peninsula near Puerto Juárez. A spectacular place, it features powdery white beaches, probably the best in the world, and clear blue Caribbean water.

A score of luxury hotels have been built at Cancún, and they offer tennis, golf, fishing, and snorkeling. Rates are comparable to those at first-class resorts in the United States or the Caribbean. Currently Mexicana and Aeromexico are operating direct flights to Cancún from Houston and Miami. You should check with a travel agent regarding direct flights from other cities. (See Chapter 9.)

Hidden Beaches. Every once in a while we get a request, often from honeymooners, for a secluded beach. Usually those desiring seclusion don't want to be too far from clean linen, hot water, and a cold shaker of cocktails. Within these limitations, we offer the following suggestions:

Las Brisas Hotel in Acapulco is really 200 separate pink cottages in the sky, each with its own pool. You can't even see your neighbor. A special "honeymoon package" for five days and four nights with breakfast, private cottage, and pool is $384 for two (not offered during peak season). See Chapter 7.

The Club Mediterranée has establishments on the Pacific at Playa Blanca near Chamela north of Manzanillo. The fabulous Cancún version has 300 rooms at the far end of the 14-mile Cancún beaches. The usual Club Med package deal is available; for information, contact their offices in major cities.

MEXICO SOUTH

A famed archeological zone in southern Mexico, and a very pleasant place to visit, is Oaxaca and the adjoining areas of Tehuantepec, home of a colorful, almost Oriental culture.

There are daily flights from Mexico City to Oaxaca that take just over an hour. If you are motoring, you can drive from

Mexico City to Puebla, right past the volcanoes, and down to Oaxaca in the same day; or you can make it shorter by taking the new superhighway to Cuautla (near Cuernavaca) and on to Oaxaca. Bus trips to Oaxaca and Tehuantepec are frequent, taking about ten hours.

Oaxaca has a pleasant, balmy climate, and is a very nice place to take a week's rest. There are several good hotels. More important, there are the famous ruins of Monte Albán and Mitla, great stone cities of pre-Hispanic times. Oaxaca is also a good city for shopping (see Chapter 19).

Tehuantepec, long known as having the most beautiful girls in the world, is in fact a dull, hot tropical town with some exotic notes worth investigation by the persistent tourist. Elements of Polynesian cultures abound, including the sarong-like garments of the sloe-eyed girls. A coast-to-coast highway to the Gulf from nearby Salina Cruz, which has good beaches on the Pacific, can be driven in three hours (see Chapter 24).

By taking the Trans-Isthmusian Highway, you can turn north at Acayucán and go to Veracruz and back to Mexico City by way of either Fortín de las Flores or the colorful city of flowers, Jalapa. Both have good roads to Mexico City. You can hire chauffeur-driven cars to travel these routes, but it will cost about $60 a day for car and driver. You can rent a drive-yourself car in Mexico City and easily make it on your own.

Two of the most scenic drives in the world are along the Yucatán coast via Isla del Carmen (with coastal ferries) or south to Tuxtla Gutiérrez, where a new paved highway south of town cuts off to Villahermosa in the state of Tabasco and provides mountain scenery reminiscent of the Swiss Alps in summer.

San Cristóbal de las Casas, a few hours south of Tehuantepec, is a picturesque colonial town set high in the mountains. It remains practically unchanged from colonial days 400 years ago, and you can see the unusual Indian tribes of this area such as the Chamulas, the Zinacantecos, and the Lacandones (see Chapter 24).

What Will It Cost?

We are writing this book for the traveler on a budget as well as for the luxury-minded. A guide might be $30 a day per person or $100 per couple for those demanding luxury. Those who wish to avoid these fairly steep prices can, upon coming to a spot they like, easily seek out an apartment by the week or month, shop in the local supermarkets, and eat in the less expensive (often incredibly cheap) restaurants, thus making their money go much further.

Since Mexico has a fantastic network of both first-class and second-class buses, you can make these wonderful trips quite inexpensively. For example, you can travel from Mexico City to Mérida, Yucatán, a distance of 1,200 miles, for $18; or south to Oaxaca and San Cristóbal for even less; or down to Acapulco from Mexico City for $8. By bus, staying at moderate hotels, you could get by on $15 per day plus travel.

To get information on bus schedules, etc., write to Guía de Transportes Aereos y Autotransportes de México, Apartado Postal 8929, México 1, D.F., México, for their current guide.

We pride ourselves on listing only safe places, and we go out of our way to nominate the best and the fanciest, too. But always with prices specified.

5

Shopping for Arts and Crafts and Other Things

TALES OF OLD MEXICO

The markets—some open daily including Sunday, and others only once a week—are the center of life in Mexico.

In many places, trails of patient women start for town the night before, sometimes lugging baskets of zapotes, jitomates, or frijoles (fruit, tomatoes, or beans) and sometimes leading laden burros.

By dawn, big white canopies are stretched over the street to shade the area. Each woman has spread out her merchandise in carefully placed piles. The market is full of chatter as gossip and various ribaldries are exchanged.

A man selling rolls will appear. He wouldn't dream of selling them all at once. "Pues, what would I do the rest of the day?" he would say.

Haggling is the order of the day. Tourists, even if forewarned, have little chance of winning this contest. The shopkeepers know they will come back. Still, it is worth the effort to start off. Prospects of the competitor selling huaraches, the woven leather slippers, or serapes, the woolen blankets, at the fat tourist price will unnerve any merchant.

By night, the ladies have sold their goods, rolled up their spread rebozos, bought what they need, and are walking home.

THE GREAT REPUBLIC of Mexico is virtually bursting with interesting and colorful goods which are a delight to the traveler from the United States.

There is fine sterling silver in handsome tea sets of both modern and traditional design, and for less than the price you would pay at home; there are beautiful woolen serapes which make colorful rugs for what two yards of carpet would cost north of the border; there is native pottery, in incredible profusion, which becomes beautiful casseroles and serving dishes; there are exotic masks and trays hand-rubbed in native black lacquer; and—my favorite—the beautiful green bubble glass.

Those who love art will not only see the great murals by the Mexican masters Rivera, Orozco, and Tamayo, but they will have an opportunity to visit galleries where both originals and excellent reproductions are sold, as well as very creditable work by newer and lesser-known artists.

From the archeological zones, immense pre-Hispanic stone cities, small idols and other stone artifacts are being recovered by the tens of thousands, and some of these can be purchased (subject to conditions noted on page 44), while the motifs—the Mayans appreciated humor and many of the little figures are laughing—have been copied widely in present-day native crafts.

There are baskets, mats, boxes and chests, fancy candelabra, wonderful chandeliers and lamps, huaraches, leather goods, and even gems to be had in the huge public markets. We shall discuss each category, describing the points to consider in buying and the pitfalls of which the buyer must beware.

SILVER OF ALL KINDS

Silver is the greatest buy in Mexico, for the simple reason that Mexico is the greatest silver-producing nation in the world.

The national government has wisely set standards for Mexican silver to give it a rating for purity equal to the best anywhere, and you are not likely to find silver on sale in any reputable store that is less than high-quality sterling. Silverplate is virtually unknown—it would be ridiculous to waste any labor on it when pure silver is so plentiful.

The government has ruled that all silver, from large pieces to the smallest earring, must be stamped with the word "sterling" or ".925" and that both of these shall mean it contains not less than 925 grams of pure silver for each 1,000 grams of weight. That means alloy content of less than 75 grams per kilogram. This is almost as pure a silver as can be worked.

The silver also usually carries the imprint of the silversmith or of the shop where it was made. And we might point out that almost all silver—even that sold in the shops of Taxco—now comes from the Bank of Mexico stocks in bar form. Practically no silversmith, despite what he may say, deals directly with a mine.

In buying silver, it is important to remember several things:

1. Judge the silver by the reputation of the shop where you buy it, but at the same time note its weight either by lifting it in your hand or by asking that the salesperson place a piece on a scale (every good shop has one). The silver should be sturdy and not inclined to bend under pressure of your finger. And look for the hallmark on the back as described above.

2. Workmanship is the important consideration once you have established the quality and weight of the silver. Workmanship is not hard to judge. Has the piece been polished smooth, or are there striations or mars from polishing? Where the design or legs have been welded on, is the work carefully finished, or has it been left with crudities? If there are hinges, do they work easily and look sturdy?

3. Style is the most distinctive element, and it is a matter of taste. Some people prefer the simple lines of the Danish silver makers, and such pieces are easy to find in Mexico today. Others prefer the traditional English and Sheffield patterns represented by bellied tea services decorated with scrolls or other embellishments. There is also rather elaborate work carrying Mexican and Indian motifs. If an original work is designed, it usually is copied in short order by all silver shops throughout the country.

4. A word of warning should be given about buying silver with inlaid stones. Silver cleaner will usually ruin the inlay, so that you cannot polish your silver without risk of harming the inlay. This applies only to cheaper artificial or semiprecious gems, of course, and silver pieces employing rosewood or ebony handles are perfectly practical.

GEMS

Despite popular opinion to the contrary, Mexico is not a great source of gems. The country produces in limited quantity only two semiprecious gems: mauve amethysts and bluish-green-to-orange opals. All others are imported. However, lower-quality stones of blue turquoise, transparent onyx, and opaque black obsidian are genuine, though not valuable enough to be called gems.

You will find combinations of "jade" and silver offered, but it must be reported that jade varies greatly in quality and type in various areas of the world. Very little high-quality jade has been found in Mexico since the conquest, although it is true that the pre-Columbian Indians did leave many jade artifacts. Where they came from is still a mystery, but the jewels found in the tombs of Monte Albán were, indeed, real jade.

The jade offered for sale in jewelry in Mexico today is almost always *nephrite*, a baser gemstone which is much darker in color and appears oilier. In less expensive jewelry, much "jade" is just glass.

The opals and amethysts are genuine, but you must be careful to get the real thing. Cut and polished, the stones can be very fine indeed. They come from the Querétaro area, and you will find them offered in many stores. Be careful about buying them in the streets, though they could well be genuine, too.

Turquoise is widely used with silver, but again you must distinguish between the good stones in reputable stores and bits of opaque bluish glass which resemble the real thing. A good hard look should do it.

Since the price of gold is set worldwide, there is only a slight advantage to buying it in Mexico, although the country does mine gold. Old gold coins of historic value can be purchased, and more recently minted heavier coins of up to 50 pesos in face value can be found. Something about the size of our half dollar in gold can be purchased for about $160. Gold bracelets are cheaper in Mexico than in the United States.

TIN AND COPPER

Tin, as you undoubtedly know, is a fine metal, and almost unrelated to the tin can. In Mexico, tin is used to make handsome trays, coffee tables, Aztec-style masks, candleholders, and even chests. Hanging lamps of glass and tin are particularly attractive. Where wood is used as a support, it is important to have a solid frame structure. Tin itself usually wears well, acquiring a dull patina, and is easy to care for. As in all crafts, workmanship varies from exquisite to shoddy.

Copper—once the favorite metal of the Mixtecs and Aztecs— is plentiful in Mexico, and it is a shame that it is not used more widely today. One small village, Santa Clara del Cobre, close to Pátzcuaro and Uruapan, which are just west of Morelia, has become famous for its copper work. The craftsmen hammer out deep kettles, pots and pans, and fine pitchers and lanterns, all made of pure copper.

But be warned that most of the so-called "copper work" you will see for sale both in shops and on the streets of Mexico is actually *iron sprayed with copper-toned paint*. This is worse than useless, as the paint peels off and you are left with ordinary sheet iron.

Some distinctive metalwork has been done recently in "wedded metals," which means the working of two different metals such as bronze with silver, brass with copper, and many other interesting combinations. These have been used in modernistic stylings for plates, vases, and ashtrays. (Note that they are called "wedded," and not "welded," metals.)

POTTERY AND GLASSWARE

The range of pottery in Mexico is limitless. It varies from the common, ordinary household pottery, sold in infinite forms in every market and used in every Mexican kitchen, to exotic work in finer potteries ranging from sculptured figures to elaborate candlesticks used for religious decorations.

Household Pottery. You can buy wonderful casserole dishes, called *cazuelas*, which are available in various sizes and shapes up to several feet in diameter, for only a dollar or two. You will find these useful dishes in every public market. They are ovenproof, made of *barro corriente*, the commonest clay, and their brown color is often decorated with a pattern in glaze of deeper brown. They are breakable and should be shipped like glass. Jars or pots (*ollas*), three-legged spice-grinding pedestals (*molcajetes*), and the soup bowls (*soperas*) from which much of the nation eats, are all available in the public markets. We have brought them back to the United States and have used them for years.

Talavera de Puebla pottery is a finer type introduced by the Spaniards; it can be easily recognized by its yellow, white, and blue colors and its glaze. It is somewhat more expensive (though still cheap) and of better quality than household pottery.

Oaxaca pottery is black in color, made from dark gray clay which contains iron oxide. Because of its black color, this distinctive pottery is most unusual. It is also fairly strong—enough so that it is used to sell a well-known brand of mezcal, a potent distilled juice of the maguey plant.

Tlaquepaque pottery is made in the little town of that name just outside Guadalajara. Some of the crudest and most vulgar of pottery is turned out here in a myriad of shapes, colors, and forms, but among it you can find some interesting pieces. For example, a popular art shop there, called El Arte Tonalteca, makes rough dinner plates with a beautiful blue horse design that has attracted wide attention. And they will ship for you.

Finer pottery can now be found in Mexico. *Maja* is produced by a Swiss woman who imports a clay and bone mixture and uses it in conjunction with Mexican talents for hand-painting to turn out beautiful white plates banded in soft pastels, grays, or mauve, with floral and bird decorations individually painted. These can be found at Sanborn's, among other places, and there are complete place settings as well as individual pieces.

Candelabra. Probably the most famous Mexican pottery items are the multicolored candelabra used for ceremonial occasions. These have a maze of arms rising like branches on an espaliered tree, and scores of smaller figures are interwoven among the gay designs. They usually tell a story, such as the fall of Adam and Eve. Unfortunately, it is a real problem to ship them home safely. Many of the best of these gaily colored candelabra as well as the popular *nacimiento* figures displayed at Christmastime come from the town of Metepec, near Toluca, which abounds in workshops where the polychromed clay sculptures have been fashioned by talented artisans for generations.

Coffee-Table Tops. Some very fine clay work has been used recently to make unusual tops for coffee tables. Some feature hand-painted bullfight scenes. They are glazed and of good quality, but are rather expensive. The shops in Puebla offer a particularly fine selection of tiles in the Talavera colors.

Mexican glassware, blown by hand in a variety of shapes and in colors ranging from brilliant blue and turquoise to pale amber and amethyst, is indeed a bargain and a handsome souvenir. Almost all glass is made in a relatively few factories in Guadalajara, Puebla, and Mexico City, the best being those of the Avalos brothers, who welcome visitors to their workshops to see glass blown in the same manner as it was centuries ago. They will ship to the States, but we recommend hand carrying when possible.

BASKETS

Almost as ubiquitous as pottery are the baskets of Mexico. They can be found in every size, shape, and color. We recommend you wait until your last day, then rush to the public market, or Sanborn's, and buy a big hamper to carry the things you can't get into your suitcase. These hampers are of various sizes, are usually fairly sturdy, and have covers that can be fastened shut. Everyone else on the returning plane will be checking one through also.

There are two main types of baskets:

The most ordinary type is woven from flat strands of reeds or palms. These are left flat to make the little mats (*petates*) on which both children and adults commonly sleep in the poorer homes. Schoolchildren use them for rest periods in fancy kindergartens, too. They are gathered together and formed into shopping bags of excellent design and utility.

Stronger baskets are made from willow reeds, stripped to bare wood, around which palm strands are wound like tape around a wire. These bound reeds are then tied one above the other to form the walls of the baskets we call hampers, which are useful for carrying goods home and for picnics later. Handles are an important feature on baskets, so examine them for durability.

LACQUERED TRAYS AND MASKS

The finest lacquered trays are produced in the Pátzcuaro region near Morelia in western Mexico. You will easily recognize these by the polished black backgrounds painted with colorful flowers. Other work, from Olinala, features a gold lacquer.

The lacquer work is similar to that for which China has long been famous, but in Mexico the original native lacquer used to be made from *chía* oil, extracted from wild sage, and from the boiled remains of plant lice called *aje*. To the mixture of these two extracts was added powdered dolomite, a mineral commonly found in Mexico, and native colors obtained from other minerals and insects. From this surprising combination comes lacquer as smooth, hard, and durable as the finest Chinese lacquer (which is made from the sap of a tree not found in Mexico).

The trays are hand-carved from soft whitewood called *tzirimu*, and in the case of masks you can turn them over and see the hand-hewn wood. The black lacquer is carefully placed on the wood and rubbed endlessly. In the finest lacquer work the design is then cut out and the lacquer peeled away, then a different color is applied to build up the surface. This ware is called *encrustado*, and it is the product of the best, though rarest, method.

On other trays the design is merely painted over the top of the original lacquer, and this procedure is known as *aplicado*. It is still an admirable method if the proper hand-rubbing has been done in the beginning. Unfortunately, the use of imported ordinary lacquer paints has been widely introduced, the polishing has been slighted or skipped entirely, and the applied designs are often sloppily done. A careful glance at the wood will tell you if it is encrustado or aplicado, and judicious observation will tell you if the work is fully polished and the design carefully painted.

While black is the commonest background, there are also chests with birds and flowers on white backgrounds, trays with colorful colonial figures on white, and the elaborately decorated large chests from Olinala. All of these can be found in Mexico City at Sanborn's and other craft shops, while you can purchase them on the scene in Quiroga, on the Guadalajara road near Morelia; in Pátzcuaro itself; or, best of all for the genuine article, in Uruapan, off the main road beyond Pátzcuaro.

SERAPES AND TEXTILES

Serapes (or, correctly, *sarapes* in Spanish) are a fine buy in Mexico as they are usually genuinely hand-loomed and make good use of the country's great talent in color and design. These blanketlike articles are almost always made of wool and are used by the Mexican country people as an overcoat and as a bedroll for the men (women carry shawllike rebozos, *not* serapes). Some have slits for wearing as ponchos. Tourists buy them for use as blankets, rugs, or to hang on the walls of dens.

In shopping for a serape, you should note the weight and thickness, examine the strands of wool to see if it is clean and does not contain other elements, and you might try the colors by asking for a dyed strand and placing it in water. Depending on the type of wool, the blanket can be either thick or thin, but it will not be flimsy to the feel unless it contains cotton.

Bargaining is in order, and prices do vary considerably, depending upon the size and quality. Usually a seller will come down in his price.

The very best serapes come from Santa Ana village in Tlaxcala and can be found for sale at roadside stands in the town of Huejotzingo just beyond San Martín Texmelucan on the main road from Mexico City to Puebla. San Martín is 34 miles from Santa Ana. Equally good serapes are made near Oaxaca, and the Pátzcuaro region also produces hand-loomed serapes. Prices range from $8 up.

Rebozos of all types, ranging from soft woolen shawls to sequin-decorated lace, can be bought almost anywhere in Mexico. Women use them as headdresses, as slings for carrying babies on their backs, or wrapped over the shoulders and around the waist in specific manners distinctive to each region. The soft, cashmerelike wool rebozos are the best.

Chaleco jackets, often called *Yucateco jackets* or *guayaberas,* are a most useful purchase for men. They are long-sleeved cotton sport shirts, usually with many pleats and pockets, and serve as dress wear without a tie in the tropics. Women find them delightful as beach jackets. Youths are fond of buying a colorful version without sleeves, called *Cortorinos.*

Heavy wool sweaters knitted from natural wool, with vivid designs, are warm and as handsome as any of the popular Scandinavian garments. They are available in Mexico for half the price in the States and can be found in markets throughout the country.

Native costumes of all varieties can be purchased in Mexico. Especially popular are the hand-embroidered *charro* or cowboy costumes for men and boys, and the feminine version, the *china poblana* costumes. Also, native women's costumes from various parts of Mexico can be found, such as the lovely, lavishly embroidered *Tehuana* or *Chiapas dresses.*

Toluca cloth, a wonderful hand-loomed cotton, can be purchased at bargain rates. This fast-dyed cloth is long-wearing and attractive.

Hand-screened cloth is beautifully made by a number of firms in Mexico and may be purchased by the meter in several shops in Mexico City's Zona Rosa as well as in most of the resort towns. Its bright colors and splashy designs are most effective for resort wear, but make sure the colors are permanent before laundering.

LIQUOR

There are good buys in liquor in Mexico, although you must keep several things in mind. First, by federal law, you cannot take back more than one quart per adult (see the Customs Allowance section, page 44, for further information). Second, liquor in bottles is heavy, and overweight charges on your flight home might cost more than the liquor. Third, Scotch is very expensive in Mexico, as are most imported items, so your really good buys will have to be local rum or tequila, or some of the liqueurs. Incidentally, for your own consumption in Mexico, Castillo rum is a dead ringer for Scotch. Try it. Costs only half as much.

Rum is sold in gallon jugs—in the supermarkets, among other places—nicely packaged in woven baskets which can later be used as lamp bases. Prices for the best rums usually run somewhere near $5 per gallon. Tequila is sold in quarts for not much more, and mezcal, the equally fiery distilled liquor, comes in handsome pottery flasks. The most popular liqueur is Kahlua, a combination of coffee and chocolate, and this is also in the same price range. Mexican brandy does not touch French standards.

THE THIEVES' MARKET

While you may hear many stories about the thieves' markets, they are not quite what the name implies, though interesting nevertheless. They are Sunday markets where many secondhand items are sold. You can find such sections at the big Lagunilla public market in the heart of Mexico City (found by going down Madero, the main street, to Isabel la Católica, then turning north for six blocks).

A special buy at Lagunilla is usually the old apothecary jars (there always seems to be a supply, although tourists have been buying them for years), which are expensive but of fine quality and usually genuine antiques. Just north of the cathedral is a smaller market, Tepito, which is said to be the real thieves' market.

LEATHER GOODS

Mexico does produce wallets, belts, and other leather goods of quality—notable for the fine rawhide used. Mexico is also a fine place to buy equestrian equipment. However, there are two things to check for in buying leather goods: First, peel back an edge somewhere and make sure it is solid leather and not a sheet of leather pasted over cardboard or another substance, such as plastic. Second, in buying briefcases, handbags, or suitcases, particularly note the clasps and hinges. These tend to be second-rate and can completely spoil an otherwise excellent purchase. Alligator is available in Mexico, although the genuine article is expensive. Again, beware of thin leather glued over other substances.

PIÑATAS

These are the fancy papier-mâché animals, usually approaching life size, gaily decorated and containing a clay pot which is filled with toys and candy. Blindfolded children are turned loose with a bat in hand and try to break the piñatas at birthday parties and at Christmas. They can be found in almost any public market. Children back home love them, too, but getting them aboard the plane is a chore. If you do buy one, check to make sure there is really a clay pot inside (reached through an opening at the neck)—some lack this most important part.

HUARACHES

The Mexican sandals are good indeed, though here again you can find many variations in quality. In many places, such as Puerto Vallarta, you can get them handmade to fit the measure of your foot. Women delight in the colored leather sandals braided into interesting patterns. Good huaraches will last a lifetime and are quite inexpensive. Try them on, for Mexican shoe sizes do not correspond to those in the United States.

PERFUMES

French perfumes are imported, and prices are somewhat lower than in the United States, although Mexico's own tariffs have substantially narrowed the gap. If you do buy perfume, by all means go to a reputable shop such as those in the big hotels. In any case, demand a whiff, and don't buy anything you don't recognize. Be especially careful not to buy toilet water bottled to look like perfume.

FINE ART AND ARTIFACTS

For paintings and plastic art, there are fine galleries in Mexico City and elsewhere which sell originals by distinguished Mexican painters, as well as some truly wonderful reproductions in silk screen, engravure, and other processes. There is nothing wrong with an excellent reproduction of a famous Rivera or Tamayo painting, and these are available. Likewise, there are numerous originals by less-known artists. An especially fine gallery is that of Mizrachi at Genova No. 20, Mexico City. He has another gallery at Juárez No. 14 as well as others elsewhere. Mexican galleries of current interest are listed once a week in *The Mexico City News*, usually on Sunday, along with a fine column by an expert on art, Toby Joysmith. Other art galleries worth noting are in San Miguel de Allende, Guanajuato, Guadalajara, and Acapulco.

Idols and other clay figures, which do in fact lie under the soil in countless archeological zones of Mexico, are offered for sale at most sites of ancient ruins, but tourists can usually presume that the chances are fifty-fifty that they are merely getting a good reproduction. However, it is possible to buy authentic stone figures carved in pre-Columbian times if you are expert enough to tell the difference.

According to Mexican law, all artifacts and works of antiquity are the property of the nation, and it is illegal to dig in archeological zones without a permit. If you do buy a valuable piece to take home, it is necessary to secure a receipt from the seller, then to take both to the Institute of Archeology in Mexico City and get a permit to remove the artifact from the country. This can be done, but the paperwork is time-consuming.

However, you are not usually bothered when small figures are concerned, although you do run a slight risk of having them taken from you at customs as you leave. Taking out something larger would call for a permit. The authorities will require a photograph of the object.

SHIPPING THINGS HOME

It is possible to have your purchases packed for shipment to you, but it is no longer possible to claim duty exemption on goods shipped in this manner. You must take them across the border to claim the exemption. However, you can have them shipped to you, either by parcel post (if they are not too large) or in care of a customs broker (the merchant will usually know one), and pay the *ad valorem* duty upon their arrival. Naturally you should be sure you are trading with a reputable dealer before paying him in advance. Paying by credit card helps to establish you did order it, and permits easier follow-up when necessary.

CUSTOMS ALLOWANCE

In November of 1978, new customs regulations went into effect which permit a duty-free import of $300 per person, so that a family of four can bring in $1,200 worth of goods duty free. Also under a program of "generalized system of preferences," a wide range of products can be brought in with, the exception of footwear, textiles, and watches. But you can bring in china, jade, leather, wood carvings, and many, many more items under this provision.

Duty-free gifts can be mailed home if valued at $25 or less per gift, and if no more than one gift is sent to any one address.

Liquor is permitted duty free at one quart per person, but federal authorities will permit as much as you can convince them is for personal or gifts provided you pay the federal taxes and applicable state taxes, which vary in almost every state. In fact certain states (California and Texas) allow only one quart per person but Florida permits up to five gallons if you pay the federal duty. A free leaflet, "Advisory for International Travelers," can be obtained from U.S. Customs Service, Washington, D.C.

6

Highway Travel

The Mexicans, as you will observe on the streets of Mexico City or even on your taxi ride in from the airport, love to get a little extra speed from their cars, and manage some rather neat manipulations in traffic. By and large, they are expert drivers and you are in good hands—so relax.

This love of speed has resulted in one of the ten major official auto races of the world, the Gran Premio de México, which is run each year in the handsome Autódromo de México, a fine closed-circuit track near the Mexico City airport.

But in days gone by, this auto championship was run on the open road in a 2,000-mile race from the Texas border to the Guatemalan border. Over 100 stock cars, often with top professional drivers, usually participated. With the cars shooting through the mountains and around hairpin bends at speeds over 100 miles per hour, this was a thrilling contest until mounting death tolls caused authorities to shift it to the Autódromo.

One year, while it was still an open-road event, an automotive publication for which I wrote asked me to cover the race in person, and I joined forces with a well-known photographer on assignment for Life. In my brand-new Mercury we drove to a stopover point where all drivers got thirty minutes to change tires, eat, and refuel. We shot pictures of this, but when it came time to leave we were told the road was closed to ordinary traffic for twenty-four hours.

When we said we would never get the race official's pictures back in time to be published, he had the brilliant idea of letting us enter the race, which on the next lap came to Mexico City, where we wished to go.

We pulled up to the starting point, my black car bearing an official press placard, and the checkered flag came down on us as well as the competitors. We roared off, and the photographer said, "Give it the gun and stay with them while I catch a picture of the group under way."

To our surprise, we drew up on the last car, and the photographer muttered intently, "Pass it!" We did, much to the amazement of the race driver, who saw a camera being poked out our window as we went by. Our car, in excellent shape and cool compared with the overheated racing engines, eventually passed fourteen of the racing cars and we moved well

*up into the middle of the pack. As we zoomed into Mexico City, we heard
the announcer at the finish line saying in Spanish:*

"Viene otro coche! Muy rápido! Muy bonito. Es coche negro. Es
numero . . . es numero . . . es coche sin numero . . . es coche fantasmo
. . . es [*as he caught sight of our press placard*] . . . es carro de prensa
. . . que milagro!"

*He had said, "Here comes a black car, nice driving, it's a car without
numbers, a mystery car, a press car— What a miracle!"*

*My wife, who was worried that I wouldn't get home to an important
dinner engagement that night, got a phone call from a correspondent who
was listening to the radio. He reported: "I think John just got home."*

MEXICO NOW HAS a fine network of 125,000 miles of paved
roads. They crisscross the country in every direction, although
many of the principal highways are spokes extending from
Mexico City to various parts of the Republic. Others run along
the shorelines, the new Route 200 on the Pacific coast and its
counterpart along the Gulf. Both have breathtaking views of
the sea. In southern Mexico a fascinating new highway cuts
through Alps-like mountains from Tuxtla Gutiérrez to Villahermosa, providing an alternate Pacific-to-Gulf route to the
famed highway across the Isthmus of Tehuantepec.

The roads north from Mexico City include the famed *Pan-
American Highway*, which is the designation most commonly
used for the road from Laredo, Texas, but which officially is the
road entering Mexico at El Paso. It makes no difference, as both
are of equivalent quality and both lead to Mexico City. The one
from Laredo is older and carries heavier traffic. It is a two- or
three-day trip to Mexico City from the border.

A new *Central Superhighway* has been completed straight up
the center of Mexico, avoiding many of the mountains encountered on the older roads. It, too, can be reached by entering at
Laredo, then traveling west at Monterrey to Saltillo, and thence
south via San Luis Potosí to Mexico City. It is considerably less
scenic than the older roads, but cooler and faster. It is not a bad
idea to enter on one of the older highways and use the faster
new road for your homeward trip. The old Laredo–
Monterrey–Valles road is one of the most dramatic tropical
routes in the world, and perfectly safe.

The new *short route*, or *Ruta Corta*, starts at Brownsville, Texas, and is convenient for tourists from the eastern United States, who can hug the Gulf coastline and save miles. The Ruta Corta goes straight down the Gulf to Tampico and Tuxpan, and then inland to Mexico City via Poza Rica and Tulancingo, a brief but moderately mountainous drive.

The old *Pacific Coast Highway* (Route 15) enters at Nogales, Arizona, and carries one down the Pacific coast section of Mexico, with interesting seaside stops at Guaymas and Mazatlán, and then to Guadalajara and Mexico City. This is a long route and takes four days of good driving.

Beyond Mexico City, principal routes are southwest to Acapulco (an easy five- or six-hour drive from the capital), east to Veracruz on the Gulf coast (about a seven-hour drive), or directly south to Guatemala via Oaxaca, Tehuantepec, and Tuxtla Gutiérrez (nine hours to Oaxaca and eighteen to Guatemala).

A fabulous new highway going along the very edge of the Pacific coast is *Mexican Highway 200*. When completed it will permit motorists to drive along the water for 1,000 miles or more. At present you can pick it up at Tepic from the Pacific Coast Highway (Route 15), go down to Puerto Vallarta and on to Manzanillo, past the new tourist zone of Chamela and Barra de Navidad. After Manzanillo the road turns inland to Colima and Zamora, then goes back to the coast at Playa Azul and south to Ixtapa, Zihuatanejo, and Acapulco. An amazingly beautiful bit of road, paved all the way.

Another breathtaking stretch of road you can already drive is north from Veracruz to Tampico, right along the Gulf of Mexico. An older but still lovely Gulf road travels from Villahermosa to Isla del Carmen and thence to Campeche along gorgeous beaches with overhanging palms.

There is now a completely paved highway running the length of the famed Baja peninsula, over 800 miles. You can enter at Tijuana and go south to La Paz at the far end, where large car ferries make daily trips to the mainland at Mazatlán and Topolobampo. At either city you can pick up the main highways north or south. See Chapters 8 and 14 for details.

Mexico is a country of constantly changing vistas, and every curve in the road is apt to bring some startling new view to your attention. The scenery is almost never tiresome, and even on the barren northern stretches of desert, the many varieties of cacti and the feeble little grass or mud huts standing stubbornly in the wind, with the small brown-eyed children playing around them in the dust, are arresting to the eye.

More often, one finds startling displays of tropical flowers along the road. Or from a highway snaking along the ridge of a mountain chain arise fabulous views stretching off for hundreds of miles. And one can hardly go far in Mexico without finding picturesque tropical scenes including palm trees, banana trees, and often parrots and other colorful birds. Life in the villages along the roads is an intriguing sight by itself.

RENTAL CARS IN MEXICO

It is not only possible but positively easy to rent cars in Mexico by the hour, day, or week, using a charge card and your U.S. driver's license. All major rental agencies not only have offices in most cities in Mexico, but you are almost sure to find a representative of one or more at a counter in your hotel. The agency representative can arrange to have a car delivered to the hotel for you at any specified hour.

Prices are higher in Mexico, largely because the agencies compute mileage in kilometers (about two-thirds of a mile), but charge the same rate they would for a mile in the States. This makes the major lessors very expensive. You can beat the high prices handily by checking out some of the very good but smaller concerns.

Most agencies will give you a travel kit including a map of the route you wish to take and information on places to stop, travel time, and points of interest to tourists. In Mexico City, some even provide a chauffeur to take you to the outskirts of the city and get you started on the highway.

Following are names, addresses, and telephone numbers of some car rental agencies in Mexico City:

Avis: Dr. Velasco 146 (566-00-99), Intl. Airport, and most hotel lobbies. Office in Acapulco. Reservations for all Mexico at 578-10-44.

Budget Rent a Car: Hamburgo 69 (514-9487), Reforma 60 (511-1235), and Intl. Airport. Reservations at all hours in thirty cities at 566-68-00.

Datsun Rent: Hamburgo 218 (525-2449), Reforma 51 (525-1173), and Intl. Airport (571-1685).

Drive Power (with chauffeurs): Insurgentes Sur 1761 (534-4457).

Hertz: Versalles 6 (near Hotel Fiesta Palace) (566-00-99) and Intl. Airport (571-3239). Offices in Monterrey, Guadalajara, Acapulco, Campeche, Cozumel, Guanajuato, and Mazatlán. Offices in most major hotels.

National Car Rental: Aeropuerto Central (571-11-08) and Reforma 240 (511-64-18).

Rente-Ford: Nuevo León 204 (564-50-64) and Intl. Airport (762-04-67).

Highway Maps and Road Logs

The Humble Oil Company has put out an excellent map of Mexico's highways, which you can obtain in Houston or other points in Texas. Texaco, Mobil, Sinclair, and others also put out good road maps of Mexico.

The American Automobile Association has a book called *Motoring in Mexico* which is good on highway travel itself, although we sometimes quarrel with its recommendations.

The most famous road log of Mexico is issued free by *Dan Sanborn* of Sanborn's Insurance in McAllen, Texas. His travelogue is individually compiled for you when you give him your itinerary. He puts various detailed, mile-by-mile guide sheets in special binders which often grow to be an inch or more thick. Many highway travelers find it becomes their Bible, as it lists all gas stations, restaurants and snack bars, hotels, and many sights along the road. He also provides a list of trailer parks. Dan, a wonderful person known widely in Mexico, expects you to buy your car insurance from one of his agents located at all principal entrances to Mexico; his rates are the same as others and his service has representatives throughout Mexico. Write to him at P.O. Box 1210, McAllen, Texas 78501, for information.

Food and Drink

First, there will be Coca-Cola (no plug) everywhere. Second, there will be the excellent ice-cold Mexican beer everywhere.

It is not, of course, recommended that you drink beer while driving.

You can usually find a satisfactory place to eat along the highways—giving yourself an hour or so leeway. With a little planning, you can go from one excellent dining room to another on the more heavily traveled Mexican routes. On the other hand, on an out-of-the-way road it is useful to know that practically every Mexican village has at least one passable little restaurant where you can order *carne asada y frijoles refritos* (a small beefsteak with mashed beans). This, with the aforementioned beverages, has gotten me through many a difficult spot in Mexico.

GASOLINE

You can be sure that all main highways, and most side roads, are equipped with gasoline stations from one end to the other. There is no reason, in my view, to even think about carrying extra gasoline, parts, etc. At the same time, it is a good practice to fill your tank at the first service station you see after your gasoline gauge touches the half-full mark.

Gasoline in Mexico is dispensed by service stations selling only the product of the national oil company, Petróleos Mexicanos (Pemex), operated by the federal government. All stations are thus Pemex stations. They are operated under franchise by private owners, much as are the service stations in the United States. It is regrettable that, with a few exceptions, they do not have immaculate appearance or facilities; however, they are usually quite adequate to passable.

Gasoline is usually sold in two grades, and the names change from time to time. At this writing, "nova" corresponds to our "regular," although with slightly lower octane, and contains lead; "extra" is nonleaded high-test (100-octane) gas. All American cars built after 1975 must use "extra" because of their engine design and the fact that the nozzle of other gasoline pumps will not fit in their tanks (most Mexican stations now have the new smaller nozzle, and those that don't, know how to circumvent the necessity for it). We found "extra" available even in the remote areas, although gas stations out of gas at any given moment are not unknown.

Gasoline is sold by the liter (3.7 to the gallon). "Nova" costs approximately 3 pesos per liter, or 60 cents per gallon; "extra" costs about 4 pesos per liter, or 96 cents per gallon. Prices, of course, are variable. Be prepared to pay cash at all gas stations. Credit cards are *not* accepted.

Some authorities advise keeping an eye on the pumps, as an occasional station is lax in starting at zero. Carefully note the bills you use in paying, and count your change as carefully as you would at home.

OIL AND GREASE

Mexican service stations generally have good equipment and are well able to service all makes of cars with efficiency and dispatch. There are locally manufactured greases and oils of good quality available at the Pemex service stations; imported greases and oils *not* available at the Pemex stations can often be obtained at garages and at well-identified shops specializing in oiling and greasing. If you are especially concerned about a new car, it might pay to search out the garages for oil changes and greasings. Most motorists, however, find the Pemex service adequate.

The attendants in the service stations may not speak much English, but they understand American cars very well and have a good grasp of proper tire pressure, etc. A small tip, from 50 centavos to a peso, is customary.

REPAIRS

In such large metropolises as Mexico City, there are, of course, many modern garages. But each village usually has a minimum of one garage and they do wonders.

Usually a tow truck can be sent out if you are in trouble. In such a case we suggest locking your car or instructing the other occupants to stay put, then flagging down the next bus and going on to the next town and getting a wrecker (called a *grúa*) to come back with you.

The Mexican government has dark green service trucks, easily distinguished by police-type white roof lights, which now patrol all roads and give free service to all motorists. Usually one will come by during a period of an hour or so.

You can count on a good supply of all makes of automotive parts in Mexico, although some of the smaller garages will have to send to distributors in the large cities to get them. They are able to make almost any imaginable repair.

Highway Signs in Mexico

A kilometer is .62 of 1 mile, or roughly 6/10 of a mile. That is, 100 kilometers equal 60 miles, 50 kilometers equal 30 miles, or 10 kilometers equal 6 miles. You will find kilometer markers along Mexican highways.

Our description of the highways of Mexico is based upon the fact that Mexico maintains white concrete markers along all its highways giving the kilometer point, in most cases the distance from Mexico City. We refer to these markers throughout the book so as to simplify our descriptions.

Otherwise, highway signs in Mexico are similar to those in the United States. The ones to note carefully are the following:

ALTO	STOP
PRECAUCIÓN	WARNING
PELIGRO	DANGER
CURVA	CURVE
PUENTE ANGOSTO	NARROW BRIDGE
TRANSITO (usually on an arrow)	ONE WAY

A narrow bridge in Mexico often means that only one car can pass, and the first car to flick its lights has the right-of-way. We suggest waiting.

Driving at night is very hazardous, and we would advise against it as a general rule. For one thing, livestock are apt to be wandering across the highway at night, and a burro through the windshield is a calamity.

Many trucks, often decrepit and without lights, park *on* the road at night, often in the main lane. More than one tourist has slammed into them with tragic results. Your lights just don't give you enough warning. Avoid night driving if you can. Otherwise drive especially slowly and alertly.

Traffic Signals

There are the usual red and green traffic signals in most large Mexican cities. There are also traffic policemen and policewomen directing traffic, and it is important to watch them (usually wearing light blue uniforms). When they are *facing you at intersections*, it is understood that *you are to stop*. When they are *standing sideways* to you, *you may proceed*. Speed limits in cities are marked, and often strictly enforced. Note that the speed limit is in kilometers.

On open highways, the speed is usually whatever you consider safe, though sometimes federal highway police will enforce limits of 100 kilometers an hour. We suggest moderate speeds, as cattle are apt to wander onto the roads, trucks and cars are apt to park on the highways, and in the villages small children will dart into the street. Out in the open, where you can see miles ahead in the daytime, it is possible to make some time. But, by and large, the way to enjoy your vacation is to take it easy.

Driver's License and Insurance

Your driver's license is valid in Mexico if you are driving there as a tourist. Be sure you have it with you. Ownership papers are also required at the border. Your U.S. insurance policy, regardless of what company issued it, does *not* cover you in Mexico, for either liability or collision; I have carefully checked this out. So it is best to buy some trip insurance at the border from one of the agents there. Specify exactly the number of days you will be in Mexico, since the insurance is most frequently sold by the day, although you can get it cheaper for longer periods. Give yourself sufficient time so that you won't be worried if you are late crossing back. The policy expires at a certain hour of the day (the hour you entered Mexico). You can get a refund for unused time if you stop at the agency's office on your way out and have the policy cancelled.

We recommend buying your insurance from one of the Dan Sanborn offices located at all entrances to the country. His rates are the same as other agents' and you get the free travelogue described on page 49.

Precautions

Car theft is as common in Mexico as it is in the United States, and we recommend that you *lock your car* when you leave it. Also remove valuables from the inside and lock them in the trunk. These precautions are not necessary when the car is within sight or in a reliable hotel garage.

Avoid Hitchhikers. It can be very dangerous to pick up strangers. We can't stress too much that you shouldn't pick up *any* hitchhikers, or even stop to help strangers unless you're sure of what you are doing. You might be the victim of a holdup.

We suggest that you keep these warnings in mind, use common sense, and start your trip with a carefree heart. Hundreds of thousands of cars course over the highways of Mexico every day, and they all seem to get along fine. So can you.

You are on your way—and you will be motoring over good roads in one of the most scenic countries in the world. Have fun!

_____*PART* 2

GUIDE TO PRINCIPAL CITIES AND RESORT AREAS

7

Acapulco

ACAPULCO IS in the tropics. There is bright sunshine the year round, tropical flowers and orchids, and even parrots. The coconut trees wave in the sunlight, and the royal palms can be seen against tropical sunsets.

Acapulco has one of the world's finest natural harbors, resulting from the immense, rugged mountains of western Mexico which tumble down at this point into the vividly blue Pacific. The dramatic hills surrounding Acapulco make for an infinite range of vantage points for homes and hotels overlooking the bay.

Hillside Homes and Tropical Sunsets. For all the rugged mountains and tropical sunsets, the main attraction at Acapulco is, of course, its beaches. They are there for the eye to feast on, but nowadays most people are content to swim at the pool, or pools, at their hotel. Still, a walking visit along the beaches can be fun. The most popular sections can be crowded, but there are also hundreds of miles of isolated beaches, almost desolate in their loneliness, to the immediate north and south, and all within a twenty-minute drive of downtown Acapulco.

Although it was once a forgotten fishing village, and then a quaint and jumbled resort town, Acapulco is now, alas, a city of 250,000 inhabitants. It possesses some twenty major luxury hotels which are probably far better than those in most U.S. cities. In addition, there are 100 other large hotels of varying facilities and perhaps 200 smaller ones.

The handsome skyscraper hotels stand in a seemingly endless curve around Acapulco Bay, and the city looks more like Rio de Janeiro every day. All hotels are air-conditioned, and each has a strip of beach where its guests can lounge on the sand, although most prefer the hotel pools with their sparkling clean water, comfortable lounges, and handy service.

It is quite fashionable for self-styled "experienced travelers"

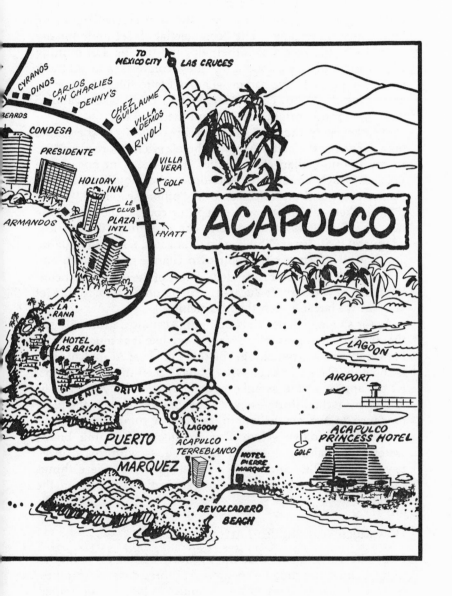

(those who usually have been to Mexico once before) to turn up their noses at Acapulco as being "too commercial" or having "too many Americans." The "commercial" label undoubtedly refers to the big hotels with their air conditioning, hot running water, and fairly good food. I like these comforts, and am frank about saying so. I have had my share of rustic village hostelries, and while they, too, can be interesting, I will take Acapulco any time for downright comfort and the good life.

Sitting beside the pool enjoying breakfast from the ample menu of one of the better Acapulco hotels is a lot more romantic, in my opinion, than chasing flies from beans in one of the villages which abound up and down the fabulous Mexican Pacific coast and are referred to as "other Acapulcos." From this blanket statement I will except, of course, the handsome new developments at Ixtapa and the charming (though less adequate) facilities at Zihuatanejo, Manzanillo, Puerto Vallarta, and Mazatlán. They have their own charm, good hotels, and scenery. But they aren't Acapulco—home of the jet set. (Cancún, the plush new resort off Yucatán, may become a rival for the jet set, but we haven't seen them switching.)

As for so many Americans being in Acapulco, I can only say that they are there, usually because they like it as much as I do. For gaiety and merrymaking, you just can't beat Acapulco! Here is the only place I've been where I have seen the international jet set appear at the swankest functions clad only in sandals and open-necked shirts—never a coat or a tie. Here is the place to dance in the gently lapping surf as a rumba band plays coaxingly till dawn. Here also are fleets of fishing boats, waterskiing galore, and even discotheques with go-go girls, psychedelic lights, and a hot beat till dawn. All these things make Acapulco one of the really extraordinary places in the world.

How Much Time Should I Allow?

I used to recommend that the ordinary visitor on a limited budget and time schedule spend two or three days in Acapulco. Now I am changing my mind. Acapulco is too big, too impersonal, and too expensive for the tourist on a modest budget. Better to take a package deal to a smaller place where you will feel more at home and less at the mercy of the sharpies of the big resort. So try a package tour to Puerto Vallarta, Manzanillo, Ixtapa, Mazatlán, or Playa Azul.

For those without any financial concern, Acapulco has fine luxury hotels, and for those with time to search out housing by the week, there are bargains to be found in Acapulco.

GETTING TO ACAPULCO

Under a new air agreement, Mexico and the United States are permitting American, Braniff, Eastern, and Western airlines to fly direct (in some cases nonstop) to Acapulco, as do the Mexican airlines, including Aeromexico, which has had a monopoly on direct flights for many years. The advantage of the direct flight is that winter travelers will find themselves under the warm sun in a matter of four or five hours from takeoff.

For those doing a complete Mexican trip, we still recommend going to Mexico City first, spending a few days there, then traveling to Acapulco by car, bus, or limousine via Cuernavaca and Taxco, two interesting Mexican villages (we recommend lunch at Las Mañanitas in Cuernavaca and an overnight at the Victoria Hotel or the Holiday Inn in Taxco). The superhighway to Acapulco passes through fascinating terrain: up to the mountains, then down to the tropics with its profusion of banana trees, mango clumps, and tropical flowers. (See Chapter 10 on Cuernavaca and Chapter 23 on Taxco.)

You can rent a car for this trip (see page 48 for a list of car rental agencies) or take a bus (make reservations at Estrella de Oro, Calzada Tlalpan Highway at south outskirts of Mexico City or the south bus terminal).

HOW MUCH WILL IT COST?

The real answer is that the best hotels are getting about $35 for double rooms without meals in the summer, and charging $60 to $80 for double rooms with breakfast and dinner in the winter season (generally December 15 to April 15). Expensive! Still, we found modest hotels charging $25 without meals for doubles, and some hostel-type accommodations for as little as $15.

There are some real bargains during the off season—places you can stay for three days and two nights, children free, for

$79. But don't look for such bargains in the winter. Such special deals are usually advertised in *The Mexico City News* as they occur, or your travel agent might know of them.

The *Condesa del Mar*, operated by American Airlines along with the nearby El Presidente and Fiesta Tortuga, is an excellent hotel right on the beach and in the center of activity. The price is $58–$64 for a double in winter plus requirement to include breakfast and dinner during peak periods at $17 per day additional. *El Presidente* is the same price, but *Fiesta Tortuga*, a fine hotel across the street, is only $42–$48 per day for a double with no meal requirements. In summer the price of rooms drops by almost half.

Las Brisas consists of "pink cottages in the sky," each with its own swimming pool, and a beach club on the shore. The price is only $36 for two in a double bungalow with pool in summer and $52 in winter, continental plan, which means breakfast is brought to your room each morning.

The *Acapulco Princess* is the largest of them all. Its pyramidlike building features nearly 1,000 rooms, each having a balcony open to the sky. It is located on the rather wild Revolcadero Beach near the airport, but it has a great eighteen-hole golf course. By making special arrangements, you can also play the Tres Vidas and Pierre courses nearby. The Acapulco Princess costs $50–$60 in summer, and $80–$100 in winter including breakfast and dinner for two.

The *Pierre Marqués,* also on Revolcadero Beach, is somewhat more isolated. A top hotel, it has doubles at $48 in summer and $80 in winter, with breakfast and dinner.

The *Plaza International*, a huge skyscraper hotel on the main beach, the *Holiday Inn*, also on the beach, and the *Paraiso Marriott* are top luxury hotels built within the last year or so. Rates generally are similar, ranging from $68 for a double with two meals in winter to $28 in summer without meals.

Some old favorites such as *El Mirador* offer European plan (no meals) with doubles from $32 in winter and $24 in summer, while the Western Hotels-owned *Caleta Hotel* has rooms at $40 in winter without meals and $30 in summer without meals. There is no charge for children in the same room with adults.

An *Acapulco package tour* is usually available in several forms. You might ask at your hotel desk in Mexico City, but Bedolla Tours, near the Hilton at Paseo de la Reforma 144G, México 6,

D.F., México, offers a typical two-night stay in Acapulco at a first-class hotel (*Hamacas* or *Casablanca Tropical*), with three meals each day and including round-trip plane ticket, for $79 per person. I would choose the Casablanca Tropical, but both are good hotels.

There are inexpensive rooms in small but often new and modern hotels such as the *Hotel Los Pericos* on Costera Boulevard near Caleta Beach, where you can get a room for $10 per day in winter and $6 in summer. The *Hotel Playa Hermosa* and the *Hotel Pacífico*, also on Caleta Beach, have doubles for $20 with meals and $12 without.

There are several hundred smaller hotels and pensions in Acapulco, including places to rent hammocks (which college students occasionally like, near Pie de la Cuesta). We no longer attempt to list them, as they change ownership and service frequently. We would recommend staying your first night in a recognized hotel and shopping around for less expensive accommodations your first day—when you can see for yourself. Some are very good and only a few dollars a day, often with meals.

Prices given in this section are estimated dollar prices. See Chapter 29 for actual prices.

MOTELS

There are not too many motels, as we know them, in Acapulco (many hotels have parking next to your room). However, three worth mentioning are the *Motel La Jolla*, not too far from Caleta Beach; the *Bali-Hai*, on the main Costera Boulevard; and the *Ritz Auto Motel*, also on the boulevard near the big luxury hotels. All have pools.

HOTEL LIST

A complete list of hotels, with general price range for both winter and summer, is included at the end of this chapter. Some motels and trailer parks are also included in the list.

WHAT TO DO IN ACAPULCO

First take a long breath, put up your feet, and prepare to change your ideas on how to live! Anything goes in Acapulco. Most people arrive about noon by plane or early in the afternoon by car. So find your hotel and have lunch (usually served from 1 until 4 P.M.) and a siesta. Our instructions start with the cocktail hour.

The cocktail hour is the key to your entire stay in Acapulco. You can have a nonalcoholic coconut-milk drink in the original shell, or have it with a jigger of gin and ice if you prefer (called a *coco loco*); or have a lemonade converted into a Tom Collins (the number-one drink in Acapulco). All the old standbys are also available.

Try taking your cocktail on the terrace of your own room (terraces are almost standard equipment in Acapulco hotels) while watching the sun sink into the Pacific as the twinkling lights of the harbor come to life. This can be quite an overpowering experience at times, giving you a mysterious sense of peace with the world. Worries and troubles seem far away. So try this some night—wearing nothing but a towel if you wish, as your terrace undoubtedly offers privacy. Or, if you still have your bathing suit on, invite your friends in, or your next-door neighbors—it is great fun and is considered good form in informal Acapulco.

About seven you can dress for the evening. Men should wear a fresh linen or cotton sport shirt and slacks or shorts. Men in Acapulco are going in for some pretty fancy embroidered sport shirts, but they never wear ties or coats. Sandals without socks will do fine for footwear. Ladies can wear cotton dresses or shorts (the latest craze is fancy evening pajamas for dinner).

While you will want to enjoy the cocktail room of your own hotel (usually beside the pool or overlooking the bay), there is no reason why you shouldn't, and every reason why you should, visit the cocktail facilities of the other hotels. Just have the desk call a cab, ask for the Caleta Hotel, and walk into its bar overlooking Caleta Beach and Roqueta Island; or have the driver take you to the Casablanca Tropical so that you can see the view from its rooftop, the most spectacular view in a city noted for spectacular views.

One night at least you will want to see the *diving boys* at El Mirador. They perform nightly at 9:15, 10:15, 11:30, and 12:30. The truly heroic dive from El Mirador's high rocky cliffs into the shallow inlet, some 150 feet below, is an impressive sight. You can view it from the balustrade down the several sets of steps from the parking area alongside the Mirador, or you can sit on the Mirador Terrace and have a drink while watching. For the best view of all, pay the 50-peso (about $2) minimum charge per person and watch it from your table in La Perla nightclub, which occupies the lowest terrace at the Mirador. Here you can enjoy a coco loco or a *pie-eye* (a hollow pineapple filled with rum and ice). The diving boys, all said to be members of one family who pass on the art (and exclusive privilege) to continually maturing younger relatives, will come around for a collection if you are viewing it from the balustrade. However, there is no additional charge if you are viewing it from La Perla or the Mirador Terrace. The divers have become demanding in recent years, but give what you wish.

Morning in Acapulco. People go to their own little beach or pool in the morning now, depending upon where they are staying. Then about noon they move down to the most popular beach of all these days—La Condesa. You can find it right between the Hilton and El Presidente on the great wide Boulevard Costera Miguel Alemán.

Here, along about noon, people begin to gather at the Paradiso Beach Club bar, or at Beto's next door, or the new "in" place, the Yes seaside restaurant. Here the tropical music is getting so hot by 1 P.M. that the police will not let it go on beyond sundown, which is roughly 7 P.M.

La Condesa. At La Condesa, you can either go to the Paradiso or Beto's and order a drink (beer or lemonade are 4 pesos, or you can get a Tom Collins, Calypso, Bali Hai, Beach Boy, Adam and Eva, or a coco loco for 12 pesos). Or try one of the four fancy bars in the Condesa del Mar luxury hotel, right next door.

There are rows of chairs, with small tables to put your things on, along Condesa Beach, and you can rent a chair and table. Look out for the occasional big wave that is apt to take even the table away.

These waves are great for surfing. The surf may be a little too much for children, so try it yourself first. Here the big breakers from the open Pacific hit the beach directly and are not caught by the arms of land protecting other areas. Try another beach if La Condesa is too rough.

Lunch. As Acapulco has tended to go to European plan (no meals included in the price of a hotel room) in recent years, people find they can eat away from their hotel. The Paradiso serves an interesting lunch; specialties include charcoal-broiled red snapper, shrimp cooked over the coals, and broiled oysters. Sanborn's air-conditioned coffee shop downtown will serve up a club sandwich, fruit salad, *enchiladas suizas*, strawberry short-cake, cocktails, or cold beer at any hour.

There are two new and interesting restaurants with beachfront locations, the Yes and the Langosta Loca.

The Yes restaurant is probably our most favorite, as it is right on the beach, immaculately clean, and has an inviting lunch menu including giant hot dogs with sauerkraut, ham and cheese on French bread, broiled shrimp plate, and the world's best apple-raisin pie a la mode. Steak, chicken, and lobster are served at night. There is a full bar, run by Carlos Romero, with Baron Jay de Laval watching the kitchen and turning out super cheesecake. Turn off Costera Boulevard by the Bali-Hai Motel or Denny's (where the old Motel Acapulco used to be) and head for the waterfront. Look for the sign which simply says "Yes!"

The Langosta Loca ("Crazy Lobster") is across Costera Boulevard from the Fiesta Tortuga Hotel near the Paradiso. The restaurant is down a short flight of stairs; attractive straw chairs are arranged around tables overlooking the bay. They accept all credit cards and are open noon and night. You can order fisherman's soup, or half a pineapple filled with fresh fruit, and broiled fish and shellfish of all kinds including lobster.

Or why not wander up the boulevard to an interesting sidewalk restaurant called La Ballena ("The Whale"). Here you can get an excellent fried-fish plate. And they not only serve the wonderful marinated seafood cocktail, *ceviche*, at 8 pesos, or 64 cents, but they will give you a printed recipe so that you can make it when you get back home. And note the mounted fish on the walls—some of the many types caught in Acapulco Bay.

Hotel Lunches. Most of the hotels put out rather a lavish smorgasbord luncheon starting at 1 P.M., and some of them, such as the one offered at La Concha Beach Club at Las Brisas, are real gastronomical *tours de force*. But you will find any hotel serving a fairly fancy lunch. And then off to a siesta and a recoup for the evening.

Caleta Morning Beach. We don't want to pass by the older "morning beach" entirely. While it no longer is so very popular, it makes an interesting visit. You can reach it by simply giving the word to the taxi driver, or by driving to the far end of Costera Boulevard.

Here also are beach chairs in neat rows, and the morning *Mexico City News* in English appears about 11 A.M. You can have a cold glass of beer, and a refreshing ceviche goes surprisingly well. The best place for these is the Bali Bar, which is at Erendira near where the bridge goes over to the Boca Chica Hotel.

Roqueta Island and the Glass-bottom Boats. You probably won't have set foot on Caleta before some barefooted sea captain tries to sell you on a boat tour. Take your time about accepting, although you will probably want to try this before you leave.

Roqueta Island has its own beaches, just as good as Caleta and perhaps a little bit better, in that the mainland beach tends to become heavily crowded. You can escape a good portion of this near-nude humanity by taking the boat trip across to Roqueta. The trip takes about ten minutes and costs about $5.

As for the *fondo de cristales*, as the glass-bottom boats are called, this, too, is worth a go, particularly if you have children along. The glass-bottom boats reveal some clear views of underwater life in myriad forms and colors. The divers who operate the boats invariably bring up sea cucumbers, or strange pieces of coral which they will give you.

I will never forget a diver placing a youngster's hook directly in front of the very purple fish the lad wanted to catch, and sure enough, the purple fish bit and the delighted young angler, watching all the while through the glass bottom, pulled him up.

Siesta. After an energetic morning at the beach, one gets back to the hotel some time after one o'clock (no use arriving before, as no lunch is yet being served), showers, dons another pair of shorts, and goes down to the dining room. After a refreshing drink and lunch, it is easy to pick up the siesta habit and sleep till cocktail time. One can begin to see the cycle of life in Acapulco!

Waterskiing. This is not half so difficult as it looks when you first see the water-skiers out on the bay. Practically anyone can water-ski! You will probably be up and skiing a half hour after you first put the big flat beginner's skis on your feet.

The training system for beginners is a marvel. With the tow boat close to shore, you stand in knee-deep water while two experts put your skis on—then run alongside you in the water, helping you to get up should you fall. An experienced skier then comes alongside and, pulled by the same boat, practically holds you up as you start off and stays right with you in case you need an assist at any time.

If you do fall, no harm results; you just float, hanging on to a buoyant ski until the boat swings around and picks you up. Putting skis back on in the water is a bit tricky, though, and usually you go back to the beach and start all over again.

Once you master this simple art, it can do wonders for your self-esteem. You begin to feel years younger, and may even come to look upon yourself as perhaps a pretty fair athlete after all. And, if you like, the boat will hastily pull you by the floating photographers' shack. If you will hold on to the tow rope with one hand for a moment and wave at the camera with the other, you can have a picture of yourself taken and printed on a dozen postcards, which will be a pleasure to send your friends back home. It might change your whole life.

The best place to water-ski is probably right at your hotel if you are in a major resort property. They have instructors well versed in teaching beginners, and the broad beginner's skis and the trained boat crews to go with them. If not, waterskiing is taught at various well-marked operations along the waterfront.

Fishing. Many people go to Acapulco especially for the deep-sea fishing. Your chances of reeling in a 100-pound blue sailfish or an equally big sierra or marlin are about fifty-fifty. Experienced crews, with boats and full equipment, are accustomed to taking out inexperienced hands and will give you all the help you need. They like to sail about 7 or 8 A.M., to get to the best fishing areas some distance out, so ask your hotel for a box lunch the night before. It's fun with a party of four or so.

You will find a fishing dock along the principal boulevard around the bay, just beyond the Club de Pesca Hotel, going toward the center of town. Here is an official government office where reservations can be made, or you can deal with any of the boat captains directly. Craft vary from small cabin cruisers renting for roughly $50 for a day's fishing for a party of four, to larger and more luxurious craft with refrigeration, ship-to-shore radio, etc., for about $100. In any case, only two persons can fish at the same time from the two swivel seats in the stern. All equipment needed for fishing is furnished. Pick a comfortable-looking boat, and if you can't afford one of the better boats you had better not go, as the poorer ones are likely to break down and delay your return.

Hunting and fishing experts say some good *inland fishing* can be found on the Papagaya or Barro de Cayuca rivers. These can be reached by jeep, and you can usually rent a boat at the mouth of these rivers. Inquire locally.

The yacht *Acapulco* leaves the municipal fishing pier at 8 A.M. each day and will take your family "bottom-fishing," including tackle, bait, breakfast and soft drinks, for a reasonable sum. This is almost sure to net you some exciting smaller fish. Skin divers are taken out at 10 A.M. by the same organization; they will pick you up at your hotel.

And be warned! Sunburns are a serious menace while fishing. Wear long sleeves, a brimmed hat, and something to cover your legs.

Hunting. For the hunter, shooting of white-wing dove can be arranged in season, which is usually between September and December. They can be found on the marshes south of Puerto Marqués and on other lagoons. Other shooting, for larger game such as ocelots, is better arranged at Manzanillo or Puerto Vallarta (see Chapters 15 and 21).

Picnicking at Revolcadero means making a trip beyond the next bay to the south, Puerto Marqués—somewhat near the airport. The charming little inlet of Puerto Marqués, once crowded with thatched-roof shops and its own sunbathers, now boasts a new luxury hotel. Somewhat farther beyond is a huge expanse of open beach with big breakers. This is Revolcadero, and it is the location of the huge Acapulco Princess Hotel, the smaller but elite Pierre Marqués, and the Tres Vidas Golf Club farther out. But there are places on this beach for picnickers, too, so don't hesitate to drive in. The surf is very strong here, and you must be extremely cautious in swimming, but a frolic in the waves is possible. The wilderness of some of the beach is breathtaking.

The easiest way to reach Revolcadero is to head for the airport and pick up road signs saying "Revolcadero." It is about a half-hour's drive from downtown Acapulco; a car can be hired to take you there. Bring a picnic lunch from your hotel. The road up over the mountain separating Acapulco Bay from Puerto Marqués Bay gives a magnificent view as you go by the strange rock formation called La Rana ("The Frog") at the crest.

Right on Puerto Marqués Bay are some grass-thatched stands which sell excellent fried fish, ceviche, and soft drinks and beer. El Mirador Hotel has a beach club here, also.

Sunset at Pie de la Cuesta is another interesting experience. Pie de la Cuesta is found by going into the center of town and out the road to the old airport, which lies to the north of Acapulco about twenty minutes from downtown. The old airport was located on a thin strip of land between an inland lagoon and the open sea. At this point, called Pie de la Cuesta ("Foot of the Coast"), there is a fine beach where you can sit in the sand and watch the huge breakers come in. As the sun sinks into the Pacific Ocean in the west, the rays are said to shine through the breakers, making them translucent. Some people even claim to have seen fish outlined in the translucent breakers. I haven't, but I still enjoy looking. You might, too. Swimming in the breakers is dangerous, as there is an undertow, and there is now a law against swimming here, although the beaches are open for picnics. I am told that hammocks can be rented in this area for a few pesos, and that more than one college student has made it headquarters. There are also several modest but modern motels here which serve excellent meals at low prices.

SHOPPING

You will find a wonderful new group of shops across from El Presidente Hotel on Costera Boulevard. These include *Lila Bath's, Vicki's,* and *Emi Fors,* all with the most chic of cottons and beachwear. There are also a beauty parlor and a men's sportswear shop in this same group. Branches of these and other shops are in most hotels. Most shops are closed between 1 and 4 P.M.

A new *Sanborn's* has been built next to the Condesa del Mar Hotel, while the older one is on Costera Boulevard just a block from the main town square on the waterfront. Both are wonderful combinations of drugstore, restaurant, cocktail lounge, gift shop, and magazine and newspaper dealer, and very much like their counterpart, Le Drugstore in Paris. Open from breakfast till 1 A.M.

The *Super-Market Costera* is a big modern food store with many sundries, including kitchenware. It is right on Costera Boulevard before the center of town as you approach from the Hilton.

A *public market*, large and airy, has been built out in a new neighborhood which you can find by turning off Costera Boulevard at the corner of the Hotel de Gante, about a mile or two south of the center of town, onto a broad double-lane side road built on each side of a drainage facility. Follow this east toward the hills for two blocks and you will come to a number of large buildings. Various sections house shops with produce, clothing, and flowers, and No. 9, if I recall correctly, has arts and crafts. Open every day and by far the best prices in town.

San Gabriel del Pueblito is another arts and crafts market specially geared for the tourists (the previously mentioned market is a true public market), but it has unusually nice goods and is worth visiting. It is just off Costera Boulevard next to the Big Boy restaurant. Here you will find goods from all of Mexico: flowers of tin from Jalisco, onyx from Puebla, carved lacquered trays from Guerrero, black pottery from Oaxaca, Moorish woven bags from Guadalajara, and a variety of leather goods, skirts, straw baskets, dolls, and more. A small plaza makes a fine resting place.

Branches of some of the Mexico City and Taxco *silver shops* can also be found in Acapulco, such as Antonio Pinedo at Hidalgo 9, Los Castillos at El Mirador Hotel, and Emi Fors modern jewelry at Costera 1999. Sanborn's also has silver.

Denny's is nearby if you need a sandwich, as are Big Boy sandwich shops and a Dairy Cream soda shop. Denny's sandwich shops are open twenty-four hours a day. The ice cream at Danesa's is excellent. Colonel Sanders Kentucky Fried Chicken is nearby.

SPORTS AND AMUSEMENTS

Bullfighting. There is a small bullring in Acapulco, holding 13,000 people, and fights are held most Sundays at five o'clock in the afternoon. Tickets usually cost several dollars. The quality of the fights is very uneven, and you can see anything from real slaughters by poor hacks to some fine bullfights by top-notch matadors. It might be wise to make a discreet inquiry. A bad bullfight is worse than none.

Jai alai, the famed old Basque game played on a huge indoor court, is more commonly called *frontón* in Mexico. Acapulco has a modern frontón stadium near Caleta Beach, where you can see the fast-moving game. It is played by opposing teams of two men equipped with baskets strapped to their arms, with which they fire the skin ball at lightning speed over unbelievable distances. It is a betting game, with the leading team being quoted at 100 against a lesser figure for the trailing team. By betting on the losing team, and then seeing them get ahead, you can hedge your bet by then betting on the other team. Thus you are sure of winning. The trick is to pick a team capable of overtaking the other.

Skin diving is the new rage of Acapulco, and the best of equipment can be rented from Aquamundo or Divers de México, both at 100 Costera Miguel Alemán, or at Arnold Brothers, Costera 106, across from Qantas Airlines (Divers de México, tel: 2-13-98; Aquamundo, tel: 2-10-41; Arnold Brothers, tel: 2-18-77). You can either chase fish with a spear gun or just explore the fabulous wonders of the tropical ocean. Lessons are given to beginners.

Sailing Trips. There are two large motor yachts that make a morning cruise usually at 10:30, a sunset cruise at 4:30, and a moonlight cruise at 10:30 on Tuesday, Thursday, and Saturday. Look for the large white ships *Fiesta* or *Sea Cloud* at the municipal fishing pier, or get tickets through your hotel. Prices are moderate, including a free bar and music. You go as far as the next bay, Puerto Marqués, in a three-hour trip. You should wear bathing clothes.

Zihuatanejo. For those in the mood for some exploring, and for those who want to get away from the Americans, you can find a fascinating native village up the coast 152 miles. Zihuatanejo (pronounced zee-wah-tan-ay-ho) has a brand-new resort center, Ixtapa, with beautiful beaches and several luxury hotels as well as the more modest hotels in the little fishing village itself (see Chapter 13).

The highway from Acapulco to Zihuatanejo is paved the entire way. Its spectacular views along the Pacific are well worth a trip. The little restaurants in town, while rustic, serve excellent seafood fresh from the bay.

There is also bus service from Acapulco to Zihuatanejo.

Dining and Dancing in Acapulco

There are an increasing number of fairly good restaurants in Acapulco, though it can by no means equal the fine cuisine of Mexico City. As winter tourists may find that their accommodations include dinner, eating out may be only for the special occasion.

The dining hours are late, and nine o'clock is about right. Call ahead of time for a table; phone numbers are given below.

Don't dress up to go out in Acapulco. Men need only an open-neck shirt, slacks, and sandals, while women can be a little more dressy if they wish. Men wearing a coat or tie, even in the fanciest places, will be stared at in addition to being uncomfortable. *This is a very informal place!*

La Perla will give you dinner while you are watching the diving boys at El Mirador. Dinner is also served at the Jacaranda supper club at El Presidente Hotel, where the famed flying Indians called Voladores de Papantla put on a show each evening at 10:30 (except Sundays).

A Word of Warning. Old-time residents of Acapulco observe that this is now a big city with many of the problems of urban areas. They suggest visitors stay on the main streets at night, do no out-of-town night driving or parking, particularly on isolated beaches.

Where To Eat Out in Acapulco

Chez Guillaume (*tel: 4-12-31*)   Moderately expensive
On Costera Boulevard across from El Presidente Hotel; very charming, upstairs with an open roof looking to the sky. Polite waiters. Probably the best food in Acapulco at our last visit. Excellent veal scallopini, filet Diana, stuffed avocado, scampi niçoise, chicken Kiev. Run by William and Victor Androti. Evenings only starting at 8:00. Call for reservations. AE, DC, and VISA.

Blackbeard's (*tel: 4-25-49*)   Moderately expensive
On waterfront at Condesa Beach next to Condesa del Mar Hotel.
Look carefully, as you can miss it. Features sizzling platters of
shrimp, steaks, and lobster served with chili beans, garlic bread.
Famed for self-service salad bar with "sexy dressings." Nautical
atmosphere. Pleasant, cheerful waiters. Owners are Gary Sinclair
and Carlos Mendoza. Open late. Very informal. Only VISA and local
bank cards.

Villa Demos (*tel: 4-20-40*)   Expensive
At Del Prado 6, up the hill directly across from El Presidente. A
beautifully appointed Italian restaurant owned by the Borzani
family in partnership with Demos Bettocchi. Wide variety of fine
Italian and continental cuisine. Good service. All cards.

Focolare Restaurant (*tel: 4-04-10*)   Expensive
In El Presidente, the twin of famed plush restaurant in Mexico City.
Atmosphere informal; wear your sport shirt tieless. No cover.
Continental menu. Air-conditioned. Opens 9:00 every night. All
cards.

Armando's Taj Majal (*tel: 4-12-33*)   Expensive
On Costera Boulevard near the Hotel Plaza International, this
fabulous place is one of the sights of Acapulco. It combines a fine
restaurant in striking surroundings with a beach club and an
adjoining discotheque. You can swim at the beach club for a modest
fee and use the huge pool surrounding the restaurant. The pool is
located in an immense arched structure of white Persian lacework
towers, which has given it the name of Taj Majal. Girls in harem
costumes serve excellent dishes such as artichokes, lobster bisque,
chicken or shrimp curries, veal Marsala, pepper steak, barbecued
ribs, and crepes Suzette. Open noon and evening. Call for reservation. Most cards.

Petit Rivoli (*tel: 4-00-64*)   Expensive
On the main boulevard diagonally across from El Presidente Hotel,
this is a lavish restaurant set in a garden with a waterfall. Owner
Jacqueline Petit (her partners are Teddy Stauffer and Dario Borzani)
serves French cuisine including stuffed baby crab, smoked salmon,
cream of avocado, steak Diana, and chicken Kiev. Closed Sundays.
Reservations recommended.

Carlos 'n Charlie's (*tel: 4-00-39*)   Moderately expensive
Upstairs across from El Presidente. A really mad place with very
good food. Jerry Ralph, a co-owner, will be there to lead the
merriment. Menu includes oysters Madrazo, stuffed shrimp, sea
bass, chicken curry, watercress salad with bacon and mushrooms,

gazpacho, pork *jalapeño*, peppered steak. Open from 6 P.M. until 1 A.M. No reservations. All cards.

Normandie *(tel: 2-38-68)*   Expensive
This austere French restaurant may have the finest cuisine in Acapulco. On main boulevard toward town in Costera condominium, has some sidewalk tables, air-conditioned inside. Run by Mme. Chauvin and her daughter. Caviar, truffles, artichoke vinaigrette, coquilles St. Jacques, snails Bourgogne, duck à l'orange, filet Rossini, pampano provençal. AE, DC.

Coyuca 22 *(tel: 2-34-68)*   Very expensive
Said to be the most beautiful restaurant in the world, and probably close to it. Does have stupendous view of city, arches, pool, palms, lovely background music. But owner's insistence on serving only three dishes (imported U.S. ribs or steak, and lobster tail) at very high prices lends uneasy feeling one is being taken. On hilltop near Del Monte Hotel; cabs can find it. You are welcome to have a drink and see view without cover. Modesto Calderón is maître d'. Open only in winter. Carnet, MC.

Sanborn's *(tel: 2-61-67)*   Inexpensive
The two handsome branches of the Sanborn chain are on Boulevard Costera Miguel Alemán near the main plaza, and also at Alemán 1226 near the Condesa del Mar Hotel. Service from fountain, bar, cocktail lounge; sandwiches to complete meals. Also newspapers and drugstore. Open breakfast till 1 A.M.

Portofino *(tel: 2-11-44)*   Moderately expensive
Across from Hotel Maris on Costera Boulevard, this is a noisy, cheerful restaurant full of confusion but with pleasant setting around small pool. Antipasto for 10 pesos, amazingly good asparagus soup, piccato, chicken parmigiana, Caesar salad, good wine. Food rather ordinary, but fun. Open 7 P.M. to 1 A.M.

Antojitos Mayab   Inexpensive
Next to the supermarket on Costera Boulevard, this is your best bet for real Mexican food in Acapulco. You sit at small bare wooden tables, but they serve wonderful tacos, Yucatán broth, roast suckling pig, enchiladas (really hot), and smoked pork chops. Special dish each day. Open noon, night, Sundays. All cards.

Yes Restaurant *(tel: 4-88-73)*   Moderate
On Morro Beach. Serves ceviche, giant wurst and kraut, cheeseburgers, broiled shrimp, sea bass, hot apple pie and ice cream; Baron Jay de Laval makes cheesecake in his kitchen. In evenings, chicken in coconut, steak béarnaise.

Finger's (*tel:* 4-70-88)   Moderate
At Costera Miguel Alemán 7777, across from El Presidente Hotel
and near Carlos 'n Charlie's, this is a good international restaurant.
Bar. Music. Open only in evenings.

El Fiaco (*tel:* 3-58-56)   Inexpensive
A typical Mexican restaurant on a modest scale but with excellent
grilled meats, cheese fondue, charcoal tacos. Located on Costera
near Las Hamacas Hotel. Only eighteen tables. Cold beer. Open
day and night.

Shangri-La (*tel:* 4-13-00)   Inexpensive
At Picuda 5, charming outdoor restaurant with authentic Chinese
cuisine. Highly recommended.

D'Joint (*tel:* 4-37-09)   Moderately expensive
At Costera 1070. Fine prime ribs, seafood, steaks. Popular with
young crowd. Features game corner. Open 7 P.M. till 1 A.M.

Denny's   Moderate
All over Acapulco and open all hours. Clean, modern. Sandwiches
and plate meals.

Colonel Sanders Kentucky Fried Chicken   Inexpensive
On Costera between Hotel Ritz and Continental, the Colonel serves
the usual. Open day and evenings.

VIP's   Inexpensive
On Costera next to Holiday Inn, this is another very modern and
very good short-order place. Sandwiches, hamburgers, pot plates,
fountain. Open days and evenings.

Tuscan   Moderately expensive
This is a restaurant at the Acapulco airport. Open practically around
the clock, it specializes in good food and fast service (a rare
combination). Air-conditioned. Gulf shrimp plate, Mexican steak
plate, turkey tacos, fruit plate, corned beef on rye, good ice-cold
draft beer, and a wondrous thing called *cola de lagarto* ("alligator
tail"), a refreshingly long cool drink (double vodka, lime, fresh
watermelon) which will get you airborne.

Beach Boy   Inexpensive

Big Boy Hamburgers   Inexpensive
These two are strung out on Costera Boulevard along the bay front.
Open early till late.

Danesa Ice Cream   Moderate
Opposite Continental Hotel. Excellent take-out ice cream.

Kosher Shalom (*tel: 2-13-98*)   Moderate
At Posada del Sol Hotel on Costera Boulevard—far out almost to the
Plaza International. Kosher food with good service.

La Ballena (*tel: 4-09-67*)   Moderate
On Costera between the Motel Monaco and the Hotel Ritz, this is
a sidewalk café whose name means "The Whale." Wonderful
ceviche, fish plate, and seafood plate. Good whaler's breakfast, too.

NIGHTCLUBBING OR SUPPER ON THE TOWN IN ACAPULCO

Windjammer (*tel: 2-41-41*)   Expensive
On the twentieth-floor roof of the Paraiso-Marriott Hotel, this is a
gay seafaring place with orchestra and usually a vocal group and
other entertainment. Fine view of the harbor. Serves an excellent
dinner, specializing in roast prime ribs, New York strip steak,
lobster thermidor. All cards.

Jacaranda   Expensive
This is the nightclub at El Presidente Hotel, located in open air on
the beach to one side of the hotel. It currently features the spectacular
"flying Indians," the Voladores de Papantla, who do their whirling
descent to Indian music nightly (except Sunday) at 10:30. Usually
a cover charge.

La Perla   Moderately expensive
At El Mirador Hotel, this is the place to go to see the world-famous
"diving boys" who drop 100 feet from the tall La Quebrada cliffs
into the water at the foot of La Perla. You dine at tables on tiers,
so everyone has a perfect view. Food is mediocre, but where else
can you see the divers while sitting down? Divers appear at 10:30
P.M. and 12:30 A.M. Minimum charge of 50 pesos per person. Small
dance floor jutting out over water is fun if there is good music.

La Joya (*tel: 4-09-09*)   Expensive
On the roof of the Continental with a ceiling that slides back to
bring the stars into view, this is probably the best supper club in
Acapulco. It has entertainment and good food. Supper can include
breast of capon, fettucine Caruso, steak Diane, sea trout, rock
lobster, and innumerable hors d'oeuvres and soups. Maître d' is
Domínguez. Open evenings until 1 A.M. Closed Sundays. Advise
reservations.

Le Club (*tel: 4-12-33*)   Cover charge
Armando's handsome new discotheque out Costera Boulevard near
naval base. Here's where the late, late action is, silhouetted against
a spectacular stained-glass backdrop. This is part of Armando's
beachside establishment, including his Taj Majal restaurant.

Charlie's Chili and Dance Hall (*tel: 4-66-08*)   Cover charge
On Costera in the set-back area opposite the Continental Hotel.
Doesn't open until 11 P.M. but has lively music and usually a large
crowd seated in fairly dark booths around a dance floor. Gypsy,
Ramón, and Fernando are managers (what, no Charlie?). Push
through the swinging doors for omelets and chili. Open till dawn.

Aquarius (*tel: 2-62-90*)
A discotheque bar at the Hotel Club de Pesca on Costera Boulevard
toward Caleta Beach. Good music, drinks.

Boccachio's (*tel: 4-19-00*)
Music, drinks, late dancing in beautiful Italian decor. Draws some
of the jet set. On Costera Boulevard near Tropicana Hotel. Opens
at 11 P.M. Runs late.

Le Dôme (*tel: 4-11-90*)   Cover charge
Across from Holiday Inn, features huge dome from which is
suspended an incredibly large chandelier. Much gaiety, loud music,
and shows. Open late.

Tiberio's (*tel: 4-07-71*)   Cover charge
Another discotheque, this one psychedelic, at north end of town.
Shows nightly at 11:30 P.M. and 2 A.M.

Le Jardin (*tel: 4-89-13*)
Directly behind Charlie's Chili, a new spot popular with the
sophisticates. Elegant styling. Open 11:30 P.M. till late.

Tiffany (*tel: 4-31-00*)
If you want to drive the thirty minutes from Acapulco proper to the
Princess Hotel near the airport, this is a luxurious and elegant spot
which features quadraphonic sound and the latest in music. Reservations.

Mil Lucas
At the Plaza International Hotel on Costera. Has continuous music
for dancing.

Dali Bar Disco
At El Presidente Hotel on Costera. Has continuous music from 9
P.M. until 3 A.M.

Cuatro Vientos
At Condesa del Mar Hotel on Costera. Shows at 11:45 P.M. and 1:30 A.M.

La Nouvelle
In the luxurious and spectacular new La Palapa condominium; the tall building is set back from Costera but easily visible. Pleasant continuous music for dancing.

A Short History of Acapulco

We purposely didn't put the history of Acapulco at the beginning. We have long since found that history is more interesting in retrospect, when you have already trod the grounds on which it was made.

Hernando Cortés, after his conquest of Mexico City in 1521, turned westward across the mountains in search of the "Southern Seas," and his men came upon the seacoast at Acapulco. The date is not precisely fixed, but it is known that a Spanish settlement was built at this precise location about 1530, with the aim of building two ships to explore the Southern Seas.

Acapulco in 1532. These two ships were built in Acapulco from locally secure materials and were christened *San Miguel* and *San Marcos.* The first definite record in Acapulco history is of the sailing of these two caravels on June 30, 1532. They were built by Juan Rodriguez Villafuerte and were acquired by Cortés for use by an expedition headed by Diego Hurado de Menoza, one of his lieutenants.

Cortés himself participated in some of the voyages, as he had been given the right by the Spanish Crown to "discover, conquer and colonize the islands which he might find in the South Sea." In 1537, two more ships sailed from Acapulco to Peru. Other ships, searching for an imaginary fabled city of Cibola, which in fact did not exist, sailed up the Gulf of California and even up the Colorado River without finding the treasured city. But at least a rough chart of Mexico's western coast was secured.

Magellan. In the next few decades, Magellan made his trip around the world and discovered the China coast. The Philippine Islands were also discovered, and valuable goods and materials were found for Spain. However, there was no easy route back from the west, and in 1565 an Augustinian monk and great seafarer, Andrés de Urdaneta, who had sailed extensively in the Pacific, sailed from the Philippines with the mission to find a "return from the west."

Four months later, on October 3, 1565, after the pilot, mate, and fourteen of the crew had died from the agonies of the long voyage, Urdaneta's galleon sailed into Acapulco harbor—marking the first crossing from the west to this point.

The China Ships. Thereafter, the so-called China ships sailed regularly from China and the Philippines to Mexico, carrying at first goods for Spain which were packed by mules or humans over the mountains to Veracruz for transshipment to Barcelona. Soon Chinese and Japanese merchants also shipped goods, and a famed fair began to be held in Acapulco with the arrival of the China ships. Acapulco's population of 4,000 often rose to 10,000 during the fairs. Here were sold spices, silks, pearls, gold and silver jewelry, and fine cloths. Each ship was said to carry over 2 million pesos in goods, or nearly that much in dollars in those days. Those participating in the trade became fabulously rich. Here, too, arrived the famed *China Poblana*, or "China Woman," said to have been brought by a Puebla merchant for his wife, and her costume is still a national favorite in Mexico.

Sir Francis Drake. It was not long before the rich China trade attracted the sea pirates of those days, and Sir Francis Drake was among those who began to raid the rich galleons. Acapulco built a number of fortifications, including San Diego Fort, to defend the port, and from then on pirate ships were unable to enter the bay. The original fort, called San Diego Castle, built in 1616, was destroyed in a terrible earthquake in 1776; its replacement, San Diego Fort, can still be seen in the irregular-shaped pentagon on Costera Miguel Alemán not far from the downtown area.

With the War of Independence of 1810 in Mexico, trade with Spain was broken off; the China trade largely ceased, and the mule trail over the mountains from Acapulco to Mexico City fell into disuse and was overgrown by jungle. For more than 100 years Acapulco was largely forgotten, until, on November 11, 1927, a new road, more or less following the old mule trail and hacked out of the mountains and jungles, was completed. It took twelve hours to traverse it at the fastest speeds then possible. In 1955 the present superhighway was opened.

A Forgotten Village. Acapulco was actually still a practically forgotten fishing village, with only one hotel or so, as recently as 1938. Then an American promoter built Las Américas Hotel (now the Prado Américas), Don Carlos Barnard built his El Mirador Hotel, and the resort business of Acapulco began. Today there are well over 100 hotels, some of fabulous luxury, and Acapulco, often called the Riviera of the West, is a world-famed playport whose name is synonymous with gaiety and sports in the tropical sun.

WHERE TO STAY IN ACAPULCO

Luxury Hotels

Acapulco Princess (*777 rooms*)   Very expensive
This $40-million hotel is on a 280-acre site on the wild Revolcadero Beach. Its huge truncated pyramid shape permits almost every room to have a balcony open to the sky. Has eighteen-hole golf course, penthouses with Roman baths, five cocktail lounges, Cocoloco nightclub, La Princesa and El Gourmet dining rooms, skin diving, waterskiing, and beach buggies. Tumbling waterfall and slide in large pool. Bruno Lugani is manager. Thirty minutes from center of Acapulco.

Fiesta Tortuga (*252 rooms*)   Moderately expensive
Author's Choice. Operated by American Airlines, this is a modern eight-story hotel on Costera Boulevard across from Condesa del Mar, which is under same management. It is a good hotel, informal and fun. The wonderful La Fonda restaurant has good Mexican food at reasonable prices as well as a general menu. Music, dancing, and lots of young people. Golf, tennis, game rooms, and convention rooms available. Not on beach, but Condesa nearby. Convenient location. Tel: 4-88-99.

Acapulco Torreblanca (*200 rooms*)   Moderate
On Puerto Marqués Bay (about twenty minutes from downtown Acapulco), this is a modern tower hotel overlooking bay and beach below. Quiet and serene. Chateaubriand restaurant. Pool. Golf. Located in lush tropical area. Tel: 4-60-50.

Las Brisas (*200 rooms*)   Very expensive
The famous "pink bungalows in the sky" on the hillside overlooking Acapulco Bay, each with its own little swimming pool. Pink jeeps available. Wonderful beach club with saltwater pool opening on sea. Bella Vista dining room with dancing. Refrigerators in each

room kept stocked with tropical fruit, drinks. No tipping permitted, but a charge is added. Now run by Western Hotels Intl. Toll-free tel: (800) 228-3000.

Condesa del Mar (*508 rooms*)   Moderately expensive
(less in summer)
Situated on a rocky promontory in the heart of Condesa Beach, this is the newest and most lavish of the hotels in the central beach area and very convenient to shops and clubs. Rooms with balconies looking out to sea, open-air cafeteria, and sky-high Techo del Mar rooftop supper club. Two pools. Near golf. Fine beaches. Operated by American Airlines as a Flagship hotel. Tel: 4-14-15.

Americana/El Presidente Hotel (*407 rooms*)   Moderately expensive
One of the largest and swankest of hotels in Acapulco, located on Los Hornos Beach. Air-conditioned. Pool, shops, and beauty shops. Top-flight Focolare restaurant and Jacaranda nightclub adjoining and run by same management. Operated by American Airlines as Flagship hotel, and next door to Condesa del Mar with same management. Tel: 4-17-00.

Hotel Pierre Marqués (*104 rooms*)   Very expensive
(less in summer)
Exclusive hotel on 167-acre site on Puerto Marqués Bay. Situated directly on open beach, has two pools, restaurant, bar, tennis, waterskiing, fishing, and two championship eighteen-hole golf courses. Completely air-conditioned. Next door to new Acapulco Princess and has same ownership. Toll-free tel: (800) 223-1818.

Elcano Hotel (*116 rooms*)   Expensive
Located on Costera Boulevard, fronting on beach, this is one of the best hotels in Acapulco. Named after famed navigator Juan Sebastian Elcano. Fully air-conditioned, pool, restaurant, tables on beach with coconut-thatched roofs. Tel. (Los Angeles): (213) 462-6391.

Ritz Hotel (*140 rooms*)   Moderately expensive
Another towering skyscraper right on the main beach. TV czar Emilio Azzcaraga, who owns it, says, "This is a rock-and-roll luxury hotel." He wants guests to have fun, and has provided "symphony of sea" mural at bottom of pool, bar with plate-glass windows showing crashing waves of Los Hornos, and balconies overlooking sea. Central air conditioning. Tel: 4-08-40.

Acapulco Continental (*500 rooms*)   Expensive
Two modern buildings on Costera in convenient location with both pool and beach. All rooms have balcony overlooking sea, and all are air-conditioned. Has very attractive coffee shop on island in

center of pool, and rooftop dine-and-dance spot with retractable ceiling open to the stars. Tel: 4-09-09.

Hotel Casablanca (*133 rooms*)   Moderate
This is one of the landmarks of Acapulco, a white three-story building sitting on one of the most prominent hilltops overlooking the bay. It has good rooms and junior suites with balconies with marvelous views of the Pacific. Meals and drinks served on balconies. Fine pool, restaurant with view, dancing on starlight roof. Tel: 2-12-12.

Holiday Inn Acapulco (*368 rooms*)   Moderately expensive
A modern round tower situated on one of the best beaches. Balconies overlooking sea or mountains, fine rustic bar immediately over beach, palm-thatched cabanas on beach, small pool. Decor garish but fun. Delfín cafeteria good and reasonable. Tel: 4-04-10 or any Holiday Inn.

Plaza International Hyatt Regency (*750 rooms*)   Expensive
At the far end of Hornos Beach, this is a huge new hotel, first-class, which has five restaurants, six bars, rooftop supper club, tennis courts, and pool surrounded by garden. Near Tres Fuentes restaurant and just down hill from Las Brisas. Fine view of sea. Toll-free tel: (800) 228-9000.

Caleta Hotel (*300 rooms*)   Moderate
Right on famed Caleta Beach, this is one of the few hotels from which you can walk to the "morning beach" where everyone gathers. Restaurant, bar. A Western hotel. Tel: 2-48-00.

Boca Chica Hotel (*40 rooms*)   Moderate
Situated on the other side of Caleta Beach, it also is very convenient to the *playa*. Relatively new, attractive hotel, with big verandas looking out on Roqueta Island. Given a good rating by visitors. Toll-free tel: (800) 223-5695.

Villa Vera Racquet Club (*25 suites*)   Moderately expensive
A set of deluxe bungalows halfway up the hillside from El Presidente. Attracts tennis fans with its fine courts. Pool has sunken bar. Usually good food. No children permitted. Tel: toll-free (800) 421-0767 or 4-03-33.

Acapulco Malibu (*80 rooms*)   Moderately expensive
Located on beach near golf club. Has popular pool, restaurant, nightclub. Tel: 4-10-70.

Maris Hotel (*80 rooms*)   Moderately expensive
On Costera with its own beach, this is one of the modern hotels. While not luxurious, it is considered good. Small pool. Tel: 2-28-00.

Club de Pesca (*123 rooms*)   Moderate
Located on Costera in dockside area, this hotel is rather uninspired modern. Location is good, though bathing is better farther out on beach area. Very convenient to fishing dock and yacht club. Pool, bar. Tel: 2-62-90.

El Mirador (*133 rooms*)   Moderate
Perched on the great cliffs overlooking the Pacific, this rambling hotel is known as one of the best. Diving boys dive from here. Restaurant, three pools, most rooms air-conditioned. Add $12 for three meals. Owned by Western Hotels. Tel: 2-11-11.

Paraiso-Marriott (*442 rooms*)   Moderately expensive
A twenty-two-story modern hotel right on the beach with famed Windjammer supper club on its roof for dining and entertainment. Coffee shop, Palenque bar, pool, barbershop, and shops. Marriott chain. Tel: 2-41-40.

Hotel Costera (*70 rooms*)   Moderate
A modern ten-story hotel smack on the beach in one of the nicest areas, but far enough off Costera Boulevard to be quiet. Air-conditioned. All rooms have cross ventilation and a view of the sea. Near golf course. Grass-roofed tables around pool. Tel: 4-01-31.

Posada del Sol (*190 rooms*)   Moderate
A three-story hotel on Costera Boulevard within walking distance of beach. Some cottages on beach. Air-conditioned. Pool, beach pavilion, coffee shop, kosher dining room. Tel: 4-10-10.

La Palapa Hotel   Expensive
An ultraluxurious hotel-condominium on the main bay just off Costera Boulevard. Lavish pool, restaurant, and many other comforts in its thirty-story building. Toll-free tel: (800) 421-0550.

Best Motels

Ritz Auto Motel (*100 rooms*)   Moderate to expensive
Owned and managed by the same group as the luxury Ritz Hotel, but is one block inland from the boulevard beachfront hotel. Modern, attractive four-story building with pool, attended parking

lot, and good restaurant. Additional charge for air-conditioned rooms and suites. Requires modified American plan in winter, which is expensive. Tel: 2-19-40 or, in Mexico City, 525-16-65.

Impala Motel (*32 rooms*)   Moderate
An attractive modern motel just off beach. Each room has balcony. Air-conditioned. Lovely pool. Run by American from Janesville, Wisconsin. Where Mexico City road hits Costera Boulevard at Diana circle, turn left 2 miles. Tel: 4-22-01.

Motel La Jolla (*74 rooms*)   Moderate
Newest motel in Acapulco with modern, comfortable, air-conditioned rooms on Costera Boulevard about a mile before Caleta Beach. Pool, grassy lawns, handsome coffee shop. Tel: 2-58-62.

Motel Bali-Hai (*112 rooms*)   Moderately expensive
On Costera Boulevard one block from Hilton. Modern, well-run, air-conditioned. Swimming pool. Near beach. Cafeteria open all hours, bar. Tel: 4-11-11.

Excellent Moderate-rate Hotels

Pozo del Rey (*20 rooms*)   Moderate
Located on the peninsula stretching out into Acapulco Bay, this is a wondrous tropical garden with orchids and palms, sparkling-clean rooms, large gemlike pool, filtered water, and good food. Managed by an American, Diane Marsallis, whose family built it. Write P.O. Box 363 or tel: 2-22-03.

El Tropicano Hotel (*140 rooms*)   Inexpensive
At end of Costera beyond Plaza International, this is a modern, air-conditioned hotel overlooking the sea. Two pools and lovely garden. Dining room, beach club, piano bar. Tel: 4-11-00.

El Cid (*140 rooms*)   Inexpensive
A block off Costera Boulevard near the Diana statue, this is a seven-story air-conditioned hotel with pool, restaurant, sidewalk cafe. Tel: 3-50-50 or 2-42-42.

Las Hamacas Motor Hotel (*125 rooms*)   Moderate
One of the older hotels recently remodeled, set in gardens near center of town and just across Costera Boulevard from older beach area. Well-run, good food served in open-air dining room, with music and entertainment. Tel: 2-61-61.

El Matador (*250 rooms*)   Moderately expensive
Above Condesa Beach on hillside, this hotel is popular with tour groups. Colonial Mexican decor. Each room has kitchenette with stocked refrigerator. Pool, restaurant, nightclub, tennis, squash. Tel: 4-32-90.

Good Inexpensive Hotels

Casino Hornos (*100 rooms*)   Inexpensive
This is a large building on Hornos Beach next to the Ritz Hotel, and it has been completely renovated and modernized to offer convenient rooms. Tel: 4-05-00.

Hotel Belmar (*68 rooms*)   Inexpensive
A well-maintained attractive four-story hotel overlooking and within walking distance of Caleta Beach. Each room has balcony. Pool. Three meals. Tel: 2-15-25.

Club Areka Suites (*13 suites*)   Moderate
A small but modern establishment off Caletilla Beach. Address: Cumbres de Caletilla 36; tel: 2-20-66.

Hotel Lindavista (*42 rooms*)   Inexpensive
Attractive, well-kept hotel overlooking Caleta Beach. Rooms with balconies. Tel: 2-27-83.

Hotel San Antonio (*14 rooms*)   Inexpensive
New air-conditioned hotel directly across from jai alai courts, near Caleta Beach. Music in all rooms. Tel: 2-13-58.

Motel Caribe (*26 rooms*)   Inexpensive
Attractive modern hotel on López Mateos Boulevard near Caleta Beach and jai alai courts. Very good if you don't mind utility-type (although all private) bathrooms. Tel: 2-15-50.

Hotel São Paulo (*84 rooms*)   Moderate
Modern rooms and kitchenettes on Costera Boulevard near yacht club, overlooking bay. Pool, bar, good charcoal-broil dining room. Tel: 2-57-90.

Hotel Los Pericos (*55 rooms*)   Inexpensive
One of the best bargains in Acapulco with three meals at modest price in a modern building. Clean and neat, within walking distance of Caleta Beach. DC, VISA. Tel: 2-40-78.

Hotel Sands (*60 rooms*) Moderate
A fine new hotel in an excellent location on Costera Boulevard across from the Continental. Fine pool, easy walk to beach. Rooms have balconies overlooking pool and garden. Clean and neat. Air-conditioned. Jeep rental. Tel: 4-22-60.

Puerto Arturo Inexpensive
Good modest hotel overlooking Caleta Beach from Boca Chica area. Tel: 3-53-32.

Leighton Hotel (*20 rooms*) Inexpensive
Older small hotel just off Costera Boulevard near ski club and within walking distance of Caleta Beach. Tel: 2-53-40.

Hotel Pacífico (*137 rooms*) Inexpensive
This is practically an institution in Acapulco, as all the college kids for generations—at least until they got rich—stayed here. Recently two new wings were added and the entire hotel modernized. Right on beach. Informal dining bar. Air conditioning $2 extra. Accepts almost all credit cards. Tel: 2-03-53.

Hotel Villa (*39 rooms*) Moderate
Handsome new hotel, each room with a balcony overlooking the sea. All rooms air-conditioned. Lovely pool, restaurant, cocktail lounge. At Roqueta 54. Tel: 3-33-11.

Bonmattie Apartments Inexpensive
If you wish to take a small apartment and save money, you couldn't do better than Ben Urbanek's place at Aguado 18, up the street from the Club de Yates. Nice bay view, clean and comfortable.

Trailer Parks

Acapulco Trailer Park (*50 spaces*) $3
At the Pie de la Cuesta Beach about 8 miles north of sea and lagoon. All hookups, showers, boat ramp. Restaurant nearby.

Carmel Trailer Park (*120 spaces*) $3
In coconut grove 5 miles north of Acapulco on Highway 95. All hookups, modern baths, purified swimming pool.

8

Baja California:
Tijuana, Enseñada, Baja Sur, and La Paz

BAJA CALIFORNIA is, of course, the huge peninsula which
extends the unbelievable distance of 770 miles in a long arm
stretching south of the border from San Diego. Its principal
cities are Tijuana, Mexicali, and the famed resort of Enseñada,
all reachable from the United States by paved highway. The
new highway running the length of the peninsula now makes
it possible to drive to a wonderful array of bathing and fishing
resorts along the great Sea of Cortés and on to the very tip,
Cabo San Lucas.

The peninsula of Baja California is still a vast wilderness,
with huge crags of mountains, barren deserts, and even huge
salt beds on which nothing lives. But it also has hundreds of
miles of lovely beaches, lagoons surrounded by waving green
palms, and some of the best fishing in the world.

Baja California is divided into two states: Upper Baja, with
its capital in Mexicali in the heart of a lush vegetable-growing
area, and Lower Baja in the more thinly inhabited southern
half, with its capital at La Paz. Many fine ranches are located
in plateau land in the mountainous area, and new hotels are
springing up along the main highway. Still, it is a long way
between gasoline stations.

BY AIR TO BAJA CALIFORNIA

You can fly from Los Angeles to Tijuana and La Paz on
Aeromexico, and Hughes Airwest has flights from Phoenix and
Tucson to La Paz. Local flights will include stops at Enseñada,
Loreto, and Santa Rosalia as well. There are now direct flights
to Cabo San Lucas by Aeromexico and by Hughes Air West,
as well as flights from La Paz to Cabo San Lucas. American
flies direct from Dallas.

88

Driving to Baja California

For a first trip, we recommend driving to Enseñada (206 miles from Los Angeles and 67 miles south of Tijuana on a paved coastal highway) and stopping in one of Enseñada's many good seaside motels (see list on page 108) for a night or a full vacation. There is good fishing in Enseñada.

Traveling by highway from the United States to the border city of Tijuana is easy. Only 17 miles from San Diego, Tijuana is a popular visiting place for Californians, although it has the disadvantages of any border community and is almost more American than Mexican. The Mexican government even found recently that United States dollars were the common unit of exchange in Tijuana rather than Mexican pesos, and certainly English is widely spoken. However, for those who cannot really explore more genuine bits of Mexico, Tijuana is an interesting one-day visiting spot, with its shops, bullfights, jai alai, and racing at Agua Caliente.

A Sunday Drive

A long Sunday drive into Mexico can be made from southern California by going down to Tijuana, then taking a Mexican highway paralleling the border to Tecate, Alaska, and Mexicali, where you can cross the border to Calexico on the United States side and proceed home. Or you can go on to Yuma, Arizona, from Mexicali. The drive from Tijuana goes through desert with mesquite and cactus and into the fertile irrigated valleys around Mexicali, through some interesting border towns.

You Don't Have To Be an Explorer!

Be it a weekend trip to Tijuana or Enseñada, or a full excursion all the way down the 770-mile peninsula to the fascinatingly isolated city of La Paz, which has preserved so much of its colonial heritage, this chapter has been designed to introduce you to a forgotten land. The network of roads between Tijuana, Enseñada, Mexicali, and San Felipe in the northernmost part is well paved and adequate for the Sunday motorist. You can drive your own car here and find good motels when you arrive.

Driving the Peninsula

It is now possible to drive the entire length of the Baja over an excellent all-weather two-lane paved highway that snakes its way for 1,100 miles from Tijuana to Cabo San Lucas—an air distance of only 800 miles, but switching back and forth across the peninsula on the way down makes the highway distance greater.

This simple blacktop highway was constructed strictly for the knowledgeable driver. For long stretches it is only 19½ feet wide, often without shoulders, and at times it winds up thousands of feet in steep grades; occasionally flash floods will cover parts of the road with water. But it is still comfortably passable by the ordinary automobile, and with a bit of advance knowledge and preparation (get the maps and booklets of the AAA of Southern California at the headquarters in Los Angeles) this trip can be one of the most rewarding of vacations.

From Tijuana to Enseñada a wide, well-banked, and easy-to-drive toll road has been in service for a number of years. It is a fast four-lane highway that runs along the coastal shore of the Pacific for 71 very scenic miles; three toll booths charge a total of $2.40 for a single car.

From Enseñada to El Rosario, the road slips back and forth from dry desert to the cool Pacific. At El Rosario, it turns inland across rough, rocky terrain, climbing into the mountains and then dropping back to vast flat wastelands.

At Punta Prieta, a well-paved offshoot road will take the adventuresome to Bahía de Los Angeles on the Sea of Cortés, as the Gulf of California is known in Mexico. The main highway continues to Guerrero Negro for its last touch of the Pacific, and then turns inland through winding roads and past some pretty barren scenery.

When you reach Santa Rosalia, the road has taken you across the breadth of the peninsula and you get your first view of the Sea of Cortés. The road turns south again along the inland coastal shore to Loreto, passing some of the loveliest of beaches and lagoons on the way.

South of Loreto, the highway again cuts inland up through some mountains to an area of plains, where the road becomes somewhat hypnotizing until the land becomes green with

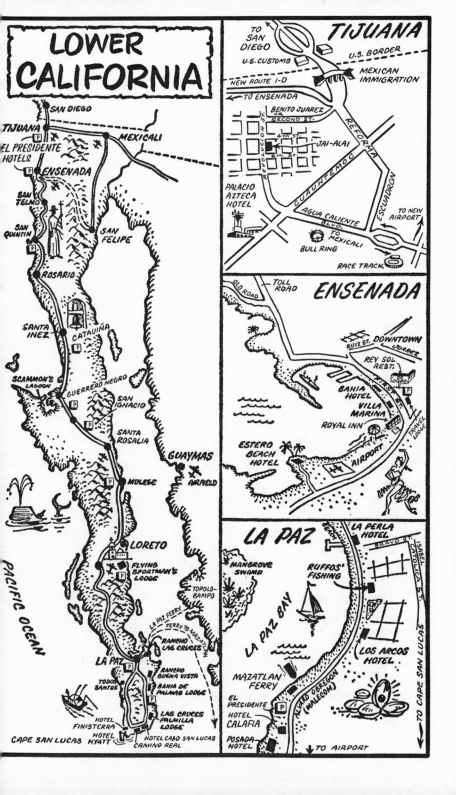

vegetation south of the village of El Cien. The road then winds down into the city of La Paz, located on a nearly landlocked bay.

You can drive on to "Land's End" at the Cabo San Lucas, which is an additional 139 miles over paved roads. You will find some truly luxurious hotels, fishing lodges, and the small town of Cabo San Lucas with more moderate accommodations.

Gasoline, Repairs, and Accommodations on the Baja Road

When the Baja highway was first completed, the road lacked many services, but now all necessities can be found and the rate at which new hotels, restaurants, and service stations are being built indicates the traveler will be well taken care of in the future.

Gas, oil, and many minor replaceable parts, such as fan belts, can be found at the Pemex stations built about every 50 to 100 miles. But should you be forced to stop on the road, almost any truck or car passing will pause to help you or give you a lift to the nearest station or town. The government has special dark green vehicles, called "Green Angels," which cruise the entire highway, ready to help motorists in distress without charge. However, they drive the same stretch of road only twice a day between 9 A.M. and 9 P.M. Personally, we found the local truckers to be more helpful.

It is best to make sure your car is in top condition and prepared to drive the desert. Make sure your tires are in good shape, have a good spare, and if your vehicle easily permits it, carry an extra fan belt, an emergency can of gasoline, and some basic tools. Check to make sure your jack is workable. Refer to Chapter 6 for further information on driving in Mexico.

The Nacional Hotelera chain has built a number of beautiful motels along the road, all called El Presidente. They are well designed and attractive, and prices are reasonable. Since service depends on local help, which is pretty thin in Baja, the food and other amenities may not be exactly what you wish, but you are usually so glad to stop without driving another long stretch to the next accommodations that you won't mind. Be thankful you don't have to drive that extra 200 miles at night.

Night Driving

As with almost all of Mexico, the same warning must be taken seriously. *Do not drive the Baja at night.* If you have trouble, you will find yourself alone and probably far from any help. There is no government patrol and few other vehicles at night. The chance of hitting a parked vehicle without lights is substantial, and many animals will lie on the warm road to avoid the cold night air. Much of the time there is no center line and certainly no side lines. So drive during daytime only.

Some Notes on Baja California

Over all this long peninsula, which the Spanish discoverers in 1535 reported to be an island, you will find desolate wilderness with stark granite mountain peaks jutting up as high as 10,000 feet. An occasional green pine forest can be seen, but largely it is a crumpled desert—huge and barren.

Here and there is an abandoned mining town, but human existence has been grim with even the original Cochimi Indians dying out despite (or perhaps because of) the efforts of the Spanish missionaries to save them. And the missions themselves, of which there were over 100, one by one were abandoned.

One of the most famous of the early missionaries was the German Father Johann Jakob Baegert who, upon his return to Europe, wrote an interesting account still preserved. It said of Baja California: "Everything concerning California is of such little importance that it is hardly worth the trouble to take a pen and write about it. Of poor shrubs, useless thorn bushes and bare rocks, of piles of sand without water or wood, of a handful of people who, besides their physical shape and ability to think, having nothing to distinguish them from animals." Anthropologists estimate there might have been 40,000 Baja California Indians at the time the Europeans arrived, but this number had diminished to 5,000 by the eighteenth century. The Guaycuras and Pericues are now practically extinct, while there may be at most 100 Cochimis surviving today.

But this bleak picture takes no account of Baja California's assets. One of the largest onyx mines in the world has been worked there, and a new salt-crystallizing operation started only in 1955 at Black Warrior north of Scammon's Bay on the Pacific turns out 600,000 tons of salt a year. Many mines (now largely abandoned) have been worked, and cattle ranches are not uncommon.

Baja California is roughly twice as long as Florida and possesses just as many or more beaches—some of which can match the most beautiful in the world. Many of them are quiet inlets where palm groves hang over the water, and nearly all of them are deserted. Miles and miles of empty beach can be seen.

The Boojum, the Elephant, and the Creeping Devil

The flora of Baja California is weird and some of the plants are found nowhere else in the world, giving credence to the notion that it was indeed once an island before an immense convulsive upheaval of some subterranean force threw up yet another land mass to connect it to the California mainland. Shells found far inland on the desert prove beyond doubt that it was once sea bottom.

Among the strangest trees in the world is the so-called "boojum" tree which is found only in Baja California, and even there in a strictly limited area. Joseph Wood Krutch, prominent naturalist, identifies them as *cirios*, and in his fine book, *The Forgotten Peninsula* (Sloane), says they look like an upside-down carrot with pencillike branches appearing helter-skelter up their 40- or 50-foot height, while they can often bend over like a giant croquet hoop and root their top in the soil again. They can exist for up to two years without a drop of rain. All the boojums in the world germinated and took root within a radius of not more than 125 miles near Los Angeles Bay in an inaccessible section just off the Gulf of California about one-third of the way down the peninsula.

Another interesting botanic specimen found in Baja California is the elephant tree, a grotesque tree whose branches are unusually thick toward the trunk and then taper off rapidly to assume the appearance of an elephant's trunk. Yet another freak is found on a desert far down the peninsula on the Pacific Coast off Magdalena Bay. This is the "creeping devil" or "caterpillar cactus," so called because a trunk the size of a man's arm lies flat along the ground and creeps forward as it grows, occasionally rising in a hump to give it the appearance of a caterpillar.

One end is said to die as the forward end progresses, sending down new roots.

LOVERS' LANE FOR WHALES

In the early spring of each year, the great gray whales, up to 50 feet long and weighing some 40 tons, make a 7,000-mile trip from their usual waters in the Arctic to seek out a natural lagoon about halfway down the Baja California peninsula on the Pacific side. This lagoon, known as Scammon's Bay after a famous nineteenth-century whaler, is off the Bay of Vizcaíno.

Here in the lagoon they mate, and after a year's gestation, during which the whales journey to the Arctic once more, they return to the same lagoon to give birth to their young. According to experts, the male mate remains celibate during the year of gestation. The whale is a mammal, not a fish, and bears its young alive. The young are actually nursed underwater.

Captain Scammon, who discovered the lagoon and astonished other whalers with the frequency and size of his whale-oil deliveries, reported that in his day the huge gray whales "huddled together so thickly that it was difficult for a boat to cross the waters without coming in contact with them. . . . They lay aground in two or three feet of water . . . rolling with apparent delight in the breakers." Naturally they became easy prey, though still dangerous, for the whalers, and the species was near extinction, until by 1910 Roy Chapman Andrews was elated to find even one. Since then they have been protected by international agreement, and the Scripps Institute of Oceanography stated that 2,286 were actually counted passing a point in California en route south. They can only travel for ten minutes below water, rising to "blow" or get more air at such intervals. They travel about 80 miles a day.

There is no easy way to get to Scammon's Bay except by private plane in which it is possible to land on the beach nearby. But it is one more of a series of fascinating aspects of Baja California.

A BIT OF HISTORY

Shortly after Hernando Cortés reached the Aztec capital in 1519, he dispatched others to explore and conquer the northwest.

From them reports came back of a fabulous island, inhabited by a race of dark-skinned Amazons, where great amounts of black pearls of value were found.

In 1533, Cortés sent out from Tehuantepec a fleet headed by one Diego de Becerra, who was killed en route by his pilot, Fortune Jiménez. Jiménez did sight land on his trip, reporting an island, and Cortés himself then proceeded there and landed on May 1, 1535, near where La Paz is today.

Cortés did find some pearls near La Paz, and they were shipped back to Spain for years, though never quite in the quantity or of the quality expected, until in the nineteenth century they finally disappeared almost completely.

The Jesuits and the Dominicans appeared and tried with unending patience and self-abnegation and -deprivation to found missions and "save" the Indian populace. But, starting with the first mission, founded in Loreto in 1697 (and not abandoned until 1822), the missions one by one were given up and left in ruins. The soil was too dry, the climate too harsh, and life was near impossible. Some missionaries were killed, many returned to Spain, and others moved to Upper California and much greater success.

American troops occupied La Paz, Mulegé, and Todos Santos during the Mexican-American War of 1848, and the American commander proclaimed it American territory, but it was returned to Mexico in the peace treaty. An American soldier of fortune, William Walker, proclaimed himself "president" of a new Republic of Lower California, but was expelled by the Mexican authorities. American land companies, one with headquarters in Hartford, Connecticut, bought huge tracts of over a million acres, and tried to sell at huge profits to gullible statesiders who had never seen the peninsula and could be convinced that it was a Garden of Eden ready for new real estate developments. Another American, Dick Ferris, in 1910 proposed to the Mexican dictator, Porfirio Díaz, that he turn the peninsula over to a commission of 100 Americans who would proclaim it the new Republic of Díaz, thus perpetuating the name of the dictator who was about to be overthrown. Needless to say, nothing came of this, either.

With the advent of modern times, reclamation projects brought water into the Imperial Valley along the border, and truck farms began to prosper in the Mexicali and Tijuana areas.

The northern part of the peninsula was proclaimed a Mexican state, while the southern part remained a territory. Even now the Mexican government is constantly building new public works for the peninsula as well as adding new schools. But the greatest hope probably lies in the new tourist business.

FISHING AND HUNTING

Baja California has been described as a fisherman's delight and a hunter's paradise. Great schools of fish are drawn to the Sea of Cortés, and especially at the junction of the open Pacific and the inland gulf near La Paz the water teems with blue sailfish, skipjacks, swordfish, tuna in many species, marlin, black sea bass, bonefish, golden dolphin, and a thousand types of smaller fish such as halibut, flounder, sole, grunt, and snapper. To these, one must add the ever-present sharks and the huge (up to several tons) giant manta rays whose bodies undulate in flapping movement.

The angler can go to Enseñada or San Felipe by car, or to any of the fishing camps such as those at Loreto, Mulegé, and Las Palmas Bay. Hotels in Enseñada are all equipped to arrange fishing excursions. Admittedly, the fishing is better if you can fly down to *Flying Sportsman's Lodge* at Loreto or *Hacienda Mulegé* at the town of Mulegé near Santa Rosalia, where they claim the "finest fishing in the world." Still better fishing is available at *Bahía de Palmas*, 67 miles south of La Paz, or *Rancho Las Cruces Palmilla* in the same area, both reached via La Paz. A new paved road connects La Paz with Cabo San Lucas, where such luxury hotels as *Hotel Cabo San Lucas, Finisterra*, Western's *Camino Real*, and others sit boldly at land's end. All have fleets of fishing boats and excellent fishing. Each has a landing strip and daily connecting flights. Lodges are described in detail on pages 123–128.

The hunter will find that the wilderness of Baja California has indeed left it a sportsman's paradise, but that there are game laws much as in the United States and he will have to observe these restrictions as well as go through the red tape involved in bringing a gun and ammunition into Mexico (much easier to rent it while there). By and large, the same agencies that arrange fishing trips will also arrange hunting. The long-horn mountain sheep are now completely protected, but in season you can shoot deer, mountain lion, antelope, wild pig, and small game such as ducks, doves, and rabbits. The Mexican consulates or the hunting and fishing organizations can provide details on the game laws, which are taken rather lightly by the ranchers of the area.

TIJUANA

Each Saturday and Sunday literally thousands of cars pour down from San Diego and points farther north on the freeway to cross the border into Tijuana.

Tijuana is a border town which has all the sins and ugliness of a border town, while offering many absorbing diversions. The city, with an estimated population of 750,000, is in a fearful race to modernity, with new boulevards and suburbs and a population explosion causing ever larger numbers to live in shanties and tin houses stretched endlessly on almost every surrounding hillside in all too evident squalor. Downtown is a shabby paved highway to the border jammed with tawdry little shops. The main street, Av. Revolución, features Mexican or imported Japanese goods of questionable quality for the border-crossing tourists, while its axis, Av. Juárez, is jammed with low-priced mass-produced American goods peddled to the Mexican population. Interspersed are many cheap night-clubs, bars, strip joints, and questionable restaurants. A typical border town, but not typical of the great country of Mexico. The government has recently announced a plan to rebuild the central downtown area.

Crossing the border is very simple. There is no formality beyond an occasional question from a customs inspector, and no papers are required. You drive across, at least at our last visit, a wide paved road that winds about in a strange manner as hordes of automobiles jockey with each other to get through. Large signs in English plainly say "To the Race Track," and inasmuch as the bullring is out the same way, both are easy to find. There are also signs pointing to the center of town, which is straight ahead.

The shops are filled with cheap souvenirs sold at high prices, and the "nightclubs" are fairly tawdry, so we can hardly recommend either. But there are some interesting things to do in Tijuana, as specified below.

Agua Caliente Racetrack is a modern, well-landscaped track equipped with totalizers. Thoroughbred races are run on Saturday and Sunday mornings at 11, though this may change. You can check on race time at (213) 272-4568 in Los Angeles and (714) 234-8343 in San Diego. There is also greyhound racing, with betting, most nights of the week, and it draws fairly large crowds of devotees.

Caliente is about a thirty-minute drive from San Diego. The track has been rebuilt after burning a number of years ago. While the buildings are splendiferous in size, the finishing touches were yet to be added on our last visit. Thus, one found big grandstands but no fancy jockey club. The restaurant was small with poor service, and obviously something better is planned.

Bullfights are not held regularly, but scheduled as prominent matadors become available for an appearance. They are almost always held on Sunday afternoons or holidays. Some of the top fighters appear in Tijuana. *El Toreo de Tijuana* is a huge bullring on the road just before the racetrack, so you can follow the same signs. The *Plaza Monumental*, the "bullring by the sea," is found by going out the Enseñada highway, which can be entered by a connecting route right at the border. For the initiates, a bullfight can be very exciting when it is good, but it can be pretty dreadful when things don't go right. Tickets are sold at box offices outside the ring, and it is best to sit in the shade.

Jai alai, an intriguingly fast game to watch, is played every night except Thursday in the big frontón building at Av. Revolución (the main street) and Seventh Street. You can't miss the huge air-conditioned structure occupying an entire block. There is a parking lot alongside. General admission is $1.25; reserved seats are $3. Both are perfectly okay from the spectator's viewpoint. Betting, in dollars ($2 and $5), is at windows under the stands.

There are two teams of two men each, usually identified by colored bands on their arms. Each player wears a basket (called a *cesta*) on his arm. The ball, which is made of Brazilian rubber wound with yarn and covered with shrunken goatskin, must be flung from and caught in the baskets after hitting the back wall of the court. The first team to score twenty-one points wins. The players hurl the ball with incredible speed over long distances.

An interesting version for tourists to follow (and bet on) is the *quiniela*, which is played twice during the evening. Here each of the six players plays for himself, the winner taking on the next man in turn until some player wins six times. The betting is similar to that on a daily double. Each man has a number, and you try to pick the two men who will come in first and second on the wins. Just buy a ticket with two numbers, and watch to see if those two come in first and second (not necessarily in that order). Then go down and collect your winnings if they do.

Cold beer and cocktails are sold in the jai alai stadium. A fairly good restaurant serving steaks and chicken at reasonable prices (but with a $1 admission charge good for a drink) is housed right in the building. Other good restaurants nearby are listed below.

Where To Eat in Tijuana

Compared with Mexico City or Los Angeles, there are no exceptionally good restaurants in Tijuana. But there aren't in Dubuque or Keokuk, either. Two merit special attention, and the others on our list range from fair to good.

The Sky Room   Expensive
  By far the best in Tijuana, this is an elaborate rooftop restaurant at the Palacio Azteca Hotel, Av. 16 de Septiembre No. 213, just off Blvd. Agua Caliente, which is an extension of the main street, Av. Revolución, curving out toward the bullring and racetrack. Serves shrimp cocktail, scampi, hearts of palm, lobster bisque, Oriental lobster, seafood Newburg, duck au champagne, pepper steak, steak martini comte, New York cut, lamb chops persille. Adjoining bar features hot combos and dancing that draws playboy set. Maître d' is José Luis Díaz García. Reservations important, as often caters to social groups taking over most of the tables. No cover; all cards. Tel: 6-53-01 or 6-54-01.

Restaurant La Costa   Moderate
  At Calle 7A No. 150, which is a side street crossing Revolución, the main street, at the frontón building. An unpretentious seafood restaurant with clean tables and usually helpful waiters. Specialties

under $5 at our last visit include Seven Seas soup, whitefish à la veracruzana, shrimp Costa Azul, and oysters Rockefeller. More expensive were lobster thermidor and crab veracruzana. Open noon till midnight. AE, DC, MC, VISA. Tel: 5-84-94.

Restaurant Reno   Somewhat expensive
Run by two brothers, Pepe and Jorge Ortiz, this is an established dining spot just off Av. Revolución, at the frontón building, at Hidalgo and Eighth Street. Well-known for its steaks (New York cut), it also serves excellent lobster Newburg, lamb chops, eels with oil and garlic, shrimp en brochette, breaded abalone, chicken *mole* (Mexican style), and enchiladas. This is an ornate place with more silver serving dishes and silver pitchers than you are likely to see outside the Ritz. Soft music, too. All prices include soup, or salad, and coffee. Carnet, MC, VISA. Tel: 5-92-10 or 5-87-75.

Coronet Restaurant   Economical
Also just off Revolución on Seventh Street, near the frontón building, this is a rather ordinary restaurant tucked in underneath a hotel, but it has clean linen and the usual steaks and lobster. Also serves breakfast. Features a fixed-price lunch at bargain rate. Serves Mexican plate, T-bone steak, filet mignon, lobster, steak sandwich, abalone steak. Piano, bar. Open until 2 A.M. Only DC accepted. Tel: 5-55-51.

Guillermo's   Expensive
On Seventh Street, directly across from the frontón building, this looks more like a nightclub than a restaurant. Serves only filet mignon or Mexican dishes. Service less than desirable at times.

Sierra Restaurant   Economical
At the Sierra Motel across from Caliente, a good restaurant with modern equipment and surroundings. Open till 11 P.M.

Caesar's   Moderately expensive
In Caesar's Hotel on Revolución, is a restaurant said to have invented the famed salad. Redecorated and now quite handsome. Tel: 5-29-23.

Where To Stay in Tijuana

Surprisingly enough, there are some pretty good places to stay in Tijuana if you know where to look for them. Staying overnight enables you to get in two days of racing rather than just one, or to get an early start on the way to Enseñada.

Palacio Azteca Hotel (*54 rooms*)   Expensive
A modern hotel in a busy part of the city, located on Highway 2,
a block and a half off the main thoroughfare on Av. 16 de Septiembre,
on road to Caliente. It is a convenient location far enough out of the
downtown to avoid parking and noise problems. Large, modern,
air-conditioned rooms and suites. Coffee shop, bar with pool, a
rooftop restaurant serving continental cuisine in lavish style, and
a rooftop cabaret with music every night. Operated by management
of famed Rosarita Beach Hotel. Sauna, barbershop, beauty shop,
and travel agency. Enclosed parking space for 100 cars. For reservations, write P.O. Box 480, Tijuana, or telephone (903) 386-5301
(in California) or 6-53-01 or 6-54-01 (in Tijuana). AE, CB, MC, VISA.

Ramada Tijuana (*200 rooms*)   Moderately expensive
A new hotel and probably the best in Tijuana. Located on Agua
Caliente Blvd. next to the Tijuana Country Club and around the
corner from the track. Only ten minutes to downtown. Air-conditioned rooms overlook golf course and racetrack. Guests have
squash, pool, golf, and tennis privileges. Hotel also has exercise
room, therapeutic pool, beauty and barber shops. El Rey Sol
restaurant serves from 7:30 A.M. until late. Discotheque has shows
at 11 P.M. and 1 A.M. All major credit cards. Reservations: (903) 386-
5000 or toll-free (800) 255-4141.

El Conquistador Motel (*100 rooms*)   Moderately expensive
Excellent new two-story motel located across from country club and
near racetrack at 700 Blvd. Agua Caliente. Rooms are spacious. Pool
with swim-up bar, sauna, barber and beauty shops. Taurus discotheque; good cafeteria serving breakfast, lunch, and dinner. All
cards. Reservations: P.O. Box 4471, San Ysidro, Calif., or 700 Caliente
Blvd., Tijuana. Tel: (903) 386-4801 and (903) 386-4805.

La Sierra Motel (*60 rooms*)   Inexpensive
Also out Av. 16 de Septiembre beyond the bullring and beyond the
Palacio Azteca, this is a modest but comfortable and well-run
motel with good dining room, bar, heated pool. Air-conditioned.
A good place to stay, fancied by much of the bullfight crowd.
Reservations at Box 888, San Ysidro, Calif., (903) 386-1601, or Tijuana
address. AE, CB, DC.

Country Club Motel (*100 rooms*)   Moderate
Directly opposite racetrack, a modern motel with restaurant, cocktail
lounge, and pool. Frequented by serious race fans. All cards, no
checks. Reservations: (903) 286-2301.

ENSEÑADA AND ROSARITA

About an hour's drive from Tijuana (you can even bypass the city by taking a sharp cutback just after crossing the border) lies Enseñada. There is now both a free route and a toll road to Enseñada from Tijuana. The toll road is beautifully maintained and one of the most spectacular bits of oceanside driving in the world. Toll is paid at three different booths and totals $2.40. The toll road is called Route 1D; the older road is Route 1. The older road is perfectly passable, paved all the way, but it takes longer and winds through some mountains, which the new road skirts.

You can drive into Tijuana and on to Enseñada without any formalities such as a tourist card, but be sure to get one if you plan to go farther south than Enseñada or plan to stay longer than seventy-two hours. Tourist cards are free at the Mexican immigration station at the border crossing; proof of citizenship—such as a birth certificate or passport, even if expired—is required. Car title, or other proof of ownership, is required to bring in a car. Mexican insurance is required and can be purchased by day ($3–$5 per day). Sanborn's has an office just before the border and provides a free detailed travelogue.

Rosarita

Some 18 miles south of Tijuana is the fancy seaside resort of the *Rosarita Beach Hotel*. This is an elaborate oceanfront establishment with manicured gardens, large pool, horseback riding, tennis, and fishing as well as a large bar overlooking the ocean and dancing and dining in the evening.

Farther along the road, 38 miles south of Tijuana, is a landmark called *La Fonda* on a bluff overlooking the sea. This is a fair place for lunch or refreshments.

There are several trailer parks along the way, some with spectacular views. They are easily visible from both highways.

Where To Stay or Eat near Rosarita

Rosarita Beach Hotel (*76 rooms*)   Moderately expensive
   A rambling hotel on waterfront still in fairly good condition. Large
   dining room with good food, dining, dancing, orchestra some

nights. Tennis courts, two pools. Take exit at 18 miles south of Tijuana. MC, VISA. For reservations (advisable) write P.O. Box 202, Tijuana.

DeAnza Inn (*25 rooms*)   Inexpensive
A modest motel with heated pool, one block from beach. Some kitchenettes. At Rosarita exit as above. CB, DC.

La Fonda Restaurant and Motel (*20 rooms*)   Moderate
Spectacular location on bluff overlooking Pacific. Bar and restaurant open 9 A.M. till 11 P.M. Mexican food and seafood. Dancing. Twenty miles beyond Rosarita. No credit cards.

Rene's Motel and Trailer Park (*40 rooms, 70 spaces*)   Inexpensive
In Rosarita, this is good motel and trailer park on beach, with restaurant, heated pool. No credit cards. Prefer to rent trailer space by month.

Motel Cantamar and Trailer Park (*25 rooms, 170 spaces*)   Moderate
On Route 1 about 33 miles from Tijuana. Has good rooms, pool, restaurant with seafood. Showers and connections. No credit cards. Rooms: $14 double; spaces: $2.

Popotla Trailer Park (*177 spaces*) $3
One exit beyond Rosarita, a fine location on beach with all hookups. Paved patios and streets. Showers, grocery store. Horseback riding and Saturday-night entertainment. Monthly rates available.

La Siesta Trailer Park (*30 spaces*) $3
In Rosarita, near beach and DeAnza Inn, it has hookups, paved patios, showers. Well-kept. No pool. No pets.

ENSEÑADA

The most popular place in Baja California from the average American tourist's point of view is undoubtedly Enseñada. It has a large number of modern hotels, some very fine beaches, and some very good fishing. And you can drive there easily.

Perhaps the greatest attraction of Enseñada is the fine seafood and fish that are served in its dining rooms. One of the restaurants in town is noted for its turtle steak, while turtle soup is found in many places.

But it would only be fair to say that Enseñada is strictly a tourist town, and that much of its appeal is somewhat superficial, for the Mexican goods (except a few baskets) must be imported from the mainland for sale, the dances are those of the nightclubs in Mexico City, and the great number of tourists have pretty well Americanized the town. Still, you can't hate Enseñada for its success in the tourist business. People wouldn't go there unless they liked it. The weather is usually sunny, although it can be too brisk to swim in the winter. It is very pleasant in the summer.

The town itself (population about 100,000) is relatively clean and neat, and the residents are pleasant and good-natured. There is a main shopping district in the center of town. A group of hotels has been built along one of the principal oceanfront streets where there once was a beach that is now blocked by a new breakwater. For this reason, several of the new hotels are built south of town in the Estero Beach area, where the beaches are still open. Most motels and trailer parks are on the oceanfront north of the town, where there are smaller beach or bathing facilities.

There is a good public beach, *Playa Hermosa*, 3 miles south of Enseñada just off the highway (a sign usually marks the road in to the beach). Refreshments are available on the beach. *Miramar Chapultepec*, a prominent hill in town, is a favorite place to visit. Any taxi will take you up there in a few minutes, and from the top you can see the whole city and surrounding area.

Fishing Trips. There are any number of fishing boat operators with business establishments along the seafront street, and it is not difficult to charter a launch for a trip to fish for yellowtail (a species of tuna), sea bass, halibut, and marlin. Group fishing is very popular, with the operator charging a flat fee per person.

Tomás Moreno (P.O. Box 104, tel: 967-560) has seven boats for charter, while the Caribe Boat House (First and Miramar) also has boats for charter and skin-diving equipment. Gordo's Bait House (Av. López Mateos 595, tel: 8-35-15 and 8-23-77) has long been favored for fishing arrangements.

Shopping. While not many high-quality handicrafts are made in the Enseñada area, this does not mean they are not sold there. In fact, there are some excellent shops. *Carlos Importers* next to the Bahía Hotel has good clothes, silver tea sets and trays, and jewelry. *Chez Dispa,* also near the Bahía, has fine women's clothing. The *Taxco Gift Shop* on First Street has a fine selection of goods from all parts of Mexico, including bubble glass, serapes, tin trays, and silver.

El Calendario on Av. López Mateos has hand-spun bulky wool sweaters, while embroidered shirts and dresses can be found at *Tesoro Bazaar,* Av. Macheros 3. *La Perla del Pacífico,* nearby at Ruiz 264, has guayabera shirts and Stetson hats. Serapes are at *Benito Curiosidades* at López Mateos 671. *Maya de México* at 149 Ruiz downtown has yard goods.

In recent years, a crush of small shops selling pure junk in the form of Mexican souvenirs or crafts (they don't deserve the word) have wedged themselves along the front street where the tourists walk. Our advice is to avoid them and particularly the cheap pottery with a glaze which probably isn't certified against lead.

Another suggestion for travelers: Try the *Panadería Ideal* on the main street. Wonderful cookies. They have developed a line of pastries that boggles the mind or mouth.

WHERE TO EAT IN ENSEÑADA

Enseñada has become filled with fast-food chain outlets, but they have poor-quality food. There are some fine places to eat in Enseñada, although by and large they specialize in seafood and steaks and not in continental cuisine. The quality is uneven, varying from the hotel dining rooms to some hole-in-the-wall restaurants in town, with the latter often serving the better food. We advise trying them both. Our favorite is the Calmarisco.

El Rey Sol   Moderately expensive
  On main waterfront Av. López Mateos across from Villa Marina in attractive new building with sprig of globe lanterns hanging over small patio. Actually it is a rather large, cavernous building with shiny ultramodern kitchen. Founded by the family of an early engineer who sent his daughter Pepita to Paris to study cuisine, it features good American-style food rather than Cordon Bleu. Good onion soup, abalone cocktail, hot garlic bread, New York steak, Mexican combination plate, abalone steak. French pastry baked on

scene is a specialty. Crowded, service slow, no reservations, but open 7 A.M. till midnight. Owner is Virginia Geofrey, a descendant of the founder. MC, VISA.

El Cid Restaurant   Moderately expensive
Next door to El Rey Sol, this is more of a supper club with music and floor show. Open 1 P.M. for lunch and until 2 A.M. Bar. No cover. Sandwiches, Mexican plate, seafood. One of the better spots in town.

Restaurant La Cueva   Moderate
In San Nicolás resort hotel on Av. López Mateos a bit south of town. Offers a limited number of special plates at reasonable prices in attractive surroundings. Hamburger plate, fried chicken, chili, Denver or Reuben sandwiches, shrimp Louis, Mexican dishes. Noon and night. All cards.

Kon-Tiki Floating Restaurant   Inexpensive
On a floating ship—perhaps "barge" might describe it better—just off the dockside adjacent to the Bahía Hotel. You can see the strings of lights on its rigging from López Mateos. A rather modest place with coffee-shop tables and jukebox music, but good bar, pleasant though desultory waiters, excellent French fries, and passable steaks. Shrimp cocktail, turtle steak, octopus and rice. Service is slow, but still this place can be fun. Open 8 A.M. till 11 P.M. Carnet and Bancomatico only.

Ramada Coffee Shop   Reasonable
Serves food twenty-four hours a day. Located at Ramada Inn on south outskirts of town. A modern coffee shop serving good breakfast including *huevos rancheros* and pancakes. Hamburgers, a wide variety of sandwiches and short orders, and an American soda fountain.

Sorrento Restaurant   Moderate
Italian food as well as Mexican and American dishes. In Cortez Motel on López Mateos. Food ordinary. Open 7 A.M. till 11 P.M. Accepts most cards.

Bahía Dining Room   Moderately expensive
There are floor shows nightly in the Bahía dining room, which is part of the prominent Bahía Resort Hotel in the center of town on Front Street (Av. López Mateos). The food (steaks and lobster) and drinks are shoved at you wholesale, but the floor show is lively and there is dancing to tropical, cha-cha, and soul music. Cover charge. Open late.

Enrique's Restaurant   Moderately expensive
About 1½ miles north of town on Route 1, this is a modest restaurant
with a reputation for good food. Offers both American and Mexican
food, and cocktails. Open 8 A.M. till 11 P.M. Closed Tuesdays.

Colonial Café   Inexpensive
Storefront restaurant in downtown area. Serves authentic Mexican
food at reasonable prices. Off-street parking. MC, VISA.

Villa Marina Dining Room   Moderate
In the Villa Marina Hotel, practically next door to the Bahía. This
dining room stays open until late in the evening, serving full meals,
and has some music. Prices are similar to those of the Bahía.

Calmarisco Restaurant   Inexpensive
Located in town at 474 Third Street, near the corner of Ruiz, this is
a very modest restaurant which will surprise you with some of the
best seafood in town. You eat with local businessmen at bare tables,
but the turtle steak is the best I ever tasted in Mexico. Cold beer
served with meals by pleasant waitresses. Open twenty-four hours
a day.

Hussong's Cantina   Moderate
This is not a restaurant, but probably the most popular bar in town.
Margaritas. At Ruiz 113.

Kentucky Fried Chicken   Inexpensive
South of town just before Royal Inn, this is a genuine version of
Colonel Sanders' chain, and carries their regular menu.

WHERE TO STAY IN ENSEÑADA

Ramada Motor Inn (*100 rooms*)   Moderately expensive
Large, modern, mission-style motel-hotel about 2 miles south of
town on Highway 1. At this writing, it was the best place to stay
in Enseñada. Rooms are large, well furnished, and comfortable;
most have terraces or balconies. Large heated pool with attractive
lounge terrace, small but effective sauna, putting green, tennis
courts. Good room service, twenty-four-hour coffee shop. Bar-
lounge with entertainment. All cards. For reservations, call (903)
399-2202.

San Nicolás Hotel (*47 rooms*)   Moderately expensive
New three-story hotel-motel on main highway in town. Along
waterfront but not on water. Heated pool, restaurant, nightclub

Palacio Azteca. Run by Nico Saad, active in local government and tourist affairs, hotel has informal and friendly atmosphere. La Cueva restaurant with inexpensive dishes open 8 A.M. till midnight. Carnet, MC, Bancamer or VISA. P.O. Box 19, tel: (903) 399-1901.

Hotel La Pinta Presidente   Moderately expensive
South of the city on Highway 1, near ocean, this is a three-story motel of Spanish-style architecture. Many rooms with balconies. Pool, courtyard, restaurant, bar, entertainment. All cards. P.O. Box 929, or Presidente reservations service, 8721 Beverly Blvd., Los Angeles, Calif., tel: (213) 657-5162 or toll-free (800) 421-0722. In California: (800) 252-0172.

Travelodge (*50 rooms*)   Moderately expensive
Modern motel around courtyard just off López Mateos at corner of Blancarte (near El Rey Sol restaurant). Pool, central air conditioning. No pets. All major cards. Reservations in U.S. at toll-free (800) 255-3050 or Enseñada (903) 393-1601.

Cortez Motel (*64 units*)   Moderate
This is a standard motel built directly on Av. López Mateos. Has some kitchenette apartments. Pool. Sorrento restaurant is open 7 A.M. till 11 P.M. All major cards. Tel: 8-2308.

Bahía Resort Hotel (*73 rooms*)   Moderate
This is an old standby in Enseñada, but unfortunately its rooms are sadly out of date and no longer first-class. Its operation also has become highly commercial and lacks good supervision or any personal touch. It still has a prominent location on López Mateos, and its dining room still puts on three lively floor shows each night. A sandbar now cuts it off from the water, but it has the best shops clustered around it. All cards. Tel: 8-2103.

Santa María Motel (*40 rooms*)   Moderate
South of town on Highway 1 just before the dry river. Modern, well-run. Heated pool. Restaurant closed on Mondays. Bancamer and MC only.

El Cid Motor Hotel (*36 rooms*)   Moderately expensive
At Av. López Mateos. Built in Spanish style, has air-conditioned rooms, heated pool. Dining room, coffee shop, entertainment. No pets. Accepts most cards. P.O. Box 1431, tel: 8-2401.

Villa Marina Hotel (*90 rooms*)   Moderate
Just beyond Bahía on López Mateos, it also overlooks ocean. Has modern rooms in motor-court style, dining room, cocktail lounge. Good. Tel: 8-3321.

Quintas Papagayos (*33 units*)   Moderate
Very handsome cottages of modern architecture set in attractive and well-kept gardens. Fully equipped kitchens. Maid service. On Highway 1, 2 miles north of town, fronting on ocean. Small beach available. No restaurant, but near Enrique's (serving three meals a day). Excellent.

Grenada Cove Beach Resort (*30 rooms*)   Moderate
On Highway 1, 3 miles north of town. Has nicely furnished units, some with kitchens. Swimming on waterfront. Pool and restaurant. Also takes trailers. Very good.

Estero Beach Resort Hotel (*46 cottages,*
                               75 spaces)   Moderately expensive
Six miles south of Enseñada on sandbar between sea and lagoon, one must turn off Highway 1 and go along winding, rather poor dirt road for several miles to end of point of land. Road is now being worked on. Resort has a handsome new office building with a very accommodating and cheerful receptionist, but sprawling hodgepodge of some good motel units intermingled with trailer spaces presents confusing picture. Still, it has many loyal devotees who like the location on the beach, boat ramps and the fishing in the lagoon, and the friendly recreation room with ping-pong and billiards, plus tennis. Restaurant. Children's playground. Television. Shops with many famous brand names as well as unusual glass and pottery. All major cards. P.O. Box 86, tel: 1380-40J.

Casa del Sol (*40 rooms*)   Inexpensive
In town on López Mateos, this has become rather run-down but is currently being renovated. Pool. Tel: (903) 398-1570.

Ramona Beach Cottages (*19 rooms*)   Moderate
Four miles north of town on Highway 1. Modest motel but attractive and clean. Pool. Fishing right on beach. Rather isolated.

Villa Carioca Motel (*15 rooms*)   Moderate
Very good motel overlooking sea on Highway 1 north of Enseñada. Rooms have balconies overlooking sea. Room service for meals, no restaurant. Pool.

Del Paseo Hotel (*20 rooms*)   Inexpensive
Modern structure at north end of town. Central air conditioning, pool, no restaurant. Major credit cards.

Hussong's Trailer Park and Cottages (*40 cottages*)   Inexpensive
Trailers charged $3 a night to use power, restrooms, beach. Cottages have kitchens. Modest.

HEADING SOUTH VIA HIGHWAY 1
TO BAJA SUR

SAN QUINTÍN

San Quintín is 125 miles south of Enseñada on Highway 1. While the town has little to offer anyone but the locals, its riches unfold at the ocean's edge, where the long, soft sand beaches are covered with sand dollars, fish, and Pismo clams for the picking. Isolated dunes and undeveloped land make this a great place for lovers of beaches. Also, during the winter months Bahía San Quintín becomes a breeding and feeding ground for ducks and geese. Fishing is excellent, but it is best to hire a local guide if you wish to do any hunting or fishing.

As you head south along Highway 1 from San Quintín, the land becomes barren and isolated as the road curves inland. *Santa Inés* is the next town along the line, 45 miles south. It offers emergency gas at the Rancho Santa Inés and has a plain restaurant and motel, El Presidente Catavina.

WHERE TO STAY IN SAN QUINTÍN

El Presidente Motel (*60 units*)   Moderate
The best place to stay in San Quintín is the new El Presidente. Located facing the water, all rooms are comfortable with twin beds; sliding glass doors open to terraces and beach. Tasteful colonial architecture is accented by a beautiful pool and displays of Mexican handicrafts. All landscaping is of local Baja origin. Las Cazuelas restaurant serves all meals; fresh lobster is specialty. While it was still under construction at our visit, the main section was finished; it is one of the better El Presidentes on the peninsula. Opened in 1974 by two Americans, Ramón and his wife Paula. For reservations, write to 8721 Beverly Blvd., Los Angeles, Calif. Tel: (213) 657-5162.

El Molino Viejo Motel (*12 rooms*)   Reasonable
A plain and simple motel, it will do if one is unable to find space at El Presidente. The owner, Mr. Vela, is also the chef of his small but pleasant restaurant. He was formerly at the Waldorf-Astoria in New York. Parking for several self-contained trailers only.

Parador San Quintín (*40 spaces*) $2.50 per vehicle
An open paved yard behind the Pemex station. Some hookups. A good place to pull off the road for the night.

Cielito Lindo Trailer Park (*42 spaces*) $3.50 for two

In San Quintín, down the road from El Presidente. A nice place to camp. Has all hookups, but sometimes has brief power failures. Directly on the beach, it has miles of open sand dunes and water. Also has three bathhouses with hot-water showers. For reservations, write to Cielito Lindo Trailer Park, 1041 N. Formosa, Los Angeles, Calif. 90046. Tel: (213) 851-2550.

El Presidente Catavina (*30 rooms*)   Moderate

A modern hotel built alongside the highway south of San Quintín near the huge and sprawling Rancho Santa Inés. This is in the center of the cirio tree area and is fascinating to naturalists. Hotel has pool and bar, with nearby restaurant, gasoline station, and trailer park. Airport nearby. Toll-free tel: (800) 421-0722.

Parador Catavina

On Highway 1, next to El Presidente. Has hookups, gasoline, restrooms.

Going through the middle of the Baja, the road brings you to *Punta Prieta*, which is just another gas stop along the way. The new Pemex station offers a space behind for camping, but no facilities. It is important to note that here the road splits. The highway heads south, but a new road is almost completed to *Bahía de Los Angeles*, an excellent spot for spending a few restful days. It's 68 miles straight west.

Continuing south, one comes to the town of *Guerrero Negro* sitting on the 28th parallel. One cannot miss this spot, as a 135-foot Monumento Águila ("Eagle Monument") sits ready to take off along the road. The monument was erected to the workers who built the great highway and marks the boundary between Baja Norte, the state, and Baja Sur. You have also traveled 445 miles from the States and still have 601 miles to the tip of the Baja peninsula.

Guerrero Negro

At present the town of Guerrero Negro has little to offer the traveler, but in years to come this will change, as the highway will bring more people to the area. The town is a small, relaxed place, plain and simple and mostly owned by the Exportadora de Suld Company. Its major industry is the salt-evaporation beds which are just outside town near Black Warrior Lagoon and provide several million tons of salt each year. Surrounding the town are great salt flats and marshes that make it quite uninviting.

Just a few miles south of town is Scammon's Lagoon, where every winter the great gray whales come to mate, calve, and play in the surf, before they return north to the Arctic waters. You can watch the whales from shore or the surrounding hills; binoculars and a good telephoto lens will enhance your viewing. The Mexican government prohibits boats in the water while the whales are there.

Where To Stay in Guerrero Negro

El Presidente Hotel Paralelo 28 (24 *rooms, 80+ spaces*)   Moderate
On Highway 1 across from the Eagle Monument, this is a modern one-story hotel. Rooms with air conditioning, shower baths, and double beds can accommodate up to four persons. We have had excellent reports on its restaurant, Las Cazuelas, open from 7 A.M. to 11 P.M. There is also a cocktail lounge. Air strip with radio. Adjoining the motel is an excellent trailer court. Spaces can accommodate any camper, and the restrooms and showers are clean and pleasant. For reservations, write to El Presidente Hotels, 8721 Beverly Blvd., Los Angeles, Calif. 90048. Tel: (213) 657-5162.

Dunas Motel (36 *units*)   Inexpensive
One mile west of Highway 1 on road into town. A modest motel with private shower baths and austere rooms. For reservations, write to Dunas Motel, Guerrero Negro, Baja California.

Driving through Baja Sur

Heading south, you are now driving through the territory of Baja Sur (Lower Baja). The weather becomes warmer and the sun much brighter. The road leaves Guerrero Negro and goes southeast through some rough wasteland to the Sea of Cortés for the first time; it will never return to the Pacific. A whole different Baja lies ahead.

San Ignacio

Coming upon the forest of date palms that surround the village of San Ignacio, one feels like the typical lost desert miner. But this peaceful oasis is no mirage. Surrounded by endless miles of rock and sand, where the only life is the mysterious boojum and cactus, San Ignacio is truly a Garden of Eden. Freshwater springs bring life to over 80,000 date palms, orange trees, and private gardens sprouting vegetables, fruit, grapes, and flowering trees and bushes.

Though the town offers little for the tourist, it is well worth a short stop. Driving into San Ignacio is a comforting change as you drive along pools of water lined with palms and arrive at the plaza.

Right at the plaza is one of the finest examples of mission architecture on the Baja. Founded by the Jesuits in 1728, the mission is well preserved. Of special interest are the ornately carved doors and stonework. With walls of stone several feet thick, the interior is cool with a high arched ceiling and ornately carved woodwork.

The coolest place in town is the newly built plaza, where a cool drink sitting on a bench beneath the shade makes one forget the harshness of the desert. If it's lunch time you would enjoy a few minutes' walk to the far end of town, where you'll find *La Posada Motel*. At the motel is a restaurant where you can grab a quick bite. The food is truly Mexican and very good. The motel and restaurant are run by Oscar Fisher and family, who are well known by Baja enthusiasts. If you are inclined to spend the night, La Posada is clean, comfortable, and reasonably priced.

On the paved highway to town 1 mile from Highway 1 is the new government-run *Motel El Presidente San Ignacio*. Complete with an oasis setting, it has a restaurant, pool, and bar. Its twenty-eight rooms have air conditioning, shower baths, and two double beds. The price is moderate. The dining room is open from 7 A.M. to 11 P.M. For reservations, write to El Presidente Hotels, 8721 Beverly Blvd., Los Angeles, Calif. 90048. Tel: (213) 657-5162.

Santa Rosalia

When the road finally crosses the Baja peninsula to the Sea of Cortés, you come to the little town of Santa Rosalia. Its wooden frame buildings with front porches make it a very unusual

Mexican village. It was originally built by a French mining company, which imported the cast iron to build the local church. The old mining installation is still worth a look. Down by the waterfront one can see the old wreck of the *Santo Domingo*, and other wrecks lie beneath the surface. You will find good fishing here, although the local beach is marred by iron slag that has been dumped on it. The famous local bakery dates back to the days of the French inhabitants. It sells *pan dulce*, cupcakes, meat tarts, and a wide variety of cookies and cakes.

On Highway 1, a mile south of town, is the *Hotel El Morro*. A modern Spanish-style hotel overlooking the Sea of Cortés, it also has a dining room and bar. Its eleven air-conditioned rooms have shower baths. Rates are inexpensive. For reservations, write: Hotel El Morro, Santa Rosalia, Baja California Sur, México. Tel: 2-01-75.

MULEGÉ

The small tropical town of Mulegé, located near the mouth of the beautiful Concepción Bay and on a lazy junglelike river, is ideally situated for fishermen and skin divers. The town itself is small and dusty, but it has palms, papayas, and mango groves which add slightly to its charm. Several good and comfortable resorts can be found here, so don't be afraid to stop. The town is interesting, and there is much that can be done and seen in the area.

River Cruise. Up the Mulegé River from the town is Mission Santa Rosalia de Mulegé. A large lava-rock structure, it was built around 1766. The Mulegé River is very much like a jungle river you'd expect to find in South America or Africa. It is the only major river in the Baja, and the only one that is navigable.

The Prison. The territorial prison is located near town. Often mistaken for the mission, the prison is located behind the town. More liberal rules than those in the United States allow most prisoners to leave for town during the day, but they must return by night.

Shopping. While not one of the great shopping centers of the Baja, Mulegé has a couple of stores that offer good crafts, necessities, and an excellent array of sporting goods. For food there is a new *supermercado* with the best supplies until La Paz.

Where To Stay in Mulegé

Hotel Mulegé (*20 rooms*)   Moderate
On a hill east of town overlooking the Santa Rosalia River, this is
a modern hotel with shower baths. Completely air-conditioned.
Fishing and hunting guides. Dining room open 7–11 A.M., 1–4 P.M.,
and 7–10 P.M. Cocktails, music, dancing. Write for reservations:
Hotel Mulegé, 12521 Branford St., Pacoima, Calif. 91331, or Hotel
Mulegé, Mulegé, Baja California Sur, México. Tel: (213) 896-2461.

Hotel Serenidad (*35 rooms*)   Moderate
On the far side of the river from town. Only twenty-five of the
rooms have air conditioning. The food is good, and there is
entertainment every Saturday night. One of the more popular of the
Baja fishing camps. Beach, no pool, small pets okay. Air strip.
Campers welcomed, but facilities are limited. No cards. Reservations: 345 N. Lincoln, Corona, Calif. Tel: (714) 644-8838.

Hotel Las Casitas (*7 rooms*)   Moderate
Located in town. It may not be the Ritz, but owner Señora Woodworth
runs an excellent place, and she serves excellent food. Ceiling fans,
patio, no pool. Good location. Small pets okay. No cards.

Serenidad Mulegé (*35 units*)   Moderate
Two and one-half miles south of town, on the Santa Rosalia River,
this ranch-style hotel has spacious rooms with shower bath as well
as two-room cottages, all overlooking river and bay. Boats for rent.
Special rates for children. Dining room open 7–11 A.M., 1–4 P.M.,
and 7–10 P.M. Cocktails, entertainment. Write to Hotel Serenidad
Mulegé, Baja California Sur, México, or Serenidad Mulegé, 4305
Douglas Drive, Long Beach, Calif. 90808. Tel: (213) 774-2257.

Hotel Terrazas (*20 units*)   Inexpensive
A motel on hillside overlooking town on Moctezuma Street. Air
conditioning extra. Tile shower baths. Write to Hotel Terrazas,
Mulegé, Baja California Sur, México.

Bahía Concepción

Located just south of Mulegé, Concepción Bay is one of the
most beautiful shorelines in Mexico. It is well protected all
around by mountains that fall right into the bay, forming
endless coves. Privacy and beauty are the attractions of the bay.
The area is still undeveloped except for a few trailer parks on

Highway 1. The bay is teeming with undersea life. Skin diving and fishing are excellent. The beaches are endless and beauty numbs the eyes.

We camped here for three great days at the local public beach. While we had nothing more than what we brought, we found roughing it to be a dream come true. We gathered fish and shellfish right out of the water. Each day a baker who lives with his family out on a point, with an adobe oven for his kitchen, drives along the beaches selling fresh breads, cookies, pies, and cakes. We lived like kings.

There are no hotels or motels here yet, but you couldn't ask for a better spot to park your van than *Posada Concepción Trailer Park*. Located 15 miles south of Mulegé on Highway 1, it has all facilities and hookups. Even has a store selling most of what you need. There are thirty spaces, and the nightly rental charge is $4 per space. This is a must stop for all campers.

LORETO

Loreto is located about three-quarters of the way down the gulf coast. Although not too impressive, it is known for its excellent fishing. Located directly on the water, it offers little in the way of anything except relaxation and some of the world's great fishing.

WHERE TO STAY IN LORETO

Flying Sportsman Lodge (*40 rooms*)   Moderately expensive
In addition to air-conditioned rooms, it has space for thirty-one campers. Reservations a must in season. The best bet till La Paz. Skin diving, fishing, hunting. Pool. Dining room open 7–9 A.M., 1–2 P.M., and 5–7 P.M. Cocktails. Office: 947 Eighth Ave., San Diego, Calif. Tel: (714) 232-7322.

Hotel El Presidente (*50 rooms*)   Moderate
This used to be the Playa Loreto. Colonial complex of two-story buildings at the far north end of town. All rooms have fireplaces, air conditioning, and balconies overlooking the water. Tennis courts, shuffleboard, horses, pool. Pets okay. Bar, dining room. AE, DC, MC, VISA. Write: P.O. Box 28, Loreto, Baja California Sur, México, or El Presidente Hotels, 8721 Beverly Blvd., Los Angeles, Calif. 90048. Tel: (213) 657-5162.

Hotel Oasis (*30 rooms*)   Moderate
An excellent fishing camp on the beach. Run by Bill and Gloria
Benzinger. Most rooms have air conditioning. Fishing boats. Tennis,
no pool. No pets. AE, VISA.

La Carreta Trailer Park (*100 spaces*) $3
Located off the beach near the El Presidente. All hookups. Patios.
Showers, bathrooms, and laundry.

NOTE: You can make reservations for all hotels in Loreto
through American Western Union by simply addressing the
message to Telegraph Office, Loreto, Baja California Sur, México.
Call toll-free (800) 648-4100.

LA PAZ

The long-isolated colonial city of La Paz, located near the far
end of the Baja California peninsula, is the capital of the
territory of Baja California Sur. It is a fine place both for fishing
and for a peaceful vacation on the beach.

Located on the bay off the Sea of Cortés, La Paz is only 51
miles north of the Tropic of Cancer. Its climate is sunny and
mild most of the year. Its summers are cooled by the *coronumel*
winds which blow in from the ocean. The winter temperature
averages 70°F.

The city faces inland on the bay, and all about it are numerous
bays, inlets, and seafront, which make for good fishing, clam-
digging, and waterskiing. In all directions interesting excursions by car or boat can be made, The deep-sea fishing is
perhaps the best in the world, while equally good hunting can
be found in the mountains not too far away.

While not too large (population 65,000 at latest count), the
city has half a dozen hotels, of which two can be counted as
luxury establishments (see page 121), while to the south some
70 miles at Cabo San Lucas are some good fishing resorts with
luxury accommodations (see page 126). It makes an ideal
vacation for rest.

How To Get to La Paz

Aeromexico and Mexicana fly daily from Los Angeles to La Paz; some flights are direct, and others stop in Tijuana. A check at the airline offices in Los Angeles (633 S. Hill St., tel: 213-626-7121), New York (500 Fifth Ave., tel: 212-563-5585), Miami, Houston, Tucson, or Toronto will give you details.

Hughes Air West flies to La Paz from Phoenix and Tucson on Wednesdays and Saturdays with jet equipment. Aeronaves has flights from Tijuana which stop at Santa Rosalia, Loreto, Los Mochis, Guaymas, and Mazatlán. Mexicana flies Mexico City–Mazatlán–Los Angeles, also with good jet equipment.

Servicios Aereos de La Paz has daily connecting flights from La Paz to the hotels on Cabo San Lucas.

Buses do run into La Paz, after having been carried on ferries from the mainland at Topolobampo. Thus it is possible, though exhausting, to take a bus from Nogales, Arizona, to Topolobampo, and there transfer to a bus to La Paz.

By ferry, one can reach La Paz from Mazatlán. Thus it is possible to fly Mexicana from Los Angeles to Mazatlán, then take the very modern ferry which leaves Mazatlán on Saturdays and Tuesdays at 5 P.M. for La Paz. The trip takes sixteen hours and costs $10 for a reclining seat, $40 for a cabin, and $64 for a stateroom. Automobiles are carried for $68. Return is on Sundays and Thursdays at 5 P.M. Excellent accommodations.

There is also a regular car ferry service from Puerto Vallarta to Cabo San Lucas using a new vessel from Germany. It leaves Cabo San Lucas at 4 P.M. each Wednesday and Sunday and arrives in Puerto Vallarta at 10 A.M. the next day. Return is usually at 4 P.M. Friday and Monday. The large modern vessel has four classes of accommodations and very comfortable facilities. Fare is similar to that quoted above for the Mazatlán trip. Allow a good amount of time before departure to secure a required car permit from customs.

As schedules and prices change, and for customs information, check on both ferries by writing or calling Caminos y Puentes Federales, Independencia 107A, La Paz, B.C., México. Tel: 2-01-09.

A Word of Caution. While you can enter Baja California without a tourist card, you definitely should have one if you go south of Enseñada, and especially if you plan to cross over to the mainland. They are easy to obtain at the Mexican immigration office at the border, or your airline can help you.

Where To Eat in La Paz

The truth is that there is no really great place to eat in La Paz. But this doesn't mean you must go hungry or brown bag it. With the completion of the highway, many people are beginning to take a closer look at La Paz for new ventures, so there may be some top-notch places to come.

Jarden Yee   Moderate
This is a new Oriental restaurant about 2 miles outside of town on the north end. Serves good Cantonese food in a pleasant atmosphere. Drinks are supposed to be the cheapest in town. Open 1 P.M. to 11 P.M. Closed Mondays. No credit cards.

Restaurant Lauryz   Moderate
Across the street from El Yate restaurant, this is a typical local establishment serving steak and seafood. Very nice with ceiling fans and old lamps. All food is prepared in an open kitchen. A good place for lunch. Bar service. Open 8 A.M. till 10 P.M. Carnet, MC.

Las Brisas   Moderate
On Obregón and Frontera. Supposed to have the best steaks in town. Also serves lobster, shrimp, and Chinese food. An open-air place on the water with live music in the evenings. Popular with the locals.

Hotel Perla   Moderately expensive
This is an open-air café and restaurant. A popular place with local businessmen. Food is ordinary, and a meal can be quite expensive, but a light lunch or snack is reasonably priced. Opens early, closes late.

Perico's   Moderate
Next to the Mar del Cortés Travel Agency on Obregón-Malecón, this small restaurant specializes in Mexican food. Owner Luis takes great pride in the place, and as anyone will tell you, he makes the best hamburger in all of La Paz. He also claims to have served many famous movie stars who come to La Paz to go fishing. Besides the hamburger, best bet is the "commercial lunch" for $2. He also has the best tortillas around.

El Patio   Inexpensive
Back through the winding streets you'll find El Patio refreshment
center at Morelos and Altamirano. It's an outdoor service-counter
place good for a quick hamburger and ice cream. We recommend
a stop here for one of their great ice cream sodas made with fresh
fruit. These are the best cooling-off drinks in town. Great for kids.

WHERE TO STAY IN LA PAZ

El Presidente (*250 rooms*)   Moderately expensive
This is the newest El Presidente. Sitting out on a point on the water
at the north end of town, its two twelve-story towers stand out
from the shorter older buildings in town. It has all the assets of a
fine resort. Tennis, boating, fishing fleet, pool, restaurant, bar, etc.
Reservations through El Presidente Hotels, 8721 Beverly Blvd., Los
Angeles, Calif. 90048. Tel: (213) 657-5162.

La Posada (*25 rooms*)   Moderately expensive
Located just up the beach from El Presidente, La Posada is the best
bet in La Paz. This tropical "inn" is gracious and very relaxing.
Everybody is extremely helpful in seeing to your needs; don't be
afraid to ask questions. All rooms have air conditioning. Large
rooms are well furnished and have fireplaces. The bar and restaurant
by the pool is open from 7 A.M. to 10 P.M. All food is cooked to
order, and deliciously so. Probably the best food in La Paz, and bar
service is always available. Garden courtyard is a mini oasis. No
credit cards, but will take checks with identification. P.O. Box 1527,
La Paz, Baja California, México. Tel: 2-06-63.

Hotel Los Arcos (*200 rooms*)   Moderately expensive
Newly expanded. New owner-manager is Luis Coppola. They will
be adding another pool, three bars, sauna, self-service cafeteria,
free parking, telephones, and maybe TV. Reports on the food were
not good. Prices are high, and service is terrible. It took one hour
to find someone who could give information. AE, Carnet, CB, MC,
VISA. No checks. P.O. Box 112, La Paz. Tel: 2-00-24 or 2-13-68.

Hotel Calafia (*28 rooms*)   Moderate
Very attractive motel 2 miles south of town on Highway 1. Air-
conditioned rooms, pool, restaurant, bar. No cards. P.O. Box 31, La
Paz.

Hotel Perla (*100 rooms*)   Inexpensive
Rooms are very basic, and somewhat clean. The help is slow, and
not fussy. Best thing about it is its location. Rooms have air
conditioning, telephones, tiled baths and showers. Shades of the
old thirties movies. Sidewalk café overlooking the harbor is a

popular hangout for local businessmen. Bar. AE, Carnet, DC, VISA. Tel: 2-07-77.

Econohotel (*120 rooms*)   Moderate
On the beach at La Paz, this is a large modern hotel. All rooms air-conditioned, each with two double beds or a king-size bed. Ice and soft drink machines, cafeteria and restaurant, bar, discotheque. Swimming pool in garden. Special rates for families. Tel: toll-free (800) 221-6509 or (800) 854-3048.

El Cardón Trailer Park (*90 spaces*) $4
The most popular in town, mainly because it is at the finish line for the famous Baja 1,000 road race. All hookups, with a two-sided hut with thatched roof over patios. Lots of shade and flowers. Pool. Coin laundry, nicely tiled showers, and restrooms. Car pit and barbecue grills. Pets okay. Well run. Located at the north end of town on Highway 1.

Tío Ed Trailer Park (*160 spaces*) $4–$5
This is the best park in the Baja. Owned and run by "Uncle Ed," it is a large, well-landscaped complex and should be quite beautiful when all the trees grow up. Uncle Ed is always concerned about his "guests" and will solve any problem you have. He keeps the place up, saying, "I've told my people I want this place so clean I wouldn't mind eating dinner in the bathrooms." Two beautiful pools, bar, all hookups, picnic tables, barbecue pits, individual light pots, store, showers, toilets, laundry, ice machines, and recreational area. Night watchman. Located at the south end of town, just off Highway 1. Tío Ed R.V. Park, P.O. Box 84, La Paz.

FISHING FROM LA PAZ

Bill Callahan, a longtime sports authority in La Paz, says, "Fishing is excellent twelve months a year for one species or another. Naturally fishing seasons vary somewhat with the year. Marlin arrive here in quantity around the middle of March and stay in these waters until October. Sailfish are usually plentiful from June until November. Roosterfish, sierra, yellowtail, etc., are plentiful all year long, although they are best in the winter months. Dolphin . . . are particularly abundant from May through December."

Jack Vélez Fleet can be reached by any hotel, or you can telephone him at 2-07-55 or write him at Box 402, La Paz. Vélez has six well-equipped fishing boats from 20 to 32 feet in length, and good crews to man them. All boats have radios. Bait, tackle, and refreshments are arranged. U.S. representative is Robert Butler, 2751 W. Lincoln, Anaheim, California 92801. Tel: (714) 821-6770.

Fred Cota, 306 Ocampo, La Paz, also has fishing boats. Tel: 2-07-98.

Salvador Morales, with an office behind La Perla Hotel, has 25-foot boats and one 40-footer. Address: Box 263, La Paz. Tel: 2-10-90.

La Paz Skin Diving Service has a 121-foot former coast guard cutter which takes sixteen passengers, and with accompanying speedboat combines fishing and diving. Address: Box 133, La Paz.

HUNTING FROM LA PAZ

There is good hunting about the area, particularly in the mountains across the bay. Experienced guides can be arranged for by any of the hotels, or by the fishing firms mentioned above. See page 97.

FISHING LODGES AND RANCHES OF BAJA CALIFORNIA

Near Enseñada, Reachable in Your Own Car

Estero Beach Resort Hotel (*46 cottages,*   Moderately expensive
75 spaces)
Six miles south of Enseñada, this resort caters to fishermen. Has both rooms and modern cabins with cooking facilities. Dining room available. See listing on page 110.

Meling Ranch   Moderate
About 100 miles south of Enseñada, just 8 miles beyond Colnett on Highway 1, a turnoff inland some 30 miles brings you to the 10,000-acre cattle ranch San José or Meling's. Practically a true-life version of an old western ranch. Special rates for children. Swimming pool, horses, hunting. Has airport. Write two weeks in advance for reservations to P.O. Box 224, Enseñada. Tel: (213) 790-4387 or (714) 466-6872.

Mike's Sky Ranch
In same area as Meling's, this is a motel-type resort at $15 per person with meals, or $95 a week. Campsites available with showers and toilets at $5 for one night, $3 thereafter. Airport 6 miles south of ranch. Write for reservations to Av. Revolución 1018, Tijuana.

At San Felipe, on Gulf, Reachable by Car from Mexicali

San Felipe is a small, isolated fishing village across the peninsula at the top of the Sea of Cortés, or Gulf of California. It is about 130 miles south of Mexicali on a good paved road that leads right into the main street of San Felipe. Behind town rise the huge Sierra San Pedro Martir Mountains with the 10,156-foot Picacho del Diablo peak.

San Felipe is right on a wide beach where the tide recedes a quarter of a mile. Great for dune buggies. There are several motels located directly on the water, and small restaurants which, while plain, serve excellent food. The best sea fishing is for dolphin, bonita, roosterfish, marlin, mackerel, halibut, and giant sea bass. There is also freshwater fishing nearby.

Small boats can be rented with tackle, or you can bring your own and there is a launching ramp. Best fishing is from November until June, with March and April best. From May to October it is extremely hot. Reservations are a must from December until Easter vacation.

Augie's Riviera Motel (*34 rooms*)   Moderate
This is a modest motel that sits on a hill across from the water and beaches, about ½ mile south of town. It has fourteen rooms in an older wing and twenty better rooms in its newer wing. Pool, dining room, and cantina bar. Open only during tourist season. Restaurant open from 3:30 A.M. until 10 P.M. in fishing season. For reservations, write to Augie's Riviera Motel, San Felipe, Baja California.

Villa del Mar Motel (*24 rooms*)   Moderate
Located adjacent to Augie's on same hill, this new motel has rather basic rooms with private baths and air conditioning. Restaurant and bar. Open only in tourist season. For reservations, write to Villa del Mar Motel, San Felipe, Baja California.

El Cortez Motor Hotel (*62 units*)   Moderate
Considered the best place in town at this writing. Located at extreme south end of town directly on beach. Units have several rooms, some with kitchenettes. Fine restaurant serves shrimp omelet for breakfast. Open all year with entertainment at the bar. For reservations, write to El Cortez Motor Hotel, P.O. Box 1227, Calexico, Calif. 92231.

NOTE: There are more than twenty camping/trailer parks in and around San Felipe. Accommodations range from a spot of sand to complete hookups. We are not able to list all. We consider the ones listed below to be the best.

Campo Turistico (*34 spaces*) $3.50 for two; 50¢ extra per person
Nice park off beach with facilities for both tenters and trailers. Thirty-four units, with sewer and water hookups at only nine. Extra charge of 80¢ for electricity and 75¢ for hot water and hot showers. Cold-water showers and bathrooms free.

Club de Pesca Trailer Park (*200+ spaces*)   Rates upon request
Most spaces have complete hookups, thatched-roof patios, some greenery. Clean bathrooms, free and pay showers. Snack shop sells beer, soft drinks, some food, candy, liquor. Nice patio on the beach serves as shade and meeting place—also as small bar in season. Game room has ping-pong, pool, darts. Bottled water and ice delivered daily (but the best ice for keeping food cold is to be found at the fish-packing plant at the north end of town). Many permanent trailers, since many people moving down to San Felipe for extended periods of time stay here. Reservations recommended. Write to Club de Pesca Trailer Park, San Felipe, Baja California.

Las Arenas Trailer Park (*50 spaces*) $2.50 per day for one spot
South of town about 1½ miles past end of paved road. Excellent location for those who want to get away from it all. Best bet is to fill up on everything you're going to need and then drive out. Full hookups with covered spaces. Good location for dirt bikes and buggies.

Ruben's Trailer Park (*50+ spaces*) $2.50 for three people
Located north of town. Go to end of paved road, up over hill, and down the other side. Continue past fish-packing plant, and ahead you will see several trailer parks. Ruben's is the best in the area, and the best next to Club de Pesca. All spaces have water and electrical hookups, patios. Clean bathrooms with showers. Restaurant and bar highly recommended by many local campers. Dogs must be on ropes and motorcycles kept outside camp. Excellent

beach, but can be crowded with campers from other areas. No reservations.

South of La Paz at Far Tip of Peninsula (Cabo San Lucas)

While La Paz is on a bay some 100 miles from the end of the peninsula of Baja California, you can easily drive or fly to Cabo San Lucas at the far end of the peninsula. Scattered along this coastline are many broad vistas, beautiful beaches, and a score of fishing lodges and luxury hotels. They are not huddled together; each is located in some isolation, usually spectacular. The first one is only 30 or 40 miles from La Paz on Mexican Route 1, while the farthest tip of land, called Land's End or Finisterra, is 139 miles from La Paz along the same highway. Air Baja and Commuter/Intrastate have flights from the La Paz airport to the towns of San José del Cabo and Cabo San Lucas, with special stops at outlying resorts which have their own landing strips. The resorts are among the most luxurious in the world, and the fishing is said to be the best. Mexicana is starting three-times-a-week jet service to Cabo San Lucas from Mexico City and the United States, utilizing a new jetport.

Hotel Cabo San Lucas (*82 rooms*)   Very expensive
This is undoubtedly the best hotel in Baja California, and probably one of the best in the world. Perched atop a rocky promontory overlooking the Pacific from the near tip of the peninsula, it is a rambling three-story structure with a red tile roof. Each room has a balcony. All rooms lavishly decorated with king-size beds, hi-fi music. Beautifully maintained with spacious bar-lounge, excellent continental cuisine, good service. Top fishing, fleet for charter, snorkeling, hunting. William Matt Parr is president, but Yee brothers—David, cashier, and Simon, manager—operate it. Call Los Angeles (213) 655-4760 for reservations, or write Los Angeles office, P.O. Box 48747, Briggs Station, Los Angeles, Calif., or Hotel Cabo San Lucas, Baja California, México. Scheduled flights daily from Los Angeles, Phoenix, and Tucson to La Paz on Aeronaves or Hughes Air West; daily connecting flights to Cabo airfield, which has 3,600-foot runway with all facilities. Paved road from La Paz takes three hours.

Hotel Finisterra (*100 rooms*)   Very expensive
At Land's End, spectacular location on ridge extending into Pacific. Structure thrusts from craggy perch, each room with balcony, while

below is private mile-long beach. Mexican decor and architecture, as hotel is owned by Luis Bulnes. Water is teeming with fish, and crews and boats are available. Horseback riding, hunting, freshwater pool. Two cocktail lounges, menu featuring fresh fruits and seafood. Private airstrip or can be reached by paved road from La Paz. Manager is Dario Ruesaga. Reservations: Hotel Finisterra, Shreve Bldg., 210 Post St., San Francisco, Calif. Tel: San Francisco (415) 397-1818 or Chicago (312) 372-1533.

Hacienda Hotel (*50 rooms*)   Expensive
A luxury hotel located on Cabo San Lucas Bay within walking distance of the village of Cabo San Lucas. Good restaurant. Tennis, fishing, waterskiing. Affiliated with Hotel Cabo San Lucas. For reservations, write to P.O. Box 48872, Los Angeles. Tel: (213) 655-7777.

Hyatt Cabo San Lucas (*125 rooms*)   Moderately expensive
Picturesque villas on a hillside by the sea. Tel: toll-free (800) 228-9000.

Camino Real (*70 rooms*)   Expensive
At Cabo San Lucas Bay, this is the former Hacienda de San Lucas just before Finisterra. Two pools, tennis courts. Manager is Emelio Calderón. Part of the Western Hotels chain.

Hotel Las Cruces Palmilla (*45 rooms*)   Expensive
Big white Moorish structure amid palms on rise overlooking sea with sandy beaches nestled between rock outcroppings. On winding dirt road turning off just before Hotel Cabo San Lucas, about 100 miles from La Paz. Pool, large dining room, bar. Fifteen fishing boats, dove hunting. Runway 6,000 feet long, approach from sea. Manager is Hector Guerena. No credit cards but personal checks if known. Discount for children. P.O. Box 1775, La Jolla, Calif. Tel: (714) 454-0600.

Mar de Cortés (*30 rooms*)   Inexpensive
Modern new hotel in the small city of Cabo San Lucas a short distance from seafront. Pool. Address hotel in Cabo San Lucas, Baja California. Tel: Los Angeles (213) 655-8708.

Hotel Bahía de Palmas (*20 rooms*)   Moderate
Located 73 miles south of La Paz by road, near Buena Vista on Las Palmas Bay. It is strictly for sportsmen, but rooms are comfortable with bathrooms; meals served ranch style in combined bar and dining room. Skiffs and cruisers, including crew, bait, and tackle. Fishing excellent. Manager is Julio Amador. Write: Hotel Bahía de Palmas, Los Barriles, Baja California. Tel: (213) 763-9041.

Rancho Buena Vista (*15 rooms*)   Moderate
Located 74 miles south of La Paz and near Bahía de Palmas. Has
landing strip (2,000 feet). This is a true fishermen's lodge and not
a luxury hotel. Brick buildings with thatched roofs, screened
windows. Food served ranch style on common table, but is good.
Road from La Paz passes through El Triunfo ghost mining town.
Hunting, skin diving, cruisers, skiffs. Fishing excellent. Write:
Hotel Buena Vista, Los Barriles, La Paz, Baja California. Tel: (714)
673-4638.

GOOD REFERENCE BOOKS ON BAJA CALIFORNIA

Lower California Guidebook by Gerhard and Gulick (Clark), 220
pages.
A mile-by-mile log of automobile trips throughout Baja California.
Includes minute details. Not for general reading but for actual use
on the road.
Log of Baja California, Mexico by Automobile Club of Southern
California.
A smaller booklet containing much general information, routes, and
pictures on auto travel in Baja California.
Yesterday's Land by Leonard Wibberley (Washburn), 154 pages.
A small book of essays on travel in Baja California. Not a travel
guide.
The Forgotten Peninsula by Joseph Wood Krutch (Sloane), 277 pages.
A naturalist's guide to Baja California by an expert.
Historia de Baja California by Pablo L. Martínez (Libros Mexicanos),
480 pages.
A detailed history of Baja California in Spanish providing a complete
account of events.

9

Cancún, Isla Mujeres, and Cozumel

FOR THOSE who wish to get away to a spectacular sunny coastline with a plethora of ultramodern hotels and miles of white beaches rimmed with waters ranging from emerald-green to turquoise to lapis lazuli, the obvious place is the new Cancún (pronounced "can-*koon*") resort built at a cost of $160 million on the Caribbean just off Yucatán.

It is not an island, though it looks like one, as it is connected to the mainland by a 200-foot causeway. The hotel area itself is isolated on an L-shaped spit of white sand with green grass and paved highways. Along its 14-mile length are strung a dozen modern new hotels, most built by recognized international hotel organizations. None are permitted to be higher than nine stories; most are lower, and some consist of cabana-type units with modern facilities.

Swimming pools are everywhere, even though the pleasant white sand beaches are powdery smooth and the water a delight to swim in. On the inland side of Cancún is Nichupte Lagoon, which has some 18 square miles of water surface itself and offers boating, fishing, and water sports.

The entire resort was built from a largely uninhabited area after government tourist promoters, on the basis of a computerized study, declared it the most potentially successful resort area in Mexico. It seemed to have everything. Fortunately, these young planners began by laying out all the proper sanitary facilities, and in fact planned an entire new city located some 12 miles from the hotel zone. Here are completely new homes and schools; the new commercial areas contain most of the shops in Cancún and some of the restaurants.

Isla Mujeres, a half-hour boat ride from Cancún, is smaller and more primitive. Cozumel is the immensely popular island off the coast of Quintana Roo some 40 miles south of Cancún. It is in no way a match for the elegance of Cancún in size or in facilities, though it does have fine fishing and a rustic flavor not found in Cancún. It still has its devotees, too.

While many of the early visitors to Cancún complained that it looked barren and there was not much to do, all this has now changed. For one thing, palms planted a few years ago are now very large and have created palm-shaded drives not only in front of the hotels but in the town as well. Meantime, there practically isn't a hotel that doesn't have a large dance floor, with entertainment every evening, while a number of restaurants and bars have opened in the town itself and the number is sure to increase. We, in fact, found there was too much to do.

GUIDE TO CANCÚN

GETTING THERE

This is a bit of a problem until the civil aeronautics boards of Mexico, the United States, and other countries can settle on more reasonable arrangements. At the moment, the only way to fly to Cancún is either by Mexicana from Miami (one hour and twenty-five minutes nonstop) or by Aeromexico from Houston with a stop at Mérida en route (about three hours flying time). Pan-Am flies three times a week from New York to Mérida, and it is a four-hour drive in rented car or bus from Mérida to Cancún.

The most accessible way from most points in the United States is to ask your travel agent if there isn't an OTC or some other group charter that will fly directly to the handsome new jetport at Cancún.

No papers are required except a tourist card, which does require you to bring a birth certificate or other proof of U.S. citizenship. Airlines can provide tourist cards on a few days' notice.

THINGS TO DO

Immediately at hand is a Robert Trent Jones course, called Poc-Ta-Pok Golf Club, which has nine holes in operation. Work is

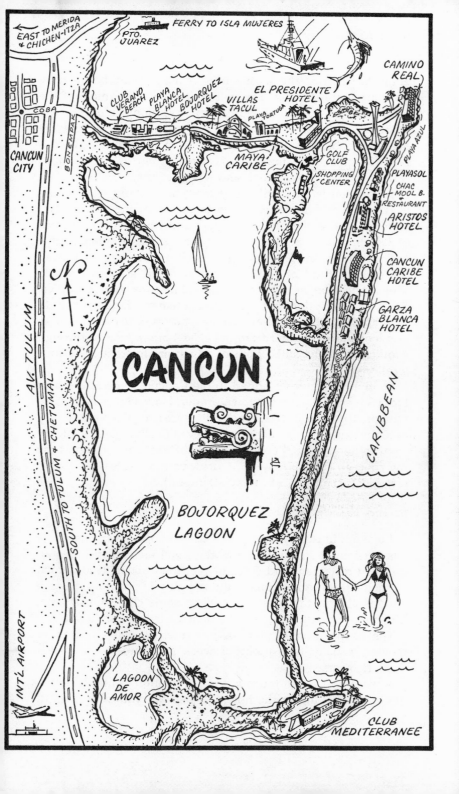

about finished on the second nine, which should be open by the time you read this. The golf course is in the midst of the hotel area on a spit of land extending along and into the adjoining lagoon. The closest hotel to the golf course is El Presidente, but it is easily accessible from all hotels, and all can play ($5 greens fee for the first nine). There is a pro shop, restaurant, swimming pool, and tennis courts.

Tennis courts are available at most hotels, and waterskiing is everywhere. Bikes or jeeps can be rented by the hour or day. Fishing trips can be easily arranged, and you have your choice of lagoon, river, or deep-sea fishing. A glass-bottom sight-seeing launch, the *Fiesta Maya*, makes a three-hour trip from the dock in front of El Presidente Hotel. It also goes to Isla Mujeres on a longer trip. The schools of brightly colored tropical fish defy description, but you can see them in a fantastic variety of shapes and colors; they virtually bump noses with you as you look at them either from the glass-bottom boat or through snorkels or scuba suits, both of which are for rent at various locations.

Bullfights have been added to the Cancún scene at the new Plaza Silverio Perez in the town proper. However, as is the case with provincial bullrings, the offerings are irregular, very chancy as to the skill of the bullfighter, and even the bull doesn't always want to fight. Still, if you can't make it to the real thing at the big rings in Mexico City or Madrid, you can at least see what it is like (usually on a Sunday afternoon).

CONVENTION CENTER

A huge auditorium with various halls, shops, and restaurants has been built in the midst of the hotel area. It includes an excellent restaurant and discotheque, the Cancún 1900, which is open late. Another smaller but delightful restaurant, Tuscan Tarr, is also in the center as well as some chic shops: Tane, L'Époque, Sportif Aire, and the famed Victor's handicrafts.

The Convention Center has an international selection of movies, usually four nights a week at 7 and 9 P.M. Ballet Folklórico comes occasionally.

A place well worth touring, the Convention Center is on the boulevard leading to the hotels. It's so big you can't miss it!

Where To Eat in Cancún

Many of the hotels use the modified American plan, where the charge includes two meals, but this is not true of all of them or, at times, of any. So you can try out some of the new restaurants both near the Convention Center and in town, or try some of the dining rooms in other hotels, most of which are fairly good and some, excellent.

Cancún 1900

In the Convention Center. A posh restaurant with some excellent food and usually music. They have a full menu from steaks and lobster to French cuisine. Prices are a bit high but not unreasonable. We found the service good. Next door, apparently under same management, is an all-night discotheque which is noisy, dark, and for the young. It does not conflict with the peace and quiet of the 1900 restaurant, fortunately.

Playa Chac Mool

Small, but a charming restaurant with glass walls overlooking the beach next to the Aristos Hotel. It is a thatched-roof building, but the food is excellent. Specialties are shrimp, lobster, and fish prepared in many ways. Open 10 A.M. till 11 P.M.

Mauna Loa

A branch of the famed Polynesian restaurant. You will find the complete range of Oriental delicacies on their menu together with an exotic selection of drinks. Dinner shows at 7 and 8:15; late show dinner optional. Cover. We recommend reservations. Closed Sundays. Tel: 3-01-22.

Las Palapas

A good Italian restaurant located in the town of Cancún on the central plaza. All sorts of pastas prepared under personal supervision of owner Giuseppe.

The Lobster House

A modest reataurant in town at Retourno 3, Manzana 22, with not only lobster but a selection of international dishes. Air-conditioned. Usually has famed *sopa de lima* (chicken soup with lime).

Chocko and Tere

Across from the Red Cross Building, which is just off Blvd. Tulum. Serves fillet of red snapper, stuffed with fresh crabmeat if you wish. Lobster at all times and often some of the typical dishes such as *pollo pibil*, which is chicken cooked in banana leaves. Open from noon to midnight.

At the Hotels

Cancún Caribe dining room

At the Hotel Cancún Caribe. We rate this as having the best food and service in Cancún. It is open to the public both at noon and evening. Food is continental, and there lurks a good chef in the kitchen. A musical group plays every night, and there is dancing until at least 10 P.M.

Restaurant Lol-Ha

At the Hotel Garza Blanca. Has been getting good reports. You will find it at the far end of the hotel row. Tel: 3-00-22, 3-00-23.

Azulejos Restaurant

At the Camino Real Hotel. Has been highly praised for its good bar service and is said to have the most interesting bar.

WHERE TO STAY IN CANCÚN

Aristos Cancún (260 rooms)   Expensive

Located on the main beach, this is a three-story star-shaped building without elevators. All rooms are air-conditioned and have fully equipped refrigerator bars. Swimming pool, tennis. Thatched huts and towel service on beach. Guests report that food is fair but service at times slow. Bar has entertainment nightly. Many tour groups stay here. All cards. Loews reservations in U.S. or Mexico City (tel: 533-05-60).

Bajorquez (69 rooms)   Moderate

A modern three-story building at the beginning of the hotel strip. Rooms have balconies. Dining room. Pool. Own beach. Write directly to Bajorquez, Cancún, Quintana Roo, México, or tel: 585-57-44 in Mexico City.

Camino Real (250 rooms)   Expensive

This is one of the best hotels in Cancún, situated at the elbow of the L-shaped spit of beach land. Its location gives it a sense of remoteness and a magnificent view. It is ultramodern with sloping walls facing the sea. All rooms have balconies, and each balcony has a hammock. Wonderful decor highlighted by macrame constructions makes it look like a modern museum rather than a hotel. There is a fine bar with exotic concoctions and free guacamole. Has several pools, shallow ones good for kids, and one of the best beaches. Golf nearby. All cards. Belongs to Western Hotels International and can be reached through any of their U.S. hotels. Tel: 545-70-75 in Mexico City.

Cancún Caribe (*208 rooms*)   Expensive
Probably the handsomest of all the new hotels and the favorite of the writer. It is run by hotelman Warren Broglie, and his expertise is apparent. Nine stories high, it is located near the far end of the island spit, where there is probably the best beach. Rooms are large, with handsome bright decor. All have balconies with view of the sea and are equipped with stocked bars and refrigerators. Has large pool and a dozen separate cabanas for parties. Tennis courts and water sports at hotel; golf nearby. Excellent dining room. Music and dancing every night. Bar with electronic games. All cards. Tel: 533-41-11 in Mexico City, or write Cancún Caribe, Liverpool 123F, México 6, D.F., México, or directly to Cancún.

El Presidente Hotel (*200 rooms*)   Expensive
One of the principal hotels in the midst of the long beach strip and immediately adjoining the golf course. A long five-story hotel with a huge white tower at one end overlooking both the beach and the golf course. Part of the huge Nacional Hotelera chain, it is run according to the high standards of the chain. Pool, tennis courts, facilities for water sports. Restaurant, two bars, and nightclub. All cards. Reservations can be made through the Nacional Hotelera at Hamburgo 135, México 6, D.F. (tel: 525-00-00), or directly to the hotel at P.O. Box 451, Cancún, Quintana Roo, México.

Garza Blanca (*56 suites*)   Expensive
A group of red-tiled buildings in a palm courtyard at the far end of the hotel group along the beach. Some of the bungalows have their own private pools. Offers a good deal of privacy. Excellent dining room and bar. All cards.

Maya Caribe (*40 rooms*)   Moderately expensive
Near the beginning of the hotel strip, this is a smaller white Moorish structure with a number of suites. Three pools, one tennis court, water sports available. Restaurant, bar, craft shop. Reservations at Inmobiliaria del Caribe, Monterrey 47-203, México 7, D.F. (tel: 525-58-93), or directly to hotel in Cancún.

Hotel Parador (34 *rooms*)   Moderate
Located in the commercial zone of the new town of Cancún built
on the mainland, this is a modern two-story hotel built in Spanish
fortaleza ("fortress") style. It has a pool and is only a taxi ride from
the public beaches. Restaurant and shopping arcade. Write to Hotel
Parador, Cancún, Quintana Roo, México.

Playa Blanca (66 *rooms*)   Moderate
This was probably the first hotel to open on the beach strip and is
just beyond the bridge from town. Built in two three-story wings
with balconies. One four-bedroom suite. Has its own beach. Tennis,
pool, boats for rent. Restaurant overlooking beach. All cards. Write
to Representaciones Cancún, Av. Chapultepec 350, México 7, D.F.
(tel: 511-34-89), or direct to Cancún.

Plaza Caribe (112 *rooms*)   Moderate
In the town of Cancún and not on the beach, this is a modern hotel
built in the commercial section. Has dining room, bar, squash
courts. All cards. Write direct to Cancún.

Villas Tacul (21 *luxury bungalows*)   Very expensive
These spacious (up to five bedrooms each), beautifully designed
and decorated bungalows in a palm garden on the beach are
probably the nicest places to stay in Cancún if not in the world. The
decor is beyond description except to mention that the Shah of Iran
stayed here. All are luxury homes with large rooms, their own
kitchens, sliding doors opening on private beaches, and a complete
staff for each house upon request. Herman Muller, a Swiss, maintains
immaculately clean and well-serviced facilities, and even the gardens
are beautifully kept. A 50-percent deposit is required upon reservation, the balance upon occupancy. Write to Villas Tacul, 924
Farmington Ave., West Hartford, Conn., tel: (203) 523-1609 or Villas
Tacul, Paseo de la Reforma 292-502, México 6, D.F., tel: 528-60-85.

Club Méditerranée (300 *rooms*)   Club rates
This is a facility of the international travel organization, and you
must sign up with the club in any of the major cities of the world
in order to become eligible for their group tours to any of their
seventy-two far-flung establishments around the world. The one in
Cancún may be the best of them all.
The club features great friendship among its guests, encouraged by
young women and men called *gentils organisateurs*, or more often
simply "GOs." The idea is to dispense with all money during this
time, using beads worn around your neck to pay for drinks, and
to consider everything else including meals as part of the package
deal you signed up for. Swimsuits are standard daytime wear,

though the wildest costumes from all parts of the world are worn at night. Entertainment is constant.

The Club Med at Cancún is large, with 300 double rooms, and is very modern but looks almost Moorish with its white stucco finish. Built around Punta Nizuc, which is at the far end of the Cancún beach, it is well isolated from the other hotels. A large lagoon serves as a central point around which have been built nearly a dozen buildings two or three stories high. A huge pool in the center is the main gathering place, and shaded tables there serve as an open-air dining room. Use of Mexican tiles and brightly hued bedspreads make the rooms attractive.

It is only twenty minutes from the new jetport at Cancún, reachable by its own road, which has yet to be improved. While Club Med has a reputation for catering to singles, many couples seem to enjoy it, too. For those with very special ideas on living.

Contact the Club Mediterranée in any major city or write to Club Mediterranée, Newton 156, 5th Floor, México 5, D.F. (tel: 545-01-11), or directly to Club Mediterranée, Cancún, Quintana Roo, México.

Trips from Cancún

Chichén-Itzá. Cancún is within easy reach (75 miles) of some of the most fabulous archeological grounds in the world. Certainly the most noted, and for my vote the most interesting, is Chichén-Itzá, which is an all-day bus trip (or you can easily drive, as there is only one road and no way to get lost). The bus tour (usually daily from your hotel) offers air-conditioned motor coaches, box lunches, and a guide for a reasonable price.

Chichén-Itzá dates back to the middle Mayan periods, well over a thousand years ago, and consists of an array of temples, ancient Mayan ball courts, religious structures, and residences of high officials. There is a spectacular underground lake, or *cenote*, where human sacrifices were made and where many great art treasures were found by divers.

All of this, as well as some adjoining areas such as Old Chichén, can easily be visited on foot once you arrive, and there are some hotels and restaurants nearby if you wish to stay longer. (See Chapter 26, which has a complete description and drawings of this fascinating zone.) This should be a "must" trip if you go to Cancún and have never seen the relics of the ancient Mayan civilization. Buses leave at 7:45 A.M. and return at 6:15 P.M. Fare is currently $24 including lunch at one of the hotels in Chichén-Itzá.

Chichén-Itzá is not alone as a relic of the Maya. There are estimated to be 6,000 similar cities, many older, many still undiscovered. Few have been as well restored as Chichén-Itzá.

Akumal. About 35 miles from Cancún on the Tulum road is a noted resort, *Club de Yates Akumal Caribe.* It has bungalows and suites for rent and an attractive main building with a restaurant and bar. Prices are high, but we understand the accommodations are very comfortable and the food is good. There is a museum exhibiting many treasures recovered from Spanish galleons still at the ocean bottom off the shore. It is possible to rent launches and full fishing equipment, and the beach is excellent for swimming. For further information and reservations, write to Calle 60 No. 458, Mérida, Yucatán, tel: 1-36-78, or 5820 Burning Tree, El Paso, Texas, tel: (915) 584-3552.

Xel Ha. Six miles south of Akumal, at a well-marked turnoff, is perhaps the only natural aquarium in the world. Called Xel Ha, it is an inlet from the open sea which is literally alive with tropical fish of every imaginable color, shape, and fin type. The name is Mayan for "the place where waters are born," derived from the fact that the porous coral permits fresh water to flow into the outlet and mix with the seawater; apparently this condition is a natural attraction for the fish. There is a 5-peso admission fee. Snorkeling is permitted and equipment can be rented, but since Xel Ha is a national park, no spearfishing is allowed. The fish are friendly, and you and your children can have the time of your lives seeing what must be the most beautiful collection of fish, swimming freely, in the world.

Tulum, another Mayan ruin, is located about 80 miles southwest along the coastline from Cancún. It is easily seen from the road, and there is a landing strip not far away. You can drive in and park; there is an admission charge of 10 pesos. Soft drinks are sold, but nothing else.

Tulum is much smaller than Chichén-Itzá, but it is the only known major Mayan ruin built on the edge of the sea and may have been a signal point to Cozumel. It has a single large temple on a hilltop surrounded by a wall.

Below the temple, sometimes called the pyramid, there are about sixty structures in various states of abandonment. However, the massive columned temple does have frescoes worth seeing. There is a small beach for swimming.

Buses to Tulum leave Cancún at 9:30 A.M., returning at 5:30 P.M. The cost is $22 including lunch at a hotel.

Coba. A car trip of 24 miles from Tulum, all over a well-paved, straight, and level road, brings you to the ruins at Coba. Restoration here has only recently begun, and as the site is estimated to cover 80 square miles and contain thousands of stone buildings, it will be a long time before the work is completed. Already some very interesting ruins have been uncovered, as well as thirty-six stelae (carved slabs), each with messages that can probably be translated. It is believed that a wide road connected Coba with Yaxuma and that a canal may have run to the sea at Tulum for the purpose of exchanging Mayan goods among the markets and returning with seafood.

GUIDE TO ISLA MUJERES

One of the most pleasant ways to spend a day is to take one of two ferries to Isla Mujeres from Puerto Juárez, which is the original settlement for Cancún. It is just a few miles down the road from the new town, adjoining Punta Sam.

The island can be a frustrating place to reach, as the ferries are irregular, not very comfortable, and no one ever seems to know when the next ferry leaves. And you are lucky if you get a seat. Still, the crossing takes only twenty minutes or so, and you will find some delightful things to explore and enjoy on the small island (population is some 7,000) which has acquired, through various legends, the name of Isla Mujeres, or "Island of the Women."

Inexpensive lobster and a wide variety of seafood are abundant on Isla Mujeres. There are also turtle pens where you can view—in fact walk around among—these giant creatures of the sea, usually bound for a canning factory.

There is a rather unusual Mayan ruin at the far tip of the island (about 5 miles from the ferry landing). It is called "the lighthouse," as apparently the Maya used it to send signals to the mainland. A modern lighthouse stands nearby. There is a fairly good road to the lighthouse which you may drive if you rent a car or a motorcycle (very popular on Isla Mujeres). It is also possible to hire a taxi (at about $5 an hour) to drive you there, but the drivers up the tariff considerably for what they consider an "island tour." Check them. But you can't win.

Another interesting means of travel on Isla Mujeres is by chartered launch, which usually costs 100 pesos per person, with a minimum of eight persons required. The launch trip will not only take you by the turtle pens, and to a fine sea view of the Mayan structure, but also to El Garrafón, a lovely coral area filled with colorful tropical fish. You are free to snorkel at El Garrafón if you wish, but fishing is prohibited.

Getting There

First you must get to Puerto Juárez or Punta Sam, by driving through the town of Cancún and heading for the shorefront. You can get a taxi from your hotel to Puerto Juárez for 50 pesos; it costs an extra 15 pesos to go to Punta Sam. Usually cabs are waiting around, but will load all the passengers they can.

There is a choice of two ferries. The one leaving from Puerto Juárez is an overcrowded ordinary fishing boat with everyone squeezing aboard as best they can and paying 10 pesos each. On our trip it was uncomfortable and crowded, but the crowd was jolly and the voyage not too long. The Puerto Juárez ferry leaves at 5 A.M., 9 A.M., noon, 2 P.M., 3 P.M., and 6 P.M. It returns at 2 A.M., 7 A.M., 10 A.M., noon, 2 P.M., 4 P.M., and 6 P.M. A modest hotel by the ferry, Villa del Mar, serves a respectable breakfast or lunch and makes a good waiting place.

A much bigger, steel-structured ferry, capable of carrying trucks and cars and with a few seats and a snack bar, leaves from Punta Sam, which is about 2 miles farther up the coast from Puerto Juárez. It costs 5 pesos per person but 50 pesos for cars. It leaves Punta Sam at 8:30 A.M., 11:30 A.M., 1:45 P.M., and 5 P.M. It returns from Isla Mujeres at 7:15 A.M., 10 A.M., 1:15 P.M., and 4 P.M.

Eating on Isla Mujeres

There are a number of small restaurants, but apparently you are out of your mind if you don't go to the famous *Kin Ha Club* run by Marie Mendez, which is why it is more commonly called "Marie's." She serves a wide variety of dishes, featuring seafood, but her specialty is lobster. It costs less than elsewhere. You can call her to deliver to your Isla Mujeres hotel, or you can have one of the launches stop at her restaurant. The taxis, for their usual outrageous prices, will of course also take you there. A small dockside restaurant, the *Tropicana*, is modest but clean and serves good seafood and sandwiches.

WHERE TO STAY ON ISLA MUJERES

There are some rather modest hotels on Isla Mujeres, but nothing at all like the luxury hotels of Cancún. So our advice is to make it a day trip and get back home. Still, there are clean but austere rooms available at several hotels.

Posada del Mar (*43 rooms*)   Moderately expensive
A modern three-story motel-type structure on main avenue along beachfront. In a coconut grove facing bay. Pleasant, well-decorated, and spacious rooms are probably the best on the island. Balconies on most rooms overlook pool and palm-lined gardens. Open-air dining room, bar with view. Good service. Reservations necessary. Address hotel at Isla Mujeres, Yucatán.

Hotel Zazil-ha (*78 rooms*)   Moderately expensive
At last viewing, this was still a compound of rather nice thatched-roof cabanas with full baths, around a central bar and dining room. It is located at the far north tip of the island among palm trees and right on one of the nicest beaches on the island. A new multistory addition was still a steel skeleton at our visit. Air-conditioned dining room, bar. Saltwater pool. Private beach. Waterskiing, skin-diving equipment for rent. Service mediocre. Reservations: Niza 67, Suite 103, Mexico City, or at Calle 60 No. 49 in Mérida.

Hotel Rocas del Caribe (*43 rooms*)   Moderate
On a rather rocky beach. Rooms very modest. For those who prefer low prices and austerity. Write: Av. Francisco Madero No. 2, Isla Mujeres, Yucatán.

Hotel Rocamar (*10 rooms*)   Inexpensive
A rather run-down but clean hotel. On a rocky promontory over-looking the open ocean but with no beach, although swimming off the rocks is possible. Rooms very austere, but have nice balconies. Bar and restaurant. Tel: 527-56-14 in Mexico City, or write to Calle 65 No. 419, Mérida, Yucatán.

GUIDE TO COZUMEL

This is the island that originally was the chic spot for many travelers to Mexico. Even now, completely outdone in terms of luxurious accommodations by its new neighbor 40 miles to the north, Cozumel still has its devotees and is filled to capacity in the winter. I found it a rather barren island, but there is lovely swimming from white sandy beaches often set among outcroppings of stone.

Located some 20 miles off the coast, the island is only 24 miles long and 8 miles wide. It has one very small village, San Miguel, and a half dozen hotels, of which three are on the beach and the others in the town. Reservations are imperative at all times, and practically unobtainable at the height of the winter.

GETTING THERE

Transportation to Cozumel is difficult. Mexicana and Aeronaves have daily flights from Mérida to Cozumel. The flight from Mérida to Cozumel takes about fifty minutes. Your first move should be to get confirmed reservations on either of these airlines both for going to Cozumel and returning. Mérida is served by Mexicana from Mexico City and by Pan-American from Miami and New Orleans. Mexicana now has a direct Miami–Cozumel flight. Aeromexico and Mexicana have both been offering seven- to thirty-day excursion flights from New York to Mexico City to Cozumel.

It is a true island some 20 miles off the coast, but it has an airport with daily flights from Mérida with connections to flights to the States or other parts of Mexico.

There is a daily car ferry from Puerto Morelos, which is about 10 miles south of Cancún. However, the ferry is small and can carry only a limited number of cars.

THINGS TO DO ON COZUMEL

Cozumel is more like the Caribbean islands (perhaps most like Antigua) than it is like any other parts of Mexico. It is low and flat, with frequent limestone outcroppings between which are little coves of powder-white sand leading into the clearest azure- and emerald-tinted waters you have ever seen.

There are several lagoons, some of them filled with shoals of brightly colored tropical fish which seem not to mind skin divers at all. Underground coral gardens can be found for snorkeling, which means any novice can slip on a rubber and glass mask and breathe through a short tube while time slips away as he views the incredible underground world of fish and marine vegetation.

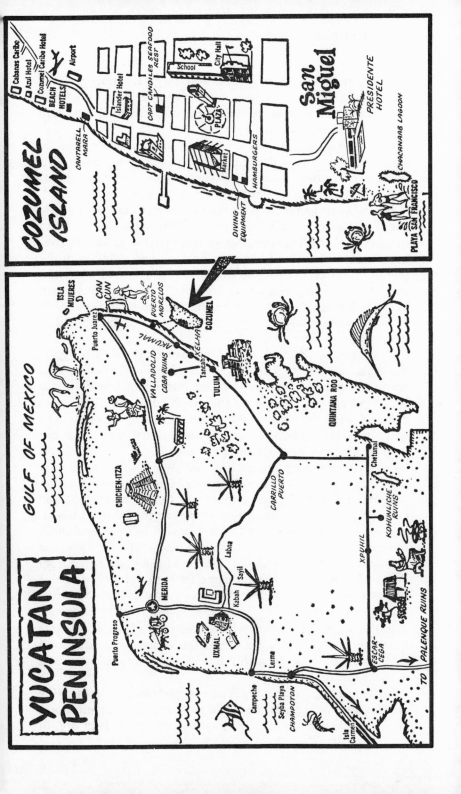

The island has excellent fishing, and the great fishing grounds near Tulum are easily accessible by chartered boat. A visit to the ancient Mayan ruins of Tulum can also be arranged. There is fine bonefishing in this area, too.

Chacanab Lagoon is the destination of many daily trips by small boats, and here the scuba diving is probably unexcelled in the world. Also, the crews will spear small lobster (*langostino*) and barbecue them for you right on the beach.

Several years ago there were no phones on Cozumel and only about one crackly radio connection, which usually made an unsuccessful effort at taking down reservations for those arriving. Practically no food is grown on Cozumel, aside from the plentiful lobster and fish, so that everything must be brought in by plane or ship. This goes for fuses for the power system, nails for the buildings, tissue for the bathroom, and every can of food on the island. So even the luxury hotels are limited in what they can offer.

Despite this, three of the hotels have reputations for good dining rooms (see page 145), while all of them take you by boat up to the famed Chacanab Lagoon and on to San Francisco Beach, where you can loll on the beach while your crew goes out and easily spears all the lobster (actually large prawns without claws) and fish you can possibly barbecue. You can help them if you like. The hotels charge $8 per person for this trip, including your lunch. You will see dolphin and other deep-sea fish leaping from the water. The beach is beautiful.

There are some nondescript ruins of the ancient Mayan civilization on Cozumel, but no roads to get to them. Instead, you can rent horses, rather humble steeds, in town and climb on the wooden saddles and make a day's trip for $5 to the uninhabited part of the island. Francis Murphy, an expert from Portland, Oregon, has spent some time studying these ruins and states they exist all over the island. You'll see many birds. Cozumel was originally Cuzamil, or "land of the swallows."

In the town San Miguel, which is usually a 12-peso taxi ride from your hotel if you are out at the beach, you will find a dusty little community with a few stores, a little plaza, and a modern market building.

In the evening, the people of San Miguel can be seen strolling around their little plaza. The little girls, mimicking their mothers, who chatter like fishwives (which many of them are, of course), are amusing. A nightclub, Tumben Maya Lumm, next to the Caribe Islander Hotel, was operating at my last visit.

When it comes time to leave, remember that the airport is not very well staffed; your plane may or may not be announced, so keep an eye on the sky. Don't try to overstay your reservation. Incoming passengers will be demanding your room, and the hotel staff will be helping you pack your wet bathing suit with friendly insistence. Such is the charm of Cozumel.

Side trips from Cozumel are discussed on pages 147–148.

WHERE TO EAT ON COZUMEL

Cozumel Caribe
In hotel of same name, welcomes the public and has extensive menu with some very interesting dishes. Charming dining room overlooking sea with good service. Various kinds of seafood. Good soups and desserts. Prices reasonable. Reservations.

Restaurant Bali-Hai
An air-conditioned restaurant on the main street in San Miguel. Extensive menu with lobster, shrimp cocktail, conch ceviche, Mexican dishes such as enchiladas. Also serves breakfast and sandwiches. Tel: 1–32.

Captain Candela's
At Calle Norte 10 in center of San Miguel. A modest but clean and very good restaurant specializing in seafood. Lobster served with garlic or any style, turtle steak or soup, seafood soup. Cold beer is served with everything. Captain Candela will welcome you himself. A charming person.

Pepe's Hamburger Shop
This is a walk-up short-order with hamburgers and Cokes on the main street of San Miguel. Preferred by youngsters. Perfectly safe.

WHERE TO STAY ON COZUMEL

El Presidente (104 rooms)   Expensive
A big, splashy two-story resort hotel about 3 miles south of San Miguel. Beautifully decorated in vivid colors, completely air-conditioned. Large rooms each with large bath and balcony. Hotel is right on its own private beach, with dining room overlooking beach area. Food is good, but room service is off and on. Lively Palapa Bar has entertainment in evening. Music in dining room. Cabanas and lounge chairs along beach and by pool. Beach buggies for rent at hotel. All cards. Part of Nacional Hotelera chain represented by Utel International. Reservations through Utel in New York, Chicago, Dallas, and Miami, or John Tetley Company in West Coast cities. Reservations, well in advance, a must.

Cozumel Caribe Hotel (*84 rooms*)   Moderately expensive
A first-class luxury establishment with ten-story building with glass
walls overlooking beach amid palms. Completely air-conditioned.
Private terraces on all rooms, and ten rooms have private bars.
Excellent dining room with perhaps best food on island, good
service, and colonial bar with music in the evening. Snorkeling,
fishing, skin diving. Operated by Barbachanos. All major cards.
Reservations well in advance at Mayaworld, P.O. Box 90, Mérida,
Yucatán, México. Tel: Mexico City 566-4644.

Cabañas del Caribe (*60 rooms*)   Moderately expensive
Out on a tip of land on beach north of airport about 2 miles. A new
two-story building with balconies for each room, all air-conditioned.
Dining room in thatched cabana under overhanging palms. Pool.
AE only. Tel: Alexander Associates, Brooklyn (212) 253-9400, or
Hotel Associates International, Dallas (214) 827-6351.

Hotel Mara (*50 rooms*)   Moderately expensive
Modern four-story hotel overlooking water. All rooms air-conditioned. Small beach and pool. Boats for fishing. Skin diving. All
cards. Tel: Alexander Associates, Brooklyn (212) 253-9400; toll-free
(800) 972-9861.

Hotel Cantarell (*60 rooms*)   Moderate
Modest three-story hotel in beach area with thin strip of beach. All
rooms have balconies overlooking sea and are air-conditioned.
Pool. All cards. Write: P.O. Box 24, Cozumel, Quintana Roo, México.
Tel: 1-09-19 in Mérida; Alexander Associates, Brooklyn (212) 253-
9400; toll-free (800) 522-0457 (New York), (800) 221-9508 (East Coast),
(800) 221-6509 (nationwide).

Caribe Islander (*31 rooms*)   Moderate
Run by the Barbachanos, this is a first-class hotel with a good pool
and dining room, but it is located in the town of San Miguel, which
means you must take a five-minute taxi ride to the beach. All rooms
air-conditioned. Built around a garden. Also known as "Isleño."

Playa Azul (*40 rooms*)   Moderately expensive
On beach just north of airport, this is a modern three-story building
set amid palms. Fully air-conditioned. Most rooms look on sea,
though some have garden view. Also two cabanas for families.
Pleasant dining room with sea view, dinner music nightly. Fishing,
skin diving, snorkeling. AE, DC. Write: P.O. Box 31, Cozumel. Tel:
Alexander Associates, Brooklyn (212) 253-9400.

Sol Caribe (*200 rooms, 20 suites*)   Expensive
A modern ten-story building on Paraiso Beach. All rooms face the

Caribbean. Water sports, tennis. Discotheque. Reservations: Sierra Gorda 374, México 10, D.F. Tel: Mexico City 540-7545.

El Cozumeleño (*80 rooms*)   Moderately expensive
A five-story building directly on beach. Most rooms have sea view. Air-conditioned. Pool, tennis, water sports. Tel: Alexander Associates, Brooklyn (212) 253-9400. P.O. Box 53, Cozumel (tel: 2-01-49).

Mayan Plaza Hotel   Expensive
Built alongside the Cabañas del Caribe and run by the same management. On the beach. Fishing. Reservations same as for Cabañas del Caribe (see page 146).

TRIPS FROM COZUMEL

Tulum. It is possible to take a charter boat trip from Cozumel to the main Quintana Roo coastline. It is largely uninhabited but has miles of lovely beaches and the notable Mayan ruin of Tulum, the only Mayan city built overlooking the sea.

Boat trips, which take about five hours, can be made in the local fishing boats, which are motor powered but have no special comforts for tourists. It costs about $55 for such a trip, but a large group can split expenses. See your hotel regarding arrangements. One must arrange to bring one's own water and lunch, as none will be available at Tulum.

Your hotel on Cozumel can also arrange for a charter plane trip to Tulum. The cost is $60 for a chartered Cessna or Lockheed which will accommodate one to four persons. A small airstrip has been built close to Tulum, and the planes from Cozumel, or from Mérida, land there. Arrangements are usually made to have a jeep from *Tancah*, a coconut ranch located about 6 miles from the airstrip, pick up passengers. It is sometimes possible for visitors interested in a longer stay to put up their hammocks in empty quarters at Tancah.

Tulum can first be seen from the sea, a stone sentry tower emerging from atop a seaside bluff. It is one of about sixty structures identified as having been built within the ancient walled area called Tulum. These partially restored courts, temples, and pyramids stand beside the beautiful blue and green sea, embracing a breathtaking view.

It was first seen by Juan de Grijalva, the Spanish explorer sailing from Cuba, in the year 1518, but it is estimated that

Tulum flourished about 1,000 years earlier. One stela carries the date 564 A.D., but the city has some Toltec influences indicating that it was inhabited up to the fourteenth century.

The most prominent building is called "the castle," and this pyramid-type building is topped by a two-story tower visible from the sea. Other buildings include a temple with inclining sides with a fine carved head of the god Kukulkan, the greatest of the Mayan deities. Visitors have called it one of the most dramatic of sights for travelers to this area.

Lovely beaches overhung with palm trees run for hundreds of miles, and ruins can be found almost anywhere along this coast. But it is deserted today. Ancient shipwrecks, some with gold bullion, have been found here.

Fishing is good the year round, although the fall can bring rough weather. Hunting for ducks (four major migrations each year tend to rendezvous here) or for deer, puma, or wild boar is possible in season. Contact George García López, Manager, Yucatán Safari, P.O. Box 236, Mérida, Yucatán, for arrangements.

Boca Paila, south of Tulum, is a narrow sea entrance to a large bay where bonefishing is said to be the best in the world and where large tarpon can be seen leaping and rolling in the sun. The bay is connected to jungle-hidden lagoons where orchids can be picked from boats navigating ancient Maya-built canals.

Chetumal. It is possible in another four-hour drive (some 234 miles) to continue on the straight paved road along the coast from Akumal and Tulum to the isolated city of Chetumal, which is located on the border of Belize.

Chetumal is a typical seaside fishing village with no great attractions and only one good hotel, El Presidente, which is quite swank if it only had some parking space. Still, El Presidente is a first-class hotel with a good dining room.

The main reason to go to Chetumal would be to take a new return road toward Escárcega; about 36 miles along this route is an access road to the newly found but already partially restored ruins of *Kohunliche.* There is a fine government road sign at this point, just beyond the town of Francisco Villa beyond Hachi-Cocum, and here you can drive into Kohunliche.

Kohunliche is currently under study, and excavation has revealed many masks of a type hitherto found only in Guatemala. There are also carved idols and what apparently is a huge plaza and temples.

10

Cuernavaca

For those who care to notice, there is an ancient cobblestoned roadway that twists over the mountains from Mexico City south to Cuernavaca.

Over this narrow roadway, in the year 1865, a royal coach, its leather supporting slings groaning, rattled along drawn by twelve white mules, preceded by a bodyguard of Austrian hussars astride their horses.

Inside the carriage His Imperial Majesty, Maximilian, Emperor of Mexico, and his consort, Her Majesty, Carlota, a dark-haired beauty, sat watching the countryside and occasionally nibbling at some breast of chicken and sipping white wine carried in a little cupboard in the carriage.

The carriage went through the little watering point of Tres Marías, later to be called Tres Cumbres, and started down into the Valley of Cuernavaca, leaving behind the pine forests of the highlands. Soon the carriage rounded a well-known lookout point, El Mirador, and there below them lay the valley in whose balmy climate grew lemons, oranges, bananas, and limes.

"Look, Max," Carlota exclaimed, "it is my golden bowl filled with sunshine and flowers."

There before them were the red roofs of Cuernavaca, the tower of the cathedral, and the great Quinta Borda, which was the vacation home for the Emperor and Empress when they left the demanding court life of Chapultepec Palace.

The grounds of the Quinta Borda were then magnificently kept, filled with formal gardens. Whispers had it that Carlota upon occasion would meet secretly with one of the tall Austrian hussars in these gardens.

Maximilian was shot in Querétaro in 1867; Carlota fled to Europe to appeal vainly to Napoleon III for aid, and died in an asylum in Europe in 1927. For two lives filled with tragedy, their happiest moments must have been here in Cuernavaca.

WHEN CORTÉS, conqueror of Mexico, was offered any part of his new conquest as his own personal property by the King of Spain, he chose Cuernavaca. It was in Cuernavaca that he built a governor's palace in 1530, erected one of the first large churches in Mexico, and set up a sugar plantation. These structures are still standing.

Cortés selected Cuernavaca for reasons valid today. And they certainly are worth consideration in planning your own visit. Chief among these is the ideal semitropical climate, which precisely fits the word "balmy." Located 5,000 feet above sea level, it is warmer than the cool, temperate climate of Mexico City, but is much milder than the hot seacoast towns. Many people consider Cuernavaca's weather ideal the year round.

Pastel-colored Town. Cuernavaca is a town of picturesque red-, yellow-, and blue-walled houses with red-tile roofs poking up among the huge old trees which shade the town. Flowers abound on all sides, and every wall is covered with huge bursts of bright purple bougainvillea, orange fire plants, and the beautiful red Christmas flower, *flor de Nochebuena*. It was discovered in Cuernavaca in 1836 by the American minister to Mexico, Joel Robert Poinsett, who successfully carried some back to his home in South Carolina—thus introducing the poinsettia to the United States.

The Plazas. In the center of the town, which has some 200,000 people but no particular industry, there are several charming plazas where people gather in the evening. Along the outskirts large homes with fine gardens have been built by wealthy families. Many retired Americans live here, and at times it has also been a center for writers and Hollywood movie stars.

Cuernavaca is only an hour to an hour and one-half (depending upon traffic) away from Mexico City, on the new superhighway, and for this reason it is a popular weekend resort for the *capitaliños*. There are even a few people who live in Cuernavaca and work in Mexico City. But the heavy traffic to Cuernavaca is over the weekend, as many people like to go down to swim at one of the many pools usually opened to the public by the hotels which maintain them, or just to sit on the veranda of one of the public places around the plazas and enjoy the balmy weather.

We recommend that you either stop in Cuernavaca for lunch, en route to Taxco and Acapulco, or that you spend a few days there. Those with unlimited time might like to spend an entire

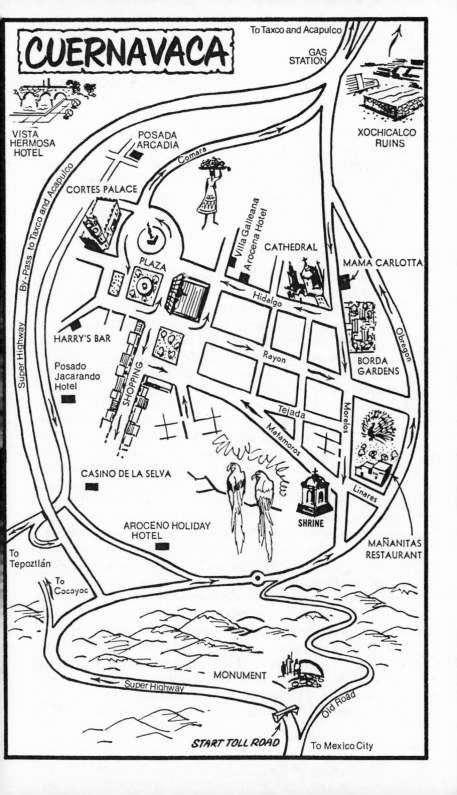

winter if they want peace, quiet, and nice weather. It is close enough to Mexico City so that the English-language papers arrive, television is easily received, and there are enough Americans so that convivialities such as cocktail parties are not hard to arrange. It was once said that on $500 a month retired Americans could rent a huge home, with swimming pool and staff of servants, and pay all their expenses. It is definitely about double that now, but it still is a fine place to which to retire.

GOING TO CUERNAVACA

From Mexico City, the easiest thing to do is to drive out to Avenida Insurgentes South, in your own or a rented car, past University City and on to the toll road (10 pesos), which sweeps right into Cuernavaca, some 40 miles away, without turn or stop. Or you can arrange for service on a fine Greyhound-type bus, with reserved seats, at Estrella de Oro, located at Calzada de Tlalpan 2205 (tel: 549-85-20), which is beyond Quevedo on the south exit from the city; nearby is the modern Centro de Autobúses del Sur at Taxqueño 1320 (just beyond the huge Gigante shopping center). You can take the underground Metro from the Zócalo station at Juárez to Taxqueño. The bus terminal is open all hours, and has fixed taxi service to any part of the city by zones. You buy a ticket at the terminal. Buses for Cuernavaca leave from the terminal on two lines, Estrella de Oro and Auto Pullman de Morelos. Fare is about 17–30 pesos, depending upon class of service. We recommend *lujo* or *super-lujo* with reserved seats. One special trip per week on super-lujo leaves Friday afternoons from Estrella de Oro's own office nonstop to Cuernavaca. Seats can be bought in advance. The railroad is old and inconvenient. There is no air service.

Two Roads. There are actually two roads from Mexico City to Cuernavaca. One, known as the old road, twists and winds through some lovely pine forests and over fairly steep mountain grades with beautiful scenery. The new road, which is the modern toll superhighway, is still scenic but cuts the travel time in half. These roads split at the outskirts of Mexico City and join again just at the entrance to Cuernavaca.

The drive to Cuernavaca is very dramatic, rising to 10,000

feet at one point and then dropping in sweeping curves down to the 5,000-foot plateau on which Cuernavaca lies. On clear days, going out from Mexico City, the twin snow-covered peaks of the two extinct volcanoes, Popocatepetl and Iztaccihuatl, can be seen off to the left. As the road heads into Cuernavaca beyond the mountain ridge, Popo again rises up majestically directly in front of you.

WHAT TO SEE

The best thing to do in Cuernavaca is to sit in the plazas and watch the people go by. But here are the sight-seeing points:

Cortés Palace. This is the principal sight in Cuernavaca, located on the main plaza in the center of town. Once the seat of the state legislature, it is one of the oldest Spanish buildings in Mexico, construction having been started in 1530, when Cortés retired from his governorship of all Mexico. The palace was Cortés's home in Cuernavaca. It is now the Cuauhnahuac Museum open from 10:30 A.M. till 7 P.M. on Saturdays and Sundays, and on weekdays from 10:30 A.M. till 6 P.M. It is closed on Thursdays; admission is 10 pesos. You can also go upstairs and out on the balcony, where there is a magnificent view of the countryside. Popocatepetl can be seen on clear days.

The balcony features a famed fresco by Diego Rivera, commissioned in 1930 by United States Ambassador Dwight Morrow, father-in-law of Charles Lindbergh. Its theme is the conquest and history of Mexico. The central figure, Morelos, after whom the local state is named, has eyes which follow you no matter where you stand. The Spanish soldiers are shown being aided by a figure in wolf's clothing in a tree—a traitor who turned on his own people. Other panels show Zapata, a local revolutionary leader; Cortés receiving tribute from the Indians; and the start of the local sugar industry.

Cuernavaca Cathedral. The spire of the cathedral can be seen from practically any part of town, so it's easy to find this fortresslike building that was constructed in 1529 in the Franciscan style of the time. One can easily imagine, gathering within its massive and severe walls, the armor-clad Spaniards, the monks with shaven heads in cowls, and the elaborately garbed royalty.

The cathedral is located on the main highway through town. Closest to the street is a small chapel, Capilla del Tercer Orden, and you pass through this to the main church. Note the aged wooden doors, the twisted old Spanish nails, the heavy iron hinges, and the huge baptismal font, said to be the largest in the Americas. At 11 A.M. on Sundays there is a special mariachi Mass. Be there by 10:30 in order to ensure a seat.

There was once a clock tower with a clock presented to Cortés by Charles V, but the clock has disappeared with the years.

The Borda Gardens, located just across the main highway from the cathedral, are more interesting today for their history than for their floral displays. You can find them behind a wall, with a small sign on one side saying *Jardín Borda.* The gardens, which are terraced down a slope, were created in colonial times at a cost of 1 million pesos by the wealthy silver baron, José de la Borda.

When the French-supported Emperor and Empress of Mexico, Maximilian and Carlota, ruled, about the time of our Civil War, they frequently drove in horse and carriage from Mexico City over the mountains to Cuernavaca on a cobblestoned trail. Carlota made the Borda Gardens one of her favorite stopping places. In fact, one novel about this period, *The Breast of the Dove,* describes a romantic meeting Carlota had with an Austrian hussar in the Borda Gardens.

Today, you pass through a small courtyard (where an attendant collects the 3-peso admission charge) and then enter the gardens proper, where you can see numerous pools, fountains, and seven or eight terraces, but, sadly enough, few flowers. It is currently being renovated. It is open from 9 A.M. to 7 P.M. daily. A small shop to the left of the main gate offers beautiful secular and religious arts and crafts made by the Emaus brothers.

The Pyramid of Teopanzolco, near the railroad station and about a mile from the center of town, is an Aztec ruin with some sculptured temple walls. Unfortunately, much of the structure was destroyed by the Spanish in breaking down the Indian religion.

The Caves of Cacahuamilpa, some 40 miles south of Cuernavaca, just off the main road to Taxco, are open to the public daily for parties arriving before 12:30 P.M. At 1 P.M., guides take a party into the caverns, where you can see gigantic stalagmite formations with picturesque names such as the King's Throne, the Organ, the Fountain, and so forth. There are plans to add a *son y luz*, or lights with music, feature.

Salto San Antón is a charming waterfall only a pleasant walk, about a mile, from the center of town. Along the stream, where tables and benches have been placed, is a nice place for a picnic.

Lake Tequesquitengo is about half an hour beyond Cuernavaca, on the Taxco road. Some people prefer to stay here while visiting in Cuernavaca, while others prefer to stay in Cuernavaca and visit Tequesquitengo. This is a small inland lake where water-skiing is the principal sport. A bit reedy for swimming.

Hacienda Vista Hermosa. The main hotel at Tequesquitengo, the Hacienda Vista Hermosa, is a sight in itself, as it occupies the ruins of an old sugar mill said to have been built by Cortés. The mill has been beautifully converted into a hotel, with an expansive swimming pool under arches of an old aqueduct. It is possible to drive there for lunch, and this is certainly a recommended trip. The hotel is first-class, and the dining room, open to the public, is usually fairly good.

To get to Vista Hermosa and Lake Tequesquitengo turn left at Alpuyeca (about K-100 on the highway marker) down the Taxco road.

The Xochicalco ruins, which lie about 26 miles south of Cuernavaca on the road to Taxco, are among the more interesting in all of Mexico and well worth visiting. Turn off at kilometer 100 (K-100 on the highway marker) at Alpuyeca, and they are 5 miles in on a side road.

Xochicalco means "in the place of the flowers." Nowadays there are only indications of most of the vast terraced buildings, although a number have now been restored. Apparently this settlement was occupied by a separate culture not connected with the Aztecs of Mexico. Very interesting carvings.

Tepoztlán is a picturesque small village about a half hour away from Cuernavaca in another direction, back on the superhighway to K-71, and 10 miles on a side road. If you have any serious sociological interest in the Mexican people and would like to see a small, unspoiled, carefully studied village, you might make one of the highlights of your trip to Mexico a visit here plus a reading of the famed pair of books, *Tepoztlán—*

A Mexican Village, by the distinguished anthropologist Robert Redfield (University of Chicago Press, 1930), and its recent counterpart, *Tepoztlán Revisited*, published by the University of Illinois Press, by another authority on the subject, Professor Oscar Lewis of the University of Chicago. Both books are serious, fascinating studies of this village and its people.

Posada de Tepozteco. Even if you don't go in for this heavy reading, you'll find it interesting to drive over to Tepoztlán one day to see the fertile valley surrounded by high cliffs, and to wander around the cobblestoned street, stopping at the old Dominican church, and up the hill to the lofty temple of Tepozteco, an Aztec god. An American, Larry Brookwell, established a modern resort hotel, the Posada de Tepozteco, in an old hacienda, and this small, quiet spot, with its good food and pool, attracts many writers. Interesting native handiwork can be purchased here.

Tepozteco, after whom the village is named, was an Aztec god whose memory is still revered by the inhabitants. He was said to have been born of a virgin, but the girl's family refused to believe in this miracle, and he was placed on an anthill to be devoured. The ants, however, fed the child instead. He grew up on the milk of the maguey plant and thus, according to one legend, was considered the son of Ometochtli, the god of pulque, the fermented juice of the cactus. He is still honored each year on September 8 in a pagan ceremony—which naturally makes some use of pulque.

The temple of Tepozteco, mentioned above, is perched on a cliff several hundred feet above town. The climb is rather steep, and you should allow two hours for it. The temple, a pyramid-shaped structure of porous volcanic stone, has an Aztec sacrificial stone with the name of King Ahuizotl and the date of his death, which indicates it was constructed in the tenth century by the Tlahuicas.

Where To Eat in Cuernavaca

Cuernavaca has some very interesting restaurants well worth a stop.

Harry's Bar, on the main plaza, is a fun place with Mexican revolutionary decor. It is part of the Carlos Anderson Shrimp

Bucket chain. International cuisine. 1:30 P.M. till 1:30 A.M. Tel: 2-76-79. Closed Mondays. Moderate.

Those with time for a leisurely lunch should by all means enjoy one of the finest restaurants in all Mexico. This is *Las Mañanitas*, on Linares Street, where the main highway from Mexico City nears the center of Cuernavaca. It is run by an American, Robert Krause. Cocktails are served on an immaculately tended lawn, with peacocks straying about. The food is excellent. Specialties are chicken curry, vichyssoise, and chocolate-bottom pie, as well as excellent Mexican dishes. Sunday luncheon is crowded. No credit cards accepted. Tel: 2-46-46.

A former colleague of Krause, Salvador Castaneda, has opened a similar establishment, *Las Quintas*, which serves equally good food in my view, and in equally charming surroundings. It is on the old Cuautla road, found by going a mile or so out behind the Cortés Palace. Signs along the way point it out. Excellent *chiles rellenos* (pepper stuffed with pork, veal, and beef). Tuna in avocado, steak Diane, pampano meunière, pomegranate salad, and orange chiffon pie are exceptionally good. Tel: 2-88-00.

Café Vienés, just beside the telegraph office one block from the main plaza, is one of the best moderate-price restaurants. It features German cooking, and the food is uniformly good.

Other places worth investigating are *India Bonita*, a small restaurant serving both noon and evening meals; *La Joya*, at kilometer 71.5 (K-71.5 on the highway marker), which has Viennese cooking; the *Casa de Piedra*, on the old Cuautla road, with a fixed menu which is good; and the *Majestic Terrace*, near the rotary coming into town. The two *Moby Dick* restaurants, at Ayala 383 and Av. Plan Ayala 383 (tel: 2-89-98), feature seafood at moderate prices. Noon till 10 P.M. except Mondays. A popular spot is the *Dance Hall 1920's* for food, music, and gaiety. *Chez Gaston* is a piano-bar restaurant that opened recently. While its restaurant serves French food, it also has a nightclub with a floor show. Located in the Hotel Suites Paraiso.

WHERE TO STAY IN CUERNAVACA

There is no single outstanding hotel in Cuernavaca. The downtown hotels are good but ordinary, while the larger and fancier establishments are slightly out of the downtown district, which is a disadvantage in a place like Cuernavaca, where half the fun is sitting around the plaza in town.

Arocena Holiday Hotel (*25 rooms*)   Moderate
A modern motel-type structure north of town on Paseo del Conquistador near the entrance of the toll road. Pleasant view of the city. Pool. Dining room, bar. DC. Tel: 3-08-00.

Hacienda Cocoyoc (*150 rooms*)   Moderately expensive
One of the top resorts in Mexico and probably the best accommodations in the area. Operated by Western Hotels. About 21 miles east of Cuernavaca on new toll road cutoff to Cuautla. Large pool, nine holes golf, horses, tennis. Mexican buffet. Restored hacienda is situated on 70-acre estate with original chapel, natural aqueduct. Said to be site of original Dominican sugar mill. AE, DC. P.O. Box 300, Cuautla, Morelos. Tel: Cuautla 2-20-00.

Posada de Tepozteco (*12 rooms*)   Moderate
In nearby town of Tepoztlán, twenty minutes northeast of Cuernavaca. A charming small hotel with pool, good food, bar. No credit cards.

Casa de Piedra (*14 units*)   Moderately expensive
A seventeenth-century colonial mansion with spacious gardens and bungalows in colonial-style decor. Pool. Breakfast served on terrace. On old Cuautla road, but still in town. Tel: 2-07-66.

El Buen Retiro   Moderate
Leandro Valle 20. A rest home that takes guests. Medical staff. Nice grounds.

Casino de la Selva (*250 rooms*)   Moderate
On old Cuautla road, a mile or so out of the center of town, this is the largest hotel in Cuernavaca. Beautiful grounds, large pool, kiddies' pool, tennis courts. Dining room. Has cottages with pools. Rather lively on weekends, with lots of young people.

Posada Jacaranda (*39 rooms*)   Moderately expensive
On old Cuautla road, about 1½ miles out of town. Very fine resort, the fanciest and most luxurious hotel in Cuernavaca. Garden, pool, good food, tennis, pitch-and-putt golf. P.O. Box 361, Cuernavaca, Morelos. Tel: 2-46-40.

La Posada Arcadia (de Xochiquetzal) (*16 rooms*)   Moderate
Leyva 200. Fine small hotel in colonial mansion. Pool. Good food. Reservations. Tel: 2-02-20.

Las Mañanitas (*15 rooms*)   Moderately expensive
Linares 107. This charming place is more famous for its food (see page 157), but it has been enlarged and now has a number of deluxe rooms opening onto its lovely gardens. Pool. Restaurant serves both noon and evening meals, with cocktails in the gardens. Call for reservations at 2-46-46.

Las Quintas (*18 rooms*)   Moderate
Hostería Las Quintas, Av. Las Quintas 107, off the old Cuautla road somewhat behind Cortés Palace area. One of the loveliest places in Cuernavaca, and probably the best-run hotel. Rooms grouped around a lovely pool. Superb food. Manager is Salvador Castaneda, formerly of Las Mañanitas. AE, DC. Tel: 2-88-00.

Casa Arocena (*12 rooms*)   Inexpensive
Hidalgo 239, in town. Garden, pool. Tel: 2-43-08.

Hotel Vista Hermosa (*64 rooms*)   Moderate
At Lake Tequesquitengo, south of Cuernavaca 23 miles. Beautiful old sugar mill. Pool. Recent reports favorable to new management. P.O. Box 127. Tel: LP 10-012.

Hotel Posada Borda (*10 rooms*)   Inexpensive
Hidalgo 22. Economy hotel near center of town. No pool. Special rates for extra guests.

Centro Las Plazas Suites   Inexpensive
On main plaza, an apartment-hotel with one- and two-bedroom units with kitchenettes. Tel: 2-61-68.

Hotel Paraiso   Moderate
Domingo Diez 1009. Has double rooms with kitchenettes. Bungalows for eight persons. Swimming pool, steam bath. Snack bar, TV. Good for children. Tel: 3-36-65.

Posada San Angelo (*14 rooms*)   Moderately expensive
Cerrada de la Selva 100. Pool, garden, attractive setting. Fine dining room. Good service.

Villa Vegetariana (*20 units*)   Moderate
A most unusual health-resort motel run by David Stry. Pool, tennis courts, gym. Grows own vegetables, which make up meals. No smoking or drinking of alcoholic beverages permitted.

11

Guadalajara

North of Guadalajara on the Nogales road, you will find huge fields of maguey plants, the broad-leaved "century plants" of Mexico.

Near the little town of Tequila, you can see dozens of peons in the fields cutting, bundling, and loading the broad leaves on burros.

The spiny maguey leaves will be pressed, and the juices will be fermented and distilled to make the fiery clear beverage, tequila, which is not unlike vodka both in appearance and potency.

Little boys will approach your car near the village of Tequila, and offer you the small wooden casks in which it is often sold. Or they will invite you to visit the tequila factory.

You will probably be offered sample drinks on the house, served in a cow's horn. The right thing is to sprinkle salt at the base of your thumb, up-end a small glass of tequila in one quick gulp, quickly suck a small quarter of lemon, and then tip the salt on your tongue.

The most famous tequila plant is that of Don Francisco Javier Sauza, the third generation to head the family business. His building has a facade showing the gods of sun, rain, heat, and lightning watching over the tequila plants. Inside, a mural of the town of Tequila surrounds the beautiful copper still that reaches up through the skylight. Around are the many diplomas, medals, and awards his product has won all over the world.

GUADALAJARA IS named after the Moorish city of the same name in Spain. It is famed for its handsome people, called *tapatíos;* for its dignity, culture, and restraint in matters political and social; and for its songs and dances, which are the best-known of all Mexican lyrics, including the internationally known *Jarabe Tapatío,* or Mexican hat dance, and the popular *canción Guadalajara.*

Guadalajara vies with Monterrey as the second largest city in Mexico, and for the moment Guadalajara holds the edge with over 1,200,000 inhabitants. Like its rival to the north, Guadalajara has considerable industry and is a trading center for the entire state of Jalisco, of which it is the capital.

Guadalajara is said to be the most Spanish of Mexican cities, and this is true in many ways. The church is especially strong here, and during parts of Mexico's history it was unbelievably wealthy. The huge cathedral and other church buildings, as well as the university, reflect this.

A Rebuilt City. The city made a determined effort to change, in 1949–50, from an old colonial town with narrow, traffic-clogged cobblestoned streets to a modern city. Entire blocks of the very center of town were completely torn down, large buildings were moved, and broad avenues were cut through as principal arteries. The project was successful, and the city today has the appearance of an up-to-date, bustling metropolis, which it is.

Guadalajara is now a mixture of modern streets and buildings and many old plazas and parks, with colonial churches and buildings carefully retained. It is a center for the pottery industry and also has a glass factory. Nearby is the village of Tequila, where the national drink of Mexico, the clear, vodkalike tequila, is manufactured from the maguey plant.

Guadalajara can be a hub from which the visitor can see the entire western area of Mexico. The drive from Mexico City by highway takes about ten hours, while the train trip is overnight and the plane flight is about an hour and a half. The road from Mexico City passes through such interesting points as Lake Pátzcuaro, a good place to break the trip with an overnight stay, and Morelia, a charming colonial city. A circle tour going north on the Querétaro superhighway toll road, then via Irapuato and Highways 110 and 90 north of Lake Chapala to Guadalajara is much faster though less scenic. This could be driven in over seven hours.

Close to Pacific Beaches. From Guadalajara, it is possible to go down to the Pacific Ocean at Barra de Navidad Beach or Manzanillo by road; or Puerto Vallarta can be reached by road or by plane. One can go north on the new Pacific Coast Highway, via Tepic, to the port city of Mazatlán, and on to Guaymas and out of the country at Nogales, Arizona. This trip of about 900 miles is one of the most interesting in Mexico.

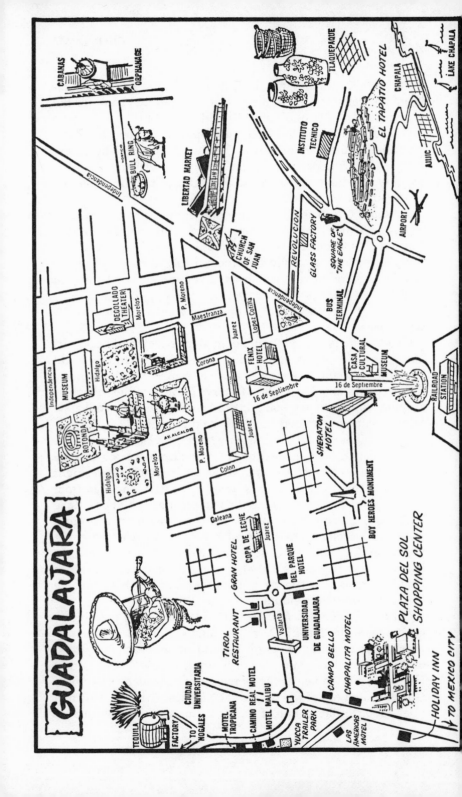

While you still have to jog inland at times, the new coastal highway 200, which already runs to Manzanillo, will be completed and you will be able to drive on to Ixtapa and Acapulco. Even now, you can jog inland (the road is very mountainous, though) to Uruapan, then back to the coast to the stretch of 200 completed not only to Acapulco but beyond. This is going to be a splendid highway with magnificent scenery, so check its progress. Our sons have already driven it in a van.

A Good Climate. In the benign climate usually found in Mexico at the 5,000-foot altitude at which Guadalajara is situated, one finds flowers, palms, and year-round good weather. Most homes are Spanish-style, built around courtyards and featuring immaculately shining red-tiled floors and patios.

Art Museums. Guadalajara is the birthplace of one of Mexico's most distinguished artists, José Clemente Orozco. Perhaps his greatest masterpiece is the swirling and vibrant-colored "Man of Fire" in the dome of Cabanas Orphanage, but others of his murals can be seen in the assembly hall of the University of Guadalajara and the staircase of the Palacio del Gobierno. There is also a collection of Murillo in the city's museum, and many fine colonial items remain from the era when Guadalajara's wealthy citizens were unequaled in collecting art treasures.

A Place to Live. Given its climate, its attractive residences, its modern services including some good schools (among them an American school), its modern shops marked by two of the largest and probably the most handsome shopping centers in the world (Plaza del Sol and Plaza Patria), its two major golf courses, its universities, and now several of the finest hotels in Mexico, it is no wonder Guadalajara has become a favorite with Americans looking for a permanent place to live.

There are many business opportunities in Guadalajara, and a number of Americans are in business there, bringing highly prized services from pure milk and some of the best ice cream in the world (Bing's) to fine china and production of agricultural machinery.

Others prefer to live on the shores of Lake Chapala, a lovely spot only a short drive away over a paved highway, and some in the quaint village of Ajijic, while others vacation at the superb beaches at Barra de Navidad, a drive in the other direction on paved highway to the Pacific.

The Guadalajara Sheraton has become a social center for Guadalajara, while outside the town the towering resort hotel, El Tapatío, has an immense spread of rooms looking over the city. Numerous luxury motels are available.

Best of all, the people of Guadalajara love gardens, boulevards, and fountains; they are everywhere and are well kept. Sitting among them are some fine public buildings such as the towering modern Casa de Cultura in Agua Azul Park near the Sheraton. A museum of archeology is nearby.

The history of the city is evident everywhere: the twin towers of the cathedral, 400 years old, rising above the flowered Plaza de Armas, its park and benches ready to accommodate all; the state palace with its murals; the dignified Degollado Theater with its Grecian portico; the circular columns of the rotunda built to honor illustrious citizens of Jalisco.

The *Grupo Folklórico* of the University of Guadalajara presents the famed *Ballet Folklórico* on Sundays at 10 A.M. and the theater when it is in town (you can ask at the box office). Ticket prices are reasonable. Also, the *Guadalajara Symphony* has won an international reputation and performs at varying dates during the year. Your hotel can help arrange tickets.

Going to Guadalajara

From Mexico City, you can fly on either CMA or Aeronaves. It is approximately a one-and-one-half-hour flight.

If you want to go by bus, take the Pullman from Tres Estrellas de Oro, located at Niño Perdido No. 19, Mexico City. Fare is $8.

By train, Nacional de México runs a fair overnight trip from Mexico City, leaving from the main railroad station, called Buena Vista. Although equipment is old, Pullman is available. Some new equipment is being added.

One can also travel to Guadalajara from California, via Aeronaves or CMA, or from Nogales by Tres Estrellas bus line. The Pacífico railroad operates from Nogales to Guadalajara as well, but while the line is being rehabilitated, this is still a tedious journey.

By highway, it is a ten- or twelve-hour drive on the old road between Mexico City and Guadalajara, but many prefer it because it permits stops in Morelia and Pátzcuaro, prime tourist sights. A much faster route is to take the superhighway from Mexico City to Querétaro, about three hours, and thence to Irapuato and Highways 110 and 90, another four hours plus, to Guadalajara. Part of this is a toll road. You can combine this latter trip with visits to San Miguel de Allende and Guanajuato, if you wish.

WHERE TO EAT AND STAY

You are fortunate in that Guadalajara in the last few years has acquired some excellent hotels and restaurants where for many years they were on the thin side. The hotels and motels are listed at the end of the chapter (pages 176–181), but we must mention at once that Guadalajara is now blessed with three outstanding hotels—the *Guadalajara Sheraton*, a modern twelve-story hotel in town; *El Tapatío*, a magnificent immense resort hotel on a hilltop just outside town on the airport road; and the *Camino Real* luxury motel at the edge of town on Highway 15 to Nogales.

The *Lafayette* restaurant at the Camino Real is outstanding, while the *Top of the Sheraton* has an exciting Mexican buffet with music and dancing on Wednesdays and Sundays. *Carnes Asadas Tolsa* and the *Las Cazadoras* restaurants serve steaks, while *Carlos O'Willie's* is a fun gay-nineties place. See our complete restaurant list on pages 174–176.

WHAT TO SEE AND DO IN GUADALAJARA

The Palacio del Gobierno (State House) and zócalo (plaza) are located in the very center of town, one block off the wide main street, Juárez, at Independencia, by the cathedral. The Palacio is used for the offices of the governor of the state of Jalisco. Special guidebooks are available at the entrance. It is best to visit the palace in the morning, when the various halls with their important paintings are open. However, a visit in the afternoon or evening can be arranged, to see just the exterior. The palace is typical of the highly ornate churrigueresque architecture. On the walls of the main stairway are frescoes by the great José Clemente Orozco depicting the heroic priest Hidalgo.

Orozco was perhaps Mexico's greatest painter, and the work on the staircase of the Palacio was commissioned by the governor of Jalisco, Everado Topete, in 1939. The mural shows a heroic portrait of the father of Mexican independence, Padre Miguel Hidalgo. He is seen holding a burning torch representing the aspirations of the people for freedom, while forces of evil are represented by serpents. Another side shows a hammer and sickle over anguished faces, while a storm rises in the distance.

Guadalajara Cathedral, on the main plaza, is a confusing mixture of many periods of architecture. Originally started in 1571, it was finally dedicated in 1618. Although it was begun as a Gothic structure, numerous reconstructions carried Tuscan, Arabic, Mudjar, Corinthian, and Byzantine motifs into the building. The Byzantine towers are 200 feet high. It is possible to enter toward the sacristy and see the church's great treasure, Murillo's "Assumption of the Virgin." The rich decoration is an indication of the great wealth that has supported this church over the centuries.

From 16 de Septiembre Street, upon which most people approach the plaza and cathedral, the church appears to have one sharp spire and a dome. Actually, there are twin spires but one is effaced when viewed from here.

While we have referred to "the plaza," actually there are four plazas, one on each side of the cathedral. There are bubbling fountains, pleasant foliage, and to one side the circular colonnade of the *Rotunda of Illustrious Men.*

Inside the cathedral, the basilica is divided into three naves with thirty columns rising gracefully to merge into the roof. The interior is of immaculate white, and beneath the last dome is the main altar. Much of this work was done by Italian artisans in Milan.

To the left of the main altar is the body of Saint Inocencia, embalmed and covered in wax, while a nearby staircase leads to a small chapel, where relics include the body of Don Francisco Gómez de Mendiola, the man who started construction of the cathedral in 1571.

The principal treasure of the cathedral is the world-famed masterpiece "The Assumption," by Estebán Bartolomé Murillo, who lived from 1617 to 1682. You can see it by descending a staircase to the sacristy, found to the right of the choir. The figure of Mary can be seen and the Tower of David. King Charles IV of Spain presented the picture in return for family silver sent to the mother country by the people of Guadalajara during the Napoleonic invasion of Spain. Nearby is a small, more attractive church, Santa Mónica, said to have the most beautiful facade in the city.

The State Museum and Library, located just north of the cathedral on Avenida Corona, has been made from a fine old monastery. It houses a collection of early Mexican paintings, with one room in the north wing devoted entirely to the famed Murillo collection.

Degollado Theater, a handsome columned building across the park behind the Palacio and the cathedral, is the home of opera, symphony, ballet, and legitimate drama in the Jaliscan capital. Built between 1856 and 1866, it is an impressive building with a facade supported by eight Corinthian columns. The new portico was only finished on September 8, 1964. Named after Governor Don Santos Degollado, who started construction of it in 1855, its grand opening was in October 1866, when the Mexican opera star Angela Peralta sang in *Lucia de Lammermoor.*

Across from the Degollado Theater on the Morelos side is the old *Church of St. Augustine,* with a charming little garden.

The State of Jalisco Library, which you pass as you walk farther down Morelos Street to Independencia, a broad avenue, is a handsome new air-conditioned structure built to hold a million volumes and with the latest microfilm equipment. The architect was Julio de la Pen, and the murals inside portraying prominent Jaliscans are by Gabriel Flores.

The Cabanas Orphanage is one of the most famous buildings in Guadalajara and should be included among the places you visit. It is only a seven- or eight-block walk from the cathedral and can be found near the bullring. Walk down Morelos Street, behind the Palacio del Gobierno, and cross wide Calzada Independencia and it will be right in front of you on Hospicio Street.

The orphanage and home for the elderly was a humanitarian gesture by the last colonial bishop of Guadalajara, Don Juan Cruz Ruiz de Cabana, who founded it in 1803. At times it houses as many as 600 children, for whom industrial and training schools are maintained. It is immaculately clean and shiny and has some beautifully kept gardens; an air of cheer-fulness is very evident.

By 1938 the central building with its famed cupola, built of local *tzontle* stone, had deteriorated to the point where it had to be restored to its original condition, and Orozco was invited to decorate the restoration. He made it the major work of his career. In the dome of the old chapel he painted frescoes depicting "The Man of Fire" which represent human evolution. The dome has the flaming man of fire, a dynamic sight, while the walls show a majestic array of kings, clergy, soldiers, and others.

There is no admission charge, but contributions can be made. Open from 10 A.M. to 6 P.M.

Libertad or San Juan de Dios public market, housed in a beautiful modernistic building with striking winged roof, is just a few steps from the orphanage. It consists of hundreds of small shops which are so close to each other, and usually selling the same goods, that it is hard to see where one stops and another starts.

A big section of huaraches—the largest such display in the world—offers a chance to buy the famed thonged sandals. Baskets are good here, also leather goods (though check closures and hardware) and clothes. Bargaining is very much in order.

Across the street from the market is the *Church of San Juan de Dios.*

The Bullfight Plaza has been moved about thirty blocks from the center of town, but a taxi can get you there. Fights are held on Sunday afternoons, usually at 4 P.M., from January to March and occasionally during the rest of the year when young fighters, called *novilleros,* perform (usually badly). The plaza holds 16,000. Purchase tickets at your hotel. Allow half an hour to find your seat (which should be on the shady side).

Tlaquepaque, or San Pedro Tlaquepaque as it is rightfully called, is the famed "clackie-packie" of tourist note. It is a small village, about 4 miles out past the Instituto Tecnológico on what is called the Calzada Tlaquepaque, and anyone can direct you there. This little town is noted for its pottery, which, frankly, is interesting and intriguingly designed, but of low quality. However, visiting some of the numerous pottery shops is fun, and they will ship to the United States for you. The prices are astonishingly low. This is also a fine place to visit on a Sunday evening, when the many mariachi orchestras go there, as do the tapatíos. Drink a beer and watch life go by.

The plaza with its covered arcades has many inexpensive souvenir shops. On Juárez Street in Tlaquepaque, there are a number of attractive and rather expensive specialty shops featuring men's shirts and women's skirts in hand-blocked prints, modern sculpture and paintings, lamps, and much pottery.

The Instituto Tecnológico, on the road to Tlaquepaque, is an ultramodern school which trains engineers and technicians badly needed for Mexico's expanding economy.

The University of Guadalajara, created at the instruction of King Charles IV in 1792, is also a fine school. It has 5,000 students studying medicine, law, and commerce. It has an assembly hall featuring Orozco's mural of man as worker, educator, creative thinker, and rebel.

Tequila, a little village northwest on the Nogales road some 42 miles from Guadalajara, is reached by a pleasant drive through some beautiful countryside. Small boys there will besiege you with tempting jugs of the native product, and you can visit a tequila factory in town if you wish. It is wise to bring a box lunch.

Chapala, a resort town of 5,000, is located on *Lake Chapala*, Mexico's largest lake. The water level, which caused some concern a few years ago by falling, is now restored, but a plague of water hyacinths has afflicted the lake in spots but in no way hinders boats from putting out. The fishing is still excellent. It is 30 miles from Guadalajara on a good road, or a one-hour bus ride from the Guadalajara bus station. The fish from the lake are famous and are served throughout Mexico, but are especially good at the restaurants in Chapala. One species resembles Lake Superior whitefish, while black bass are being seeded.

The *Camino Real del Chapala* is a large luxury motel on the shores of Lake Chapala about 1 kilometer from Ajijic. Fully air-conditioned, with bar and dining rooms plus pool and other resort facilities, it makes a fine place to stay. It is operated by Western Hotels. A kilometer away is the *Motel Chula Vista*, much more modest but with bar, restaurant, and a fine view of the lake (although it is not on it). The *Villa Carlo Hotel*, nearby and very attractive, has fifty-one rooms and thermal baths.

Ajijic, which is another easy name to pronounce once you get it (aah-hee-HEEK, or just a double hiccup), is a picturesque little village on the shore of Lake Chapala only 38 miles from Guadalajara. Once noted for its Bohemians, would-be writers, and would-be artists, it has now acquired some serious talent. One of them is former advertising executive James Kelly, who writes: "It's an unhectic town where nobody is waiting to discover it. The bloom, such as it was, is now off and perfectly sensible simple living is right here for the taking." The Kellys, like other Americans, have found it reasonable to rent a Mexican-style home with a patio and garden, and live the quiet life they seek.

The *Posada Ajijic*, with a lovely location looking out on the lake, has changed hands a number of times, but at this writing is run by an American, Booth Waterbury. Its rooms, while Mexican styled, have modern new bathrooms and cozy fireplaces. The garden is filled with flowers and tropical birds in cages, and there is a swimming pool. A fine fish lunch is served on the patio. The *Posada Rancho Santa Isabela*, six blocks east of the small plaza, has inexpensive cottage-type units.

Jocotepec is an unspoiled fishing village on the west end of Lake Chapala. You can go there either from Ajijic or by taking the Mexico City road, Highway 15, from Guadalajara to K-623, where you turn left half a mile. Jocotepec has a lovely fiesta in January, and its cathedral has a carved statue of Christ. The villagers are largely fishermen, but also weave beautiful white serapes. A small hotel, *Hotel La Quinta*, is a great favorite with visitors. It is said to be the oldest operating hotel in the entire country. It is an authentic country inn, with lovely patio and polished floors; good food is included in the modest price.

El Salto de Juanacatlán is a spectacular waterfall, said to be the largest in Mexico and second largest on the American continent when at its fullest. It's good to visit only in the summer months when there is enough water to make a show. It is out on the Chapala highway, 13 miles from Guadalajara, where a junction leads 7 miles over a gravel road to Juanacatlán.

The Barranca de Oblatos is a 2,000-foot canyon where a breathtaking trip can be made by cable car to a power station down below on the Santiago and Verde rivers. The car goes down at 8 A.M., 12 noon, and 4 P.M. *La Toma,* nearby, is also pretty for a picnic. Go out Calle Belisario Domínguez to Huentitan, some 5 miles.

Barra de Navidad ("Christmas Beach") is a wonderful beach area, with a huge sandbar and very clear water, only four hours from Guadalajara by paved road to the Pacific. Take Highway 80 west (it runs along with Highway 15 to Mexico City for 15 miles) from Guadalajara. The road is paved all the way, but goes through some interesting villages, past lakes and then gorges and mountains as it drops down to sea level. One fair-sized town, Autlán, has a Motel Autlán, with a pool.

As you come to the Pacific coast, the road turns south on a new stretch of what will be the Pacific coast highway 200. At this point, you can find the Hotel Melaque and the famed beach of Barra de Navidad by going down a side road for 1 kilometer. There are several modest motels in the immediate area—such as the El Dorado, the Monterrey, and the Del Sol—and some bungalows, such as the Villa Mar.

Manzanillo is only 30 miles farther south on Highway 200. It is a larger port town with two very good hotels and other lesser accommodations. It also has nice beaches. (See Chapter 15.)

Puerto Vallarta, to the north, can now be reached by Highway 200, which will soon be completed the entire length of the west coast. Puerto Vallarta is also accessible by plane. (See Chapter 21.)

Sports

The country club, located just off Zapopan Road, has golf, tennis, and swimming. Tourists may get monthly membership.

Santa Anita Golf Club is an eighteen-hole course where many of the American colony play. Its 6,617-yard, par-72 course has some interesting holes. A plush clubhouse was recently built.

Bullfights are held in season on Sunday afternoons at four o'clock. The plaza is located about thirty blocks from downtown, so take a taxi. Tickets can be purchased at your hotel.

Shops

Native Goods

Casa de las Artesanías de Jalisco, in Agua Azul Park at Independencia and Gonzalez Gallo, has fixed prices and an excellent display of all manner of handicrafts of the area.

Boutique Demian's, in the Plaza del Sol shopping center, has exceptionally fine leather goods ranging from coats and slacks to painted suede purses and accessories.

Instituto de la Artesanía, Alcalde and Ávila Camacho, has a modern building with a fine display of handicrafts from all parts of the state.

Galeria Elena, in Tlaquepaque at Independencia 258, has brass scales and dolls.

Alfareria, in Tlaquepaque at Juárez 130, has Indian arts, lamps, and pottery.

El Águila Descalza, in Tlaquepaque at Juárez 20, has expensive women's clothes, furniture, brass, and pottery.

Bazaar Hecht, in Tlaquepaque at Independencia 158, has a dozen rooms full of antiques, furniture, lamps, chests, and tables. The owners, Armando and Enrique Hecht, are very pleasant to deal with.

Jewelry

Helena's, at the Sheraton and Tapatío hotels as well as downtown at Juárez 424, has fine jewelry and other finely crafted gift articles.

Tlaquepaque Silver Factory, in Tlaquepaque at Independencia 211, has silver, brass, gold, and jewelry in a wide range of designs. You can watch silver being worked here.

Ceramics

Sylvia Ceramics, López Costilla 94.

Palomar, on the boulevard before Tlaquepaque, has distinctive stoneware, serapes, native rugs, and a factory with kilns in operation.

Kristian, in Tlaquepaque at Juárez 109, has modern ceramics and hand-blocked cloth.

Tequila

Herradura, Juárez near 16 de Septiembre, also sells fancy groceries.

Photography

Laboratorios Julio, 16 de Septiembre 125, is a Kodak agency.

HISTORY OF GUADALAJARA

Some four years after Hernando Cortés had completed his conquest of the Valley of Anáhuac (the present site of Mexico City), some of his lieutenants pushed out to the west looking for still further conquests. One of these lieutenants was Nuño Beltrán de Guzmán. He was able to bring under control a wide area, including the present states of Michoacán and Jalisco and nearby coastal lands.

One of Beltrán's men is said to have founded a city near Nochistlán which was named Guadalajara after the Moorish city in Spain. Trouble kept breaking out with the Indians, and the location of the city was moved several times. One last great battle with the Indians, on the eve of San Miguel Day in 1541, was won by the Spaniards, and is celebrated to this day in Guadalajara.

Because of its fine climate and fertile land, Guadalajara drew large numbers of Spanish colonists, and it became one of the most Spanish of the Mexican cities. The city preserves much of the architecture of Spain. The Spaniards also maintained strong church ties and fostered cultural interests, which meant buying and preserving many Old World art treasures.

Modern Guadalajara got its impetus when the Southern Pacific, one of the strongest of the United States railroads, completed a new line down the West Coast into Mexico, arriving at Guadalajara in 1927. This was then called the *Sud Pacífico de México*. When in 1950 the Mexican government realized the railroad was losing money and rapidly deteriorating, it arranged to buy the railroad from its American owners. This was done, and much has been accomplished to modernize the line since then. It serves to haul cotton, tobacco, and many other important products both to the United States and to such ports as Mazlatán.

Where To Eat in Guadalajara

Lafayette Restaurant   Fairly expensive
Located in the Camino Real luxury motel at Vallarta 5005, which is the highway from town to Nogales, this is an ultraswank dining spot among several this fine hotel maintains. Service by excellent waiters under the eye of manager Carlos Azpetia. Food from the kitchen of chef José Borrallo includes coquilles St. Jacques, lobster bisque, veal chops with green peppers, tournedos grillé béarnaise, fillet of sole normande, coq au vin, scampi sauté creole, fillet of trout, and poached sea bass. Special dishes upon request. Open till midnight. Music. All cards. Tel: 21-72-17 for reservations.

Los Colomos   Expensive
High on a hill overlooking Guadalajara, this is part of the fabulous El Tapatío resort hotel 4 miles outside the city on the road to the airport. Its dining room looks over the lights of the city, and its menu is deluxe with the finest of dishes. Music and dancing. There is also a bar and nightclub here. All cards. Tel: 35-60-50 or 17-80-00 for reservations.

Top of the Guadalajara Sheraton   Expensive
Rooftop restaurant at the Sheraton Hotel. Has music, dancing, and full menu. Mexican buffet Wednesday and Sunday nights for flat charge of $6. Good mariachis and couples dancing Mexican hat dance. All cards. Tel: 12-51-51.

Carlos O'Willie's   Moderately expensive
At Unión 59 near Vallarta is one of the lively, fun restaurants with excellent food. Run by Carlos Anderson of Shrimp Bucket fame in Mazatlán. Gay-nineties atmosphere, singing waiters. All cards. Tel: 16-78-89.

El Tirol   Bargain
At Brasil 25, across street from Gran Hotel, which is block off Vallarta just inside gateway. Excellent German and Mexican food at modest prices served in interesting open porch or air-conditioned interior. Ham hocks and sauerkraut, German sausage, breaded veal, hamburger. T-bone steak for $3. Excellent draft beer. Also open breakfast and lunch. Very clean. No credit cards.

Las Cazadoras (*seven branches*)   Moderate
At Américas 759, Unión 405, and other locations. Serves good steaks from charcoal grill; also pork, chicken, and fondue. Open kitchen, music. All cards. Tel: 15-88-78.

El Buen Gusto   Moderate
Next door to Focolare at Vallarta 2452, and in town at Juárez 2452. Excellent seafood paella. Connected to a great French pastry shop. Tel: 15-30-46.

Copa de Leche   Moderate
Located at Juárez 414 in the heart of the city (on the main street), this is a three-tier restaurant with something different on each floor. The ground floor is now a bar, the second floor a balcony with short orders, either from the fountain or the bar, while upstairs is a restaurant serving fine international dishes amid quiet music. Good for breakfast or to have a drink or a snack whiling away an evening. Tel: 13-17-42.

Los Arcos   Very reasonable
A clean modern restaurant in the new Sears near the Sheraton (16 de Septiembre and González) serving fine breakfast from 9 A.M. through dinner to 10 P.M. Has a Sunday buffet at noon. Sandwiches, short orders, plate lunches. Cheerful waitresses.

Tai Pak   Inexpensive
Authentic Cantonese dishes at the best Chinese restaurant in Guadalajara. Located at 16 de Septiembre No. 427. Takeout orders too. Noon to midnight. Closed Thursdays. Tel: 3-96-08.

Posada Ajijic   Moderate
If you want one of the nicest lunches in the area, take time to drive to Lake Chapala (about an hour) and in the village of Ajijic ask for the lakeside *posada*—a small inn. Twenty pesos get you a four-course lunch: juice, soup, entrée (choice of roast pork, shrimp with avocado, or whitefish from the lake), and wonderful coconut pie for dessert. Bar service. Kids can ride horses. Tel: Ajijic 25.

Chalet Suiza   Moderate
A fine restaurant opened by a Swiss couple. Off Vallarta five blocks before Minerva traffic circle at Hidalgo 1983. Serves sauerbraten, cheese fondue, veal Cordon Bleu, and a mixed German plate as well as steaks. Bar. Open 1 P.M. to midnight. Closed Tuesdays. Tel: 15-71-22.

Chez Pierre   Moderate
Av. España 2095 near the Niños Héroes monument. A small French restaurant which is intimate and friendly and will make you feel comfortable while serving veal, fish, and onion soup. Tel: 15-14-77.

Kri-Kri   Moderate
A fun place in the Zona Chapultepec at López Cotilla 1500. You will find outstanding dishes such as Cornish hens, shrimp curry, and steaks while being served by a friendly staff. Tel: 15-19-98.

Portofino   Inexpensive
An Italian restaurant with an open terrace at La Paz 1992 near Chapultepec. Serves veal scallopini, pasta, shrimp scampi, and seafood Newburg. Lunch and supper. Tel: 25-18-56.

Recco   Moderately expensive
A real Italian restaurant in a restored colonial mansion at Libertad 1973, just off Chapultepec. Chicken cacciatore, lasagna, and shrimp Casa Mona. Tel: 25-07-24.

Sakura   Moderate
At Av. Vallarta 2777, near the Minerva traffic circle. Has sukiyaki and tempura as well as other traditional Japanese dishes. Tel: 15-47-68.

Denny's   Inexpensive
At the corner of Juárez and 16 de Septiembre, this is one of the chain of hamburger and soda shops that dot much of the United States and Mexico. Another is at the Plaza del Sol shopping center. Open twenty-four hours and serves breakfast, lunch, and dinner.

Pizza Hut   Inexpensive
In the Plaza del Sol shopping center, this is part of the chain that serves cold beer as well as a variety of pizzas.

COMPLETE LISTING OF HOTELS, MOTELS, AND TRAILER PARKS FOR GUADALAJARA, LAKE CHAPALA, AND BARRA DE NAVIDAD

Hotels in Guadalajara

El Tapatío (*250 rooms*)   Expensive
One of the most fabulous resort hotels in Mexico. Located on a hilltop 4 miles outside Guadalajara on the superhighway to the airport. Rooms charmingly decorated with beams and touches of colonial decor have air conditioning, refrigerators stocked with drinks, piped-in FM music, and windows overlooking the city.

Eighteen-hole golf course, tennis, transport, children's playground, pool with island bar. AE, CB, DC, MC, VISA. Tel: 17-80-00.

Guadalajara Sheraton (*222 rooms*)   Expensive
This is a handsome hotel, styled with colonial beams, hand-blown glass, native textiles, and local ceramics. Very lavish, very comfortable. Heated pool, steam bath. Several dining rooms, one with dancing. Rooftop bar with music. Decor by Pablo Fantonet. Located conveniently in town. All major credit cards. Tel: 12-51-51.

Camino Real (*200 rooms*)   Moderately expensive
Beautifully laid out two-story motel set in tropical gardens at edge of city at Vallarta 5005, Highway 15 about 3 miles from center of Guadalajara. Most rooms have private terraces or balconies. Three heated pools, wading pool, playground, tennis, putting green. Gourmet dining room. Camichin nightclub, Diligencia bar. Western Hotels-operated. All major credit cards. Tel: 21-72-17.

Hotel Plaza del Sol (*200 rooms*)   Moderate
New top-flight hotel situated in the Plaza del Sol shopping center. Modern decor, air conditioning, TV, private bar, restaurant, and poolside grill. Convention and banquet facilities. Parking and watchman. AE, CB, DC, MC, VISA. Tel: 21-56-11.

Hotel del Parque (*77 rooms*)   Inexpensive
Fair hotel, just out of downtown area on Juárez Street. Easy parking, fair restaurant and sidewalk café, bar. AE, CB, DC, MC, VISA. Tel: 25-28-00.

Hotel de Mendoza (*104 rooms*)   Inexpensive
Very good colonial-style downtown hotel, near historical landmarks: the Degollado Theater, museum, state capitol, and cathedral. Has garage, heated pool, air conditioning, TV, dining room, rooftop cocktail lounge open till midnight. On Venustiano Carrenza 16. Major credit cards. Tel: 13-46-46.

Holiday Inn (*208 rooms*)   Moderately expensive
On Highway 15 to Mexico City, edge of town near Plaza del Sol shopping center at Av. López Mateos 2407. Attractively landscaped. Pool, playground, putting green. Dining room and coffee shop. Tel: 21-24-00.

Gran Hotel (*55 rooms*)   Inexpensive
Old hotel, uptown at Morelos 2244, recently rebuilt and modernized. Enthusiastic visitors say one of best in Mexico. Olympic swimming pool. Tel: 15-01-86.

Hotel Aranzazu (*64 rooms*) Moderate
Modern new hotel off Av. Corona near the Degollado Theater between Kunhart and Av. Héroes. Coffee shop.

Hotel Fénix (*250 rooms*) Moderately expensive
An older hotel with a new section which is air-conditioned. Convenient location at Av. Corona 160 in the heart of town. Good restaurant with international cuisine. Servis-bar in all rooms. Most cards. Tel: 14-57-14 or toll-free (800) 421-0000.

Econohotel (*100 rooms*) Moderate
Modern air-conditioned hotel in Plaza del Sol shopping center, convenient to 240 fine shops. TV, ice machine on each floor, heated pool, restaurant, cocktails, and dancing to live entertainment. P.O. Box 31-444, Guadalajara, or toll-free (800) 854-3048.

Hotel Genova (*60 rooms*) Moderate
At Juárez 123. All bedrooms air conditioned, with TV and stereo. Refrigerator bars in many rooms. Restaurant serves Mexican and continental food. Coffee shop, drugstore. Tel: 13-75-00.

Hotel Morales (*100 rooms*) Inexpensive
Downtown at Av. Corona 243. Interestingly modernized colonial with solarium. Built around courtyard. Tel: 13-29-69.

Hotel Frances (*40 rooms*) Inexpensive
Colonial gem downtown, at Maestranza 35. Fair.

Motels in Guadalajara

American Motel (*24 rooms*) Inexpensive
On Highway 15 and 80 at López Mateos 631. Good two-story motel. TV. Coffee shop serves breakfast only. AE, CB, DC, MC, VISA. Tel: 15-28-30.

Motel de las Américas (*100 rooms*) Inexpensive
Four miles south of town on 15 and 80 at López Mateos 2400. Very good with attractive rooms with balconies, swimming pool, dining room, bar, kitchenettes. AE, CB, DC, MC, VISA. Tel: 21-36-51.

Motel La Estancia (*40 units*) Moderate
Four miles south on 15 and 80 at Glorieta Mariano Otero 2407. Off highway, new, pleasant rooms, pool. AE, CB, DC, MC, VISA. Tel: 21-05-02.

Motel Malibu (*200 rooms*)   Moderate
Three miles northwest on Highway 15 to Nogales, at Vallarta Prieto
3993. Nice two-story motel set in gardens with heated pool and
wading pool, TV. Plus high rise with eighty rooms which are new
and nicer. Tel: 21-75-17.

Tropicana Motel (*28 rooms*)   Inexpensive
Six miles northwest on Highway 15 at Vallarta 6075. Remodeled
bungalows in rural area. Pool, riding horses, dining room, bar. Pets
welcome. AE, CB, DC, MC, VISA. Tel: 21-11-51.

Posada del Sol Hotel (*200 rooms*)   Moderate
Four miles south on 15 and 80 at Glorieta Mariano Otero at López
Mateos 4205. Good hotel with pool, coffee shop, bar. Suites with
kitchenettes. Adjacent to ultramodern Plaza del Sol shopping center.
AE, CB, DC, MC, VISA. Tel: 21-01-71.

Motel Suites Caribe (*42 rooms*)   Moderate
Three miles south on 15 and 80 at López Mateos 2128, near Plaza
del Sol shopping mall. Air conditioning, attractive decor, pleasant
lounge. Heated pool. Restaurant open till 10 P.M., bar. Very good.
Tel: 21-69-95.

Motel Chapalita (*85 rooms*)   Inexpensive
At López Mateos 1617 on Highway 15 to Mexico City. Clean austere
rooms. Pool. Tel: 15-08-76.

Hotels and Motels at Lake Chapala

Camino Real del Chapala (*100 rooms*)   Moderately expensive
On Mexico's largest freshwater lake, 35 miles from Guadalajara out
airport road on Highway 94 to kilometer 52. A brand-new two-
story structure overlooking lake. Luxury rooms. Some suites with
private pools. Restaurant, bar. Olympic pool, fishing, waterskiing,
boating, golf, horseback riding. Run by Western Hotels. Tel: 5-24-
13.

Motel Chula Vista (*30 rooms*)   Moderate
Across highway from Lake Chapala, a mile beyond the village of
Chapala and before Ajijic. Modest motel with fine view, good pool,
modern rooms, bar, restaurant. Box 75, Chapala. Tel: 5-22-13.

Posada Ajijic (*18 rooms*)   Inexpensive
Well-established Mexican-style inn set in tropical gardens on Lake
Chapala. Pool, fireplaces. Pets allowed. Dining room and cocktail

lounge have beautiful view of lake, fine food, and good service. Stop in for dinner. AE, DC, MC, VISA. Located on Calle 16 de Septiembre (Box 12, Ajijic). Tel: 5-25-01.

Hotels and Motels in Barra de Navidad (on Pacific)

Hotel Melaque (*200 rooms, 7 bungalows*)   Moderate
Located on the lovely Barra de Navidad Bay, whose white beaches nestle between jagged rocky islands on each side, this is a rambling three-story structure, painted pink, yellow, and blue. Rooms are austere and without air conditioning, but all have cross ventilation and terraces looking on the ocean. Has two large pools, one for children, breezy dining room on second-floor veranda where food, featuring fish, is good. About four- or five-hour drive from Guadalajara over interesting paved Highway 80. At junction with coastal highway 200, look for small 1-kilometer entrance road to Melaque just before village of Barra. Office in Guadalajara: Prisciliano Sánchez 437. Tel: 14-56-05.

Puerto Viejo Chamela (*60 rooms*)   Moderately expensive
Up the coast between Barra de Navidad and Puerto Vallarta is a new recreational area still very much in the wilderness. Here a sixty-room condominium has been opened, and an airstrip and marina are planned. Mary Bishop of Guadalajara is manager. Write to Puerto Viejo Chamela, Chamela, Jalisco, for details.

Club Méditerranée West (*100 rooms*)   Moderate
Also up the coast a bit from Barra de Navidad is one of the famed seventy-two worldwide vacation clubs. You must join at club offices in a major city and arrange a package group tour. Features life in a bathing suit without money except for beads (as you have paid in advance). This one is pretty isolated.

Motel del Sol (*10 rooms*)   Inexpensive
Small new motel on highway. Pool. Walk to beach. No credit cards.

Monterrey Hotel (*28 rooms*)   Inexpensive
Modest two-story structure on beach. No pool. No credit cards. Same owners as Motel Malibu in Guadalajara.

Trailer Parks in Guadalajara and Lake Chapala

Yucca Trailer Park (*130 spaces*) $3
Off Highway 15 from Nogales or Mexico City at corner where Camino Real Motel is located, two blocks in on Boulevard Calzada de las Torres. At edge of city about 3 miles from downtown.

Excellent court with every site landscaped with flowers. All facilities, pool, laundry room, bathhouse, community hall. Markets nearby, deliveries, newspapers. Busy in winter. Write P.O. Box 1320, Guadalajara. Tel: 15-36-00.

Guadalajara Trailer Park (*150 spaces*) $3
Three miles north on Highway 54 to Zacatecas. Well-run large court with connections, cement patios, large heated pool, barbecue pit, bathhouse, hot water, laundry, recreation room. Beer and soft drinks sold. Three-hole golf course. Reservations in winter. P.O. Box 2062, Guadalajara. Tel: 14-63-17.

Paradise Trailer Park (*57 spaces*) $2
Three miles south on 15 and 80 at López Mateos 1470. All connections. Showers and toilets. Takes campers. Tel: 15-91-52.

La Floresta Trailer Park (*140 spaces*) $3
Half mile from Camino Real del Chapala on Highway 94 by Lake Chapala just before village of Ajijic. All facilities, showers, restrooms. Swimming pool. Operated by Western Hotels. Write % Camino Real, Chapala.

12

Guanajuato

TALES OF OLD MEXICO

In Guanajuato there is a charming little street, only 78 centimeters wide, called the Street of the Kiss (El Callejón del Beso)—one of many narrow steep streets in this mountainside colonial gem lined on both sides with eighteenth-century houses in pinks and creams with wrought-iron balconies almost touching across the cobblestones. A romantic legend handed down over the generations explains how the little street got its name.

In the eighteenth century there lived in this small callejón two lovers named Doña Ana and Carlos. He was a poor miner; she, the daughter of a rich Spaniard. Carlos wished to marry Ana, but her family had finer plans for their daughter—she was betrothed to a wealthy Spaniard.

Carlos, however, rented the narrow house across the street with 18 hard-earned pieces of silver, and the young lovers continued to meet. One night Doña Ana's father surprised the couple kissing from balcony to balcony and threatened to kill them if he found them together again. Headstrong Ana thought her father was joking, and the next night he found them embracing again on the balconies across the narrow lane.

Without a word the irate father drew his dagger and stabbed his daughter in the back. With her last ounce of strength the dying girl stretched her arm out to her lover on the far balcony; he seized her limp hand in his and gave her a final kiss on the upturned palm.

The pretty legend is typical of the songs, stories, and poetry written about this fascinating and romantic old town.

GUANAJUATO is one of many charming mountain mining towns in Mexico, and its hillside location, clean cobblestoned streets, and red-tiled roofs have given it much favor among tourists. It is situated in a narrow mountain gorge in the Sierras, four or five hours north of Mexico City.

It is the capital of the state of the same name, and its 50,000 inhabitants divide their attention almost equally between the silver mines and the heavy tourist trade.

Guanajuato, once one of the greatest mining cities in the

world, was said to have supplied the entire world with over two-thirds of its silver as well as large quantities of gold and lead. In those days the city had a population of nearly 100,000 and was one of the most prosperous and bustling communities in all Mexico. Those great days are still reflected in such unusual possessions as an opera house and handsome churches.

GOING THERE

Guanajuato is off the main El Paso–Mexico City highway just beyond Salamanca (Highway 45, free, or 45D, toll) and can be reached by starting from Mexico City on the Querétaro toll road north. It is about a four-hour drive. From Mexico City, limousine service is offered daily by Corsarios de Bajío, located at Buenavista No. 4, or your hotel can arrange for a car and driver. Fair bus service is offered regularly by Transportes Chihuahuenses or Tres Estrellas de Oro; all buses leave from the new Terminal de Autobúses on Insurgentes Norte in Mexico City. It is also possible to take the National Railways of Mexico, which runs a streamlined overnight Pullman to Guanajuato. However, car or bus is usually more convenient and is recommended.

WHERE TO STAY

Guanajuato has made a genuine effort to make the tourist comfortable. It has a good climate, and it is a fine place to stop overnight or for a week of exploring and enjoying the ever-present sun. Hotels do demand cash deposits, and refuse refunds unless they have three to ten days advance cancellation. The city has several very good hotels and some acceptable smaller ones, as well as a number of small pensions and boardinghouses which take in tourists. On the whole the best place to dine is probably in your hotel, or another hotel dining room.

The *Hotel Real de Minas* just south of town, built in the colonial style with a lovely enclosed courtyard, is without doubt your best choice. Its comfortable rooms are handsomely furnished in rustic colonial style, and its pleasant dining room features good service.

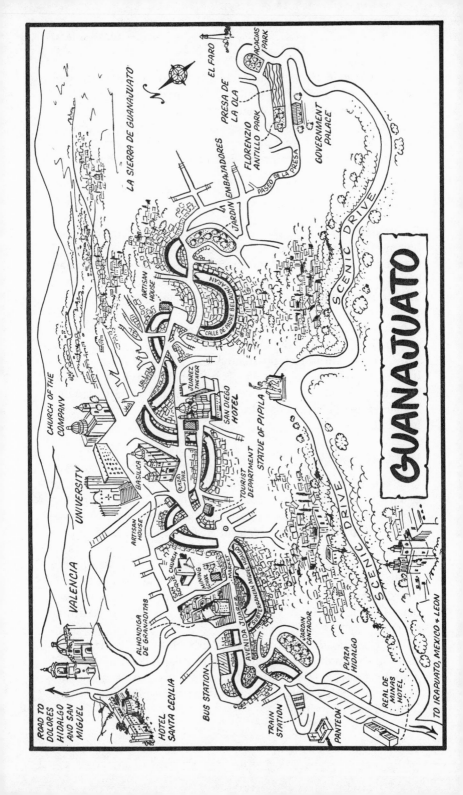

We recommend the *Castillo de Santa Cecilia* for its beautiful location in a castlelike structure sitting on a mountain peak overlooking the city, yet within walking distance of the downtown area. Sometimes, however, its service is erratic.

The *Parador San Javier* is an old hacienda set in beautiful gardens. The dignified *Hotel San Diego* downtown is a modernized seventeenth-century convent complete with Spanish wine cellar.

HOTELS AND MOTELS IN GUANAJUATO

Castillo de Santa Cecilia (*100 rooms*)   Moderately expensive
An old castle, turrets and all, with modernized rooms with baths, some fireplaces (necessary to take the chill off). Gardens, small heated pool. Large dining room open 8 to 10 A.M., 1:30 to 4 P.M., and 7 to 10 P.M. (open to public). (Ask for the a la carte menu unless you wish the fairly expensive table d'hôte meal.) Deposit refund notice ten days. On Valenciana road overlooking city, about 1 mile from center. All cards. P.O. Box 44. Tel: 2-04-85.

Hotel Real de Minas (*175 rooms*)   Moderately expensive
On Route 110, the largest hotel in Guanajuato. Attractive colonial-style hotel with large rooms, some balconies. Small pool, bar and restaurant with music, beauty parlor, conference rooms. Four floors with modern elevators. Tel: 2-14-60.

Parador San Javier (*109 rooms*)   Moderately expensive
An old hacienda with lovely gardens just down the hill from the Santa Cecilia on Plaza Aldama overlooking city. Heated pool. Fine dining room and bar, El Pozo. Serving bars in each room. All cards. Tel: 2-06-26.

Hotel San Diego (*43 rooms*)   Moderate
Authentic seventeenth-century convent with modernized rooms. At second exit of subterranean expressway in town, on Jardín Unión. Elevator. Spanish wine cellar, music nightly, dining room. P.O. Box 8. Tel: 2-13-00.

Hotel El Carruaje (*43 rooms*)   Moderate
Opposite the Castillo. An attractive colonial-style building with pool, pleasant dining room and bar. Tel: 2-21-40

Motel Guanajuato (*12 units*)   Moderate
On Dolores Road above town. Modern in colonial style, fine view, small rooms. Restaurant with excellent food, bar. Tel: 2-06-89.

Hotel Valenciana (*45 rooms*)   Moderate
On Dolores Road above city. A modern building with pool, fabulous
view, restaurant, bar, music on weekends. Tel: 2-07-99.

La Motel de los Embajadores (*20 rooms*)   Inexpensive
Ordinary motel with excellent food in town at the end of the
subterráneo, at Parque Embajadores. No credit cards.

THINGS TO SEE

Guanajuato is one of those wonderful towns where you can
wander about on foot, seeing an interesting view at almost
every turn. Ask for a map. The twisting streets will confuse
you.

The zócalo, or central plaza, is called El Jardín de la Unión
and is distinguished by its very small size. It is a charming
spot, offering the weary tourist a choice of lacy white ironwork
benches to rest on beneath a canopy of carefully pruned laurel
trees, while university students stroll by or catch up on the
day's news at the brightly awninged café on the corner. As
with any zócalo in Mexico, the townspeople like to gather there
in the evening, especially on Sundays, Tuesdays, and Thursdays
when there are concerts in the Victorian bandstand and strings
of bright lights sparkle in the trees.

To go elsewhere in town, it is important to know several
things. Guanajuato has a unique subterranean highway which
runs the length of the city, hurriedly carrying traffic from one
end of town to the other. This is an old drainage canal, now
replaced by underground tubing, which has been converted to
a broad depressed expressway. (See map.)

You can take the Presa-Estación bus from one end of the town
to the other for 50 centavos, first class, and see a lot of the city.
Another bus, the Valenciana, goes up the hill past the hotels to
the famed Valenciana mine, and then returns. Both are fine for
sightseers.

A scenic drive can be found by going out the Paseo de la
Presa, returning past the statue of Pípila, and back into town
on the Irapuato road.

The Alhóndiga de Granaditas is a massive stone warehouselike
building that one passes near the market before starting up the
hill out of town. It bears a plaque saying that construction on

it was begun in 1798 by the Spaniards. Ostensibly built for grain storage, it was almost immediately turned into a fortress by the Spanish when the War of Independence broke out in 1810. It was the scene of a bloody struggle on September 28 of that year when the revolutionary troops, led by Hidalgo, fought their way in, step by step, while missiles and hot oil rained down on them from the walls. The day was saved when a young miner called Pípila (meaning "scrawny turkey"), protected by a slab of stone on his back, charged the door and started the fire which destroyed the large wooden north door, allowing the revolutionaries to enter and kill all the Spanish defenders. Later, the Spanish recaptured Guanajuato and caught Hidalgo in Chihuahua. They executed Hidalgo and sent his head and those of three other leaders to be hung on the four corners of the Alhóndiga from October 14, 1811, to March 28, 1821, as a warning to future revolutionaries.

Turned into a jail by Maximilian, the Alhóndiga later became the state penitentiary and is now a handsome museum, not to be missed, depicting the history and culture of the state of Guanajuato. Allow an hour to wander through it. It is open from 9 A.M. to 2 P.M. and from 4 to 7 P.M. Closed on Mondays. Admission is 3 pesos, 5 with a camera.

A mural by José Chávez-Morado, the museum's director, adorns the walls, and his collection of pre-Hispanic art is on display. Startlingly effective is the "Masks of the Revolutionary Heroes" display.

The churches of Guanajuato have been considered among the most magnificent in Mexico, although they are now somewhat neglected. *La Compañia*, a Jesuit church until the Jesuits were expelled in 1767, is probably the most beautiful, although severe in lines. Only a short distance from the center of town, it is worth visiting to see the huge naves, with the largest in the center in Roman style. In its sacristy are two large paintings by Cabrera. On the Plaza de la Unión is the *San Diego Church*, with its lovely churrigueresque facade, started by the Franciscans in 1663. On the adjoining Plaza de la Paz is *La Parroquía*, officially named the Basilica of Our Lady of Guanajuato. In the church's chapel is the Sanctuary of the Virgin of Guanajuato, a wooden statue brought from Spain in 1557 as a gift from the King of Spain.

Also on the Plaza de la Paz are the former Government Palace, where the state legislature meets, and the former handsome home of the Conde de Rul, once owner of La Valenciana mine.

Juárez Theater, or the Opera House, on the main plaza, was completed in 1903 in the heyday of Guanajuato. Money was lavished upon the structure during its construction, and the dictator of Mexico in those days, Porfirio Díaz, attended the opening, which was a performance of Verdi's *Aïda.* The best opera companies in the world gave performances there. Note its facade of green stone columns over which are the muses: Melpomene (Tragedy), Thalia (Comedy), Polymnia (Rhetoric), Terpsichore (Dance), Euterpe (Music), Clio (History), Calliope (Poetry), and Urania (Astronomy).

The University of Guanajuato, located in a modern building near the center of town, has been open only in this century. It is housed in modern buildings dominated by a principal building of white stone with a Moorish turreted facade which can be seen rising above the old city. It is evidence of the community pride and culture that are very much alive in Guanajuato. The city did have a college dating back to 1732 when the Jesuits started the Hospicio Escuela de la Santísima Trinidad in the former home of a leader of society, Doña María Josefa Teresa de Busto y Moya. It later was a seminary, then a treasure house in the regime of Agustín de Iturbide in 1821.

Mummies. The mummies at the cemetery have come to be one of the sights of Guanajuato. For those with a strong stomach, or plain scientific curiosity, this is a macabre but thrilling visit. Buses from the center of town will take you there.

Entremeses Cervantinos. If you visit Guanajuato in the spring you must see the Entremeses Cervantinos, a series of productions of sixteenth-century plays, many by Cervantes. They are staged in the streets and plazas of the town, with many of the residents in costume.

NEARBY EXCURSIONS

Marfil. The ruins of Marfil are only 5 miles down the highway toward Silao and are worth visiting. Before one enters the ghost town, one can see the *Presa de los Santos* off to the side of the road. A small but interesting dam, it bears across its top curious stone statues which decorate what was actually a reservoir.

In Marfil itself are the ruins of what was once the luxurious summer retreat of the wealthy mine owners of Guanajuato, where they entertained on a lavish scale in beautiful villas. Picnickers now frolic where the wealthy played, though some effort is now being made to restore some of the once handsome homes, deserted when floods and a declining silver market sent their owners scurrying back to the city.

La Valenciana—which stands for both the famous church and the mine of the same name—is on a hill above the Castillo de Santa Cecilia, a distance of 3 miles from town. As this is rather a steep walk from town, a taxi ride might be a better idea. The church, built by the mine owner, Don Antonio de Obregón y Alcocer, later the first Count of Valenciana, is one of the finest in Mexico. The miners are said to have contributed generously of the silver they produced, even to putting some in the foundation. The actual name of the church is Santo Cayetano, but it is better known as La Valenciana, due to its association with the mine. It has three beautiful altars, one carved of wood and one encrusted with tortoiseshell and ivory.

The statue of Pípila is another steep though pleasant hike up a mountainside—this time behind the Juárez Theater off the zócalo. It honors the stout Indian who carried the stone on his back to brave the missiles of the Spaniards defending the Alhóndiga.

Dams. The *Presa de Olla* and the *Presa de San Renovato* are about a quarter mile up the hill beyond the Hotel Orozco and the Posada de la Presa on the Calle de la Presa. This is another pleasant walk, and carries you by a beautiful park with many flowers. These dams are part of a series which hold the city's water supply. The first dam was built in 1742 by the son of the Marquis de Rayas. The park is called *Las Acacias* and has a statue to Hidalgo in its center.

Dolores Hidalgo, a historic little town often called "the cradle of Mexican independence," can be reached by a well-paved mountain road running a distance of some 20 miles. This is a scenic drive and good fun. If you are driving, the road starts up past the Castillo de Santa Cecilia. Or you can take the local bus.

San Miguel de Allende can be reached by the Dolores Hidalgo road or by turning back to Silao on the main road, down to Celaya, and into San Miguel de Allende. San Miguel is a beautiful town with good hotels (see Chapter 22).

Ixtapa and Zihuatanejo

THE PERFECT RESORT may have been devised at last on the white coral sands of the long-isolated Zihuatanejo area, where a new development, Ixtapa, with luxury hotels built along a completely virgin strip of beach, is just 10 miles north of a picturesque century-old fishing village which is being discreetly modernized without losing any of its native charm. The area is 125 miles north of Acapulco on the Pacific coast.

Zihuatanejo and Ixtapa are being developed together, one very old and one very new, as a single government-sponsored project. Hopefully they will be free of many of the problems that face their big neighbor to the south, Acapulco.

The beaches are as nice as or nicer than those at Acapulco, and the palm trees are even thicker. Ixtapa Bay is being kept pollution-free because the government took over the entire area, which had never been inhabited, and began by building all sanitary facilities as they laid out the resort and a new community to go with it. A huge jetport, with a monumental terminal building, has been built just south of Zihuatanejo and can serve both communities with daily jet flights by Aeromexico and hopefully by American airlines, too.

IXTAPA

Ixtapa has open at this writing two luxury hotels, El Presidente Las Palmas and the Aristos, and nine holes of a planned seventy-two-hole Robert Trent Jones course. A paved road leads 10 miles south to the old village of Zihuatanejo. El Palmar Beach at Ixtapa is one of the nicest in Mexico, stretching out in a 1½-mile-long arc. Swimming is good when the water is quiet, but heavy surf brings up red warning flags. We found no difficulty swimming in a moderate surf when we were there.

There are pools at both luxury hotels, and both have excellent restaurants and coffee shops. Perhaps the edge for elegance is held by El Presidente, a cluster of red-tile-roofed structures no more than three floors high built in a U around the pool. The Aristos is an ultramodern eleven-story hotel whose rooms are comfortable but less luxurious than those at El Presidente. However, each Aristos room has a nice balcony, and most of them have sea views.

ZIHUATANEJO

Zihuatanejo is a very old fishing village which has long been isolated from the rest of Mexico, and looks more like a scene from a South Seas movie than anything else. It is located on its own almost landlocked bay, Zihuatanejo Bay, and its wharves and waterfront serve the fishing industry which has harvested these rich waters for so many years. Shrimp, oysters, bonita, red snapper, and larger game fish abound here.

Until 1972, Zihuatanejo was a little town of 4,000 people, but now its population is twice that and will continue to grow. The town consists of just a handful of streets in an orderly pattern of squares around the waterfront, which has three cafés and some other stores. Several other restaurants, all modest, are located in various dwelling-type buildings scattered about the village, where practically no building is more than one story high. All are whitewashed in native style, with red-tiled roofs.

To make sure that the wealthy new development (the government is spending millions on the entire project) of Ixtapa did not overwhelm the little village of Zihuatanejo, both are being incorporated in a general plan, but that for Zihuatanejo is to preserve its rustic appearance while at the same time giving it the same good sanitation and well-maintained streets that can handle the new traffic. The streets are being repaved with cobblestones, and no new building in Zihuatanejo can be higher than the existing structures. The parks are being landscaped with flowers and palm trees and equipped with new stone benches.

On the south side of Zihuatanejo Bay, a long arm stretches out which contains three beaches: La Madera, closest to town; then La Ropa; and, farthest out, Las Gatas. Along this stretch of three beaches, but perched up on the hillsides with steep descents to the beaches, are a number of older hotels, some of

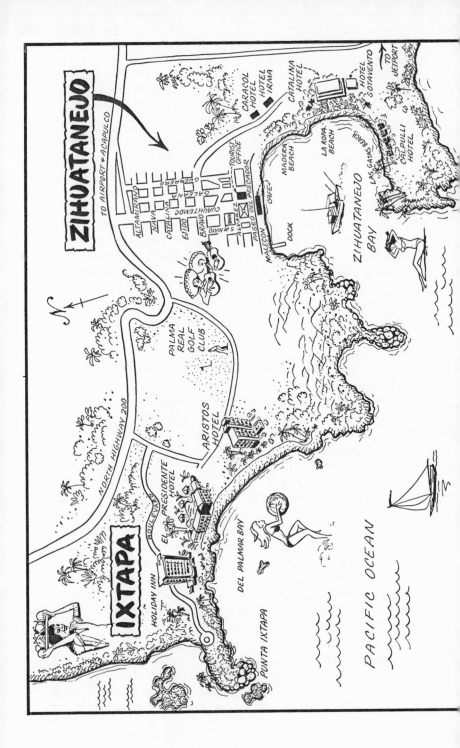

which are pretty good. But they are completely different from their new luxury-hotel neighbors to the north at Ixtapa. They are traditional Mexican seaside resorts, usually offering rooms with meals on the American plan and serving limited but good meals in open-air dining rooms looking out on the scenic bay. I would mention the Hotel Sotovento and the Catalina, run by the same management, and the Hotel Irma and Posada Caracol as the best of the group. There are others.

Boats for fishing can be chartered at the fishing wharf on the other arm of the bay, and marlin, sailfish, dolphin, and bonefish are among the many game fish caught here. Or one can simply take a small boat from the wharf in the town out to Las Gatas Beach on the far end of the point (hard to reach by a ridge-top road), where several informal open-air restaurants will serve you a broiled red snapper wrapped in palm before cooking, or plates of oysters, shrimp, and ceviche. Nice for a picnic.

In town, the small wharfside restaurants are pretty casual and likely to have rickety tables and lots of flies, but they serve a delicious plate of small lobster, actually langostino or crayfish, as well as other seafood. Or you can get a small steak and refried beans, a typical Mexican dish.

How To Get to Ixtapa and Zihuatanejo

There are flights daily from Mexico City on Mexicana and Aeromexico. At this writing, Aeromexico has three daily flights between Ixtapa and Mexico City; flight time to Ixtapa is 45 minutes. Return flights leave at 4:50 P.M. Mexicana has flights every day, except Tuesdays and Thursdays, leaving Mexico City at 6:50 P.M. and departing for Mexico City at 8 P.M. Taxis charge $8 from the airport to the Ixtapa hotels (a 12-mile ride), or there are minibuses which charge $3. American Airlines has direct flights via Mexico City from Dallas–Fort Worth. Other flights can be had from Los Angeles.

Buses (Estrella de Oro and others) make frequent trips each day from Acapulco to Zihuatanejo. There are buses from the airport to town, and on to Ixtapa.

A new highway direct from Mexico City via Toluca is under

construction, but in the meantime one can drive to Acapulco and then turn north for something under four hours on a completely paved and extremely scenic highway along the Pacific to Zihuatanejo and Ixtapa. Eventually Route 200 will also connect Ixtapa with its neighbor to the north, Manzanillo, but this is still abuilding. Driving from the north, it is possible to cut inland from Manzanillo to Uruapan and then descend on a twisting but passable mountain road to connect with the Zihuatanejo road. My sons drove it in a van, which must prove it is possible for any vehicle.

WHERE TO STAY IN IXTAPA

El Presidente Las Palmas (*313 rooms*)   Expensive
Located on the lovely Playa Palmar of Ixtapa, with miles of white sand and blue surf, this is a truly deluxe hotel built in a number of three-story mission-style buildings grouped in a U shape around a huge free-form pool. All rooms are air-conditioned and have phones. There are two tennis courts, and the Palma Real Golf Club with its Robert Trent Jones course is close by. There is poolside dining as well as a luxury restaurant and room service. It is operated by Nacional Hotelera, the government-supported hotel chain. Reservations through any of the El Presidente chain, including offices in large cities in the U.S. All cards.

Aristos Ixtapa (*226 rooms*)   Moderately expensive
Next door to El Presidente stands this handsome seven-story ultramodern structure of somewhat Moorish design with shaded balconies looking out over the Pacific. Its rooms are all air-conditioned and quite comfortable but a bit more austere than those at El Presidente and less expensive. It is a first-class hotel. Does not operate room service, but has a fine dining room and coffee shop with excellent food, and a bar with entertainment. Pool, gift shops, water sports. It also is on Palmar Beach. Operated by Aristos chain of Mexico City. All cards. Tel: (905) 533-05-60.

Camino Real Ixtapa (*200 rooms*)   Expensive
A new hotel scheduled to open by the time this book is published. It will be a completely modern deluxe hotel with pool and sports facilities, overlooking the fabulous Playa Palmar and adjacent to the Palma Real Golf Club. Operated by Western Hotels. Reservations through Western Hotels at toll-free (800) 228-3000 in the U.S.

Ixtapa Holiday Inn (*251 rooms*)   Moderately expensive
A new ten-story hotel right on Palmar Beach next to El Presidente.

Large pool. Coffee shop and restaurant. Reservations through Holiday Inn chain.

Famitel *(130 rooms)*   Inexpensive
On the Ixtapa beach, this was under construction at the time of writing. It is planned to offer special suites for families at reasonable rates.

Ixtapa Pacífico *(250 rooms)*   Expensive
One of several additional deluxe hotels planned for the main beach in Ixtapa. Check with your travel agent.

Viva Ixtapa *(110 rooms)*   Moderate
A white-and-red-roofed three-story hotel at the west end of the bay. Air-conditioned. La Resaca Restaurant set in garden. Bar. Lighted tennis courts. Manuel García, manager.

WHERE TO STAY IN ZIHUATANEJO

Hotels Catalina and Sotovento *(44 and 26 rooms)*   Moderate
On the bay near the little fishing village, some 3 miles south of Ixtapa, these are older but in many ways more charming hotels (run by same management) than their new neighbors to the north. They are set among dense palm groves on the steep hillside well outside the village but within possible walking distance to the village. Rooms and dining room are not air-conditioned, but a steady breeze makes it livable. Pool. Stairways directly to the beach, where swimming is good in the protected bay. Hammocks on terraces with fine view. Offer both European and American plans at reasonable rates. Good food. Bar. All cards. Write directly to hotels at Zihuatanejo, Guerrero, México. Tel: 4-21-37.

Hotel Irma *(30 rooms)*   Moderate
Also on Zihuatanejo Bay, somewhat out of town. Modest hotel on beach. American plan. Write P.O. Box 4, Zihuatanejo. Tel: 42-025.

Posada Caracol *(53 rooms)*   Moderate
Stone structure across roadway from beaches with courtyard and two pools. Small, easygoing place but restful. A block walk to beach. Restaurant and discotheque. All cards. Tel: 42-035.

Hotel Calpulli *(76 rooms)*   Moderate
Farthest out on the arm of land around Zihuatanejo Bay, at far end of La Ropa Beach. Near Las Gatas Beach also. Bungalow-style rooms, restaurant, bar, pool. No cards. Tel: 42-166.

Bungalows Pacífico (*6 units*)   Inexpensive
Very clean furnished bungalows run by a Swiss woman. Serves no
meals, but it is easy walk to many small restaurants in town. On
La Madera Beach. Tel: 4-21-12.

Where To Eat in Ixtapa and Zihuatanejo

In the little town of Zihuatanejo there are three or four small
restaurants worth mentioning, plus some informal beach services that can only be called open-air dining. The restaurants
are small, and the hours inexact. But some have delicious food.
The wharfside eating establishments are very rustic but serve
good food. In Ixtapa one would have to go to the dining rooms
in the large hotels.

From 6 A.M. to 11 P.M., buses run the 10 miles between
Zihuatanejo and Ixtapa every 15 minutes for a 3-peso charge.
Taxis are much more expensive.

El Presidente Las Palmas Hotel dining rooms   Expensive
At Ixtapa in the large hotel, a fancy multilevel dining room called
Los Caracoles serves breakfast from 7 to 11 A.M., lunch from 1 to
4 P.M., and dinner from 7 to 11 P.M. Features four kinds of steaks,
lobster and shrimp in five styles, and a Mexican buffet on Sundays
from noon on with regional dishes from all parts of Mexico,
including Yucatán, with pork pibil, chicken marinated in orange
juice, and enchiladas and tamales of all kinds. A poolside snack
bar, the Vagabond Clam, serves hamburgers, fruit plates, and
shrimp in pineapple as well as drinks. Entertainment.

Aristos dining room   Moderately expensive
At Ixtapa in the hotel of the same name, there is a coffee shop/
restaurant looking out over the beach, and it is the perfect place to
take the family. Special attention is given to children, and there are
big tables and booths to accommodate them. Open from breakfast
till 10 P.M. Menu varies from club sandwiches and ice ceam sodas
to fish and steak dinners. Cocktail service, too. Prices are moderate,
and the food excellent. Entertainment.

The Captain's Table   Reasonable
In Zihuatanejo, two blocks from beach at center of town on Bravo
Street. A modest residential-appearing building with reputation for
good food, open noon and evenings. Bean soup and oyster stew,
sashimi (fresh fish) Japanese-style served with an omelet, rice
Cantonese, seafood plate, captain's special lobster, top sirloin, and
barbecued ribs. Owners are Oliver and Luz María. Tel: 4-20-27.

La Tortuga y La Rana   Reasonable
In Zihuatanejo at 5 de Mayo and Álvarez streets, another modest
restaurant with all kinds of seafood including the famed Mahawa
oysters found nearby, lobster, crayfish, red snapper, and sea bass,
as well as standard meals. Run by what is proclaimed to be the
"Tortuga Gang" (*tortuga* meaning "turtle"). Open 1:30 P.M. till
midnight. Tel: 4-2323.

La Bocana   Inexpensive
In the very center of Zihuatanejo on the waterfront, this is a rickety
restaurant—alas, with some flies—but they have broiled lobster,
the huge oysters, ceviche, and ice-cold beer. You can also get
Mexican-style steak and beans here. Very rustic, service catch-as-
catch-can. Most prices are low, but lobster is expensive.

Las Brisas   Bargain
One of several restaurants along La Madera and La Ropa beaches.
About a mile out of town following the shore to the south arm of
the bay, near the foot of the Hotel Irma. Here tables are set up
under thatched-palm roof right in the sand. They serve a delicious
seafood soup, giant shrimp cooked in garlic butter, ceviche, other
fish from the broiler, and cold beer. Daytime only.

THINGS TO DO IN ÍXTAPA AND ZIHUATANEJO

The Tourist Information Office is located in the modern two-
story municipal building in the center of Zihuatanejo. It is
managed by Salvador Hernández, who will provide information
on boats, shops, and sports.

Boat Trips to Las Gatas. A trip from the downtown wharf
across Zihuatanejo Bay to the practically isolated but lovely Las
Gatas Beach can be had for $3 or $4. It is ten minutes across the
bay, and the boat will take your entire party for the price. Las
Gatas has a coral reef, and the snorkeling is good. Open-air
restaurants sell clams, oysters, and grilled fish in banana leaves,
which is locally called *una talla.* You can rent snorkeling and
scuba equipment from a Frenchman, Carlo Duran, at the scene.
There is a bar in what is called Las Gatas Beach Club, and some
palm-covered cabanas.

Golf and Tennis. At the Palma Real Golf Club in Ixtapa, nine
holes of a planned seventy-two-hole Robert Trent Jones course
are in operation. It is a beautiful course across the lagoon from
the hotels. Greens fees were a nominal $8 and cart rental the

same. The clubhouse has a very pleasant bar and restaurant. Tennis courts in the same area are $5 per hour and have lights for nighttime use (double charge then).

Fishing. The best place to charter a fishing craft is the wharf on the waterfront of downtown Zihuatanejo. Prices vary greatly with the size of the boat. Rental agencies also have equipment and can put cold drinks aboard. It's best to bring a box lunch from your hotel (they all supply them on request). There is deep-sea fishing for sailfish, marlin, tuna, and dolphin, and smaller fish such as roosterfish, bonefish, and red snapper. Spearfishing is illegal.

Shopping. There are many shops both in the hotels at Ixtapa and in the town of Zihuatanejo. They feature everything from handmade clothing, straw goods, and sandals to silver, jewelry, and sophisticated Mexican sportswear. If you need bathing suits, slacks, or Yucateco jackets, they are here.

14

Mazatlán, Guaymas, Hermosillo, Álamos, Los Mochis, Topolobampo, and San Blas

MAZATLÁN

ON THE GREAT Pacific Coast Highway of Mexico, an outstanding port and resort city is Mazatlán, about halfway down the coast from the United States to Mexico City. Travelers coming from Arizona and the West will find themselves going through the capital of Sonora state, Hermosillo, and the long-famed fishing port of Guaymas on the Gulf of California. The new seacoast highway 200 will eventually be completed and offer an alternate route through much of this area.

Mazatlán has always been considered a fine fishing and hunting resort, and its carnival just before Lent each year has been the gayest in Mexico. But now Mazatlán is getting some real luxury hotels on its beautiful beach and has turned into one of the best places in Mexico to spend a vacation.

Mazatlán is famous for its sunsets, being at a latitude (just 25 miles south of the Tropic of Cancer) where the pinks, blues, and yellows play on the evening sky in a fabulous manner, lighting up Olas Altas Bay.

In the older central part of town, a long boulevard called Paseo del Centenarios has been constructed along the bayfront, and the little *arañas* or horse carriages trot up and down under the boulevard lights, giving the port city a rakish continental touch.

Mazatlán has something of Rio de Janeiro about it, for in addition to both cities being famous for their Mardi Gras, they each have imposing hills rising from the sea (called "Sugar Loaf" in Rio and "Crestón" and "Faro" in Mazatlán). A lighthouse atop Faro is the second highest natural lighthouse on the American continent.

Mazatlán is a tropical town with fair weather most of the year. It has a stretch of open beach just north of town that is unexcelled anywhere, and a fantastic array of modern hotels has been built along this strip, called North Beach. The fishing is as good as at any point on the west coast, with marlin, tarpon, sailfish, and scores of other denizens of the deep. Good launches are available. There is also hunting with guides to take you out for duck, pheasant, and doves most of the year and occasionally ocelots and deer. (The name *Mazatlán* means "place of the deer" in the native tongue.) Alligators are seen in the rivers.

More and more Americans are finding they can easily drive from the western United States through Nogales, Arizona, down to Mazatlán and have a really luxurious winter vacation at reasonable costs. The trip is usually broken with an overnight stay in Guaymas or Culiacán along the way.

Mazatlán has the exotic air of a seaport that deals regularly with Japan, the Philippines, and the Orient. Behind the resort part of the city, fronting on the ocean, there is a harbor protected by three islands where oceangoing ships dock, and you will find crewmen of many other nations there loading chicle, cotton, sugar, shrimp, tomatoes, and hardwood while bringing in sheet plate, machinery, and petroleum.

The city dates back to time immemorial, with the Cocoyama tribe inhabiting the area until the arrival of the Spanish conquistadores. It was charted by Domingo de Castilla in 1541 in one of the oldest known maps of the entire hemisphere and mentioned by geographers in 1633 as "two small islands called Mazatlán back of which is a harbor of the same name." Its good port attracted freebooters and pirates, and Spanish colonizers used it as a base from which to explore the California region.

How To Get to Mazatlán

By Car. The Pacific Coast Highway (No. 15) runs from Nogales, Arizona, to Guadalajara, Mexico, and passes directly by Mazatlán, which is 764 miles south of Nogales and 325 miles north

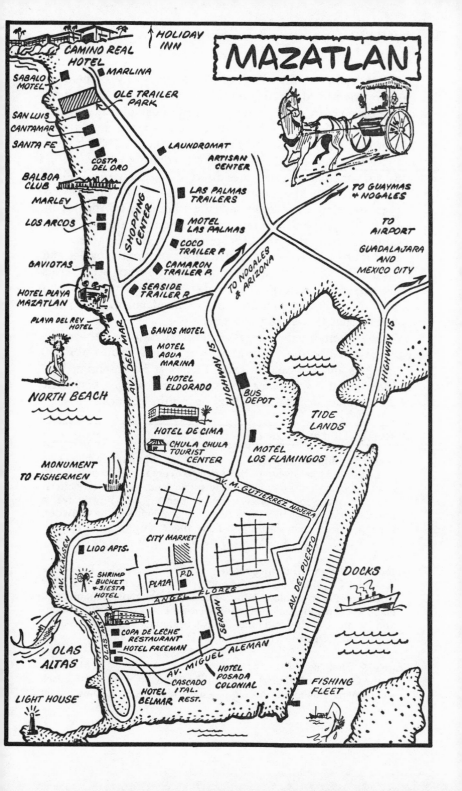

of Guadalajara (or 747 miles north of Mexico City). Thus it is easy to drive to Mazatlán from Nogales in two or three days over a paved road, with good stops at Hermosillo and Guaymas (see pages 210–219) or other points such as Culiacán, Ciudad Madero, or Los Mochis (see pages 219–224), all of which have modern hotels. (See also Chapter 6 on motoring.)

By Air. American Airlines flies direct to Mazatlán from Dallas–Fort Worth. Both Mexicana and Aeromexico fly from Mexico City to Mazatlán. Mexicana will bring you from Los Angeles on a nonstop flight, and Aeromexico flies nonstop from El Paso. A large new airport is 15 miles southeast of the city.

By Bus or Train. Air-conditioned buses run from Nogales and from Mexico City (Tres Estrellas line has reserved seats on its Pullman-service buses). The Pacífico Railroad from Nogales passes through Mazatlán en route to Guadalajara, and it is a possible, though wearing, journey.

By Sea. There is a deluxe passenger ferry running between La Paz, Baja California, and Mazatlán. It has cabins for 150 passengers and 115 cars. It leaves La Paz at 5 P.M. and arrives in Mazatlán at 9 A.M. Same hours in reverse coming back. Tel: 24-25 Mazatlán or 2-04-18 La Paz, or inquire at dock.

WHERE TO DINE IN MAZATLÁN

La Siesta Shrimp Bucket   Moderately expensive
In La Siesta Hotel in town, but open to everyone from early till 10 P.M. Caters to families. Has lively music and humorous waiters. The "in" place for people-watching, operated by Chuy Juárez, a popular local personality. Specializes in seafood, serving chowder, shrimp creole, charcoal-broiled fish, and a shrimp salad special. Also steaks, chops, and Mexican plate. All cards. Tel: 63-50

Hotel Playa Mazatlán dining room   Expensive
At Hotel Playa Mazatlán at far end of North Beach, about 5 miles from center of town along boulevard. This is the most romantic and elaborate of dining facilities, with open-air tables overlooking palms and Pacific. Dancing and music. Bar. Cocktail lounge. Lunch served at poolside. Open to visitors. All cards. Tel: 23-23 or 37-73.

Ernie's & Chato's   Moderate
In the Chula Chula tourist center on the highway along North Beach as it enters the town. A colonial-style restaurant specializing in

seafood and Mexican food, including steaks. Open 11 A.M. till midnight. Mariachi band begins playing about sunset. Good place to relax.

Hostería Mendoza   Moderately expensive
On Av. Alemán behind Freeman Hotel. A refined, quiet dining room with excellent food prepared by a Pennsylvania woman. Lobster, fish, and plate specials. Usually closed July to September. Tel: 45-13.

El Patio   Moderate
Swinging open-air restaurant and bar one block from Hacienda Hotel with view of bay. A good place to lift the spirits and watch the sun set. Try the lobster, Mexican plate, or Swiss-style enchiladas. Special attention from "Jesús, your host," whose after-dinner drinks will make your evening.

Lafitte Restaurant   Expensive
Located in the Camino Real Hotel, this pirate's gourmet restaurant offers many specialties: roast prime ribs, jumbo shrimp, excellent local fish and lobster.

Señor Frogg's   Bargain
On Av. del Mar next to the Sands Hotel, this popular spot offers all you can eat or drink from the daily menu for about $5. Lively atmosphere and they'll play your favorite album on the stereo.

Hongkong Restaurant   Inexpensive
At Zaragoza 16, corner Aquiles Serdán in town, where road from north goes through town. Open twenty-four hours. Oriental decor. Clean. Shrimp chop suey, eggs fu yun (which is the way they spell it).

Pekin Restaurant   Inexpensive
Across from cathedral, at Juárez 4, and near new municipal market. Chinese food. Open until midnight.

Copa de Leche   Moderate
At Olas Altas 33, next to Belmar Hotel. Modern and handsome coffee shop and dining room open from 6 A.M. for breakfast until midnight. Try their soups. Bar open until 1 A.M.

Chuy's Chew Choo   Moderate
In the Océano Palace, this colorful spot offers up railroad atmosphere with a wide variety of Mexican dishes.

Cascada   Moderate
  Italian restaurant on downtown waterfront next to Belmar Hotel.
  Serves pizza, spaghetti. Open 4 P.M. till 2 A.M. Food to go.

Cazadores   Moderate
  Part of a chain in western Mexico featuring charcoal-grilled steaks,
  regional cuisine.

WHERE TO STAY IN MAZATLÁN

The place to stay in Mazatlán is on North Beach, just north of
the center of town, and on the three beach areas beyond—
Gaviotas, Camarones, and Sabalo. This wide, sweeping stretch
of beautiful white beaches is lined with dozens of good hotels
and motels. Reached by following Avenida del Mar and then
Boulevard del Sabalo northward are such outstanding hotels as
the Camino Real, far out on Sabalo, the nearby Océano Palace,
the new resorts El Cid and La Palapa, and the long-popular
Hotel Playa Mazatlán.

In town, on Olas Altas Beach, where the swimming is not as
desirable but the shopping is fun, are the older hotels like La
Siesta, where the popular Shrimp Bucket restaurant is located.

Mazatlán also offers a number of well-equipped trailer parks.
Outstanding among them is the Olé Trailer Park far out on
Sabalo Beach.

HOTELS AND MOTELS IN MAZATLÁN

Camino Real Mazatlán (*170 rooms*)   Expensive
  Built on a rocky precipice overlooking a fine playa on the North
  Beach strip, this is a modern three-story building with a spectacular
  view from each room. Terrazas restaurant, Sabalo nightclub. Water
  sports, tennis, golf available. P.O. Box 538, Mazatlán, Sinaloa,
  México, or care of Western Hotels. Tel: 2-33-22.

Océano Palace (*200 rooms*)   Moderately expensive
  Modern luxury hotel right on Sabalo Beach with large solar-heated
  pool, restaurant, and shops. Family plan available, with children
  under eighteen free. All cards. P.O. Box 411, Mazatlán. Tel: 3-31-11.

La Palapa Mazatlán (*300 rooms*)   Moderately expensive
  A new resort center on the beach with one wing for condominiums.

Close to town. Two pools, tennis, golf. Tel: toll-free Utel (800) 223-9868 in the United States or 5-33-59-53 in Mexico City.

Hotel Playa Mazatlán (*300 rooms*) Moderately expensive
This is undoubtedly the best hotel as to location and service. Fine beach location, top dining room, cocktail lounge overlooking sea, good shops, honeymoon suites with lovely view. Heated pool and whirlpool. Waterskiing, tennis, golf. Mexican fiestas twice weekly. Hunting and fishing. American management. Reservations necessary. Well worth visiting for dinner on terrace overlooking sea. Bob Vient, manager. P.O. Box 207. Tel: 1-44-99.

Hotel de Cima (*130 rooms*) Moderate
Modern four-story hotel on North Beach. Balconies, pool, music in the bar nightly, shops, tunnel leading to the beach. Informal atmosphere. Discount rates in the summer. AE, DC, MC, VISA. Manager: Sergio de Cima. Tel: 1-41-19.

Playa del Rey (*158 rooms*) Moderate
A three-story modern motel-type structure located on Gaviotas Beach just before Playa Mazatlán. Attractive rooms mostly air-conditioned, some with balconies. Two pools, airy outdoor dining room overlooking the bay. Music and dancing nightly. AE, CB, DC, MC, VISA. Tel: 1-75-20.

Don El Guía (*103 rooms*) Expensive
New nine-story condominium run as a resort hotel. All rooms have kitchenettes, living rooms, and balconies with ocean view. North of the Camino Real, it has its own marina, large pool with swim-up bar, tennis. Laundry and maid service. Restaurant. Jesús Hizarraga, manager. Reservations a must. AE, CB, DC, MC, VISA. Tel: 2-17-77.

Azteca Inn (*74 rooms*) Moderate
Located on Sabalo Road near Playa Mazatlán. Modern two-story, nicely furnished, air-conditioned motel with bar and poolside restaurant. MC, VISA. Tel: 1-68-40.

Holiday Inn (*350 rooms*) Moderate
Offers all the typical Holiday Inn attractions—pool, bar, and restaurants. Right on Sabalo Beach. Tel: 2-11-88.

Cantamar Motel (*25 units*) Inexpensive
On Gaviotas-Sabalo Beach beyond Playa Mazatlán, this is a modern three-story motel with good service. Pool with bar. Major credit cards. Tel: 1-50-28.

Motel Marley (*16 units*)   Inexpensive
On Playa Gaviotas, new colonial-style motel with its buildings
amid palm trees but several directly on beach. All units have
kitchenettes. Pool. Tel: 1-59-77.

Posada Santa Fe (*28 units*)   Inexpensive
Two-story motel at far end of Gaviotas Beach next to Cantamar.
Ceiling fans, some air conditioning. Efficiencies and housekeeping
apartments available. Pool. No cards. Tel: 1-56-27.

El Cid Hotel (*120 rooms*)   Moderately expensive
New, very modern three-story resort hotel, beautifully landscaped
with fountains. Several pools, eight lighted tennis courts, eighteen-
hole golf course, and horseback riding. Rooms are large and
attractive, with roomy baths. Restaurant, bar, discotheque, bar and
grill at pool. Forty villas along the golf course. Across the street
from Sabalo Beach, near Olé Trailer Court. All cards but DC.
Guillermo Bernal, manager. P.O. Box 884. Tel: 1-75-40.

La Siesta Hotel (*59 rooms*)   Inexpensive
An American-run older hotel in the Olas Altas section in town
across boulevard from seafront. Accommodations somewhat austere
but comfortable. Convenient to shopping; has an American newsstand. Famous Shrimp Bucket restaurant located on the street level.
Remodeled rooms air-conditioned. Tel: 1-26-40.

Motel Aqua Marina (*100 rooms*)   Inexpensive
On North Beach, modern hotel with restaurant, bar, pool, shops,
aquarium, TV, protected parking. Across boulevard from beach.
Comfortable, informal. AE, MC, VISA. Tel: 1-70-80.

Sands Hotel (*60 rooms*)   Inexpensive
Located on Av. del Mar 2½ miles from city. Informal and clean.
Pool, garage, restaurant, bar. Fifteen-percent discount in summer.
AE, DC, MC, VISA. P.O. Box 309. Tel: 2-00-00.

Belmar Hotel (*200 rooms*)   Moderate
On Olas Altas, facing seafront. Older hotel with quite a bit of style.
Pool, restaurant. Air conditioning in newer section only. Major
cards. Tel: 1-42-99.

Hotel Las Brisas (*70 rooms*)   Moderate
Av. del Mar 900, across the street from beach. Plain, clean, pleasant
with balconies overlooking bay. Pool, restaurant, air-conditioned.
MC, VISA. Tel: 1-76-60.

Hotel Posada de Don Pelayo (*105 rooms*)   Moderate
Motel 3 miles north of town on Av. del Mar. Air conditioning, pool, parking, and dining room. Major cards. Tel: 1-75-02.

Apartamentos Lido (*28 rooms*)   Moderate
Beautifully decorated new apartments in building on North Beach. Modern kitchens, maid service. American plan only in winter. Write for rates: Apartamentos Lido, Av. Klausen, Mazatlán.

Hotel Hacienda Mazatlán (*104 rooms*)   Moderate
Directly on beach at Av. del Mar and Flamingo. Modern nine-story hotel with El Capitán restaurant open twenty-four hours. TV in all rooms. Reservations: P.O. Box 1468, Nogales, Ariz. Tel: 1-69-89.

Posada Colonial (*31 rooms*)   Inexpensive
Charming and beautifully kept Spanish-colonial-style building around a tropical garden pool. Four blocks off beach in residential area at Av. Alemán 11. Good restaurant attracts outside trade too. Specializes in serving five kinds of shrimp.

Trailer Parks in Mazatlán

Olé Trailer Park (*100 spaces*) $4 for two
About 2 miles beyond Hotel Playa Mazatlán on Sabalo Beach. One of the best-located trailer parks in the world, with sites right on a lovely white beach. Connections, showers, toilets, groceries. Palm-tree shade. Good surfing. Reservations a must during peak season (November–May). P.O. Box 382, Mazatlán, Sinaloa, México. Tel: 1-57-99.

Camarón Trailer Park (*66 spaces*) $3
On Sabalo Beach, just north of Holiday Inn. Trailer connections, baths, toilets, laundry. Reservations: P.O. Box 233. Deposit required.

Las Canoas (*90 spaces*) $2
Farthest out of all on Sabalo Beach, this is new with only water and power connections at last report. Surf fishing. Reservations and deposits required. P.O. Box 429.

Holiday Trailer Park (*200 spaces*) $4 for two
New, modern, and 9 miles from downtown. All hookups, baths, showers, laundry, groceries. Recreation room, shuffleboard, salt-water pool, and concrete patios. Open year-round. Reservations: P.O. Box 682.

Playa Escondida $4 for two
Under same management as Holiday Trailer Park across the street

in a great tropical setting directly on the beach. Reservations: P.O. Box 682.

Sea Side Trailer Park (*56 spaces*) $2
In palm grove across from beach, at Playa del Rey. Trailer connections, showers, laundry, toilets, barbecue pits. Reservations and deposits required. P.O. Box 362.

Las Palmas Trailer Park (*105 spaces*) $2
An older court built in well-established grove of palms with nice gardens. About two blocks to beach. All connections, patios, showers, toilets, laundry. Recreation room, soft drinks. Well run. Near Hotel Playa Mazatlán and Gaviotas Beach. P.O. Box 310.

Things To Do in Mazatlán

Swimming and Sunbathing. The swimming and sunbathing are always good in Mazatlán. North Beach is by far the best and is open to all anywhere along its 5- to 6-mile length. The newer Gaviotas and Sabalo beaches, still farther out, are now even more popular, particularly with the surfboarding set. All beaches are open to the public and not in any way private. Watch for warning flags when jellyfish are in—they can sting. There is also some swimming along Olas Altas in town, but the shore is narrow and rocky and lacks any real beach.

Fishing. Mazatlán has been rated one of the best deep-sea fishing spots in the world by experienced anglers. From November through April, striped marlin running to 140 pounds are caught; from May to November, sailfish weighing 100 pounds or more are caught; and black marlin are found in the summer months. Dolphin are caught year round, as are many kinds of small game fish such as yellowtail, red snapper, rooster, and sea bass. Well-equipped fishing launches with crew cost $75 to $125 a day, or small boats can be rented for $10 per hour. Any hotel can arrange such reservations, or try Bill Heimpel's fleet of first-class boats (tel: 20-37 or 35-37) or Ernest Coppel's fleet (tel: 36-40; reservations at P.O. Box 204, Mazatlán).

Hunting. Good hunting of ducks and doves is found in the marshes some 60 miles to the south of Mazatlán. Duck season is from November 15 to March 15, and the limit is fifteen ducks per person. The Ávila Brothers arrange hunting, furnishing licenses, guides, and guns for duck, doves, deer, or jaguar.

Write to P.O. Box 221, Mazatlán (tel: 27-56 or 37-28). To bring your own guns, you must get a permit from the Mexican consulate in advance. Balboa Club de Mazatlán has a private duck-hunting preserve, and any member of a recognized private club in the United States can arrange to stay there and use club facilities, which are top-notch. Write to Balboa Club de Mazatlán, Apartado 402, Mazatlán, Sinaloa.

Jungle and Harbor Cruises. Boats leave twice a day from the fishing pier, going past the busy harbor and then up an inlet to a point where you transfer to smaller passenger boats for a trip through a palm-, banyan-, and cypress-covered area to an isolated river island. You can usually see many colorful birds and unusual fish. A brief stop for refreshment is made on the island. Most hotels sell tickets for under $10. The trip takes three hours. A two-hour harbor trip, no jungle, costs less.

Bullfights. During the winter, bullfights are usually held on Sundays at 4 P.M. Mazatlán has a small 3,000-seat ring. Check with your hotel.

Golf. A nine-hole course is available for play at the Club Campestre de Mazatlán, on the outskirts of town on the highway south. A new course, El Cid, located on Sabalo Road at the hotel of the same name, has eighteen holes. At both courses, greens fees are reasonable, caddies are available, there is a pro, and clubs are for rent. There is a tennis club near the Club Campestre.

Shopping. The usual variety of Mexican goods and crafts can be purchased in Mazatlán, and you will find any number of good stores on Olas Altas Boulevard. La Siesta Hotel has a good gift shop and also carries a big stock of English-language newspapers, magazines, and books, as well as postcards. A new *Arts & Crafts Center* has been opened across from the Playa del Rey Hotel on Gaviotas Beach with excellent goods and craftsmen at work. Open 9:30 A.M. to 7 P.M.

The *new municipal market* near the cathedral in town has fine goods and will save you lots of money. Try bargaining. There are several *modern supermarkets*, one just off the North Beach boulevard and another, much bigger one downtown on Serdán off Zaragoza. Make local inquiry. They carry a wide range of packaged and canned goods, frozen food, and, best of all, good fresh lobster and fair steaks at less than half stateside prices.

Trip to Copper Canyon. For those who wish a very special adventure, there is a railroad route north of Mazatlán 272 miles at Los Mochis. It is equipped with modern engine and cars and goes through the magnificent Barranca de Cobre ("Copper Canyon"), which is said to be larger than the Grand Canyon and even more awesome. You can simply drive to Los Mochis, or go by bus. For details, see page 221.

Trip to Baja California. An easier and no less fascinating trip is the ferry that goes daily over to the tip of the Baja California peninsula and the ancient port of La Paz. The ferry is an ultramodern luxury ship of considerable size with cabins, pool, theater, restaurant, and cocktail lounge. Cabin class is $24, with berth and private bath, while a deck chair costs only $4. Cars can be taken and are very useful at the La Paz end. The ferry leaves from municipal docks at the south end of the city near El Faro. The Chula Chula tourist center on the North Beach boulevard sells tickets.

GUAYMAS

Travelers driving down the Pacific Coast Highway from Arizona or California are apt to spend their first night in Guaymas, which is only about 260 miles from Nogales, after passing through the capital of Sonora state, Hermosillo. Either place has good accommodations and is within striking distance of Mazatlán for the second night. Guaymas is well worth visiting for a weekend by itself. Hermosillo makes a good luncheon stop.

Guaymas has a variety of places where you can stay, although none of them can pretend to be luxury establishments. But, in their way, they are good. They vary from the older Playa de Cortés, a mission-type hotel, to the very new Posada de San Carlos with pink bungalows overlooking San Carlos Bay. Hermosillo has one luxurious new motel, the Valle Grande, and other fair motels and hotels.

Guaymas is for the weekender who wishes to stay in a cottage and fish, or for a pleasant overnight stop. It is not a resort, at least at this writing, where you will find the amenities of Acapulco or Mazatlán. There are several good trailer parks on

San Carlos Bay about 10 miles north of Guaymas—Casas Moviles with patios right on the water is notable.

Guaymas has one of the more interesting harbors in the world, with the small village clutched in an encircling ring of mountains. Some mornings the water is mirror-smooth and reflects with unbelievable reality the ships in the harbor. The evening sunsets display myriad hues which impart a particular glow and charm to the bay.

The beaches are shifting and pebbly, and the two main hotels, the Playa and the Miramar, are located away from town and across a ridge on the beach at Bocachibampo Bay. They can be reached by leaving Guaymas to the north and, just outside town, taking the paved, well-marked fork to the left.

The full name of Guaymas is Villa de San Fernando de Guaymas. It has been primarily a fishing village since its founding in 1769. There are some 25,000 people living there today, most of them active in the shrimp and oyster trade, a large commercial business engaged principally in shipping to the United States. The government has recently built a petroleum-shipping facility in Guaymas and is endeavoring to build up the port program. The rail line from Nogales to Guadalajara passes through the Guaymas junction, 5 miles away.

Going to Guaymas

Presumably most persons going to Guaymas will either be weekend visitors from Arizona, or en route on the Pacific Coast Highway south to Mazatlán and possibly Guadalajara and Mexico City. Guaymas makes a fine stop. Transportes de Norte de Sonora runs air-conditioned buses to Guaymas from Nogales, and Tres Estrellas runs buses from Mexico City to Guaymas. The Sud Pacífico Railroad carries passengers, but accommodations are not too comfortable. Aeromexico is the principal airline flying to Guaymas.

Restaurants in Guaymas

Playa de Cortés dining room   Moderate
  In hotel of same name about 4 miles out of town to the north. Food once had great reputation. Still good. Fresh seafood a specialty. Good air-conditioned bar.

Las Playitas Restaurant   Moderate
On 20th Street in town head west to road to naval base that circles
Guaymas Bay; restaurant is about 5 miles out. A popular and
picturesque restaurant that many say is the best in town. Serves
steaks, seafood, Mexican and Oriental food. Clean. Bar. Open 8
A.M. till midnight. Music in evening.

El Paradise   Inexpensive to moderate
At No. 32 XIII Rodríguez Street (turn off main street in town at
Banco Nacional toward west one block) near Hotel Malena. This is
a top-notch seafood restaurant, extremely clean, but small with only
eight tables. Lobster, shrimp, frogs' legs are among specialties.
Good fish soup. Catch their own seafood. Air-conditioned. Open
10 A.M. till 10 P.M. VISA.

HOTELS IN GUAYMAS

Playa de Cortés (*71 rooms*)   Moderately expensive
Older hotel 4 miles north of town on bay. Air-conditioned. Excellent
dining room. Dancing. Heated pool. Fishing, waterskiing, pitch-
and-putt golf. Operated by Gandara Hotels, P.O. Box 66, Guaymas,
Sonora, México. Tel: 20-121.

Posada de San Carlos (*50 rooms*)   Moderate
A group of four-room villas and air-conditioned motel rooms about
13 miles from Guaymas on the beach at Bahía San Carlos. Modern,
attractively decorated. Maid service, restaurant, cocktail lounge,
pool. Near Guaymas Yacht Club. Turn off Highway 15 seven miles
north of Guaymas. All cards. Reservations: P.O. Box 57.

Miramar Hotel-Motel (*100 rooms*)   Inexpensive
Just north of Guaymas then 2 miles off to edge of Bocachibampo
Bay on Gulf of California on well-marked side road. Modern two-
story motel wing has air-conditioned rooms, many with balconies
overlooking sea. Beach immediately available and good fishing.
Restaurant, nightclub, cocktail lounge of modest type. Also has
older bungalows, and trailer park with seventy-five spaces. All
cards. Write to María Elena Dávila, P.O. Box 31. Tel: Guaymas 2-00-
36.

Motor Hotel Valle Grande Triana (*33 units*)   Moderate
On Bahía San Carlos; turn into San Carlos 7 miles north of Guaymas
on Highway 15. On beach. Pool. Most cards. No pets. Air conditioning. Bar. Reservations recommended. P.O. Box 911, Guaymas.
Tel: San Carlos 29 or Hermosillo 4-45-70.

Guaymas Inn (*24 rooms*)   Inexpensive
On main highway north of town. Air-conditioned. Restaurant, bar.
Pool. Small, modest, nice gardens.

Casitas Catalina   Moderately expensive
On San Carlos Bay 6 miles north of Guaymas on Highway 15, then
7 miles west to edge of bay. Air-conditioned two-bedroom luxury
apartments. Maid service. Beach a short drive away. Good view of
harbor. P.O. Box 615, Guaymas, for reservations.

San Carlos Bay Apartments (*36 units*)   Moderately expensive
On San Carlos Bay with good view of harbor and fishing vessels.
Air-conditioned two-bedroom units with kitchenettes. Discount by
week. Offers fishing safari: three days, two nights, five meals,
tackle, boat, guide. Write to 21 Elias Street, Nogales, Sonora, México.
Tel: Nogales 2-27-86.

Motel Flamingos (*42 rooms*)   Inexpensive
In Colonia Loma Linda. Small, austere.

Armida Hotel (*27 rooms*)   Inexpensive
On highway in town. Older, worn. No cards.

Hotel Rubí (*110 rooms*)   Inexpensive
Commercial-type hotel in center of town.

TRAILER PARKS IN GUAYMAS

Casas Moviles de San Carlos (*178 spaces*) $4–$5
Turnoff 6 miles north of Guaymas going 7 miles west on paved side
road to San Carlos Bay. Near Guaymas Yacht Club. Sites are terraced
up from beach, a bit rocky but fine for swimming, and many have
flowers or palms and all connections. Excellent informal patio
restaurant and bar well worth slow service. Laundry. Boat launching
ramp. No pool. No cards. Write to Apartado 212, San Carlos,
Guaymas, Sonora, México.

Tecalai (*180 spaces*) $3 for two
Five miles west of junction with Highway 15, and then west 7½
miles on access road. All hookups, showers, laundry. Pool. Beach
across street. P.O. Box 89, San Carlos.

Teta Kawi (*115 spaces*) $2 for three
Beyond Tecalai (see directions above). Paved slots, showers, laundry,
recreation hall, boat ramp. Near beach. P.O. Box 671, San Carlos.

La Bahía Trailer Park (*80 spaces*) $4
Turn west in town on 20th Street and circle Guaymas Bay toward
naval base. Modern establishment with all hookups, long-term
discounts, showers, boat launching. P.O. Box 375, Guaymas.

Las Playitas Trailer Park (*46 spaces*) $4
Same location as La Bahía (above) on far side of Guaymas Bay but
a mile farther on. Has excellent restaurant with steaks, Mexican
food. All connections. Showers, toilets. Concrete patios. Boat launching, barbecue pits. Cocktail lounge. P.O. Box 327, Guaymas.

WHAT TO DO IN GUAYMAS

Swimming and fishing are the prime attractions. You can rent
boats and tackle at any of the hotels or at the docks in town.
One of the things to do is to enjoy the fine seafood at the
restaurant at the Playa de Cortés, which is open to the public.
There are also some fair restaurants in town.

From Guaymas, you can fly on Aeromexico to La Paz in Baja
California on every day except Sunday, at a round-trip fare of
less than $50. There are flights three days a week to Nogales
and on other days to Tijuana. There are also flights to Mazatlán
and Hermosillo. Hughes Air West also serves Guaymas.

Flying to La Paz can be an entire vacation in itself. Across the
Gulf of California, also known as the Sea of Cortés, lies the
long, mountainous, and rugged peninsula of Lower California.
Baja California is no longer one of the really isolated preserves
of old Mexico, but is still filled with little-known villages and
bays. The fishing and hunting are extremely good. (See Chapter
8.)

HERMOSILLO

Hermosillo, capital of the state of Sonora, is 90 miles north of
Guaymas on the road to Nogales, and is an optional stop for
visitors traveling on this road.

It is a modern city which has prospered as one of the principal
trading centers for the fertile northwestern area of Mexico. From
this area come great crops of wheat, cotton, and corn. Modern
irrigation projects in the Yaqui Valley and the Mayo River Valley,

plus thousands of heavy-flowing deep wells, have helped to recover vast areas of desert.

Hermosillo is a city of over 100,000, with modern, air-conditioned hotels and a bustling atmosphere. It has fine homes and country clubs, and is not unlike the prosperous towns north of the border. At the same time, it still has much of the frontier atmosphere.

The city was named for José María González Hermosillo, a revolutionary leader in the war for Mexican independence. Many of the buildings are old Spanish colonial in style, but at the same time the ultramodern buildings of the University of Sonora, especially the strikingly handsome Abelardo Rodríguez Museum on the campus, are well worth seeing as examples of the best in modern Mexican architecture. The museum is named after a president of Mexico who came from this area and did much to promote industry here.

RESTAURANTS IN HERMOSILLO

Restaurant del Mar   Moderately expensive
In town at Serdán and Calle 17 six blocks west of main plaza. Complete menu. Cocktails and entertainment. Open noon till 11:30 P.M. Closed Tuesdays. Most cards. Tel: 2-02-26.

Valle Grande coffee shop and dining room   Moderate
Located on main highway toward north of town in huge new motel of same name, this is probably the best dining place in Hermosillo. American food. Open for breakfast and until midnight. Coffee shop prices moderate, dining room expensive.

Merendero Colores   Moderately expensive
At Matamoros and Jalisco, within short distance of motel row at north part of town. Pleasant outdoor patio dining under exotic yucca trees. Specializes in barbecued steak served in heaping splendor. Hot sauce, tortillas. Fancy fruit soft drinks, cold beer. Music Sundays at noon. Good service. Captain is José Savedra.

Las Playitas Restaurant   Moderately expensive
On Playitas peninsula 5 miles south on Varadero road, a local favorite with seafood, Mexican and U.S. dishes. Bar. Open 7 A.M. till 11:30 P.M. Tel: 2-27-27.

Merendero La Huerta   Moderate
At No. 105 San Luis Potosí, also near motel row. Very plain restaurant

with bare tables, but serves excellent seafood at reasonable prices. Air-conditioned. English thin, so point.

El Petate   Inexpensive
In town at Monterrey 29. Modest air-conditioned restaurant with Mexican dishes.

Jo Wah   Inexpensive
A good, clean, modern Chinese restaurant just beyond the civic auditorium on main street in town. About four blocks from San Alberto Hotel. Open noon and night. Reasonable prices. Carnet, VISA.

Mexican-Italian Club   Moderate
Upstairs in building diagonally across from San Alberto Hotel in center of town, over Bona Gift Shop. Fine Italian food. Open to public.

La Posada de Kino   Moderate
In town at Veracruz and Segunda. Serves good steaks and features a trio.

HOTELS AND MOTELS IN HERMOSILLO

Motel Valle Grande (*104 rooms*)   Moderately expensive
This is a big, new, handsome Spanish-style motel with luxurious rooms in colonial decor, fully air-conditioned. TV. Pool in center of courtyard. Bar, dining room, nightclub with dancing, coffee shop open early till midnight. On main highway at north end of Hermosillo. All cards. Reservations at Apartado 988, Hermosillo, Sonora, México. Tel: 4-45-70.

Hotel Internacional (*110 rooms*)   Expensive
An ultramodern hotel and at the moment the best in Hermosillo. Located in town on Route 15 at Rosales and Moselia. Well-furnished air-conditioned rooms, some TV. Pool and wading pool. Secured parking. Dining room and bar open 7 A.M. till 11 P.M. Entertainment. P.O. Box 686. Tel: 3-89-60.

Motel Gandara (*100 rooms*)   Moderate
Its newer section with central air conditioning is one of the better places in Hermosillo, older section bungalow-type improved and less expensive. In motel row on Highway 15 north of town. Pool in garden section. Dining room and coffee shop open 7 A.M. to midnight. Cocktail lounge. Rental TV. All cards. Reservations at Apartado 686. Tel: 3-68-85.

Motel Bugambilia (*53 rooms*)   Inexpensive
An older motel in motel row on Highway 15 north of town. Neatly landscaped grounds and bungalow-type rooms. New section of sixteen rooms. Air-conditioned. Coffee shop. Most credit cards. Tel: 3-89-20.

El Encanto (*42 rooms*)   Inexpensive
On Highway 15 north of town, this is an old colonial-type structure with rooms on modest side but comfortable. Small pool among shade trees. Air-conditioned. Restaurant. All cards. Tel: 3-75-50.

San Alberto Hotel (*130 units*)   Moderate
On main highway in very center of town, a modern air-conditioned commercial-type hotel. Pool, dining room, coffee shop. Most credit cards. P.O. Box 181. Tel: 2-18-00.

TRAILER PARKS IN HERMOSILLO

Mazacoba Trailer Park (*30 spaces*) $3
On Highway 15 at north end of town. All connections. Wall-enclosed spaces. Concrete patios, barbecue pits. Purified water, laundry, toilets, bathrooms. Recreation room with TV. P.O. Box 318. Tel: 3-70-32.

El Capitán Trailer Park (*70 spaces*) $3
On Highway 15 north of town. All connections. Landscaped grounds, purified ice, bathhouse, barbecue pits, free emergency auto service within 20 miles. P.O. Box 328. Tel: 3-43-39.

THINGS TO SEE IN HERMOSILLO

The Plaza Zaragoza, in the center of town, has the cathedral on one side. The *Parque Madero* with its gardens is a fine place for a stroll. Hermosillo has always grown a wide variety of fruits, and one can see date palms as well as orange, fig, and pomegranate trees.

The business center features the modern building of *Banco de México*. It is always fun to sit in the terrace restaurant outside the *San Alberto Hotel*, over a coffee, watching the passersby.

The University of Sonora, the finest college in northwest Mexico, is some 2 miles northwest of downtown. An outstanding sight on the university campus is the *Abelardo Rodríguez Museum*, an ultramodern structure of white marble.

The Rodríguez Dam, reached via the country-club road, is one of the largest earth-fill dams in Mexico.

The country club offers golf, tennis, and swimming. It is possible to arrange for a guest card.

TRIP TO KINO'S BAY

A 69-mile side trip from Hermosillo to a beach and fishing area at Kino's Bay can be easily made over a paved road, Highway 16, leaving from Highway 15 in Hermosillo at Transversal Boulevard just before the university.

There is actually a New Kino and an Old Kino, and accommodations and beaches are at New Kino. The beaches are not the world's best, as there are frequent outcroppings of rock, but the swimming is good and the fishing is excellent. Boats for fishing can be rented at the Posada del Mar Motel. Shore fishing is popular at the Caverna del Seri beach area restaurant, where red snapper, mackerel, sea bass, crabs, and grouper are caught.

Near Kino's Bay are a number of islands, of which the largest is Tiburon or Shark Island. The bay is named after a Jesuit priest who was the first to explore this area, and who spent the years from 1680 until his death in 1711 establishing twenty-five missions in this wilderness. He was a remarkable horseman, cartographer, sailor, and priest. His remains are on view in the village of Magdalena near Santa Ana on Highway 15.

MOTELS AND TRAILER PARKS AT KINO'S BAY

Motel Kino Bay (*25 rooms*)   Moderate
  Six miles north of Old Kino on beach highway. Air conditioning, shower baths. Has own beach. Restaurant open 7:30 A.M. to 8:30 P.M. Reservations: P.O. Box 857, Hermosillo, Sonora, México. Tel: Hermosillo 4-14-92.

Posada del Mar (*48 rooms*)   Moderate
  One mile north of town on beach highway. Two-story motel with air-conditioned rooms, shower baths. High over beach, with pool, fishing, paved landing strip. P.O. Box 314, Hermosillo. Tel: Hermosillo 3-36-81.

Kino Bay Trailer Park (*120 spaces*) $4
  Six miles north of town on beach highway across from beach.

Connections, patios, bathhouse, laundry, grocery store, restaurant.
Reservations: P.O. Box 857, Hermosillo.

El Saguaro Trailer Park (*46 spaces*) $3
Five miles north of town on beach highway. All connections,
covered patios, bathhouse, laundry. P.O. Box 694, Hermosillo.

ALONG THE ROAD TO MAZATLÁN

In addition to the good motels and hotels in Hermosillo or
Guaymas, you have an opportunity to stop at other places
between Guaymas and Mazatlán, which is a fairly hard day's
drive and perhaps more than some care to attempt.

Ciudad Obregón, which is 80 miles south of Guaymas, has a
new luxury motel, the *Valle Grande,* with ninety-six air-conditioned rooms. It has a pool and wading pool, a restaurant, a bar
of first quality, and dancing and music most nights. Tel: 3-71-
40 or P.O. Box 39. The *Motel Costa del Oro,* also on the main
highway, has eighty-one rooms with air conditioning, pool,
dining room, and cocktail lounge. Tel: 3-70-75.

Navajoa. Forty miles farther on, in Navajoa, there is a thirty-
eight-room *El Rancho Motel* with air-conditioned rooms in a
rustic setting and with a pool. Tel: 2-00-04. The *Nuevo Motel del
Río,* open all year, has a pool and a restaurant open from 7 A.M.
till 10:30 P.M. that serves beer and wine. Tel: 2-03-31. *Alameda
Trailer Park* has fifty-one spaces.

ÁLAMOS

Just 33 miles off Highway 15 at Navajoa, you can find the lost
village of Álamos, a colonial gem of a onetime prosperous
mining town, once the capital of the area.

Álamos was founded in 1534 by the Spanish because of the
rich silver mines in the surrounding Sierra Álamos. At that
time, it was on the royal highway from Mexico City to San
Francisco. Large homes, many in Moorish style, were built to
house the wealthy governors and miners, and there was an
attractive plaza with an austere but commanding mission church

topped with a three-story bell tower. Cobblestone streets were laid.

When the mines were exhausted, Álamos was forgotten, and the new highways no longer passed through it. But its magnificent climate in winter, invigorating but warm, caused a colony of Americans to reclaim the ancient manor homes and restore them. Most famous is the Casa de los Tesoros, a block-square one-story colonial building with an inner courtyard surrounded by rooms. It is now used for a hotel (open only in winter).

The Hotel Los Portales was once the home of Don José María Almada, a wealthy Spaniard who owned one of the largest of the some forty silver mines, La Quintara. Los Portales was the scene of many lavish parties for the thirty-six children of Almada's several marriages.

His son, Cholo Almada, who in turn operated the silver mines, built a twelve-room mansion which was purchased and restored by a Californian. Another mansion, Los Delicios, once owned by another Almada, is open to the public for visits to see the beautiful manner in which it has been restored.

The last interesting note is that a native of Álamos grows a type of bean with small worms inside that became known in the United States as "Mexican jumping beans." His name is Joaquín Hernández, and he has earned a comfortable living selling to the United States market. In Álamos, they are known as *brincadores*.

WHERE TO STAY IN ÁLAMOS

Casa de los Tesoros (*16 rooms*)   Expensive
   In the center of town, a block and a half from the plaza. A true colonial building with many of the furnishings of the period. Rooms nicely kept. Small pool. Restaurant and cocktail service, fine food. Reservations imperative (open only October 1 to May 1). P.O. Box 12, Álamos, Sonora, México. Tel: 8-00-10.

Hotel Los Portales (*10 rooms*)   Moderate
   Older hotel, somewhat run-down but comfortable, with pleasant patio where drinks are served. P.O. Box 15. Tel: 8-01-11.

Dolisa Motel-Trailer Park (*5 rooms, 80 spaces*) $3
   On the highway as you come into the village. Pleasant walled

courtyard run by helpful Mexican couple. Pure water. All connections.

El Caracol Trailer Ranch (*24 spaces*) $4
Eight miles before you reach Álamos, this is a real fruit and cattle ranch but has patios and trailer connections, modern bathhouse. Restaurant open 7:30 A.M. to 9 P.M. Cocktails and beer served. Riding at extra charge. Open only October 1 to May 1.

Acosta Trailer Ranch (*30 spaces*) $4
One mile beyond the town of Álamos, this is part of a large ranch which offers trailer parking and camping, with hunting, fishing, riding, and bird-watching. P.O. Box 67.

LOS MOCHIS AND TOPOLOBAMPO

One of the most scenic train trips in the world can be found passing through Los Mochis, a point some 94 miles beyond Navajoa on Highway 15. Los Mochis has some fair accommodations, and the nearby coastal town of Topolobampo, a typical fishing village, is worth visiting.

Train to Copper Canyon. The train, operated by Pacífico Railroad, stops at Los Mochis after originating in Topolobampo at 1:30 A.M. every day except Monday. It is a modern diesel engine with air-conditioned cars, a lounge, and bar car. A flatcar will carry your automobile if you wish to cut over to Chihuahua on the central highway.

You can take a four-hour ride past the scenic canyon, said by some to be four times larger than the Grand Canyon, to the Divisadero lookout point over the canyon, incredibly deep and rugged, and catch a return train in half an hour. There is a local hotel, *Copper Canyon Lodge,* forty-five minutes from Creel, and *cabins at Urique* where horseback riding, hiking, and motoring tours are available. The *Hotel Nuevo,* in front of the railroad station in Creel, also has modest but clean rooms at low rates.

Or stay on the train to Chihuahua, a twelve-hour trip, and return immediately. Round-trip fare is approximately $20. One of the great travel bargains in the world.

Los Mochis itself (the name means "The Turtles") is a market center for 250,000 prosperous farmers, thanks to new systems of irrigation from huge dams plus deep wells. They grow sugar cane, rice, cotton, and winter vegetables. Los Mochis was only a group of four huts in 1903 when Benjamin Johnston arrived from Philadelphia and started to grow sugar cane and later built a sugar mill (now owned by the Aaron Saenz group), one of the biggest in Mexico. Johnston laid out the streets, built a huge mansion, and saw Los Mochis grow fantastically. It now has 65,000 citizens. You can see the huge mansion, although its state of disrepair prevents tours.

Topolobampo is a rather scruffy little fishing village 10 miles away, but it has year-round swimming, fishing, and hunting (ducks love the rice fields). Nearby Las Animas Islands is a breeding place for sea lions, and fine for sunbathing and spearfishing. A five-minute canoe trip will get you there. Motor canoes can be rented.

Fishing can be excellent at Topolobampo with skipjack, yellowtail, Sierra mackerel, and roosterfish. From July until November, sailfish and marlin can be found. A new car ferry plies between Topo and La Paz, Baja California.

RESTAURANTS IN LOS MOCHIS AND TOPOLOBAMPO

México Restaurant   Inexpensive
Downtown in Los Mochis. Modest but has good grilled shrimp and other seafood.

Santa Anita dining room   Moderate
In hotel of same name in center of town. Features seafood. Cocktails. Open 7 A.M. till 11 P.M.

Bahía Restaurant   Inexpensive
A real wharf-type restaurant in Topolobampo. Serves shrimp scampi and fillets of fish. Very informal. Tables overlook port.

WHERE TO STAY IN LOS MOCHIS AND TOPOLOBAMPO

Holiday Inn (*100 rooms*)   Moderately expensive
A brand-new Holiday Inn on a hilltop on Route 15 in Los Mochis, with a view of El Fuerte Valley. Restaurant, pool, bar. Children under eighteen free. Reservations: Holiday Inn chain. Tel: 2-48-52.

Santa Anita Hotel (*130 rooms*)   Moderate
Modern fairly luxurious hotel in Los Mochis, fully air-conditioned. Good dining room featuring fish fillets. Also a colonial-decor supper

club with music and dancing. Arranges tours to Copper Canyon, fishing, hunting, and local sight-seeing. Reservations recommended. P.O. Box 159, Los Mochis, Sinaloa, México. Tel: 2-00-46.

El Dorado Motel (*43 units*)   Moderate
Two miles off Highway 15 on road into Los Mochis. New three-story building completely air-conditioned. Dining room specializes in charcoal-broiled steaks. Music and dancing nightly. Cocktail lounge. All cards. Manager: Bill Poulos. P.O. Box 412. Tel: 2-01-79.

Motel América (*42 rooms*)   Inexpensive
In Los Mochis on south side of town, near medical center. A modest but good two-story motel. Extra charge for air conditioning. Fair restaurant. All cards.

Chapman's Hotel (*42 units*)   Inexpensive
On road into Los Mochis at north end. A fairly good air-conditioned hotel, with good dining room featuring seafood and game in season. All cards.

Posada Real Motel (*26 units*)   Moderate
At north end of Los Mochis. A clean, well-run colonial-style motel. Good dining room. Pool. All cards.

Río Fuerte Trailer Park (*43 spaces*) $4
About 10 miles north of Los Mochis off Highway 15. All hookups. Bathrooms and showers. Pool, laundry. Tree-shaded area well guarded. Hunting and fishing available. Reservations through Chapman's Hotel.

Don Juan Trailer Park (*42 spaces*) $3
On Highway 15, 1½ miles north of Los Mochis. All connections. Bottled water, shower, laundry, groceries.

Topolobampo Yacht Club (*21 units*)   Moderate
In Topolobampo, 10 miles from Los Mochis. Operated by Santa Anita Hotel management. While modest, has air-conditioned rooms, a dining room, bar, pool. Fishing boats available. All cards. P.O. Box 159, Los Mochis.

CULIACÁN

At Culiacán, only 144 miles north of Mazatlán, there are *Motel San Luis* and *Motel Los Tres Ríos*, which are fair, and the *Motel Los Caminos*. All have pools and are air-conditioned. Just south of Culiacán you will cross the Tropic of Cancer.

We must note that many new motels are being built along the stretch of road between Culiacán and Mazatlán, and you will undoubtedly find new ones we don't list. We have only attempted to assure you that you will find at least one good motel in the town you set out for; if you find others, so much the better.

SAN BLAS

San Blas is probably the least-known of the Pacific seaside resorts, but next to Mazatlán, it is the most easily reached (on a paved road, surprisingly) from the interesting town of Tepic on the main northwest highway, halfway between Guadalajara and Mazatlán. You turn off 22 miles north of Tepic and go down Route 46 about a half hour's drive to San Blas. It is a little tropical town on the water, surrounded by lagoons, with only 1,800 population.

The drive is especially interesting, going through tropical forests, with huge palm trees on both sides of the road creating a green canyon. Just before reaching the coast, the road breaks out on a marshland.

San Blas is plagued by small gnats, which can be bothersome at certain times of the year. Insect repellents (bring your own) handle them nicely, however. And on my last visit there were none. So take your chances.

Hotels are scarce to nonexistent. But one drawing favorable comment is the *Casa Morales*, run by an American schoolteacher and her husband with the aid of their son. It is located in town, and rates are moderate. Table d'hôte meals are excellent. Trailers can park in the weed-grown yard in front of the *Playa Hermosa Hotel* about 2 miles south of the little town on the best beach (actually a large sandbar) in the area. The Playa Hermosa is too far gone to recommend, but with its whirling fans and its quiet bar (still serving good drinks), it is part of the tropic atmosphere, I guess.

Other trailer parks are scattered about. A hotel in an old mansion, *Los Flamingos Hotel*, has trailer parking across the street. The *Casino Colón*, on a gravel road on Matanchen Beach 2 miles off the highway, has full hookups and showers. *Los*

Cocos Trailer Park, in a palm grove near the beach, and El Dorado Trailer Park, on the road to the Playa Hermosa, also have full hookups and showers.

In town one good restaurant, the Torino, was functioning and served shrimp cocktail, filet Mexican style, broiled lobster, fish fillet, shrimp in garlic butter, chicken tacos, and an enchilada plate. Spaghetti could be cooked to order, as could turtle steak. The menu carried no prices, but we found the cost reasonable.

The beauty of San Blas somehow makes up for the lack of good accommodations and food. High on a rise of ground behind the little village, the stark stone ruins of the fortress and ancient mission church still stand looking out to sea. This was once the waterfront. Now the village is built on sands that drifted in, far below. But once these old Spanish cannons commanded the bay.

A guide can take you up to the old ruins, which have been partially restored and are well worth the visit. Banyan trees climb over everything. The bell has been removed, as it was cracked, and is now down in the town. But the old cannons are still very much in evidence. In fact, an entire old Spanish town was once on this site. Our guide was Jim Mendoza, usually to be found at the Playa Hermosa Hotel or the Buccanero Hotel.

Those who like San Blas—and they tend to be fanatically in favor of it—like it for the easygoing Utopian life the natives enjoy, each with his patch of ground given the village people under the land-reform laws decades ago. Coconuts are easily gathered, and crops such as papaya, bananas, and mangoes are so easily grown as to be constantly available for the picking.

Sue Cross, a trusted correspondent, reported after visiting San Blas: "If you want to feel like Humphrey Bogart and Katharine Hepburn, then it's San Blas. The bugs are awful, tropical heat and no air conditioning, everything moldering, the local people are not congenial, and we crossed a quarter-mile sandbar to the beach."

What To Do in San Blas

Aside from the usual swimming and sight-seeing, this is a fine place for deep-sea fishing, as the local fishermen, equipped with slow but seaworthy craft, really know how to fish. If an engine breaks down, they have sails to get them to shore.

A most interesting trip is one by dugout canoe to the tiny island of *Mexcaltitlán*, a dot in the mouth of the San Pedro River. Your hotel can make arrangements. On the island are a miniature fishing village, perfect in its simplicity, and a stately church with cracked bells in its tower.

The ruins of the old Spanish town are on the crest of a hill overlooking San Blas. If you walk over to see the ruins of the old town and what is left of the old church, you might like to think of this extract from Longfellow's poem, "The Bells of San Blas," which was the last poem he wrote (in 1882):

What say the bells of San Blas
To the ships that southward pass
From the harbor of Mazatlán?
To them it is nothing more
Than the sound of surf up the shore;
Nothing more to master or man.

But to me, a dreamer of dreams,
To whom what is and what seems
Are often one and the same,
The bells of San Blas to me
Have a strange wild melody
And are something more than a name . . .

They are a voice of the past;

Of an age that is fading fast;
Of a power austere and grand
When the flag of Spain unfurled
Its fold o'er this western world,
And the priest was lord of the land.

The chapel that once looked down
On the little seaport town
Has crumbled into the dust,
And on an oaken beam below
The bells swing to and fro
And are green with mold and rust. . . .

15

Manzanillo, Barra de Navidad, and Chamela

MANZANILLO, halfway down the west coast of Mexico between Puerto Vallarta to the north and Acapulco and Ixtapa to the south, has long been considered a bustling port city in a tropical setting with beaches and some small hotels. The mountains dip down to a seacoast with some fabulous beaches of white sand overhung with thick groves of palms, but Manzanillo was a fairly difficult place to travel to until some recent changes.

Now it is no longer a forgotten and isolated paradise. There is a new multimillion-dollar jetport just north of the city with regularly scheduled flights by Aeromexico. There is a spectacular new coastline highway, Mexico 200, paved all the way to Puerto Vallarta, and work is going on to eventually link it with Acapulco to the south.

The construction of one of the most fantastic hotels in the world, the Hotel Las Hadas, on Peninsula de Santiago, 6 miles north of the city of Manzanillo, has brought to the area its own jet set and turned it into a major tourist attraction. Hotel Las Hadas is operated by a sophisticated chain, the Princess Hotels, which also has leading resort hotels in Acapulco and Bermuda.

Las Hadas was planned and financed by a Bolivian tin millionaire, Antenor Patino. Built on the hillside overlooking the bay, it is a group of buildings resembling an *Arabian Nights* village with clusters of villas, all with balconies looking out on the beach below and the bay beyond, all dripping in purple and red bougainvillea. Adjoining the hotel is an eighteen-hole golf course. There are swimming pools and a fleet of electric carts (no cars permitted) to get you about.

Manzanillo is known as perhaps the best sailfishing port in the world, and an international sailfish tournament is held there each winter. Las Hadas has become famous as the scene of the world backgammon championship.

Manzanillo is almost south and slightly west of Guadalajara, a distance of 230 miles. It is possible to drive there over an all-weather road which leaves the Guadalajara–Mexico City highway at two points. One is only 27 miles from Guadalajara, and the other is 100 miles from Guadalajara at the little village of Jiquilpan. Both roads wind down through Colima, the capital of one of Mexico's smallest states, and on the shoreline where tropical hills jut out to form the Bahía de Santiago at Manzanillo.

By Air. American Airlines has direct flights via Mexico City to Manzanillo. Aeromexico flies regularly from Mexico City to Manzanillo, usually via Guadalajara, while Aeromexico has direct flights between Manzanillo and Los Angeles.

The beaches of Manzanillo lie largely to the north of the city. They include the Playa Azul, the Playa Santiago, the Santiago peninsula, and the famed Audiencia Beach, which is the best in Manzanillo. Audiencia is about 7 miles north of town and off on a cobblestoned road leading a mile or so down to the beach, which is open to the public. The entire scene is delightful, with the arms of the bay extending around a rock island rising in the very center of the bay and called "the pulpit"; hence the surrounding land is the "audiencia." Several thatched-roof trailer parks are here.

Santiago Bay just north of Audiencia has a less attractive beach, but there are several hotels on the beach. Between the port and this area, the Bay of Manzanillo has the beaches of Playa Azul, Olas Altas, and Playa Miramar, where surfing is the best. Along this stretch of road, called locally "the strip," one finds a number of motels and restaurants. Most are fairly modest, but there are indications that the new condominiums arising on the hillsides in the area will bring with them some fancy restaurants and nightclubs. Playasol Condominium at Las Hadas is the largest; Roca del Mar and Palomar, though smaller, are also attractive. They usually have apartments by week or month. There are few phones along the strip, and taxis are rare but possible. Buses do go from Playa Santiago into town.

Trips can be made to beach areas somewhat farther away, and there you will find remoteness and privacy. These are at Melaque to the north, where the great Barra de Navidad beach is located (see Chapter 11), and Cuyutlán to the south, where at certain times of the month 30-foot-high waves come crashing in. They are known as the "green rollers" and are not only impressive to look at but downright dangerous. They usually occur in April or May.

Fishing is done from the wharf in town, where a number of stores have tackle and boats for rent, or you can charter a craft with experienced sea captains by going to the Fishing Boat Owners Association, Niños Héroes 543, right in the port area on the waterfront.

Boating. There is a marina capable of handling 100 yachts at Las Hadas, while you can launch smaller craft at a ramp in the port area. Luxury steamers plying between Los Angeles and Mexico's west coast and as far as Panama often stop in Manzanillo.

The Town. In the town there is a pleasant tree-shaded plaza with benches, and you'll enjoy a pause there on your way down for the morning newspapers. Along the road one can see coconut and banana plantations. Going into town involves a bit of maneuvering, for a new ship basin causes the highway into town to take a detour. Once you are in the port town (population 40,000), you find a typical Mexican coastal city but one marked by a number of steamers, tankers, and large areas of oil storage tanks. All in all, it is rather commercial with small crowded streets. The plaza is worn, and the Colonial Hotel, while good for fishermen, is ancient. It does have a dining room serving good seafood.

A Port City. Manzanillo has been a seaport since the days of Cortés. Later it was used for the Far East trade. Since then, it has been used to ship copra, coffee, hardwoods, and bananas.

Today Manzanillo is said to be the busiest port on the west coast of Mexico, as it has the best rail connections to the interior of Mexico. Thus, coastal tankers load here, cotton is shipped to the Far East, and copra, coffee, bananas, and other traditional exports are sent from here, while machinery and consumer goods are brought in.

There is said to be buried treasure in the Manzanillo sands; the steamer *Golden Gate* caught fire near here on July 21, 1862, while carrying $1,500,000 in gold bullion and silver specie, and her captain headed her for Manzanillo, where she foundered in the heavy surf and the treasure disappeared under the shifting sands. In 1900, an American, Duncan Johnston, led an expedition which recovered some $500,000 in gold, but the rest of the treasure is still there. One chest alone, according to the U.S. Treasury Department, contained $35,000 in $50 gold pieces, part of the only octagonal coins ever minted by the United States, and worth several hundred dollars each today.

RESTAURANTS IN MANZANILLO

Legaspi   Expensive
The gourmet restaurant at Las Hadas, noted for its distinguished continental cuisine. Has a splendid view to be enjoyed while dining. Expensive.

El Terral   Expensive
Also at Las Hadas. A more moderately priced open-air restaurant offering grilled steaks and seafood, game such as rabbit and duck, and turtle steaks.

El Penasco   Moderate
At Hotel Vida del Mar. A good restaurant open for breakfast, lunch, and dinner. Has an ocean sea-cliff view.

Manolo's Restaurant   Moderately expensive
At Las Brisas. Very popular. Noted for its langostino, or crayfish.

Crown and Trident   Moderately expensive
A new restaurant just south of the Santiago peninsula in the Las Hadas area. Rated good. Closed Sundays.

Mesón de los Perros   Moderate
Located 1½ miles northwest on Playa Santiago highway, across from Playa Azul. Serves seafood specialties and also Mexican, German, and American dishes. Cocktail lounge. Open 1 P.M. to 1 A.M. AE, DC. Reasonable.

La Chiripa   Moderate
A tropical open-air restaurant, American-run. At kilometer 3 on main highway by Manzanillo Bay. Wonderful shrimp in garlic butter, small lobster broiled, sea bass, Mexican plates. Ice-cold draft beer. Open noon and night, closed Mondays. Near Hotel La Posada. No cards.

Hotel Playa de Santiago dining room   Moderately expensive
Overlooking sea and open to public. Serves very fine seafood morning, noon, and night. On Santiago Bay about 5 miles from town.

Colonial Hotel dining room   Inexpensive
While a run-down hostelry, the Colonial does have a fairly decent dining room built in Spanish style. Serves some good seafood and is apt to have seafood soup, turtle steaks, or more unusual fare.

El Dorado Restaurant   Inexpensive
On the far end of Playa Azul on the strip as you drive toward Las Hadas. A popular restaurant with good prices. Noted for its soups and excellent food in general.

Red Snapper   Inexpensive
Small fish restaurant on the strip, facing Playa Azul.

La Hamburgesa   Inexpensive
In town. Serves good hamburgers, French fries, ice cream.

The Hatchet Cover   Inexpensive
In town. Serves a variety of pizza.

La Red (*Barra de Navidad*)   Moderately expensive
A large fish restaurant, but all the way to Navidad (about 20 miles). Has marvelous lobster, shrimp, and fish.

Nightclubs in Manzanillo

La Palapa
At Las Hadas. By far the fanciest in the area, but also expensive. Dancing nightly in a tropical garden.

El Cangrejo
On the Playa Azul road. A popular spot with spectacular lighting, stereo sound, and late hours.

El Staril
A Polynesian-type nightclub beyond Arco Iris on main highway. Very picturesque with palm roof and towers, and a pool inside the gate. Band and dance floor.

Morocco and **La Jirafa**
Two discotheques in the Las Hadas area.

Hotels and Motels in Manzanillo

Hotel Las Hadas (*200 rooms, 50 bungalows*)   Very expensive
Luxury establishment built on the hillside overlooking Tesoro Bay, which is the north ring of the main Manzanillo Bay. About 6 miles from town and 1 mile west up steep hill. Amid palms, rooms look

out on lovely view of bay. Enlarged in 1971 to have 200 new rooms plus the 50 former white Moorish-style bungalows. Open-air dining room. Pool. Fishing. Eighteen holes golf. Tennis. Scuba diving. Write for reservations: Apartado Postal 158, Manzanillo, Colima, México. Or contact any Princess Hotels International offices in major U.S. and Mexican cities. In Mexico City, tel: 566-22-11. Tel: 2-00-00.

Hotel Vida del Mar (*200 suites and villas*)   Expensive
On a hilltop peninsula overlooking the Pacific. Own beach. Tennis courts (two lighted), golf, water sports, fishing. Restaurants, bar. Toll-free tel: (800) 854-3380; in Calif. (800) 432-7045. Tel: 2-01-86.

Hotel Playa de Santiago (*85 rooms*)   Moderate
On the beach outside town. Also bungalows. Fishing boats. Open-air dining room and cocktail bar. Accepts DC. P.O. Box 90. Tel: 2-00-55.

Hotel La Posada (*23 rooms*)   Moderate
Six miles north of town, 1 mile off Highway 200, and right on Playa Azul beach. A rather informal place with an honor system bar. Cottage units share bath; hot water only in showers. P.O. Box 135. Tel: 2-08-05.

Casa Blanca Alamar (*58 rooms*)   Moderate
On Santiago Beach just off Highway 200 as it approaches Manzanillo from north. Two-story hotel set in well-kept gardens. Rooms not air-conditioned. Open-air restaurant with good food. Large saltwater pool. No cards. Apartado Postal 237.

Posada del Sol (*10 rooms*)   Inexpensive
On main bay on Highway 200, right on beach. Small rooms with kitchenettes. Clean pool. No cards.

Motel Playa del Tesoro (*10 units*)   Inexpensive
On Treasure Beach, about 6 miles from Manzanillo on Santiago highway, then 1 mile south to beach. Modest rooms, but secluded beach is good. P.O. Box 158.

Motel Marbella (*10 units*)   Moderate
On Playa Azul 4 miles north of town on Highway 200. Shower baths. Small pool. Open-air restaurant from 3 to 6 P.M. P.O. Box 232.

TRAILER PARKS IN MANZANILLO

Audiencia Trailer Park (*55 spaces*) $3
Must be one of the most fabulous locations in the world, with trailers parked under palms, the lovely Audiencia Beach immediately in front, and the Audiencia Bay with its high rock island.

Located off Highway 200, 6 miles north of Manzanillo, 1 mile west to coast. All connections. Very busy in winter. Write for reservation.

Don Felipe Trailer Park (*20 spaces*) $2
Six miles north of Manzanillo on Highway 200. Connections, shower, laundry, pool. Near beach. Reservations necessary in winter.

La Bahía Trailer Park (*20 spaces*) $2
Three and one-half miles north on highway. Connections, shower, laundry, groceries, bottled gas, ice. Near beach.

BARRA DE NAVIDAD AND CHAMELA

Barra de Navidad ("Christmas Bay") is a small resort area about 30 miles north of Manzanillo on Route 200. It is popular with people in Guadalajara, which is about 150 miles away on Highway 80. Barra de Navidad has a fine beach sheltered by some islands, and a few modest hotels, of which the best is the Hotel Melaque, which is right on Melaque Bay and Barra de Navidad. It is a popular, moderately priced family hotel with 200 rooms. The dining room looks out over the sea and serves all types of fish and seafood. Offices are in Guadalajara, Prisciliano Sánchez 437 (tel: Guadalajara 4-56-05).

At Playa Blanca, still farther north, is located the Pacific coast version of Club Méditerranée. Contact Club Méditerranée in any major city. They arrange full charter flights for their members as part of the overall fee.

Chamela is a brand-new resort area that is only now under planning, but which many observers feel will be a major tourist point in the future. It is a coastal stretch north of Barra de Navidad and reachable by Highway 200. Those with campers can find some wonderful beach areas here, but at this writing we do not have any first-class hotels to recommend.

For additional information on the Barra de Navidad area, see Chapter 11.

16

Mexico City

Diego Rivera, certainly the best known and among the greatest of the Mexican muralists, could be seen in my day sitting on a scaffolding in various public buildings, wearing his overalls and his floppy hat, and one could interview him while he worked. There was always a story for a journalist in need.

On his great mural, "Sunday in Alameda Park," which can now be seen in a handsome lobby chamber in the Del Prado Hotel, he painted among other things a banner saying DIOS NO EXISTE, or "God Doesn't Exist." This provoked demonstrations culminating when Catholic students broke into the hotel and knifed out the offending phrase. Later he was prevailed upon to repaint it with the words indecipherable. This satisfied everyone. Diego was, of course, referring to Mexico's rebellion against the Church, and the promulgation of the anticlerical laws which still exist.

Another time Diego, who looked a bit like a giant toad to some, painted a portrait of a beautiful, though somewhat bohemian, young poetess named Pita Amor. It was duly shown in a highly publicized exhibition in the cultural center of the country, the Palace of Fine Arts. Only then did some reporter, perhaps tipped off, look behind the portrait of Pita. There Diego had scrawled, "On this day, this portrait being finished, Pita and I gave ourselves to each other without any restraint whatsoever."

Juan O'Gorman, my favorite Mexican artist, who is noted for having done the natural-stone exterior of the twelve-story University of Mexico library, built himself a home in a cave in San Angel, and furnished and landscaped it delightfully. When I once stopped by to ask how to find Rivera's museum, O'Gorman, who is as self-effacing and kind as one can be, took time to draw me a little map, and illustrate it with priceless sketches of things along the way.

THERE IS NO DOUBT that the dynamic hub of the entire Republic of Mexico lies in its capital—Mexico City. It is not only the largest city and the seat of the federal government, but historical development of the nation, even in pre-Hispanic days, evolved about this particular site, for it was also the Aztec capital, Tenochtitlán.

Lying in a long valley high in the mountains of central Mexico, the capital is one of the world's largest cities, with a population, including the suburbs, now estimated at 12 million—larger than New York City. It is a city of broad boulevards and parks with multihued flowers. It has many modern skyscrapers, their glass fronts glistening in rows down the famed Paseo de la Reforma. One skyscraper, located at Madero 1, is forty-three floors high, the tallest building in Latin America.

There is opera, the symphony, ballet, and art museums. There are fine continental restaurants and places to dance. There are relics of Aztec days and historic buildings such as Chapultepec Palace, where Emperor Maximilian made his home. Outside the city there are the mysterious and centuries-old Pyramids of the Sun and Moon built by the Toltecs, while the ultramodern University of Mexico has an architecturally striking campus just south of the city on an old lava bed, spewed out of Ajusco volcano before the time of Christ.

As Mexico City has grown, with a rush of population from all other parts of the Republic, it has encountered the problems of many big cities in other parts of the world. There are monumental traffic jams to the point where one must advise visitors not to attempt to move about the city between 5 and 8 P.M. on weekdays (Saturdays and Sundays the city is almost deserted). At the same time, limited-access high-speed traffic arteries are being built, usually ringed about the city, and the afternoon rains and brisk breezes sometimes clear the air to make it look like the bright, flowery Mexico City we have always known.

THE WEATHER

Winter travelers from the United States come to Mexico City to warm up, summer travelers to cool off. Capitaliños themselves call the climate "eternal spring."

The tropic sun warms Mexico City at an altitude of 7,400 feet, and pine trees and palms, like winter and summer tourists, thrive in a delightful harmony of temperatures averaging 70 degrees. A rainy season begins usually in May and ends in

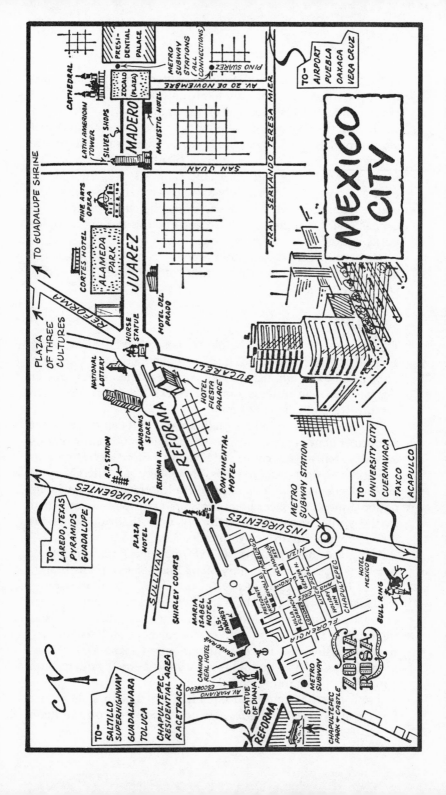

October. The summer rains fall in midafternoon and sometimes in the evening. Mornings are almost always sunny, and many visitors like the lush foliage of the rainy season. While the winters are usually dry, there is smog as well as occasional dust storms from the dry bed of Lake Texcoco. There is an unfortunate temperature inversion that holds a blanket of smog from the many new factories and the traffic exhausts over the city for days at a time, causing a heavy overcast even on days when the sun is shining brightly, and obscuring the snow-covered volcanoes. Winter weather is good for visiting the pyramids or parks without fear of a downpour.

Residents wear woolen suits the year round, but rarely get out a topcoat or a hat. Bring lighter cotton clothes for midday wear if you wish.

THE HOTELS

There are several hundred hotels in Mexico City, the best being as good as any in the world. If they are distinctive, it is because of onyx lobbies, mosaic murals, tropic gardens, silver drawer clasps, or Mayan numerals on the clocks (which nevertheless run on twentieth-century time).

One hotel has leaping fountain sprays in its suites, another a gourmet banquet room for ten which will put its entire chef's crew (also ten) at your command if you can afford such attention.

Engineers, doctors, physicists, archeologists, United Nations assemblages, and trade fairs have made Mexico City an international meeting place; hotel registers are especially crowded in the winter months. We strongly urge that you write for reservations a month or two in advance.

Along the main boulevard, Reforma, one finds big luxury hotels such as the twelve-story *María Isabel Sheraton*, the brand-new *El Presidente Chapultepec* (in the park), and the towering *Fiesta Palace*—whose five bars and five restaurants are the center of much activity. Just off Reforma are such fine luxury hotels as the original *El Presidente*, convenient to shops and restaurants, or, a bit farther out, there is the immense *Camino Real*, whose several mission-type buildings are scattered about gardens with a number of swimming pools.

Just a notch behind, and equally good though smaller, are *Del Paseo, Alameda, Reforma, Aristos, Bamer*—all on the main *paseo*—and also on the Reforma, but bigger, the *Del Prado*. The Del Prado has long been one of the leading hotels and has in its lobby the huge Diego Rivera mural, "Sunday in the Alameda" (park).

A second group of hotels can be called first-class but not luxurious, and their rates are decidedly lower. These include the *Genève* (long the queen of the famed "Pink Zone" or *Zona Rosa* with its fancy shops and good restaurants), the *Monte Cassino* nearby, the *Montejo* on Reforma, the *Purua Hidalgo* farther downtown, and such old favorites as the *Luma* and *Meurice*. A far-out in styling hotel right on Reforma is the redecorated *Emporio*—really wild! A convenient hotel in the Zona Rosa is the *Holiday Inn*. There is also one at the airport. The new *Florencia* is very Mexican in styling and located on the street of that name in the Pink Zone.

By far the best of the surviving colonial gems—if you like antique settings—is the *Gran Hotel* on the zócalo; others are the *De Cortés*, built around a sunny patio across the park from the Del Prado, the *Majestic* on the historic zócalo, and the *María Cristina*, off the lower Paseo de la Reforma. If you like a quiet hideaway right in the choice Genève district where the good shops and restaurants are, try the luxurious *Le Havre Internacional* on that street, whose extra-large rooms are commodious and comfortable.

The best motel in the very center of the city is the *Park Villa Motel* near Chapultepec Woods. A very good motel, *Atlauco*, can be found near the Churubusco Country Club. Other modern motels can be found on the highways entering the city, such as the *María Bárbara* or *Dawn* on the superhighway from the north, or the *Holiday Inn* at the airport.

A list of accommodations is given at the end of this chapter. Letters will reach most hotels addressed simply México, D.F., México. Actual prices are listed in Chapter 29.

RESTAURANTS

It is possible to order French bouillabaisse, Mexican enchiladas con mole, Swiss fondue, Polynesian curry, Italian cannelloni, or American-style sirloin steak all within Mexico City's smart new supper-club district. Here can be found some of the finest restaurants on the continent.

The *Rivoli*, at Hamburgo 123, next to El Presidente Hotel in the Genève district, is our favorite. It has quiet elegance, tasteful decor, soft music, and its lobster soufflé is out of this world. Dario Borzani is the owner. Telephone 5-25-68-62 or 5-28-77-89 to make sure you have a reservation.

Fine French cuisine and continental elegance can be found at *Les Moustaches*, Río Sena 88, just off the Reforma behind the American Embassy. The restaurant is a charmingly converted old mansion with a glass-covered courtyard. Requires coat and tie. Music. Closed Sundays. Accepts all cards. Telephone 5-33-33-90 for reservations. *Les Ambassadeurs*, Reforma 12 (tel: 5-35-57-14), has crystal chandeliers and plush chairs. *Delmonico's* at Londres 87 (tel: 5-10-40-40) has fine steaks and the best martinis, or you can get piano music with a quiet supper at Bill Shelburne's *El Paseo*, Reforma 146; we recommend the filet fondue bourguignonne. *Les Bon Vivants*, out in the wealthy residential district at Av. de las Palmas 726, serves gourmet food, and has a guitar player. Telephone 5-20-22-99.

The splashiest restaurants, if you are going for a big evening, are the *Del Lago*, an ultramodern dining spot in Chapultepec Park with an immense fountain jetting water sky-high, and top cuisine at top prices (call 5-15-95-85 for must reservations), open noon and evening and accepting all cards, or the more Mexican *Hacienda de los Morales*, in a restored great house off Reforma, where amidst torches and music a big menu includes many Mexican dishes (tel: 5-40-32-25). In the fabulous El Presidente Chapultepec Hotel, *Maxim's de Paris* is managed by the famous Parisian restaurant of the same name and offers the same four-star cuisine and service. Reservations are imperative. Call 254-00-33 or 254-00-25. *La Cava*, far out Insurgentes Sur (No. 2465) opposite the Obregón monument, is newly relocated in a large colonial-style structure and has an attractive courtyard, excellent food, and good service. Open from 1 P.M. till 1 A.M., it has Mexican and continental dishes. All cards. Telephone 5-48-82-75.

The most fun restaurant has to be *Anderson's*, at Paseo 400, where singing and joking waiters make fun of their actually very good food, including shrimp bisque and oysters Rockefeller (tel: 5-11-51-87). Also great fun is the *Mauna Loa*, out by University City, where they outdo Trader Vic's with Cantonese and Polynesian dishes and exotic drinks (tel: 5-48-68-84). All cards. *Los Comerciales,* out Insurgentes Sur at 2383, and in Ciudad Satélite, is another spot with clowning waiters and good food. Tel: 5-50-69-00.·

If you wish Mexican food, the Mexican dishes are unexcelled at *El Refugio,* Liverpool 116. A fine seafood restaurant which also offers true Mexican dishes is the *Colonial Loredo,* Hamburgo 29, near the Hilton. One of the best traditional restaurants in Mexico is *Prendes,* downtown at 16 de Septiembre No. 10, where excellent waiters serve the finest seafood amidst murals of Mexican history. Busy at noon. Yucatán food can be had at *Circulo Sureste, Lucerna,* and *Bucareli.* And almost all restaurants will carry some Mexican dishes such as *carne tampiqueña,* which is steak cooked with peppers and diced vegetables. Mexican food is seasoned to be hot, so have some cold beer ready to go with it. Sanborn's many restaurants have both a "Mexican plate" and enchiladas suizas, the latter being one of our very special recommendations. Try also the chicken enchiladas at the *Carmel Restaurant* at Genova 30, in the Genève district. Excellent.

If you like Spanish cuisine, a fascinating restaurant built in medieval style is the *Mesón del Cid* at Humboldt 61. It is like an old-world tavern, but its cuisine is authentic Spanish, from roast suckling pig (their specialty) to young lamb. Extremely fine wines. Tel: 5-21-19-40.

If you like skyline dining, we highly recommend the *La Joya Supper Club* atop the Continental Hotel, where you can dance and dine with the lights of Mexico City at your feet. On Thursday nights they have a gala buffet.

If your mood is for some pleasant evening in a country inn, you couldn't do better than to try *San Angel Inn,* about twenty minutes out Insurgentes Avenue, with a very gracious table. Reserve at 48-67-46. This inn is one of the most charming places in Mexico, open noon and evening, and accepts all cards. The *Del Prado Hotel Grill* has an excellent charcoal broil at reasonable prices. And, of course, *Sanborn's, Denny's,* and *VIP's* can be found all over town—on Reforma, in the Pink Zone, by the María Isabel, on Madero, and other places. These coffee shops are often open twenty-four hours a day and will not only whip you up a club sandwich with a thick malted milk, but also serve ham and eggs, hamburgers, and apple pie a la mode (and everything's immaculate, too). A pastrami on rye at *Kineret*, at Hamburgo and Genova, is good. They also have bagels and lox.

If it is Italian food you want, *La Gondola 21* will have it. *Cardinis*, Madrid 21, is a fine little Italian spot where you can dine inexpensively on spaghetti and a bottle of good red wine. Swiss food is at *Chalet Suizo*, Niza 37; Hungarian food at *Czardas*, Atoyac 93; German food at the *Bellinghausen* on Londres in the Pink Zone (also excellent seafood). *La Calesa* across the street on Londres is one of the best restaurants in the city.

A LARGER GUIDE TO MEXICO CITY

There are many other good restaurants in Mexico City, and you will find them all listed (with actual prices and reproductions of menus of forty top restaurants) in a separate volume, for it requires a complete book to handle the lot. *John Wilhelm's Guide to Mexico City* is on sale at magazine stands throughout the city; the entire volume is devoted to Mexico City. There is also a complete section on the many nightclubs in Mexico City, as well as opera, ballet, and burlesque. A subway map is included. *NOTE:* This companion guidebook, published by Editorial Tolteca in Mexico City, gives thirteen special trips about the city, with individual maps so that you can do your own walking, or driving, tours by yourself. Look in your hotel newsstand. If you do not find it available, write Dimsa, Apartado 1767; México, D.F., México.

THE SUBWAY AND BUSES

Mexico has a new underground transport system, known as "El Metro" and indicated by a large *M*, and it has been called the finest subway in the world. There are three lines, interconnecting. One runs from Chapultepec Park, roughly paralleling Reforma, to the airport on the other side of the city, while other lines shoot off at right angles and head south toward Xochimilco and toward University City. Biggest stations are at Insurgentes and Chapultepec (near the Pink Zone and convenient for tourists) and at the zócalo, or main plaza, by the government palace and cathedral. Fare is 1 peso and 60 centavos. Worth seeing for its decor alone.

Buses run along most avenues. Those with a red stripe on white are called *delfínes* ("dolphins"), charge 2 pesos, and limit boarding to seats available. Larger buses with blue fronts and white sides are *ballenos* ("whales") and pack everyone possible aboard for 1.5 pesos. You are welcome to jump aboard. *Pesero* taxis pick up as many passengers as they can crowd in. They cruise along the main avenues and charge 4 pesos or more, depending upon their route. A man holding up a finger is usually a pesero driver. Wave him down.

Intercity buses to all parts of the Republic originate in three new bus terminals, Central de Autobúses del Norte, out Insurgentes Norte to Cien Metros, Terminal Central del Sur, on Taxqueño off Calzada Tlalpan or Terminal Oriente on the Puebla Road. An interterminal trolleybus, painted red, called Trolebús El Equipajero, runs between these two on a circular route with stops at the Insurgentes Metro station just off the Reforma a few blocks. Route 1 goes one way, and route 2 in the opposite direction, both making all stops. Fare is 3 pesos. Runs from early morning (4:35 A.M.) until past midnight.

SIGHTS OF MEXICO CITY

The National Museum of Anthropology, located on Paseo de la Reforma near Chapultepec Park, is one of the finest museums in the world. It is new, handsome, and fun, and a very good starting place for any tour of Mexico City. Its interesting rooms with stone treasures from ancient cities will give you a background for your other sight-seeing. The museum is open from 10 A.M. to 6 P.M. (8 P.M. on Fridays) from Tuesday through Friday. On Saturdays and Sundays, 10 A.M. to 6 P.M. Closed Mondays. Entrance fee is 10 pesos.

The Pyramids of the Sun and Moon, located about an hour away from the center of the city off the Laredo highway, are impressive. A taxicab will take you there, stopping en route at the Basilica of Guadalupe, the religious focal point of Mexico, named after its Patroness, the Dark Virgin. Cost would be at least $20.

The pyramids can also be visited in the evening during the winter, or dry season, with buses leaving from the Monument to the Revolution, behind Sanborn's Reforma, at 5:30 P.M. Cost is $2 or $3, and they get you to the pyramids in time for a "light and sound" show which presents, to symphonic background, a reenactment of the days of the Toltecs, who occupied the huge religious city of Teotihuacán. It can be cold, so bring a sweater.

The pyramids, along with that at Cholula, are considered the largest artificial mounds on the American continent. They are estimated to date from 400 A.D. to 800 A.D. Inside are older, smaller pyramids, which may date back to before the time of Christ. An entire city has been partially excavated around the pyramids, showing where the priests lived and where they held ceremonies, replete with flaming torches, dances, and human sacrifice.

An avenue has been uncovered between the two main pyramids, and along here is a structure called the Temple of the Butterflies. Nearby is the Ciudadela, or Temple of Quetzalcoatl, where the ceremonies were held. Serpents' heads carved in stone are very evident. A museum and restaurant are available in the pyramid zone. There is also a fine new restaurant-hotel, the Villas Arqueológicas, near the pyramids. It has a dining room seating 200 and service almost around the clock.

The Shrine of Guadalupe, mentioned as being on the route to the pyramids, can also be visited separately; buses (usually marked "Guadalupe") from Bellas Artes and Reforma go to the shrine. The original shrine dates to December 9, 1531, when a humble Indian, Juan Diego, saw a vision of the Virgin Mary, who told him a church should be built on that spot. She told him to pick some roses and carry them in his shawl to the bishop. When Juan Diego opened the shawl to present the roses, the image of the Virgin was on it.

The Basilica of Guadalupe, the holiest spot in Mexico, was completed in 1622. Here Catholics from all over the country come to worship and ask for the Virgin of Guadalupe's help, many making the last of the trip on their knees. A modern building has recently been completed to display the holy mantle upon which the figure of the Virgin appeared to Juan Diego in 1531; it is located on a site adjoining the present shrine. Across the plaza is the original basilica, which over the centuries has sunk so far into the ground as to be in danger of toppling. Nearby is a small chapel covering the Pocito, a bubbling spring to whose waters are attributed miraculous healing powers. The mantle is now spectacularly displayed against a gold background in its new setting, but the old church still retains the feel of those thousands of humble peasants who approached the Virgin with awe and love over more than three centuries.

Chapultepec Castle, located on a hill in Chapultepec Park with magnificent vistas of the mountain-ringed capital, is worth visiting. Here again a taxi is handy. The castle was at one time the home of Emperor Maximilian and Empress Carlota and still houses their furnishings as well as the *Historical Museum.*

Chapultepec Park. Chapultepec Park itself offers many delights. The *Museum of Modern Art* near the park entrance just off Reforma offers a fine collection of works by Mexico's big three—Rivera, Siqueiros, and Orozco—as well as a growing collection of other outstanding modernists including Rufino Tamayo. There are children's playgrounds, picnic grounds, a fine zoo, botanical gardens, a lake for boating, bicycles and ponies to rent, charro riders on Sundays, and polo matches. In the New Park a huge amusement area has one of the world's largest roller coasters. Nearby are the *Museum of Anthropology* and the *Museum of Natural History.* At the edge of the park on Avenida Molino del Rey is the famous old mill which was the scene of a battle in the Mexican-American War, and next to it is Los Piños, home of the Mexican president.

University City, located south of the capital on the road to Cuernavaca, houses the four-centuries-old National University in Mexico's most striking futuristic buildings. It has some forty spectacular structures, many with exterior murals. The library, encased in radiant natural-stone mosaics on four sides, is a masterpiece.

Zócalo and National Palace. The old zócalo, main plaza of the city, can be found by walking down Madero Street to its end. Here one sees the National Palace, which contains the offices of the Presidency. From the balcony at the front of the colonial building the President of the Republic rings a bell on the Anniversary of Mexico's Independence, which sets off wild jubilation in the crowd-filled plaza below. Inside the National Palace, in the stairwells, are history-laden murals painted by Diego Rivera over a twenty-five-year period.

The Alameda is the historic park in the downtown area across from the Del Prado Hotel on Avenida Juárez. In the days of the Aztecs, it was the site of one of the markets of the pre-Hispanic city of Tenochtitlán. During the colonial years the Spanish rulers permitted its use as a burning place for the fearsome inquisitions, and hundreds of persons died there. Later it was turned into the principal recreation area of the colonial city, and for many years crowds gathered to hear band concerts. Today the beautiful park is filled with flowers and high-shooting fountain displays which leisurely residents and visitors admire from graceful tiled benches of the colonial period.

The Palace of Fine Arts, or Bellas Artes, is the white-marble opera house located at the far end of the Alameda at the corner of Avenida Juárez and San Juan de Letrán. In addition to serving as an auditorium for opera, symphony concerts, ballet (and Mexican presidential inaugurals), the Palace of Fine Arts houses one of Mexico's most distinguished art collections, including some of the largest murals by Diego Rivera, José Clemente Orozco, David Alfaro Siqueiros, and Rufino Tamayo. One is the replica of the Rockefeller Center mural commissioned of Rivera in New York City and later ordered removed because it contained an unflattering portrait of the patron. The murals may be seen from the second- and third-floor balconies of the main foyer. The Palace of Fine Arts was begun in 1900 and finished in 1934. The heavy Italian marble resting upon the unstable Mexico City subsoil has caused the building to sink more than 15 feet, giving it a noticeable slant.

The famed Ballet Folklórico is presented at the Bellas Artes on Sunday mornings and several evenings of the week. The box office is open during the day for information or tickets. They can also tell you if the Mexican National Symphony or any visiting orchestra or company will be appearing during your stay.

The National Cathedral, located down Madero Street on the zócalo, occupies virtually the same site as the principal Aztec *teocali*, or temple, which was destroyed by the conquerors. Construction of the Christian church was begun in 1573 and completed in 1667. It is the largest cathedral on the North American continent and is open to visitors. Nearby is the newly discovered (1978) huge 10-foot, 8-ton Aztec circular stone excavated at the corner of Seminario and Guatemala streets. Open now on Saturday mornings, later more.

The racetrack, known as the Hipódromo de las Américas, is open from October to June with races Tuesday, Thursday, Saturday, and Sunday. Taxis will take you there, and you have a choice of buying general admission or a seat in the clubhouse. On special request it may be possible to visit the swank Jockey Club. Admission is nominal.

The Floating Gardens of Xochimilco may be visited at any time, but the flower-decked canals are at their best on a Sunday morning. They are half an hour by taxi from the city. A nice Sunday trip is to visit the Palace of Fine Arts (Bellas Artes) about 9 A.M. and see the murals, then watch the Ballet Folklórico (native dances) starting at 9:30 A.M. Then go by taxi after the dances to Xochimilco for the rest of the morning, lunch at the Fonda Santa Anita restaurant (Mexican food) near the bullring about 2 P.M., and watch the bullfights at 4 P.M. A full day, but worthwhile. If you have time, it is not too far away to the San Angel Inn, off Insurgentes on Altavista, where you can lunch at one of the finest restaurants in Mexico. Telephone 5-48-67-46 for reservations, as it is popular on Sunday.

THE BULLFIGHTS

One of the fascinations for tourists is to join the colorful Sunday bullfight crowds in the *Plaza México*, world's largest bullring, or *El Toreo Plaza* near the racetrack. *Corridas* take place on Sundays at 4 or 4:30 P.M., with the professional fighters appearing in the winter months and the apprentice *toreros* in the summer months. Tickets should be purchased in advance through your hotel, or you can buy them more cheaply at the ring if you speak some Spanish. Specify the shady side—unless you enjoy fistfights in the aisles and intermittent showers of flour or water tossed by heckling aficionados. Be on time, as the bullfights begin promptly and finding your seat among 50,000 may take half an hour. A good bullfight can be thrilling even to the uninitiated spectator, while a bad one is just bad. But the sight is worth seeing even if you don't approve of the "art." It is not called a sport!

SHOPPING IN MEXICO CITY

Among the great joys of visiting Mexico City are the endless shopping possibilities. There is something for everyone, whether your taste runs to straw baskets and embroidered blouses from the street markets or to leather jackets and silver jewelry from the chic boutiques. The Zona Rosa, or Pink Zone, is the fashionable place to shop. Here, amid the best hotels and restaurants in midtown, at shops ablaze with paper flowers and adorned with fabulous handwoven rugs and handsome ceramics, can be found one-of-a-kind pieces of gold and silver jewelry set with precious stones, onyx pieces in a variety of sizes and shapes, leather sandals, and hand-painted fabrics.

Among the most reliable places to shop for gifts to take home are the many branches of Sanborn's, the ubiquitous gift shop-newsstand-restaurant where most tourists change their money and buy their hometown papers as well as their postcards and stamps. Here you can find everything from $200 necklaces to dolls in typical native costumes for $1.50. Clerks speak English and are particularly helpful with customs declarations.

Perhaps the most fun for the shopper or even the browser is to visit one of the many markets scattered throughout the city. The easiest to find is the public market in the Pink Zone on Liverpool between Genova and Amberes near the Genève Hotel. The largest in town is the San Juan Market, whose craft displays can be found in a beautiful modern building on Ayuntamiento Street. Lagunilla Market, with everything from antiques to just plain junk, should be visited on Sundays. Bargaining is still the rule at most market stalls. For the ultimate in sophisticated handicrafts, spend a Saturday at the Bazaar Sabado in San Angel out near the university; it's an outing not to be missed, complete with buffet lunch and strolling musicians in the patio.

When you still haven't found quite what you are looking for, or are shopping for items in quantity or wish to buy things to be shipped home, try the Green Door at Cedros 8. It's hard to find—take a cab and ask for Mercantil Brictson—but worth the trip, for you'll discover a storehouse full of crafts of all kinds—a real grandmother's attic with a most understanding owner at your service.

A warning note: Be sure to keep your sales slips. They will be useful if customs questions arise.

Side Trips from Mexico City

There are any number of interesting day trips which can be made from Mexico City, apart from the longer ones described in Chapter 4.

Cuernavaca makes a nice day trip. Driving there in your car, or going by bus or limousine, takes about forty minutes on the superhighway. You can have a swim, lunch, and do some shopping. A complete description of this trip can be found in Chapter 10.

Taxco, that old gem of a mining town, is a bit farther, taking at least an hour and a half each way, but you can do it for lunch and return if you wish. See Chapter 23.

Toluca is an interesting colonial mountain town about an hour from Mexico City on the Guadalajara highway, which you find by going out Reforma. It is best on Fridays, when natives from surrounding villages come into the public market. The huge Nevada de Toluca volcano is easily seen as you approach the town, while you can visit the pre-Aztec ruins of Calixtlahuaca just beyond Toluca if you wish. Inquire locally. You will need a guide.

Ixtapán de la Sal is a garden of flowers with its famed mineral baths in the center. The modern and well-run Hotel Ixtapán is a wonderful place for a quiet rest. Its office in Mexico City is at Reforma 132 (tel: 35-76-22). Good restaurant, fine private baths. About an hour beyond Toluca on a side road.

A Selection of Hotels and Motels in Mexico City

Hotels and motels in this section are listed according to quality and size.

Modern Luxury Hotels

El Presidente Chapultepec (*753 suites*)   Expensive
This is the newest major hotel in Mexico City and, like the older El Presidente, part of the Nacional Hotelera chain. This is a true luxury hotel set in the woods of Chapultepec Park on Reforma at Campos Elíseos 218, Colonia Polanco. Has a number of fine dining rooms and bars, shops, and luxury accommodations. Each of thirty-

two floors takes the theme from one Mexican state for its decor. Tel: 5-20-86-12.

María Isabel Sheraton (*850 rooms*)　　　　　　Moderate to expensive
At Reforma 325, this is one of the biggest and most luxurious hotels in Mexico City. Good location. Splashy red carpet and white-marble decor. Sanborn's moderate-priced restaurant immediately next door, and shops. Tel: 5-25-90-60.

Americana Fiesta Palace (*700 rooms*)　　　　　Moderately expensive
A new twenty-five-story hotel smack in the heart of Mexico City at Reforma 80 at the Colón Circle. Operated by American Airlines. Air-conditioned, pools, five restaurants and bars, much activity. Rooms are comfortable though on the small side. A very convenient place to be. Excellent staff and services. Manager is Francisco Zinser. Tel: 5-66-77-77.

Camino Real (*720 rooms*)　　　　　　　　　　Expensive
At Mariano Escobedo 700, a cab ride from most places but in a quiet location and within walking distance of Reforma and Chapultepec. Several mission-style buildings are sprawled about gardens and amid pools with interconnecting walks. Large rooms with balconies and roomy baths. A number of excellent restaurants and nightclubs, and a cafeteria. Operated by Western Hotels. Tel: 5-45-69-60.

El Presidente (*300 rooms*)　　　　　　　　Moderately expensive
This is a luxury hotel with just about every comfort available, including the best beds the author has ever tried. In middle of new shops and restaurants. At Hamburgo 135, just off Paseo de la Reforma. Tel: 5-25-00-00.

Hotel Mexico Hyatt (*1,000 rooms*)　　　　　　　Expensive
Mexico City's newest hotel. A fifty-story skyscraper under construction with revolving rooftop dining room, spectacular views, and Polyforum Museum with Siqueiros murals. On Insurgentes Sur.

Holiday Inn (*400 rooms*)　　　　　　　　Moderate to expensive
At Liverpool 155 at the corner of Amberes, in Pink Zone, at a very choice location. Has a new tower section. Swimming pool, roof garden, across street from restaurants. All cards. Tel: 5-33-35-80.

Del Prado Hotel (*600 rooms*)　　　　　　　　　　Moderate
Once the biggest hotel in Mexico City, it is still one of the best. Located at Juárez 70 in heart of city, it has modern rooms, Sanborn's coffee shop, and handsome lobby with Diego Rivera mural. Tel: 5-18-00-40.

Reforma Hotel (*250 rooms*)   Moderate
The famed hotel on the corner of Reforma and Paris where Hollywood stars came for many years. Now, after a million-dollar
redecoration, operated by Dubin Hotels. Good restaurant, bar, fine
location, good service. Tel: 5-46-96-95.

Hotel Aristos (*360 rooms*)   Moderately expensive
A modern hotel at Reforma 276 in Pink Zone shopping and dining
district. Comfortable rooms, nightclub, sauna baths, gymnasium,
dining room, and coffee shop open twenty-four hours. TV. Reservations necessary and even then misplaced. Tel: 5-33-05-60.

Continental Hotel (*400 rooms*)   Moderately expensive
Located at Reforma 166 at the intersection with Insurgentes, this
was once a Hilton. Notable for incorporation of true Mexican decor
and motifs throughout. Rooftop dancing, etc. Tel: 5-18-07-00.

Alameda Hotel (*150 rooms*)   Moderate to expensive
In the heart of the downtown area at Juárez 50 across from Alameda
Park. Close to many of the sights and shops. Rooftop pool and sun
deck. Restaurant and nightclub. Owned by Western Hotels. Tel:
5-18-06-20.

Del Paseo (*100 rooms*)   Moderate
Chosen by discriminating travelers and very popular. Has rooftop
pool, cabanas, good restaurant with view. Located at Reforma 208
in top area. Tel: 5-25-76-00.

Bamer Hotel (*150 rooms*)   Moderate
A modern hotel in heart of city at Juárez 52 overlooking Alameda
Park. Breakfast and cocktails served at roof club. Bar restaurant. Tel:
5-21-90-60.

First-Class Moderate-Rate Hotels

Genève Hotel (*450 rooms*)   Moderately expensive
Located at Londres 130 in the very heart of the new shopping and
fancy restaurant section just off Paseo de la Reforma, this has long
been a favorite with visiting Americans. Good restaurant, bar. Has
new and old section with greatly varying rates; check at desk. Fine
bookstore, newspapers. Tel: 5-25-15-00.

Montejo Hotel (*54 rooms*)   Inexpensive to moderate
At Reforma 240, this hotel is older but has top location. Rooms
modest, but good. Tel: 5-11-98-40.

Alffer Century Hotel (*142 rooms*)   Moderate
A first-class hotel in the downtown area a block off Av. Juárez at
Revillagigedo 18 and near the Del Prado. Romano management.
Tel: 5-18-09-20.

Ritz Hotel (*135 rooms*)   Moderate
At Madero 30 in heart of town. Old but renovated and comfortable.
Tel: 5-33-62-15.

Monte Cassino Hotel (*200 rooms*)   Moderate
At Genova 56 in best shopping area of town near good restaurants,
this has long been a modest but popular hotel. Owned by Dubin
Hotels chain. Tel: 5-25-15-80.

Hotel Internacional Havre (*50 rooms*)   Moderate
This is a chic hotel in Pink Zone on Le Havre Street. It is French
provincial in styling with commodious rooms and baths. Coffee
shop and bar. Pleasant and quiet. Tel: 5-33-23-00.

Regis Hotel (*300 rooms*)   Inexpensive to moderate
An older hotel directly across from Del Prado Hotel at Juárez 77 in
downtown. Recently redecorated. Good. Tel: 5-18-08-00.

Plaza Florencia (*150 rooms*)   Moderate
Good new hotel at Florencia 61 in the Zona Rosa. Ponte Vecchio
restaurant and Bobol bar. Tel: 5-33-65-40.

Hotel Bristol (*126 rooms*)   Moderate
Another new hotel about three blocks off Reforma at Plaza Necaxa
17. Well-furnished rooms. Color TV. Dining room open twenty-four
hours. Tel: 5-33-60-60.

Hotel Casa Blanca (*200 rooms*)   Inexpensive to moderate
At Lafragua 7 just off Reforma near main Sanborn's. Attractive
rooms and suites. Rental TV. Small rooftop pool. Dining room and
cocktails. Tel: 5-46-06-64.

Luma Hotel (*94 rooms*)   Inexpensive to moderate
At Orizaba 16, slightly out of center of town, this is a fine hotel for
families, as some suites have kitchenettes. Tel: 5-11-97-20.

Meurice Hotel (*42 rooms*)   Inexpensive
At Marsella 28, this is a good hotel also slightly out of the heart of
town. Good service. Tel: 5-66-07-00.

Francis Hotel (*68 rooms*)   Inexpensive to moderate
At Reforma 64, this is a rebuilt building which has been turned

into a good hotel in convenient location. Restaurant, coffee shop, bar. Tel: 5-66-02-66.

Hotel El Ejecutivo (*120 rooms*)   Moderately expensive
Off Reforma at Viena 8 near center of town (near Fiesta Palace and Continental Hotel). Large, tastefully furnished rooms, and suites. TV. Garage. Small pool. Tel: 5-66-44-36.

Hotel del Angel (*100 rooms*)   Inexpensive to moderate
At Lerma 154 just off Reforma, a modern hotel with rooftop dining room, rooftop swimming pool, air conditioning, TV. Tel: 5-33-10-32.

Emporio Hotel (*70 rooms*)   Inexpensive to moderate
Rebuilt hotel at Reforma 124 with far-out decor bordering on the sensational. For those who want something different—like rugs up the wall! Good baths, etc. Tel: 5-66-77-66.

Guadalupe Hotel (*75 rooms*)   Inexpensive
Modern hotel at Revillagigedo 36 in busy, crowded part of older downtown. Tel: 5-26-58-86.

Premier Hotel (*100 rooms*)   Moderate
Modern hotel conveniently located at Atenas 72, one block off Reforma near Insurgentes. Tel: 5-66-27-00.

Hotel Sevilla (*50 rooms*)   Moderate
Popular with students, this is a modest side-street but well-run and clean hotel in a central location off Sullivan Park at Serapio Rendón 126. Very comfortable rooms, good inexpensive coffee shop, roof garden with view of city. Walking distance from Reforma and many restaurants. VISA only. Tel: 5-66-18-66.

Plaza Vista Hermosa Hotel (*86 rooms*)   Moderate
At Insurgentes and Sullivan 1, this hotel was built in unusual semicircular fashion to give all rooms a view. Conveniently located, but it lacks luster. Tel: 5-46-45-40.

Hotel Metropol (*165 rooms*)   Inexpensive
At Luis Moya 39 in business district, block and a half from Alameda Park. Has fair rooms well kept, dining room, garage, some TV. Tel: 5-10-86-60.

Purua Hidalgo (*250 rooms*)   Moderate
This is a modern and very attractive hotel built on the new prolongation of Reforma near the center of town. AE, DC. Tel: 5-85-43-44.

Mexican-Colonial-Style Hotels with Modern Facilities

Gran Hotel Ciudad de México (*130 rooms*)   Moderately expensive
Right on the zócalo at 16 de Septiembre 82, this is a restored hotel
done beautifully in style when wealthy Mexicans fancied French
period furniture. Convenient to many sights, but a cab ride away
from the Pink Zone. Has Del Centro restaurant serving fine food
from 8 A.M. to 1 A.M. Air-conditioned. Charges for TV. Tel: 5-10-40-
40.

De Cortés Hotel (*30 rooms*)   Moderate
This is a charming little hotel, built around an open patio where
you can eat and where entertainment is held. Has modern baths.
Across from Alameda Park at Hidalgo 85. Tel: 5-85-03-22.

María Cristina (*80 rooms*)   Moderate
At Lerma 31 in the fashionable area near Paseo de la Reforma, this
is an older hotel built in colonial style and furnished accordingly,
but has modern baths. Tel: 5-46-98-80.

Majestic Hotel (*77 rooms*)   Moderate
An authentic older hotel, right on the historic zócalo at Madero 73.
Fine rooftop restaurant with view. Rooms modest. Tel: 5-21-86-00.

Good Hotels in Outlying Residential Districts

El Diplomático (*105 rooms*)   Moderate
On busy Av. Insurgentes Sur 1105. A modern ten-story building.
Restaurant. Tel: 5-63-60-66.

Aeropuerto Holiday Inn (*208 rooms*)   Moderately expensive
Opposite Mexico City International Airport terminal at Puerto Aéreo
502. Three-story motor inn decorated in Mexican motif. TV. Pool.
Dining room, coffee shop open twenty-four hours, entertainment,
cocktails. Tel: 7-62-40-88.

Polanco Hotel (*42 rooms*)   Inexpensive
In fashionable Polanco residential area at Edgar Allan Poe 8. Many
shops, restaurants nearby. Good hotel. Tel: 5-20-60-40.

Good Motels and Motor Courts in Mexico City

Park Villa Motel (*45 rooms*)   Moderate
A good motel in an excellent location near Chapultepec Park.
Enclosed, modern. From Toluca or Querétaro road, hit Constitu-

yentes and off at side street Gómez Pedraza 68. From other highways come in on Reforma, keeping left at Chapultepec Park. Dining room. Rental TV. Tel: 5-66-44-36.

Dawn Motor Hotel (*42 rooms*)   Moderate
Seven miles north on Route 57 (the Querétaro superhighway at the Naucalpan exit). Modern but undistinguished. Heated pool. Rental TV. Dining room and cocktails. Tel: 5-76-19-00.

Motel Atlauco (*46 rooms*)   Moderate
At General Anaya 52 in Churubusco section near country club, this is difficult to find. Phone 5-49-31-80 if you are lost. It is new and has attractive rooms and suites, some with housekeeping facilities. Well worth finding.

María Bárbara Motel (*80 rooms*)   Moderate
On main superhighway from Querétaro (57) about 12 miles north of Mexico City (use Satellite north exit or Santa Mónica Viveros exit). Good two-story motel. TV. Pool. Restaurant open 7 A.M. to 11 P.M. Tel: 5-62-43-66.

Villa Eldorado (*14 rooms*)   Moderate
At Belmont 2, near Chapultepec Golf Club, 6 miles north of Mexico City on Highway 57. Attractive motel with dinette cottages, pool. Tel: 5-20-91-75.

TRAILER PARKS IN MEXICO CITY

El Caminero Trailer Park (*100 spaces*) $3
South of Mexico City on way to Cuernavaca via Tlalpan; on Highway 95D near tollhouse as you leave Mexico City. Laundry and showers. Pool. Accepts pets.

Cabello Trailer Park (*45 spaces*) $3
A modern, well-run trailer park at Hortensia 235, just off Av. Universidad, leading to the new University of Mexico campus, south of Mexico City. Services and showers. Laundry nearby. Monthly rates. Tel: 5-24-29-20.

KOA Trailer Park (*50 spaces*) $3
Some 22 miles north of Mexico City on Highway 57, the superhighway from Querétaro. Turn off at Tepotzotlán exit near tollhouse, following KOA signs through villages of Tepotzotlán and Aurora to Cuautitlán for about 6 miles in all. On Cuautitlán River. Laundry, showers. Pool, game room, lounge.

TALES OF OLD MEXICO

One can wander about the streets of the fashionable Genève district of Mexico City, just off the tree-lined Reforma, and feel as much a boulevardier as anywhere in the world.

I never go by the rather austere and dignified front of the famed Rivoli *restaurant without thinking back to the late 1940s when Baron von Marx was running a delightful candlelit dining room in the María Cristina. As he gained well-deserved fame, he built the Rivoli as his dream restaurant, and its elegance today is a tribute to his taste. Now my good friend Dario Borzani, a leading New York restaurant man, owns it and runs it well. The good Baron spends most of his time back on the continent. But the Napoleon plates he installed are still at the Rivoli. And so are the quiet music and fine service.*

At the Loredo, *just around the corner from the Continental Hotel, I think kindly of scholarly José Inés Loredo, descendant of a famed Mexican innkeeping family, who saved me from a terrible gaffe. I had mistakenly read the wrong notes, and stated he served a dish, "Fountain of Youth," consisting of a platter heaped high with chilled crab, lobster, et cetera. To save me embarrassment, as I could not correct the book immediately, he invented such a dish and put it prominently on the menu. It was a great success, and is still there today. It even rivals his unexcelled seafood soup.*

At the Jena, *long one of Mexico's poshest restaurants, the owner, Serafín Suárez, is inclined to be a bit distant and cool to guests. But one day in a jovial mood he sat down at my table. I had long been a nut about maps of all kinds, and was fascinated by Señor Suárez's tablecloths, which had a handsome red and gray print of the Battle of Jena in the center of each. I told him I would like to buy a set and hang them as curtains in my den, where I am writing this. He told me they were constantly replaced for the slightest flaw, and if I would accept used ones, they were mine. So I write surrounded by old Jena tablecloths hanging in my den. Very colorful!*

And of course there is El Paseo *restaurant, alongside the University Club. For a number of editions the owner, Bill Shelburne, burned slowly as I listed his place merely as a bar. Finally he cornered me at a soiree in New York at the home of Marion Patmore, and insisted I was wrong. I went into El Paseo on my next trip, sampled the extraordinarily good food, heard Bill singing at the piano, and agreed I was completely wrong. His has been on my list of ten best restaurants ever since.*

17

Monterrey and Saltillo

MONTERREY

MONTERREY IS A bustling industrial city on the plains of northern Mexico, sitting beneath a 5,700-foot mountain, Cerro de la Silla, or Saddle Mountain.

While it has the traditional Spanish architecture, the colonial plazas, and much of the picturesque atmosphere of old Mexico, these are somewhat misleading. Monterrey is a place of hard-working, penny-wise industrialists, and they have built some of their country's largest plants and factories.

One side of the city has a sixty-year-old steel mill, Fundidora de Monterrey, which is constantly being modernized and has the latest type of rolling mills. On the other side of the city stands the country's largest brewery, Cervecería Cuauhtémoc, which turns out one of the finest pilsener-type beers in the world. German experts were once imported as brewmasters to help accomplish this. These two industries are bulwarked by some 1,500 lesser ones making glass, cement, furniture, buses, trucks, and chemicals; for this reason Monterrey is sometimes called "the Pittsburgh of Mexico."

It also has what is possibly Mexico's finest school, the Monterrey Institute of Technology, which is directly patterned after the Massachusetts Institute of Technology. Monterrey also has an older, more traditional university, the University of Nuevo León. Monterrey is the capital of the state of Nuevo León.

Old Monterrey. Monterrey has a population of 1,499,700 and is the third largest city, if not the second, in the country after Mexico City and Guadalajara. It was established on September 20, 1596, by Captain Don Diego de Montemayor. His predecessor, Don Luis de Carbajal, who explored the area after landing in Tampico in 1576, was named the first governor of the area, but he was denounced during the Inquisition and burned at the stake in Mexico City. His successor, Montemayor, with twelve companions and their families, came upon the spot Carbajal had unsuccessfully tried to colonize, called San Luis, and there they founded *La Ciudad Metropolitana de Nuestra Señora de Monterrey*, which was quite a title for a village of twelve families. However, it was to prove worthy of the name.

Many Wars. Monterrey was sorely tried by various Indian attacks during its early years, but managed to survive. During the War of Independence in 1810, Monterrey passed briefly into the hands of the insurgents, but was restored to loyal forces; thus began forty years of sporadic revolutionary fighting. In 1848, General Zachary Taylor took the city with United States forces after fierce fighting, and they remained there until a peace treaty was signed. The American troops fought a battle at the hilltop Bishop's Palace in Monterrey, then went on to Saltillo, where they suffered a rout by Mexican forces at La Angostura, but eventually prevailed.

Industry. Monterrey's future as an industrial center was started in 1888, when the state officials had the happy thought of providing a tax exemption for new industries. The first, in 1889, was a new foundry and a mining company which became the famed Peñoles mining firm. The brewery was started in 1891, and turned out 5,000 barrels the first year. Today, it is part of a beer industry that turns out 2 million bottles per day to supply consumption needs in all parts of Mexico. Even the glass bottles themselves are a Monterrey product.

A Tale of Two Families. Monterrey is really the story of two prominent families who founded many of the first industries and who continue to influence all of Mexico. One of the families introduced modern supermarkets to Mexico, and now run a score of the latest type of such markets in Mexico City and elsewhere. The same family, which sent its sons to the Massachusetts Institute of Technology, also provided the impetus for the present technical institute at Monterrey. These two families are the Sada family, which holds the brewing interests, and the Garza family, which is strong in real estate and banking and which fostered the supermarkets.

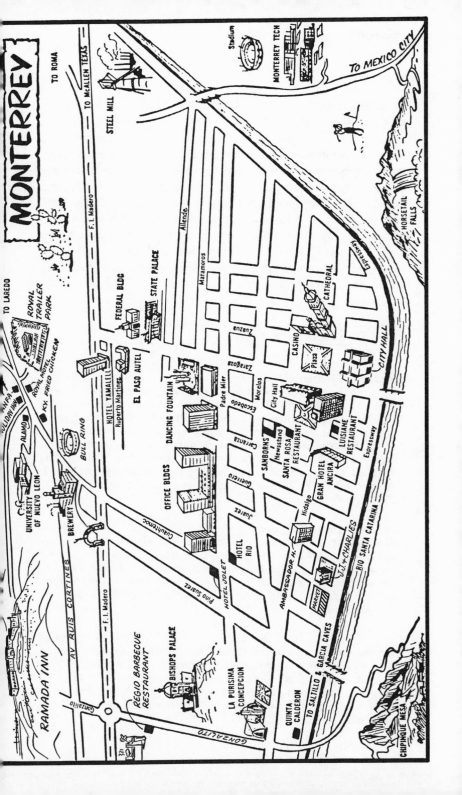

How To Get There

Probably almost everyone who goes to Monterrey will be an auto tourist crossing into Mexico via the Laredo or McAllen highways. It is about a two-and-one-half-hour drive from the border to Monterrey. Transportes del Norte runs modern Greyhound-type buses from Mexico City to Laredo, via Monterrey and with connections with Greyhound in the United States. Mexicana Airlines has flights to Monterrey leaving Dallas each morning and San Antonio each afternoon. You can drive on to Mexico City by two routes: a scenic, mountainous, paved road through Ciudad Victoria, Tamazunchale, and Valles; or the fast, cooler, but less scenic route via Saltillo, Matehuala, San Luis Potosí, and Querétaro.

Where To Stay in Monterrey

Ramada Inn Monterrey *(145 rooms)*   Moderate
Overlooking old Monterrey from a hilltop alongside the main Laredo highway 6 miles north of the city, this is a handsome white hacienda-type structure with pool, arcades, tennis courts, horses, and a restaurant casino style. Music and dancing nightly. Very Mexican decor with colonial chairs, handwoven bedspreads, and marble baths and vanities. Unfortunately, unrestricted housing has been built up around the hotel, and the hotel is poorly maintained. All cards. P.O. Box 249, Monterrey, Nuevo León, México. Tel: 52-22-70.

Gran Hotel Ancira *(365 rooms)*   Moderate
The biggest and most distinguished hotel in Monterrey. All rooms air-conditioned, fair dining room, bar, drive-in reception area for motorists, garage. Old building redecorated by famed Pani. In center of town, reachable by coming in main street, Morelos, then turning right on Escobedo to Hidalgo. AE, CB, DC. P.O. Box 697. Tel: 43-20-60.

Monterrey Holiday Inn *(218 rooms)*   Moderate to expensive
On the Laredo highway north of town, a sparkling new structure built in two-story mission style. Completely air-conditioned. Restaurant, pool, cocktail lounge. Look for standard Holiday Inn sign on green background as seen in the United States, as other hotels have used a similar name. Reservations from other Holiday Inns. All cards. Tel: 52-24-00.

Anfa Motor Inn (*106 rooms*)   Moderate
A very nice older court set in gardens. All rooms air-conditioned. Rental TV, pool. Coffee shop, restaurant, cocktails. On Laredo highway north. All cards. Tel: 52-18-08.

El Paso Autel (*60 rooms*)   Inexpensive
Older motel in town on Zaragoza Street No. 130, reachable by coming in Morelos and turning left on Zaragoza. Pool, restaurant, car park. Tel: 40-06-90.

Ambassador Hotel (*300 rooms*)   Moderately expensive
Modern hotel in center of town on Hidalgo and Carranza streets. Handsome new addition with drive-in parking. All rooms have TV and air conditioning. Good luxury restaurant, small pool. Probably the best hotel in Monterrey. All cards. Tel: 42-20-40.

Hotel Río (*360 rooms*)   Moderate
Very modern, air-conditioned hotel. Garage. New addition has pool. In center of town at Padre Mier No. 194. All cards. P.O. Box 35. Tel: 42-21-90.

Jolet Hotel (*77 rooms*)   Moderate
A new but uninspired hotel on Padre Mier downtown near Hotel Río. Air-conditioned. Coffee shop. Free garage. All cards. Tel: 40-55-00.

Hotel Yamallel (*106 rooms*)   Inexpensive
At Zaragoza and Arteaga. An eleven-story building slightly out of main downtown area. Air-conditioned. Bar, restaurant. AE, DC. Tel: 75-35-98.

Alamo Courts (*38 rooms*)   Inexpensive
On the Laredo highway coming into Monterrey. Modest, clean motel. Air-conditioned. Coffee shop. DC, MC, VISA.

Royal Courts (*21 rooms*)   Inexpensive
On highway north of Monterrey, this is a pleasant little spot with cheerful management. Has modest rooms. Some units have gas plates and refrigerators. Pool. Handy to stores.

Royal Trailer Park (*100 spaces*) $3–$4
Just off Highway 85 to Laredo north of Monterrey at edge of city. Turn east opposite Anfa Motor Inn onto Reforma, then go two blocks in and left one block on Zona Poniente. Don't be discouraged by poor entrance road. Behind walls is nice green lawn, shrubs, paved streets, good pool, all connections, and hot water. Tel: 52-10-80 and 52-39-08.

Where To Eat in Monterrey

J. J. Charlie's & Rami's   Moderately expensive
A fun-filled top-flight restaurant run by the Carlos Anderson group
of Mexico City and Acapulco, etc. In city on Constitution Expressway
corner of Serafín Pena, in a rebuilt old green mansion with horse
on roof, just off public markets and amusement park. Excellent food.
A taste sensation is special shrimp broth. You can get oysters in
four versions on one plate, bean-pot soup, grilled red snapper,
stuffed shrimp, curried chicken, barbecued ribs, and ten kinds of
steak. Guests can leave their ties for the restaurant's collection on
display. Jim Hopps, a Welshman, is part-owner and manager. Open
12 noon to 12 midnight except Sunday. All cards. Tel: 44-46-66 and
44-07-09.

Luisiana   Expensive
The fanciest restaurant in Monterrey, with silver serving plates and
tuxedoed waiters. Service is friendly, and the food is good. Vichyssoise, turtle sherry consommé, shrimp en brochette, broiled lobster,
duck à l'orange, Chateaubriand, oysters with crabmeat. Famed for
baked Alaska in individual coupé. Hidalgo 530 near Ancira. All
cards. Tel: 43-15-61.

Ramada Le Chateaubriand   Moderate
On the highway north at the Ramada Inn. Fancy dining room in
a two-story casino room with beams and panels giving it an air of
old Spain. Have a drink at their barside pool and see the lights of
Monterrey. Music, dancing. Cover charge. All cards. Call for reservations: 53-86-70.

Ancira dining room   Moderate
In the Gran Hotel Ancira in the center of town. Welcomes the
public, and has music at cocktail hour. Off-and-on service and food.
Serves beef Tampico, steak Diane, shrimp meunière, veal escallopin,
chicken parmesan, tongue. Specialties include lasagne, lobster cardinal, breast of chicken Montpensier, ceviche, chicken enchiladas,
and roast kid. AE, DC.

Ambassador Hotel dining room   Expensive
In the hotel of the same name, down Hidalgo Street two blocks from
the Ancira. Restaurant has glass windows overlooking pool. Probably the plushest decor in town. Quiet, with good music and
service. Specializes in tournedos of beef, canneloni Rossini, pork
loin in adobe, and seafood. Most cards.

Santa Rosa   Inexpensive
On Escobedo Street near the Ancira, this is a contrived but charming

native restaurant with rustic atmosphere and an open, and very clean, colonial kitchen. Serves a Mexican plate, chicken in mole, enchiladas, and sirloin at very moderate prices. Dinner only. AE, DC.

Sanborn's   Reasonable
At Av. Morales 464, this is one of the huge Sanborn's chain which is part dining room, part soda fountain, and part drugstore. Has a good breakfast (try *huevos revueltos à la mexicana*), lunch, dinner.

Merendero Los Jacales   Moderate
A big, sprawling place where Mexicans love to go for charcoal-broiled steaks and chicken. Menus in English and Spanish. Beer. Good but busy Sunday noon. South of town on Highway 85. Open 11 A.M. till 1 A.M. All cards.

Mesón del Angel   Moderate
Air-conditioned restaurant in town on Carranza off Constitution Expressway. Moderate prices for steaks. Open 11:30 A.M. till midnight.

Restaurant Regio   Bargain
This is a dining experience worth your trip to Monterrey, for it has the true Monterrey spirit and food to match. It is an outdoor barbecue, with an indoor restaurant (air-conditioned) attached. Specialty is T-bone steak with salad. Also roast kid and iced beer. It is about 4 miles from the center of town out the road to Saltillo (Highway 40) to Libertad, then right on Libertad to the corner of Gonzalito and Vancouver. Manager is Carlos Garza. Open noon till 1 A.M. Tel: 43-37-44.

Restaurant Mirador (*in Chipinque*)   Moderately expensive
If you wish a magnificent view from the Chipinque Mountains, a forty-five-minute drive to the south of Monterrey, this is well worth the trip. The restaurant is a chalet-type building with huge windows adjoining Motel Chipinque. Specialty is a Sunday buffet with overwhelming selection including many Mexican dishes. Beer and wine available. Other days onion soup, Caesar salad, T-bone steak, red snapper, and cheeseburgers for children. Take Constitution Expressway to Hidalgo exit, following signs saying "Chipinque." Open 7 A.M. till 10:30 P.M. Most cards except DC.

WHAT TO DO IN MONTERREY

Zaragoza Plaza is located in the very heart of Monterrey, with the cathedral on one side and the Palacio Municipal on the other side of the square. The city's social club, the Monterrey Casino, is beside the cathedral. The plaza is an authentic touch of old Spain and is still very much used, with the young couples strolling around and around (called the *serenata*) on Thursday and Sunday nights while a band concert is held. It is fun any night of the week to sit on one of the benches and watch the people go by.

Hidalgo Plaza, separated from Zaragoza Plaza only by the Palacio Municipal, is smaller. It is adjacent to the hotels Ancira and Colonial and actually has become, unfortunately, more the hangout for vendors to tourists than anything else. The *Palacio Municipal,* of colonial vintage, is worth a look inside, with its old well in the courtyard. It still houses the city government.

The Monterrey Cathedral, on Zaragoza Plaza, is a typical Mexican church structure dating back to 1790. Its one tower and its austere construction show that it did not have the lavish wealth poured into it that was poured into similar structures in the rich mining districts of the Republic. It has some modern frescoes by Angel Zarraga, finished only in 1945.

The Monterrey Casino is the low, modern building on one side of the cathedral with winding stairs going up to a haughty entrance. It is the social center of the city, and many fine balls for debutante daughters, wedding receptions, and other important events are held there. At noon on Sunday, members like to gather there and sip an aperitif, dressed in their best to see and be seen and talk over the night before. A piquant tripe dish called *menudo* is served and helps one to recover from excesses of a previous night. The casino was recently redecorated at a cost of nearly a million dollars by the famed Mexican architect Arturo Pani. A visitor's card is necessary to visit the casino. Dinner dances are held on Sunday evenings.

La Purísima Concepción. This ultramodern church, for which Monterrey is probably more famed than for any other, is well worth making a special trip to see. It is about a five-minute cab ride out Padre Mier Street, one of the main avenues, then on to the road toward Saltillo. This handsome church, whose plain arched roof slopes to the ground to form its walls, has a row of modern, impressionistic carved statues of the Apostles across its facade. It was constructed after World War II, with the help of a wealthy woman. It contains the "patron saint" of Monterrey—a figurine which a native woman is said to have placed in front of the threatening Santa Catarina River, which flows through the city, thus averting a flood which would have destroyed the municipality. Purísima's prize-winning modern architecture has been the keynote for much of the new building which has since flourished in Monterrey and throughout Mexico. The architect was Enrique de la Mora.

El Obispado Viejo, or the Bishop's Old Palace, is one of the chief sights in Monterrey. It is located on the crest of a small hill overlooking the city, and the view alone is worth the trip. The old structure has been restored, and a museum inside can be visited. The old building was constructed to the order of Don José Rafael Verger in 1782, to give work to unemployed Indians. It was used for Mexican troops during the War of 1848, and United States troops fought there in one of the hottest actions of the battle when the Obispado held out for two days after all else was lost in Monterrey. There are many bullet holes in the old structure. From the esplanade it is possible to see the Monterrey Country Club, Sacred Heart College, the city in the distance, and in the far distance the Saddle Mountain which dominates the area.

Cuauhtémoc Brewery, located in that part of the city where the road comes in from Laredo, is one of the largest breweries in Mexico and one of the best in the world. Its Bohemia and Carta Blanca beer are considered some of the world's best by beer lovers. Regular tours are conducted through the brewery at 9, 10, and 11 A.M. and at 2 and 3 P.M., Monday through Friday. Free beer is served in the garden to visitors.

Nightclubs. There are some new discotheques in Monterrey, of which the most popular at this writing are *Sgt. Pepper's* at Río Orinoco 105 Oriente in the Colonia del Valle section (tel: 56-02-08; Ricardo Romero, manager) and *El Gaucho* and *Las Pampas* on Av. Garza in town.

The *Ramada Inn* has a swinging cabaret (cover charge) with both individual performers and combos—loud, noisy, and late. Down on Hidalgo Street near the Ancira there are some nightclubs with floor shows.

The Ciudad Universitaria, which houses the University of Nuevo León, has a strikingly modern new campus on the highway from the north near the airport. Worth driving in for a look.

El Tecnológico de Monterrey, on the outskirts of the city on the road to Mexico City, is perhaps most easily seen as you depart southward toward the Mexican capital. It is a group of modern school buildings, much like any university, but several are decorated with colorful exterior murals that are worth seeing. A large sign over the gate confirms the fact that you are looking at the MIT of Mexico. A football stadium off to one side is evidence of the fact that *futból americano* is played here.

ROOSEVELT-CAMACHO MEETING

When Franklin D. Roosevelt came by train to Mexico on April 20, 1943, to meet with President Ávila Camacho of Mexico, their conference was held in the Governor's Palace on Benito Juárez Plaza. A plaque on the wall commemorates this meeting, which fixed the solidarity policy of the two nations during World War II. Inside the Governor's Palace there are stained-glass windows with portraits of General Mariano Escobedo, Fray Servando Teresa de Mier, Hidalgo, Zaragoza, Juárez, and Ocampo.

To reach this location, one can walk down Zaragoza Street from the center of town to Juárez Plaza. Adjoining it are the Plaza de la República and the Federal Building, which houses the post office. Between the two plazas there is a statue of General Mariano Escobedo, the Mexican hero who defeated Maximilian's last devoted Mexican generals, Miramón and Mejía, at Querétaro and who was a trusted advisor of the great Mexican leader Benito Juárez. Beneath the statue is an underground library and theater maintained by the University of Nuevo León.

PLACES TO VISIT OUTSIDE MONTERREY

García Caves can be reached by going out the Saltillo highway 13 miles and then turning north 17 miles on a paved road to Villa de García. The caves are said to be among the largest and most beautiful on the American continent. Just beyond the power plant in the village, burros are waiting to take visitors to the caves, which were discovered in the middle of the last century but were not really explored until 1946 when a *regiomontano* (as residents of this area are called), Pedro Wood, installed lights, a stairway, and a *teleférico* (cabled wagons). Eyeless fish are said to be living in the lakes of the caverns.

Chipinque Mesa, at 4,200 feet, is an area of homes and cabins located high on the mountains looming 2,500 feet above Monterrey. The weather is cooler here than in the city during the hot summers. Some wealthy residents live in Chipinque (chee-PING-kay) during these months. It is a forty-five-minute trip on a paved winding road which starts at the Hidalgo exit of Constitution Expressway in the city. The road is steep and twisting, but safe. There is a 5-peso toll charge. The Motel Chipinque and the Mirador Swiss-chalet-style restaurant are near the top, and the view of Monterrey is magnificent. The Mirador serves a splendid Sunday buffet (see page 263). Well worth the trip! Follow the signs.

Huasteca Canyon is also reached by going out the Saltillo highway to the village of Santa Catarina, somewhat farther on than the Chipinque turnoff, and going 2 miles south from Santa Catarina on a side road which is marked "Huasteca." Remarkable formations of rock in the 1,000-foot gorge make it a fine site for a picnic.

Horsetail Falls is a fine place to go for an overnight stay in some real wilderness and to see some beautiful scenery. It is 22 miles south of Monterrey on the Mexico City highway, where at K-166 you come to the little village of Villa Santiago, or El Cercado as it is locally known. Turn off to the west on a paved toll road and drive 4 miles to where there is a parking space. Here mules can be rented or you can walk another mile and hike up to the falls. The road winds up a mountainous approach with entrancing vistas, passing three small falls called the "Three Graces," and finally on to the main falls. There are a restaurant, pool, cabins, and picnic grounds, to make it an overnight stop; or Greyhound Tours, which has an office next to the Ambassador Hotel, has tours leaving downtown at 9 A.M. and 2 P.M.

SHOPPING

Monterrey is noted for its leather goods, but, generally speaking, the silver and other goods come from other sections of the country. In shopping, it is wise to consider well the advantages of buying in the place of manufacture. Of course, if Monterrey is the terminus of your trip, you can indeed find a well-rounded display of goods from all parts of Mexico.

SALTILLO

Saltillo was founded in 1775 and has been the capital of a huge territory which at one time included the state of Texas. It is still the capital of the state of Coahuila, and has a population of over 100,000. It is blessed with a sunny and dry climate, and at an altitude of 5,100 feet it tends to have cool evenings.

Although now on the main central highway (Route 57) to Mexico City, it is still a remote and somewhat colonial town. It is often called the "largest adobe city," as its buildings tend to be low in profile, and it is noted for its serape makers. It is only 50 miles from Monterrey over a fine divided highway. The highway connects with Route 57 going south at an intersection outside the city. Several hotels are located at the bypass, as well as a Kentucky Fried Chicken.

A drive into the town is interesting. You can tour the crowded downtown (the Arizpe Sainz Hotel is in the center of town and a good place to eat), and you can visit the markets at Carranza and Allende to shop for serapes (they are noted for their unusual colors, including ombré shades). There are silver shops also, near the Arizpe Sainz. The cathedral on the main plaza (started in the late 1700s) is the only structure of real interest.

At the far end of Victoria Street, where the Arizpe Sainz is located, one comes to the Alameda Park, which is lined with palms and has a lake made in the shape of Mexico. At one side is the state normal school, and not far away is the Inter-American University, which attracts U.S. students. At one corner of the Alameda is the Herradera Steak House.

About a half hour outside Saltillo is the Buena Vista battlefield, where a decisive battle of the Mexican-American War occurred in 1847. General Zachary Taylor with 5,000 U.S. troops confronted the Mexican General Santa Anna, who had a larger force, but Taylor carried the day. Several thousand men, the majority Mexican, were killed, and it resulted in control of the north by the Americans until a peace settlement was achieved the next year and they withdrew to the present borders.

WHERE TO STAY IN SALTILLO

Rodeway Inn Los Magueyes (*16 tower suites and 44 rooms*) Moderately expensive

Just beyond where the bypass connects to Highway 57 going south, you will find this ultramodern hotel with its huge tower and adjoining cluster of luxury rooms. The rooms are very comfortable, although the ultramodern Mexican decor comes as a shocker. It has a fairly good restaurant, a fine pool, and lovely gardens. The coffee shop is open all hours and offers Mexican dishes, chicken, steaks, and club sandwiches. There is also a rooftop supper club. Tennis and golf. Juan Manuel Vasconzelos is the hotel manager, and Sergio Peña the submanager. The hotel was designed and staffed by Howard Brown, U.S. hotel expert. All cards. Tel: 5-10-10.

Camino Real (*90 rooms*)   Moderately expensive
Also on Highway 57, across the road from the Rodeway Inn. A modern, well-landscaped stone hotel with swimming pool, adjoining bar with poolside service, nightclub and restaurant open late. Putting green. Operated by Western Hotels. All cards. P.O. Box 55, Saltillo, Coahuila, México. Tel: 3-81-90.

Arizpe Sainz Hotel (*55 rooms*)   Moderate
In the heart of Saltillo, at 418 Victoria Street, this is a charming two-story colonial hotel built around two courtyards. It is well maintained, and for long was the best place in town (once a stagecoach stop). As it is on a busy street, you can park for unloading and then put your car in garage next door (very narrow entrance). It has a small heated pool and a good restaurant, plus a "quick lunch" coffee shop open 7:30 A.M. till 9:30 P.M. Tel: 3-80-00.

Bermea (*23 rooms*)   Inexpensive
Near normal school and Alameda Park, this modest hotel caters to students and is an economical place to stay. On Route 40 going through town.

Sierra Vista Motel (*36 units*)   Inexpensive
On Highway 57 south of town beyond Rodeway, this is a modest motel popular with students going to the Inter-American University.

San Antonio Trailer Park (*35 spaces*) $3
Five miles south of town on Highway 57. Situated on a fruit farm, this is a fairly new facility with all hookups, showers, and toilets. Purified water available. Narrow entrance can be hard to find.

Quinta Colina (*12 spaces*) $3
On Highway 40 just beyond bypass junction from Monterrey. Enclosed grounds with all hookups, bathhouse.

18

Morelia, Pátzcuaro, and Uruapan

The Mexicans are fatalists, who accept death naturally. Their rituals for the dead encompass more of beauty and joy than do those of many other cultures.

One of the loveliest of their ceremonies is held on what is called "the Day of the Dead," or Día de los Muertos, on November 1.

At Janitzio Island, a lovely isle jutting from Lake Pátzcuaro near Morelia, the custom is for the entire family to dress in their finest, the women packing a picnic basket, then go just before midnight to the cemeteries, where they light candles for each of their dead. So many candles are lit that the light makes a glow in the night, during which one can see the soft features of the women under their rebozos as they kneel at the graves. From time to time they sing alabanzas.

Later there is a picnic held in the cemetery, where it is not unknown for the men to have a ceremonial drink or so. In fact, to offset the chill, more than a little is taken, as the family stays till dawn. The children find candies offered by peddlers, on which little skulls and bones have been formed in icing, while the bakeries produce a special bread for the Day of the Dead.

It is not uncommon for children to be given miniature funeral processions for toys, while broadsides called calaveras are printed carrying special verses, often humorous, for the Day of the Dead.

The next day, All Saints' Day, is the second of the two holidays celebrated universally in Mexico.

Mourning is carefully observed, and a man losing a wife or his mother or father will very likely wear a black band on his arm for a year thereafter. Women dress completely in black, and after the assassination of President John F. Kennedy, who had not long before made a highly popular visit to Mexico, many Mexicans in the tiniest villages appeared in black in his honor.

WEST OF Mexico City on the Guadalajara road lies the charming colonial city of Morelia, famed for its superb climate and delicate pink-stone architecture, as well as its cultured people and important role in Mexican history. Nearby is fascinating Lake Pátzcuaro and village and the island of Janitzio. Pátzcuaro brings to mind pictures of the butterfly-net fishermen floating on the deep-blue surface in their dugout canoes, but it also is the center of the Tarascan Indians—a stalwart race which still speaks its native tongue. They make fine lacquer works, carve interesting wooden masks, and perform the dance of *los viejitos*, or dance of the old men, a sprightly performance well worth seeing.

It is a scenic trip of some five hours through pine forests from Mexico City to Morelia, over paved roads, and it is about another hour or a bit more to Pátzcuaro. Uruapan is off two hours on a paved side road near the famed, now extinct Paricutín volcano.

This means you can drive to Morelia one day, spend the next morning in Pátzcuaro, and be back in Mexico City the second night. However, this does not leave you proper time to see these interesting points at all well, and we recommend spending the first night in Morelia, the second night in Pátzcuaro, and returning the third day (or the fourth or fifth, if the fancy strikes you, as it might).

If you start late, you can lunch at San José Purúa, a resort hotel and spa 10 miles beyond Zitácuaro, and 5 miles off the road (marked by a sign), whose food is sporadically excellent and ordinary. If you start by eight, you can arrive in Morelia in time for a late lunch (the dining room of the Virrey de Mendoza on Morelia's main street by the plaza is good, or the Restaurant Normandie on the main street across from the cathedral, or up the hill on Virrey Mendoza Street to Restaurant Casino Charro, or farther up to the Villa Montaña, which has the best cuisine in Mexico but admits the public only by special arrangements—such as inquiring if you can dine there).

MORELIA

Morelia is a quiet city, with some 200,000 inhabitants, whose cobblestoned streets are overhung with ancient trees, while the

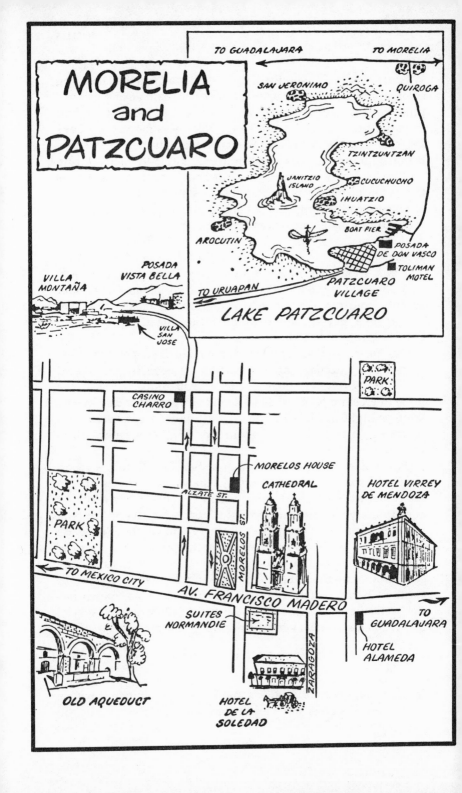

pink spires of the cathedral poke through the greenery to be seen from miles away on the flat plateau, and the tolling of the cathedral bells is heard in distant cornfields.

It is a city of schools and schoolchildren, while its Colegio San Nicolás, founded in 1540 (making it second oldest on the continent), has given it a reputation for scholarly achievement.

It has long been known also, to Mexicans themselves, as a politically conservative city with strong Catholic influences. Much of this traces back to the days shortly after its founding.

Don Antonio de Mendoza, first viceroy from Spain, founded the city on April 20, 1541, and named it Valladolid after his home city in Spain. It began to draw some of the more distinguished families of colonists, much as Virginia did in the American colonies. Many of these families are still community leaders.

Viceroy Mendoza's administration produced numerous accomplishments. In 1536 he established the first printing press in America and edited the first books in the New World. He also launched a campaign to eliminate discrimination against the Indians and was the first to mint copper and silver coins.

The cathedral, originally started in nearby Pátzcuaro by the first bishop of the See, Vasco de Quiroga, was removed to Morelia in 1553. The present cathedral building was started in 1640 and its bell towers finally completed in 1744. It is an outstanding example of plateresque style.

Still known as Valladolid, the city was renamed Morelia in 1828 in honor of its most famous son, and one of the country's most celebrated heroes, José María Morelos, a village priest who commanded one of the armies in the great revolution of 1810 and in 1813 established the first Mexican Congress. He was later captured by the Royalist forces, and was blindfolded and shot on December 22, 1815. The birthplace of Morelos, a humble house near San Augustín Church, is one of the sights of Morelia today.

Where To Stay in Morelia

Some very modern, in some cases luxurious, motel villas have been added to the Morelia scene, and it now affords a type of accommodation that the city has previously not offered visitors. Three of these are in a colony on the hills of Santa María which overlook Morelia from the south and offer a spectacular view of the city. They are only five or ten minutes from the center of the city. You can find them by taking a side street at a large park where the main highway enters the city near the aqueduct (see map, page 272). The best route is off Madero Street, then up Virrey Mendoza Street past the Casino Charro, where signs indicate the way.

The *Villa Montaña* was the most elegant of these at the time of my last visit, its cabanas being furnished with real collector's items as well as modern beds and baths. It has a large swimming pool and a fine dining room. Raymond J. Cote is owner-manager. The *Villa San José* across the street was of the same general level, while the *Posada Vista Bella* had somewhat plainer, though still very good, accommodations and welcomes children.

There is also a new deluxe hotel in the center of the city of Morelia. This is the *Hotel de la Soledad*, a fine old colonial structure which has been completely rebuilt inside to give it modern rooms with modern bathrooms. It was originally the city's first inn, having been built by the Augustín monks, used principally for a coach station. The remodeling has been done with splendid taste to re-create much of the old flavor of the coach station. It is one block off the main street, Madero, on a side street, Zaragoza, not far from the principal plaza.

The *Suites Normandie* are located in a colonial building on the main street. The eleven luxury suites are large, completely decorated in antique period furniture, and well kept with good baths and color TV.

The *Hotel Virrey de Mendoza*, also located in a handsome old colonial structure directly on the plaza, has long been one of the city's principal hotels, though of a period decor, and still offers first-class accommodations. Its rooms have small balconies from which one can imagine the señoritas gazing out on the street below—there are small seats for them. Probably has the best dining room in town. It is now operated by Western Hotels, Inc.

The *Hotel Alameda* is large, relatively modern, and also offers first-class accommodations. It is not modern enough to compete with the new Santa María villas, nor does it have the charm of either the Soledad or the Virrey. The *Hotel Presidente*, at Aquiles Serdán, is operated by the Hotel Alameda.

Hotels in Morelia

In Town

Hotel Virrey de Mendoza (*75 rooms*)   Moderate
Old colonial inn on main plaza and main street, but still the biggest
hotel in town. Well kept. Good restaurant, bar. Operated by Western
Hotels chain. All cards. Tel: 2-06-33.

Hotel de la Soledad (*60 rooms*)   Moderate
Restored old inn with modern baths, charming rooms. On Zaragoza
Street just off main street and plaza. Excellent. All cards. Tel: 2-18-
88.

Hotel Alameda (*70 rooms*)   Moderate
A more modern and more ordinary hotel, on main street across
from Virrey. All cards. Tel: 2-20-23.

Hotel Presidente (*89 rooms*)   Inexpensive
An older building at the end of the aqueduct, completely modernized
to make a comfortable, attractive, but modest hotel. Nightclub with
entertainment. All cards. At Aquiles Serdán 647. Tel: 2-26-66.

Suites Normandie (*11 suites*)   Moderately expensive
On main street across from cathedral, landmark former colonial
mansion converted to luxury suites with period furniture, color TV.
Carnet, VISA. Tel: 2-16-70.

Hotel Mansión Acueducto (*36 rooms*)   Inexpensive
Nice middle-class hotel on Av. Acueducto 25 on main highway.
Informal but pleasant service. Reasonable prices on meals. Garage
and pool. Tel: 2-20-20.

At Santa María Hills, South of Town

Villa Montaña (*57 rooms*)   Moderately expensive
An unusually fine guest ranch tastefully decorated with Mexican
works of art. Very comfortable rooms, lovely view. Excellent cuisine
served only fixed menu at fixed hours. Cocktails noon–1:30 P.M.
and 6–7:30 P.M., beer at other times. Attractive pool. No TV.
Children discouraged. No credit cards and no commissions. Write
direct: Apartado 233, Morelia, Michoacán, México. Tel: 2-25-88.

Villa San José (*17 cottages*)   Moderate
Next-door neighbor of Villa Montaña and similar. Also has good

view overlooking Morelia. Guests are very loyal and speak well of service, food, and hospitality. Garden but no pool. Jack and Sylvia Fox, hosts. No cards. P.O. Box 162. Tel: 2-25-81.

Posada Vista Bella (*42 rooms, 15 apartments*)   Moderately expensive Also on Santa María Hills, this is a pleasant, attractive, modern, motel-type structure with pool, restaurant, bar, shops. Welcomes children. AE, MC, VISA. P.O. Box 135. Tel: 2-26-24.

Hostal de las Camelinas (*60 rooms*)   Inexpensive Looking like a bit of ultramodern Habitat from Expo 67, this hotel on the Santa María hillside is directly across the street from the Casino Charro. Restaurant, bar, pool. All cards. Tel: 2-03-41.

Where To Eat in Morelia

Frankly, there are few good places to eat in the Michoacán capital, charming as it is, and those few are modest. The dining room of the *Virrey de Mendoza*, on the main street at the center plaza, is open at meal hours (usually from 1 to 4 P.M. for lunch and 7 until 10 P.M. for dinner) and is the most reliable, year in and year out.

Restaurant Normandie on Madero Street in the center of town had an elaborate menu when I was last there, with strip sirloin, seafood soup, Pátzcuaro whitefish, and stuffed Mexican pepper. Open for breakfast, lunch, and dinner. Prices are moderate.

Casino Charro on Virrey Mendoza Avenue halfway up to Santa María Hills is an elaborate country-club-type building housing a gentlemen's riding club, but its restaurant and bar are always open to the public. The extensive menu includes T-bone steak, filet mignon, shrimp en brochette, red snapper or whitefish fillet, the famed turkey *mole poblano*, as well as ham and cheese sandwiches for as little as 10 pesos.

Things To See in Morelia

As has been mentioned, the principal charm of the old Castilian city lies in its tree-shaded streets, its fine old colonial buildings of rose stone, and its superb climate: 57–69° F year-round; sunny, dry days; and cool, crisp evenings.

The old aqueduct built in 1785–1789 runs parallel to the highway on the eastern edge of town on the road to Mexico

City, coming into the city near the Bosque. It stands 30 feet high and its arches, of which there are 254, have a width of 20 feet. It is one of the remarkable engineering works of the time, and is still in good condition.

Calzada de los Penitentes and the Bosque. Along the aqueduct is a pleasant walk called Calzada de los Penitentes ("Avenue of the Penitents"). Nearby is the Bosque, the city's largest park. From here, a road runs up to Santa María Hills and the colony of new motels. There is a fine view of the city from Santa María, and the road continues, curving back to the city and into the central plaza again.

The cathedral, situated beside the main plaza in the center of town, is built of rose-colored stone with a delicate plateresque design. Its two towers rise above the ancient trees around the plaza, and its tolling bells are heard for miles about. Begun in 1640, it took over 100 years until the towers were finally completed in 1744. The interior is little different from other churches you may have seen in Mexico.

The house of Morelos, the great revolutionary hero after whom the city is named, can be found on Morelos Street off the main street near San Augustín Church. Here José María Morelos, the son of a carpenter, was born on September 30, 1765. It is now a museum, and there is a small admission fee. Other famous houses in Morelia are the residences of Melchor Ocampo, another great Mexican hero, and Don Santos Degollado, who once lived in the city.

The Plaza Principal, or main plaza, is where young people stroll about in the evening in an event called the serenata, while band concerts are performed on Thursday and Sunday evenings. A statue to Morelos is here with an interesting inscription detailing the historic events in his life.

La Universidad Michoacana de San Nicolás de Hidalgo. Morelia's famed institution of higher learning is the second oldest university on the American continent. It was established in 1540 (in Pátzcuaro) and moved to Morelia in 1880. It offers courses in engineering, medicine, dentistry, agriculture, and arts.

Palacio del Gobierno and Muséo del Estado. The Palacio del Gobierno, the state capitol building facing the cathedral, can be visited. The Muséo del Estado, which occupies an eighteenth-century palace near the main plaza, contains a collection of

Tarascan sculptures and ceramics but is small and uninspired and hardly worth visiting. Admission is 2 pesos.

The Palacio Clavijero, connected now by an archway to the Farias Dulce market, was originally built by the Jesuits in 1681 as a school. In the late eighteenth century, when the Jesuits were expelled from Mexico, the building was abandoned. In 1970 it was refurbished by the state and named as a lasting monument to Fray Francisco Javier Clavijero (1729–1787), a man called the most learned in New Spain. This restored colonial building has a great organ, and concerts in the open air are given.

The public market has been rebuilt as Independence Market on Lázaro Cárdenas Street about four blocks behind the cathedral and three blocks over. While little different from a hundred other public markets in Mexico, it is still as good as any to visit.

The Las Rosas Conservatory of Music, on Las Rosas Park, which is two blocks up Prieto Street from the Virrey Hotel, has a famed boys' choir whose reputation is comparable to that of the renowned Vienna Boys' Choir. Concerts are often given in the park. As of this writing, they can be heard from 5 to 7 P.M. Monday through Friday during rehearsals.

PÁTZCUARO

Perhaps more in Pátzcuaro than anywhere else in Mexico you get the pungent impression of having come to the very heart of the great Indian nations, to the home of the immutable and stoical people who have given Mexico not only much of its arts and skills, but its mystery, its courage, and its picturesqueness.

Pátzcuaro has a note of strangeness about it.

The village itself is perched on a hillside overlooking the deep-blue lake, the cobblestoned streets being buttressed so as not to fall into the water, the heavy carved beams and the even heavier stone pillars and walls seeming to be weighted under the centuries of history.

It is high, and there is a coldness about the air of the pine forests even though the sun shines brightly. The grinding poverty which has oppressed the patient Tarascan Indians for generations beyond knowledge is all about you. The plazas are bare, and dust-covered. Yet the women going to the well to draw water gossip and sometimes laugh. The men are more dour and have little to say.

Yet this is the land of the butterfly-net fishermen, whose shadowy outlines seem to be a misty vision upon the lake—and compose perhaps the best pictures you will have an opportunity to take in Mexico.

The name *Pátzcuaro* means in Tarascan "place of delights," and some authorities say this is related to the fact that there were once as many as 250 species of hummingbirds about here. The natives developed a now-forgotten art of placing the colorful plumage precisely upon copper plates to form pictures of unusual beauty which were sent back to Europe by early colonists.

Out in the large blue lake appears a sizable island from which towers an immense white figure, looking like another "Christ of the Andes," dominating the surrounding countryside. This is the famed island of Janitzio, and the statue is a modern sculpture of the revolutionary hero José María Morelos. Janitzio Island, which is easily visited by launch (see pages 282–283), is much favored by tourists, as it offers a boat trip on the lake to get there, a visit to a colorful fishing village on the island, and then, if you are up to a steep flight of stone stairways, a visit to the Morelos monument, which actually is six stories high, hollow, and has a mural inside portraying the life of Morelos.

The Pátzcuaro area is also known for its handicrafts, of which the lacquered trays, boxes, and masks are the best known and most highly prized. The lacquer is said to still be prepared from the crushed bodies of purple insects, which give it a handsome deep finish and great durability, as it incorporates a wax element. (See Chapter 5 for useful, detailed description of the various forms of lacquer work on sale.)

The trays are seen in many places in Mexico. They usually have a black background on which carefully etched flowers of many bright colors have been overpainted. There is a difference of opinion as to their beauty, some people finding them most tasteful while others have called them ugly. Some even doubt the genuineness of the supposedly ancient lacquer, implying that Mr. Du Pont has been called in upon occasion by some unscrupulous artists.

Our view is that the wood carving is beyond dispute a laborious hand process (examine the inside of the masks, for example, where the raw strokes show), and that the trays are not only gay and colorful, but obviously painstakingly finished with great care. The trays make fine wall pieces at home for a Mexican motif, and I think they are quite a bit better than most native handicrafts lugged home from other parts of the world. The masks have gotten downright clever (although many of the cruder older type are still on sale), while we confess we are completely puzzled as to what people do with the little boxes.

But this is good shopping country, and you will find a large display at shops in Quiroga, the town on the Guadalajara–Mexico City road at the point you turn into Pátzcuaro (5 miles farther on the side road), or in Pátzcuaro itself, while the source of supply, Uruapan, is only 40 miles away on a newly paved road through a pine forest, passing five villages. Bishop Quiroga of the Second Audiencia of Spanish times taught each village one trade. Santa Clara does fine copper work; Uruapan, lacquerware; Paracho, guitars; and Quiroga itself, colorful masks.

For those not driving, Pátzcuaro can be reached by comfortable bus. Tres Estrellas de Oro has a first-class bus leaving Mexico City each day at 1 P.M. from the Central de Autobúses del Norte off Insurgentes Norte, or take the trolley from town (see page 243, Chapter 16).

WHERE TO STAY IN PÁTZCUARO

Posada de Don Vasco (*70 rooms*)   Moderately expensive

A long-famed hotel which seems to wish to frustrate its guests with poor service. Operated now by Hostales de México, this large hotel is named after the original missionary who came to the area and later became Bishop of Michoacán, Don Vasco de Quiroga. The Posada retains much of the atmosphere and flavor of the area, but at the same time is comfortable. The food is usually very good, although not elaborate. Located on the road between the lake and the town. Reservations necessary. Call toll-free (800) 351-6035 from the United States, or 5-25-90-81 in Mexico City.

A motel section, owned by the same group, is across the street from the Posada. It is somewhat more modern, but the building has carefully been done in colonial style. Prices are the same as the Posada.

Mesón del Cortijo (*16 rooms*) Inexpensive
Hotel on main road north of town; turn off at the statue of the Tarascan Indian. It is a very attractive modern inn with handcrafted furniture and fireplaces, built around a flower-filled courtyard. Has a good restaurant specializing in Pátzcuaro dishes. Owner is Rafael Orozco. Tel: 2-95.

Motel San Carlos (*12 rooms*) Inexpensive
New motel in Swiss style near the lake and about 500 yards from junction of the Uruapan and Pátzcuaro roads. Pleasant management. MC, VISA. Tel: 3-49.

Motel Pátzcuaro and Trailer Park (*8 rooms, 12 spaces*) Inexpensive
Small, modest, but good establishment near the Posada Don Vasco. Nice rooms. Pool. All hookups.

Posada de San Rafael (*60 rooms*) Moderate
In the center of town. Colonial-style rooms. Not too comfortable but acceptable.

Motel Chalamu (*8 units, 12 spaces*) Inexpensive
At the edge of the lake. Neat and tidy motel with fireplaces and pool. All hookups for camper spaces.

Posada de la Basílica (*10 rooms*) Inexpensive
A modest hotel on a hill in the center of Pátzcuaro village. Cannot offer luxury quarters, but it does have a charming little bar with big windows looking out on a handsome view of the town and the lake. The rooms, each having a fireplace, are clean and good; the dining room is modest.

WHERE TO EAT IN PÁTZCUARO

The Posada Don Vasco dining room serves the public during meal hours (lunch from 1 to 4 P.M. and dinner from 7 to 10 P.M.), accepts credit cards, and has good food (although guests do complain about service). Pátzcuaro whitefish is their specialty.

Restaurant San Felipe, on the main road next to Vicki & Rafael's, is open from 11 A.M. to 12 midnight, and accepts all credit cards. They have a wide variety, with three styles of local whitefish, Tarascan soup (tortilla soup with cheese), jumbo shrimp, filet mignon with mushrooms or Mexican-rancher style, grilled pork chops, fried chicken or chicken with Mexican mole sauce. Or just a plate of tacos if you wish. Moderate to inexpensive.

TRIP TO JANITZIO ISLAND

Janitzio Island is undoubtedly the number-one sight for a Pátzcuaro visit, and it also serves to give you a launch ride on the lake and past the butterfly-net fishermen. You can get a launch at any time of day, but a morning trip is usually the nicest, as the water is smoothest then (storms sometimes blow up briefly in the afternoon).

The landing where you can get boats is back out on the road you used to enter town from the main highway. The turnoff is not only well marked but cluttered with would-be guides who will not only offer their services, but persist until you choose one. They, of course, get a commission for bringing you in.

You yourself can easily go right to the dock and make a bargain for either a ride on the lake or over to Janitzio, which you can easily see. There are launches holding ten or twenty persons which ply the waters regularly, and you can ride here for a few pesos. But you can rent an entire launch for a reasonable price.

The trip takes about a half hour each way (going is slow in the stretch of shallow water and reeds that mark the first part of the voyage). You can ask the pilot to take you over by the fishermen for pictures if you wish; they pose willingly (and usually expect a tip).

The picturesque little village of Janitzio, being a fishing village, is huddled close to the docks. Nets are always drying up and down the cobblestoned streets, while girls and women are busy mending old nets and spinning new ones. Many little models of the fishermen's gear are on sale as souvenirs.

By walking up the cobblestone steps, you come to the village school and a small church. Climbing on up beyond the church, you come to a zigzagging stone walkway which ultimately leads to the huge statue of Morelos on the bluff above. While it is a strenuous walk, it can be done, with occasional rest stops, and the view is worth it. I would not recommend it for older people or those of delicate health.

The huge hollow statue is entered from the rear. A winding staircase going up the interior is walled with a lengthy mural depicting the life of Morelos from his birth in nearby Morelia on September 30, 1765, through his days as a country priest and schoolteacher, and finally to his participation in the epic battles against the Spanish colonialists, leading to Mexico's independence as a nation. Morelos himself was shot before a firing squad by the Spanish.

The statue was begun on November 8, 1933, with General Lázaro Cárdenas, later one of Mexico's important presidents, on hand. In fact, it was at his instigation that the statue was built (he came from the Michoacán area himself, having a home in Pátzcuaro).

Visiting the Town of Pátzcuaro
If you are staying out at the Posada Don Vasco, you are actually halfway between the town of Pátzcuaro and the Janitzio boat landing. It is only a few minutes down the road to the south and into the village of Pátzcuaro and, of course, a visit here is something you must do. It is, in fact, the point of your trip.

Pátzcuaro, a village of over 24,000 people, was founded in 1540. It consists largely of one-story adobe or plaster-over-brick buildings with red-tile roofs. The streets are cobblestone, and often in disrepair. While you can drive into town fairly easily, the poor streets make it wise to use a taxi to spare your own car.

Interestingly enough, one of the first and largest projects of UNESCO was carried out in Pátzcuaro. An extensive program of educating illiterate Indians was carried on, while simultaneous studies were made of possible ways to improve their livelihood. The program was housed in the family mansion of the late Don Lázaro Cárdenas, a president of Mexico and leader of the reform series of governments. This huge home, overlooking the lake from a hillside beyond the town, is easily seen.

The town markets are gathered around two squares or plazas a block apart in the center of the village. The largest plaza is shaded by ancient trees, and on Fridays, Indians from all the surrounding area come to display, sell, and exchange their wares. Large areas called *mesónes* are nearby on Calle Nacional, where there are places for the burros and horses of the peasants to be tied and for men to spread out their straw mats or serapes for a night's rest. While the market is especially throbbing with life and color on Fridays, it is well worth a visit on any day. You can find stores selling handicrafts for tourists.

The Popular Museum, or Museum of Popular Arts and Archeology, is also in the center of town, not more than a few minutes from the plazas. It is very quaint, but its obviously unendowed rooms have been prepared with loving care by a native artist, Rodolfo Ayala, and they have some very interesting exhibits. We are particularly fond of the complete Mexican colonial kitchen built into the museum, while other rooms tell of Mexican handicrafts such as carvings, pottery, and weaving, and some contain artifacts found in the area. It is housed in the former school of Vasco de Quiroga, which looks like a typical colonial house built around a garden, and this structure alone makes it worth visiting.

Casa del Gigante. The so-called "House of the Giant," from a huge sculpture in the patio, can be found by asking one of the small boy guides.

O'Gorman Mural. Tourists usually stop to see the public library (*biblioteca*), as it contains a mural by one of the country's leading artists, Juan O'Gorman, which portrays the history of the state.

La Colegiata Church, originally planned to be the cathedral of the entire state, is still the most interesting of the buildings in Pátzcuaro. Sitting on a rise of ground before a broad plaza, it has a commanding position overlooking the lake.

Posada de la Basílica. If you have time, it is interesting to drop in for a cup of coffee in the morning or a refreshing drink in the afternoon at the Posada de la Basílica, even if you are not staying there. It is not far from the church or the market. It has a charming bar with windows looking out over the lake.

Dance of the Viejitos, the famed "Dance of the Old Men," is something tourists hope to see. It is usually done at the Posada Don Vasco on Wednesday and Saturday nights at 9:30 P.M., although you might check the time. It can also be arranged upon request at other times and places, or right in the plaza. Ask a guide. This is a famed and very lively dance in which small boys don masks of old patriarchs, hunch over canes, and for all the world look like some very gay old cutups having a last creaky fling.

Excursions about the Pátzcuaro Area

Tzintzuntzan, an even smaller village you pass on the way into Pátzcuaro, has a name which means "place of the humming-birds" in Tarascan. It is said to have once been the center of the Tarascan kingdom, but today it has only one small church surrounded by olive and cedar trees. It is said that a famous painting was kept in the church, but was burned in a fire that destroyed the interior of the church in 1944. The town has turned into a fair shopping area with good pottery and woven-reed goods.

Cucu Chucho, another small village off the road but accessible, is only a short way from Pátzcuaro, and you can see the famed Dance of the Viejitos there if you missed it at the Posada Don Vasco.

Jaracuaro, another lake village, is noted for its musical people and its fine gardens and orchids. It too is close enough for a day trip while stopping in Pátzcuaro. Taxis from Pátzcuaro will quote you a price on this trip.

Quiroga, mentioned on page 280, can be visited on the way either to or from Pátzcuaro, as it stands at the entrance to the main Mexico City highway. It has the largest display of lac-querware.

Santa Fe de Laguna, Eronguaricuaro, and Tacambaro. Possible to visit if you have more time is Santa Fe de Laguna, where Don Vasco de Quiroga founded a hospital that is still function-ing. Eronguaricuaro, across the lake, has barter markets and hand-loomed textiles. Tacambaro lies at the terminal point of the road some 25 miles south of Pátzcuaro, where the road drops to a tropical area and very interesting vegetation begins to appear.

Santa Clara, about 13 miles from Pátzcuaro, is the copper town. By some great quirk—for Mexico is one of the world's greatest sources of silver, lead, and zinc—the copper at Santa Clara does not come from the mine directly, but rather is reclaimed from scrap which is melted down in furnaces you can see. The two foundries at Santa Clara belong to the two Pureco brothers, but the art really lies in beating the copper into pans, pitchers, and bowls, which the artisans do with great style. Prices at the foundries or the nearby Exposición Permanente, where articles are also for sale, are about the same and not much lower than in the States. But you do get good, thick, solid copperware undoubtedly hand-beaten.

Paracho, just north of Uruapan, is the city of guitars. Taught by the early Spanish priests, the residents for centuries have put together fine guitars—each family having a special task. You can see them throughout the area, but in Paracho every other store is a guitar store. Bargain, as prices are flexible.

URUAPAN

Uruapan, which means "place of flowers" in Tarascan, is only 40 miles from Pátzcuaro by a new paved highway which goes through five villages and a pine forest. The new highway from Pátzcuaro lets you make a day trip to Uruapan. It is also possible to stay overnight there, or to continue by a different road which will bring you to the Guadalajara road at Carapan, 24 miles closer.

Uruapan is a rather large (population over 100,000) city jumbled together in a hilly setting, but many of its old buildings and its sprawling market are fascinating. You will find it a very different kind of community from Pátzcuaro, as it is the commercial center for a large agricultural area and the market there is much larger. You can find good buys in lacquerware, embroidered blouses and dresses, and pottery and copper. There is a very busy plaza in the center of town with the market behind it, and numerous places to stop for coffee or a meal.

La Roca Restaurant in Uruapan is at a beautiful site beside the flowing Cupatitzio River where it crosses Cupatitzio Street, which leads out from the main plaza (about five blocks beyond the Victoria Hotel). Typical Mexican food with the big crowd at noon. Filet mignon and chicken mole poblano every day. Cold beer and bar.

Uruapan is only 5,200 feet high, lower than Pátzcuaro, so it is warmer, while not hot. The surrounding area is much lower and tropical, with many flowers giving it the name of "the garden land of Mexico." Coffee, oranges, avocados, and bananas grow here, and frangipani, orchids, and jacaranda flowers can be seen. A national park borders the Cupatitzio River, which has some attractive walks along its banks.

At the village of *Angahuen*, you can go to a spot called *El Mirado*, where you can see the *Paricutín volcano* at 4 miles' distance. The volcano burst forth from a cornfield on February 20, 1943, and for almost a decade vomited huge rivers of molten lava in cascading red streams while blasting giant boulders into the sky as if they were pebbles. This fantastic show ended eight years later, after a cone 2,000 feet high had been built up and ashes yards deep had covered nearby villages and fields. It still has the appearance of a landscape on the moon. A village submerged in lava with only a church spire projecting is visible. You can rent horses and hire guides to go to this village and see the actual lava flow, now solidified. The trip takes about six hours altogether. The taxi costs less than $10 from Uruapan to Angahuen, and the horse for the one-hour ride to the volcano site is usually about $5.

WHERE TO STAY IN URUAPAN

Motel Pie de la Sierra (*47 rooms*)   Moderate
One of the finest regional hotels in all of Mexico. Located on the outskirts of town where the highway from Carapan and Guadalajara comes in, on a hilltop overlooking the city. Charming rooms with immaculate private baths, a fireplace in each room. The style is Spanish colonial. Large swimming pool, bar, dining room overlooking the pool, and a playground for children. All cards. Write Apartado Postal 153, Uruapan, Michoacán, México, for reservations. Tel: 2-15-10.

Hotel Victoria (*60 rooms*)   Inexpensive
A modern five-story commercial hotel in the center of the city at Cupatitzio 11 just off the plaza. All rooms have private baths. Bar, dining room, garage, and sun terrace. AE, CB, DC, MC, VISA. Tel: 2-15-00.

Hotel Hernández (*50 rooms*)   Inexpensive
Facing Plaza Morelos, an older modest hotel with a restaurant. AE, DC, MC, VISA. Tel: 2-16-00.

Hotel Paraiso (*64 rooms*)   Moderate
New motel-type hostelry 2 miles east of town on the Pátzcuaro road. Heated pool, restaurant. DC, MC, VISA. Tel: 2-24-21.

Joyita Trailer Park (*5 spaces*)   Inexpensive
  A left turn before the Pepsi factory on Highway 37 heading out of
  town. Hookups, showers, and toilet.

TRIP TO PARACUARO, APATZINGAN, AND INFIERNILLO

The entire area south of Uruapan is under development, with
a huge new dam near Infiernillo. The drive south is worthwhile,
as you go through a series of parks along the canyon of the
Cupatitzio River—a dashing mountain river. Be careful of the
slippery roads at this point. There is a crafts museum, La
Huatapera, on this road, and many fine places for a picnic.

The paved road goes all the way to Playa Azul on Route 37,
which brings you to the Pacific coast and a connection with the
great new Pacific coast route 200, which goes along the coast
to Ixtapa, Zihuatanejo, and Acapulco. Although the road is in
fine shape, the drive is rigorous through hot, dry flatland with
endless curving inclines. The area is unpopulated except for a
few villages. It is a full day's drive to the coast, but there you
find lush, bountiful fruit orchards and heavy palm groves. A
worthwhile drive!

19

Oaxaca

We always enjoyed visiting Oaxaca both for its pleasant and extremely neat people and its many fascinating ways of life. They have a festival of radishes, they have a day of toys, they make the best green pottery, and of course it is the home of mezcal.

On one trip I was told to look in on an American couple who supposedly were living in Huitzo, a tiny village just north of Oaxaca and off on a side road. We had reports that a young American couple, on their honeymoon, had adopted some Mexican children. My editors thought it would make a story.

We drove down the rutty dirt road into Huitzo, inquired for this young couple, and were immediately told they were living in the big hacienda near the railroad station.

There we found a happy household: a young Texan and his wife, whom he had met at an eastern school and married only a few months before, and no less than half a dozen Mexican boys ranging in age from two to twelve whom they had "adopted."

It seems they were painting landscapes when a little chap hung around with a terrible limp. Upon examining his foot, they found it infected and offered to clean it and apply a proper dressing. Soon he was completely cured, but he didn't stop hanging around. Then another boy showed up, whose family had abandoned him after beating him, and he was taken into their room.

They were by then so crowded they decided to rent the old hacienda, and then two more boys suddenly appeared—cousins of the first two. The young Texan put them to willing work helping to clean the house and plant a garden. He taught them lessons in the morning and basketball in the afternoon.

Another boy showed up and then another, and it was eleven children who sat down to lunch while we were there.

It was such a joyous group that we were moved to have a cameraman make a television news feature which showed the young family. Then we wrote an article which appeared in the Reader's Digest *(December 1954) and was reprinted in seventeen languages and read all over the world.*

Finally it was changed into a television drama, and this time played by actors. The screenplay looked very curious to us, but we were impressed with how far a little story from Oaxaca had gone.

I suppose the boys are all grown now, and I am sure they received a good education. We often think of the young couple who so unselfishly had their "honeymoon in Huitzo."

OAXACA IS A day's journey to the south of Mexico City on the Pan-American Highway. Located on an immense plateau at the optimum altitude of 5,000 feet, it is a land of quiet sunshine, ancient ruins unexcelled in archeological interest in Mexico, and a quiet race of people from whom have sprung some of Mexico's greatest leaders.

Many people who know Mexico well go to Oaxaca to achieve a certain peace and tranquillity which seems to exist there. Perhaps it is the fine weather and the blue skies; perhaps it is the impressive dignity of the beautiful surrounding mountains. More likely, it comes from the stoical nature of the modest and moral people who have sprung from the great tribes which started the immense cities of Monte Albán and Mitla a thousand years before Christ.

There is a song title that helps describe Oaxaca. It says, "If you love me in Wah-hah-kah, as you did in Cuernavaca, Adios." Something more is expected in Oaxaca, obviously.

Monte Albán. Whether you go to Oaxaca to spend several months in sun-filled meditation, or whether you go for a day's visit to see the stone ruins of Monte Albán, it is a pleasant trip. The hotels are good; one can sit around the plaza and hear the local band concerts; and there are wonderful side trips, such as to the Isthmus of Tehuantepec, the narrow neck of Mexico to the south with its picturesque women (see Chapter 24).

Benito Juárez. Two of Mexico's greatest presidents came from Oaxaca, which has given it the name of "cradle of patriots." By far the most outstanding was a Zapotecan Indian, from a village to the north of Oaxaca, who became a lawyer, governor of Oaxaca, then leader of rebellion forces against the French invaders of Mexico, and finally president of Mexico—Benito Juárez. He is regarded as the Abraham Lincoln of Mexico, both for his important role in the country's history and for his intrinsic humanitarianism. Many of the country's most impor-

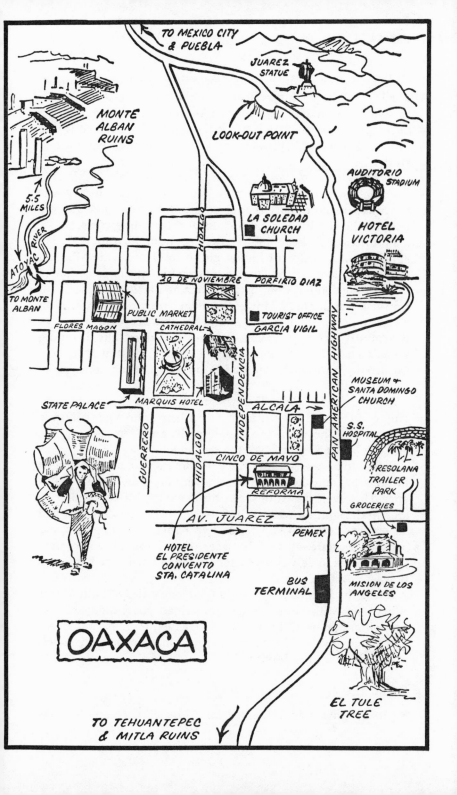

tant legislative achievements, including the Constitution of Mexico and the country's all-important Reform Laws, exist today because Juárez personally supported them. A great statue of Juárez stands on a high hill looking over the city, alongside the Pan-American Highway, and this is an impressive place to stop.

Porfirio Díaz. The other *oaxaqueño*, as the people of this area are called, who is an outstanding figure in Mexican history was a fearless revolutionary leader as a youth, but subsequently became the country's great dictator for thirty-five years.

Porfirio Díaz' dictatorship extended from 1876 to 1911. He sprang from a different Indian group in Oaxaca, the Mixtecs. Originally a fearless military leader who fought alongside Juárez in resisting foreign domination, Díaz as president became an iron-fisted strongman. However, his rule provided Mexico with an all-important era of law and order and peace, which gave the country its first great chance to grow economically, bringing with it an influx of foreign capital which did much to help Mexico by providing railroads, modern mining, and some industry.

Zapotecs and Mixtecs. The two great tribes of the Oaxaca area date back to many centuries before Christ, and their origin is lost in time. They were the Zapotecs, the great temple builders, and the Mixtecs, who were the craftsmen.

Before them the shadowy race of Olmecs seems to have been in the area, and the Mayans from Yucatán show similar influence. However, the earliest records show the Mixtecs ruling an area to the south toward Tehuantepec, while the Zapotecs had an empire near Oaxaca. These two tribes were enemies and consant warfare existed between them, except when they joined forces to defy the invaders from the north, the fierce and powerful Aztecs.

It was the Zapotecs who built the stone cities of both Monte Albán and Mitla, but the Mixtecs gained possession of these holy cities and used them as tombs for their more exalted dead. The famed jewels of Tomb 7 at Monte Albán are actually jewels placed there by the Mixtecs.

GOING THERE

By road, Oaxaca is 341 miles from Mexico City on the Pan-

American Highway, going east to Puebla, then south to Oaxaca. It is roughly an eight- or nine-hour drive. There are plenty of gasoline stations, but it is wise to take a box lunch. *Turismo* cars also drive there, while Autobúses del Sureste, located at Central Autobúses del Sureste, Fray Servando 350, Mexico City (tel: 5-42-42-10), runs first-class buses to Oaxaca. Autobúses de Oriente (ADO) also runs first-class buses directly to Oaxaca, leaving from Buenavista 9, Mexico City. Trip is $4 each way. A new central bus terminal in Mexico City has recently been completed to service Acapulco, Oaxaca, and other points. It is called Terminal Central del Sur and is at Taxqueño 1320, near Calzada Tlalpan Highway.

A CMA flight leaves from the Mexico City airport every morning. The trip takes an hour and a half and costs about $40 round trip.

WHERE TO STAY

Oaxaca now has one major luxury hotel right in town, *El Presidente Convento de Santa Catalina*, only a few blocks from the main plaza. This is by far the best hotel available, part of the government-run El Presidente chain. Immediately on the plaza is the much older, noisier, and more modest *Marqués del Valle*.

The *Victoria*, out of town on the Pan-American Highway, perched on a hillside overlooking the town, is a first-class hotel-motel attractively built with gardens and pool; it is run by Western Hotels. The former Oaxaca Courts, now called the *Misión de los Angeles*, is of lesser quality but has a small pool and offers American plan.

Smaller but good establishments in town are the *Casa Colonial*, about a ten-minute walk from the center of town but highly recommended, and the *Calesa Real*, a new hotel in a quiet area.

HOTELS, MOTELS, AND TRAILER COURTS IN OAXACA

El Presidente Convento de Santa Catalina (*92 rooms*)   Moderate
   In town five blocks from main plaza at Av. 5 de Mayo at the corner of Plazoleta Labastida, a new hotel converted from a colonial convent said to be 400 years old. Spacious rooms with attractive decor, large modern baths. Balconies around two courtyards, one with a pool and one an open-air dining room adjoining bar and cocktail lounge. Over $1.5 million was spent in modernizing the

hotel, which covers an entire city block. Excellent food. Air-conditioned. All cards. Toll-free U.S. number: (800) 421-0722; Mexico City: 5-18-00-40; or write to hotel in Oaxaca, Oaxaca, México.

Victoria Hotel (*151 rooms*)   Moderate
On Highway 190 as it passes east of the city, this is a large three-story hotel high on a hillside overlooking Oaxaca. It is part of the Western Hotels chain, and a very comfortable and well-run establishment. Half of the rooms have windows with a view of the city. Two cocktail lounges, large outdoor heated swimming pool, fine restaurant, rollaway beds. Restaurant open 7 A.M. till 11 P.M. Children under eighteen free. American plan available at extra charge per person. All cards. Reservations: P.O. Box 248. Tel: 32-19.

Misión de los Angeles (*63 units*)   Moderately expensive
A group of cabana-type units built in gardens around an old hacienda, this place has its charm although no longer its once good food and service. Has a small pool and a pleasant dining room with modified American plan available. Owner is Raul Ubando Fernández. Directly on Pan-American Highway across from principal turn into town. P.O. Box 17. Tel: 6-15-00.

Marqués del Valle Hotel (*84 rooms*)   Moderate
A commercial-type five-story hotel in the center of the city on the plaza and immediately adjacent to the cathedral. Very convenient, much atmosphere, but noisy. Well-run and fair restaurant of its kind. All cards. Tel: 34-76.

Casa Colonial (*12 rooms*)   Reasonable
About seven blocks from the plaza, at Miguel Negrete 105. A plain pension-type house with rooms built around a pleasant garden-patio. Excellent food. American management. Owners-managers are Herbert Madsen and wife. Write for reservations. Tel: 9-19-51 or 6-52-80.

Calesa Real (*77 rooms*)   Moderate
In town in a quiet area at García Vigil 306, three blocks from the main plaza, this is a new hotel in colonial style with comfortable rooms, pool in a garden, cocktail lounge, dining room, coffee shop. Manuel Ruiz Mendez is manager. Write for reservations. Tel: 6-55-44.

Monte Albán (*30 rooms*)   Moderate
An older hotel on adjoining plaza, León 1, which was once the bishop's palace. Very acceptable rooms, some with balconies overlooking plaza. Patio dining room. Famed Oaxaca folk dancers perform here Wednesday and Saturday nights at 8:30 P.M. AE, DC.

Margarita Motel (*55 rooms*)   Moderate
Two-story modern motel at north edge of town just off highway, Madero 1254. Rollaways. Tubs and showers. Nonfiltered pool. Nice gardens. Cocktails, dining room. Children free. AE, DC. P.O. Box 25. Tel: 40-85.

Hotel Senorial (*91 rooms*)   Moderate
At Portales de Flores 6, on side of main plaza in town. A café on one side obscures the hotel, but rooms inside are modern and attractive. Well-run, good dining room in back. Small pool.

Oaxaca Trailer Park (*100 spaces*) $3
Off Pan-American Highway south of Oaxaca, found by turning east across from large soccer stadium onto Voleta Street and going approximately seven blocks. A fine new trailer park with all hookups, patios, tile restrooms and showers, small recreation room, laundry room, pool, enclosed area.

La Resolana Trailer Court (*31 spaces*) $2
Off Pan-American Highway at corner of Misión de los Angeles, up side street three blocks and to your left. Fine trailer park in courtyard with many old trees, paved patios. Baths, toilets, laundry. Reservations to Ester Ortiz, Porfirio Díaz 18½.

GOOD RESTAURANTS

By far the best place to dine in Oaxaca, which is unfortunately not blessed with many restaurants, is at *El Refectorio* restaurant in El Presidente Convento de Santa Catalina on Av. 5 de Mayo in town. They have an elaborate menu with both continental and Mexican dishes. You eat inside around a courtyard. Prices are moderate to expensive.

Merendero del Tule is an upstairs restaurant on the west side of the main plaza in Oaxaca, and you can find there typical Mexican dishes as well as grilled meats. It is very popular locally and prices are modest. It is also possible to eat in the dining rooms of the *Marqués del Valle* or *Monte Albán* hotels nearby. A pleasant little coffee shop under the arches on the plaza is *Café Guelatao*. *El Patio*, just off the plaza on a side street, offers steaks and seafood from noon till midnight.

In Mitla, 25 miles south of Oaxaca at the ruins, you will find an old hacienda, *Restaurant La Sorpresa*, on one side of the plaza, which has unusually good Mexican food as well as American-style food. It serves cocktails and is open for lunch and dinner until 8 P.M. It has a few hotel rooms also.

WHAT TO SEE AND DO

The zócalo, or the main plaza in the center of town, is the best place to start your sight-seeing. This is a lovely, tree-shaded old square where concerts by the state band are given every Tuesday, Thursday, and Sunday evening, and local crowds come to hear them play in the bandstand under the trees, with the four fountains splashing and the cathedral clock counting the hours with its wooden clapper. It is worth getting a table at one of the many soft drink and coffee shops under the arches around the plaza and watching the people going by while listening to the music. Marimbas, those wooden xylophones with their melodic music, play on Wednesdays, Fridays, and Saturdays.

The Regional Museum of Oaxaca should be visited to see the famed Monte Albán jewels, consisting of hundreds of pieces of gold, pearls, turquoise, jade, coral, and tigers' teeth carved and worked into exquisite necklaces, rings, diadems, and other adornments. It is located in the former convent adjoining the ornate Church of Santo Domingo five blocks from the center of town on Calle Alcalá on the corner of Allende. Hours are 10 A.M. to 1 P.M. and 4 P.M. to 7 P.M. except Mondays when it is closed. Admission is 10 pesos.

The jewels were found in Tomb 7 of Monte Albán and are the work of the Mixtecs. Although the Zapotecs originally built Monte Albán, the Mixtecs later occupied it. The curator of the museum proclaims his exhibits as "the greatest treasure ever found in the Americas." Local shops sell facsimiles of some of the smaller pieces.

The Church of Santo Domingo itself is an early colonial structure standing next to the museum. It was started in 1575 and completed 100 years later. While simple in appearance on the outside, its interior features extremely ornate gold works in a vaulted ceiling and is considered one of the greatest baroque works of the Spanish period. Worth visiting.

The cathedral, alongside the Marqués del Valle Hotel on the plaza, is worth noting, as it is the oldest of the twenty-four churches in Oaxaca. The original building was finished about

1544, but the present building, which is larger, was started early in the eighteenth century and finished in 1733. It is a low building of solid appearance, and its interior is not particularly unusual.

The Rufino Tamayo Museum of pre-Hispanic art is located at Av. Morelos 503 just a short walk from the zócalo. Tamayo, an internationally celebrated contemporary painter, has established this handsome museum, with black marble floor and walls in strong lively colors he favored, in five salons around the various patios. Here you will find his lifetime collection of centuries-old stone figures and ceramics created by the ancient Toltecs, Mixtecs, Zapotecs, and Mayans as well as many other cultures. It is a group of amazing works showing humor, passion, and the goddess of death.

Juárez Market is a permanent public market consisting of hundreds of stalls, each selling its own assortment of baskets, pottery, and other goods. It is one block south of the zócalo. Note that the first section you come to may be devoted only to food, while farther on are other sections for crafts. Baskets are at the far end. Oaxaca is noted for its dark green pottery, and prices are very low. The interchange between shop people and customers is fascinating. A new market has been built farther away on the riverfront, but the merchants have refused to move.

The Auditorio Guelaguetza is built on the Pan-American Highway to the northeast of town. It is a huge modern stone structure located on the exact spot where the *Fiesta del Cerro* has traditionally been held on the first two Mondays after July 16 of each year. During the fiesta, regional dances are performed in a Zapotec tradition designed to bring neighbors together and to aid those in need. Legend has it that once human sacrifices were made, but now it is a merry occasion. Usually exhibits of local crafts are set up. It may be that such occasions will be repeated during the year for tourists, but you must inquire.

A new meteorological center has been built nearby with a gift from Oaxaca's sister city of Palo Alto, California.

San Felipe, a small village just out of town, makes a pleasant half-day hike if you feel up to it. You walk up Juárez Street, cross the Pan-American Highway, and continue up the narrow street in front of the Misión de los Angeles, and so on out of town. San Felipe is about 1 mile out of town. Then follow the old aqueduct, which leads to a small creek. Return to the Hotel Rancho San Felipe for lunch.

La Soledad. Aside from the walk to San Felipe, which is really a hike, you can make some interesting excursions around the town itself. The Sanctuary of the Virgin of Solitude (*La Soledad*) can be seen by walking down Independencia, the street in front of the Regional Museum, some four blocks. The story goes that a mule carrying a sculpture of the Virgin had mysteriously joined a pack train and that the mule fell at this spot and could not be moved. The muleteer could not remember having such a mule in his train. When the sculpture was removed, the mule was able to rise, then fell dead. The people decided to build a church on this spot; it was begun in 1602 and finished in 1690. The church is a good example of Oaxaca baroque styling, with many interesting carvings in stone. It is now used as a music school.

Other interesting churches are the former *Monastery of San Augustín*; the former *Monastery of the Company of Jesus*, which occupies the whole block next to the State Government Building; and the beautiful *Church of San Felipe Neri*, where Benito Juárez married Margarita Maza in 1843.

Juárez House. At García Vigil 609, six blocks from the main plaza and across the street from San Felipe Church, is the Juárez House museum. Actually, the great Mexican patriot only lived here for ten years as a servant of Padre Salanueva, but it was the start of his illustrious career. It contains some good portraiture of Juárez and also is an interesting view of a house of the period, as it has been preserved as it was. A national monument, it is open to visitors from 10 A.M. to 2 P.M. and from 4 to 6 P.M. on weekdays, and from 10 A.M. to 3 P.M. on Sundays. Admission is 1 peso.

If you did not stop and see the *Juárez monument* on your entry to Oaxaca, it is a spot you should visit. Here is the best place to take pictures of the city, in panorama, as the view is a commanding one. The monument is directly on the Pan-American Highway as it bypasses the city.

Ocotlán. About 20 miles south of Oaxaca, this little town of 10,000 has an Indian market every Friday, and is overwhelmed by those from the surrounding area anxious to sell produce, livestock, and a wide variety of goods. Every inch of space is occupied by makeshift stalls where campesinos' tomatoes, fish, rope, tortillas, and other goods are being sold. The market is very colorful and includes a wonderful collection of primitive roulette wheels.

San Bártolo Coyotepec. En route to Ocotlán it is possible to stop at San Bártolo Coyotepec, where the village has an entire mountain of black clay from which the famed black pottery is made. While all the villagers are potters, the doyenne of them all is Dona Rosa, who is said to have made a fortune in the business and owns two cars.

MONTE ALBÁN RUINS

How To Get There. Monte Albán is about 5½ miles from the center of Oaxaca. The road is paved. You can hire a taxi to take you there for about $8, or minibuses leave from the terminal at Arista and Díaz Ordaz at 9:30 A.M., 12:30 P.M., and 4 P.M. daily, or you can drive your own car there easily. Driving, one should leave the main plaza by Bustamente Street, turn right at Arista, left at 20 de Noviembre, and then go straight ahead across the railroad tracks and bridge. The road begins shortly thereafter to wind up the mountainside directly to the hilltop, some 1,200 feet above Oaxaca, where the ancient ruins are located. An admission fee of 10 pesos is charged. Maps showing how to get there are distributed by the Yalalag crafts shop at Alcalá 104 or the tourist office at the corner of Independencia and García Vigil a block from the zócalo. There are guides on the scene.

Seeing Monte Albán. Park your car, get out, and start a walk around the site which will take you either a half hour or a half day, depending upon your interest. About you is spread the immense Valley of Oaxaca, and the dramatic clouds and mountains are undoubtedly little different from those which caused the ancient builders to pick this spot for a "city of the gods."

This is what Monte Albán actually was. While it eventually took in 25 square miles, with an estimated 40,000 persons living there, the city was intended to honor the gods of the dominant Indian tribe, the Zapotecs, and their predecessors.

How these ancient people carved off the top of these bleak mountains, securing the level space on which they moved the gigantic hewn stones for the group of noble buildings, with their symmetry and handsome proportions, remains a mystery.

Monte Albán was a Mecca, a holy city, for the great tribe of the Zapotecs, and some of the carved stones can be interpreted by archeologists to tell the history. They say there is evidence that the first building began over 2,000 years ago.

The first period, estimated at some time before 500 B.C., is called the period of the *Danzantes*, or dancers, because the only indications left of this period are numerous carved slabs of stone with figures in grotesque dancing postures. These figures give some indication of a system of numbering, with bars and dots, which indicates a culture borrowed from the Mayans. These slabs, with their figures in shapeless postures and idiotic grins, can be seen in a building called the *Temple of the Dancers.*

The second period of Monte Albán, about 250 A.D., brought the *Observatory* building to the group. Some time between 400 A.D. and 1000 A.D., the immense structures of courts and palaces were built.

The huge *Central Plaza* is 1,200 feet long and 600 feet wide. At the east side are the great steps which lead to the ball court. If you climb these steps you will find behind them a gymnasiumlike structure where a ball game not unlike basketball could have been played. The object was to get the ball into a niche in each end, and players could use only elbows or hips to move the ball.

An enormous *South Platform* closes the plaza at the far end. On the west, from south to north, is the Temple of the Dancers. In the center the Observatory can be seen; it is notable because it is not in line with the axis of the other structures and several other temple buildings.

At the north end, near the entrance, is the great *North Platform* with the vestige of pillars on its summit. These steps can be climbed. Beyond them is the *Sunken Plaza*, which is a second group of buildings. All of these are believed to have been temples of a sort in which rites were practiced in worshiping the gods. Caretakers and priests lived here, but the people lived in the surrounding five hills, not actually on the scene of the temples.

Many beautiful urns and stelae (carved stones) have been found, with carved artwork that shows the people of the time, richly dressed, with helmets, carrying feathers, wearing heavy necklaces, and with stretched holes in their earlobes adorned with jewels for high castes or just clay for common people. The people have the thick lips, broad noses, and Oriental eyes characteristic of the native people still found in the villages today.

Monte Albán was also used from its earliest times, evidently, for burial of important priests and nobles. Tombs were carved beneath the rocks, and the bodies were placed there, often with rich treasures and even servants buried with their masters to show the deceased's position.

It was the Zapotecs who principally built Monte Albán. They did not withdraw from Monte Albán until the period of their decadence, after the year 1000, when they were defeated by their bitter rivals, the Mixtecs.

The Mixtecs took over Monte Albán and for the next 500 years used it, not as the holy city, but as a city of the dead. It was a place for burial. They removed many of the remains from the Zapotec tombs, or else drove the burial chambers deeper and then decorated them much more elaborately.

It was the Mixtecs—master craftsmen with a knowledge of smelting and working gold, copper, and silver; carving jade, crystal, and obsidian; and other arts—who placed in the tombs the lavish offerings which have been discovered there.

Discovery of the Jewels. Monte Albán first became known in present historical times when a French captain, Dupaix, discovered the archeological area in 1867. However, not until 1916 did the Mexican government begin any scientific exploration. In 1931, one of Mexico's leading archeologists, Alfonso Caso, began the first really systematic exploration of Monte Albán. He began excavating the first of some 500 tombs, and the initial group revealed only a few clay vessels and skeletons, as they had already been opened by unknown raiders.

But, beginning work on what is called Tomb Number 7, Caso's party cleared away debris and broke through a roof beneath two layers of stucco. Their flashlights revealed a surprising discovery. Beneath them in the darkness was a treasure that became one of the richest archeological finds ever discovered. There was a fabulous collection of gold breastplates, solid gold masks, carved jade, pearls as big as pigeon eggs, necklaces, fans, bracelets, and belt buckles made from various precious stones and metals.

There were also nine skeletons, and intensive study indicated that one must have been a high priest who was hunchbacked and probably had a brain tumor, while the others were his servants. Altogether, 500 items were taken from this one tomb, each was carefully marked as to where it lay, and every inch of ground was measured. The news was on the front pages of newspapers around the world.

The jewels were at first claimed by the national government, but they were later relinquished to the state government and are in the Regional Museum of Oaxaca (see page 296), where they can be viewed.

Going to Mitla, Tule, and Tlacolula

How To Get There. Mitla, the other great ruin of the Oaxaca area, is mentioned along with the famed Tule Tree and the little village of Tlacolula because Mitla lies 25 miles to the south of Oaxaca, on the Pan-American Highway, and one can easily pause a minute at the Tule Tree en route. If it is a Sunday, a stop at the fine market of Tlacolula is interesting and on the way. There is a fair restaurant in Mitla, La Sorpresa (see page 295).

Tule Tree. Just a few miles out of Oaxaca, one comes to the little village of Santa María del Tule; here is the giant ahuehuete or green cypress Tule Tree, which is said by naturalists to be 3,000 years old. Under its branches Cortés and his men are said to have rested on their way to Honduras. It is 135 feet high and its branches spread 140 feet. It is one of the oldest living things in the Western world.

Tlacolula. Three miles beyond Tule, a sign points to a side road which will take you to Tlacolula. On Sundays, you can drive into this town and visit the interesting markets, if you have an hour to spare.

Mitla. Twenty-four miles from Oaxaca, where there is a turnoff from the Pan-American Highway, a paved road off to the left goes 3 miles into Mitla. Youngsters on the scene are glad to guide you through the village streets to reach the ruins. In the village there is a small museum and a crafts school founded by an American couple, Mr. and Mrs. E. R. Frissell. Mr. Frissell is no longer living and the museum was given to a university, but is still managed by Mrs. Frissell. She is an expert on Mitla, and can be prevailed upon to discuss it at times; in any case, you can see their impressive display of relics gathered from the region.

A cluster of rickety shops has been built outside the ruins, offering everything from blankets to shirts. In the town of Mitla, better goods are available at Albert's Hand Crafts, Morelos 38.

The Ruins at Mitla. While Monte Albán was an impressive city built high and open to the winds, Mitla was called in Zapotec *Lyo-Baa*, "Place of Rest," and it was intended as a tomb for kings, high priests, and the very noble.

Nowadays, Mitla is a hot, sun-baked little village, but the ruins, on the far side, while partially leveled by the early Spaniards who seized upon them as building materials for the Christian churches, are much better preserved than those of Monte Albán. This is partly due to the fact that Mitla was still being used in the early seventeenth century.

Mitla was originally Zapotec, but it came under the Mixtec influence earlier than did Monte Albán, and many authorities consider it more Mixtec than Zapotec. The Mixtecs began to dominate the area from 1350 A.D. onward, and Mitla was evidently begun only about the twelfth century by the Zapotecs.

The architecture of Mitla is very intricate, and the use of the Greco pattern is found only at Mitla and Yagul, which is also nearby at Tlacolula. The patterns are made by cutting stones about 4 inches in length and fitting them together so perfectly that they hold together without cement of any sort. This is precision which would baffle modern stonemasons.

The ruins consist of four principal palaces, with lesser ones surrounding them, each having a patio in the center and rooms on all sides but the west. The palaces have wide steps ascending to them, and the angular and severe doorways (there are no arches, as this was a device not yet discovered by the native builders of that period) contain some fifteen different mosaic patterns which are unique among pre-Columbian ruins.

Under many of the palaces there are tombs. One cruciform underground chamber, which a guide will show you, contains a huge monolith called *La Columna de la Muerte*, "The Column of Death," which will tell Zapotecs, at least, how many years they have to live if they embrace it and then count off the remaining space with their fingers. It doesn't work too well for gringos, who can reach too far and usually find they are already living on borrowed time.

The most remarkable sight is the *Hall of Mosaics*, where all four walls are covered with a continuous sculptured design. The other spectacular sight is the *Hall of Columns*, a building supported by six massive monoliths, plus some others nearby which are lying on their sides, showing how the early invaders attempted to remove them for use in newer buildings.

Yagul. On the way to Mitla, one can visit some newly excavated ruins at Yagul, where tombs are still being opened. While difficult to reach, it can be done by taking a turn 5 miles before Mitla.

Where To Shop

Oaxaca is one of the best places in Mexico to shop for certain goods, among which can be listed the dark-green glazed pottery of Ozumpa, the black unglazed pottery of Coyotepec, cotton and woolen shawls, blouses, serapes (which, while less colorful than those of Puebla, are heavier and better suited for rugs), baskets in profusion, and fine steel hunting knives. Bottles of mezcal, the version of vodkalike white lightning, come in hand-painted black flasks.

Yalalag, at Alcalá 104, just off the zócalo, is by far the best arts and crafts shop in town. They have several rooms, each featuring one of their specialties—blouses, shawls, pottery, wood carvings, frames, and other Indian crafts. They will pack and ship to the United States. They also hand out as good a map of Oaxaca as can be found.

Casa Cervantes, Porfirio Díaz 5, has the best collection of local goods; ask for one of their maps of the city.

Ramona's, downtown at Hidalgo 807, is one of the top shops for local textiles in original and classic designs.

Platería Ortiz, Independencia 36, sells reproductions of the Monte Albán jewels.

Joyas Regionales, on Hidalgo Street one block from the main plaza, makes and sells very handsome jewelry of high quality. Also knives and swords of fine steel with engraving.

Artesianas Victor, Porfirio Díaz 111, has a varied selection of woven goods including napkins and tablecloths.

Casa Schondube S.A., on the Pan-American Highway near the Victoria Hotel, tries to find local artwork of some merit for purveyance to museums and art galleries.

Guillermo Brena, Pino Suárez 700, sells only hand-loomed textiles made by their own workers; their work is among the best.

Adela Jiménez, Zaragoza 402, has the most colorful pottery in Oaxaca.

Mezcal del Valle, Madero 438, sells mezcal in black flasks and also the maguey worms that can be served with it.

La Predilecta, Bustamente 115, just off the zócalo, is the most complete drugstore.

La Primavera, facing the cathedral, has twenty-four-hour photographic service.

20

Puebla

The studied politeness and courtesy of the Mexican people are in good measure part of the tradition brought from Spain, but perhaps in Mexico they are carried to even more rigid forms than in the Spanish motherland.

Madame Calderón de la Barca, wife of the first Spanish minister to Mexico after the country won its independence, wrote in a very witty volume of memoirs some comments on the manners of Mexico in 1842.

When Mexican ladies greet each other socially, she wrote, one must embrace each lady who enters the room. Then the following dialogue is de rigueur:

"How are you (Cómo está?). Are you well?"

"At your service (A sus ordenes), and you?"

"Without novelty (Sin novedad), at your service."

"I am rejoiced, and how are you, Señora?"

"At your disposal, and you?"

"A thousand thanks, and the Señor?"

After much more of the same about other members of the family, the conversation then concludes:

"Madam, you know that my house is at your disposal (Aquí es su casa)."

"A thousand thanks, madam. Mine is at yours, and though useless, know me for your servant, and command me in everything that you may desire."

Withdrawal is always made by saying, "Con su permiso" (With your permission). This is still good form today.

PUEBLA OFFERS you either a day's trip from Mexico City or an overnight stay en route to either Veracruz or Oaxaca. It is about a two-hour drive from Mexico City. On the way to Puebla you pass very close to both of the huge snow-capped volcanoes, Popocatepetl and Iztaccihuatl.

Mexico's fourth largest city, Puebla has clean streets, charming churches, and some exquisite architecture, and very possibly deserves more attention than it receives. It has its own industry, being the principal textile center of the country, and is a trading center for the extensive agricultural areas on all sides which grow apples, oranges, plums, cattle, wheat, and, of course, corn.

Puebla's population is over 750,000. It is located at over 7,000 feet in altitude, which means it has a coolish temperate climate; but, like Mexico City, it is also blessed with a good deal of bright, warm sun the year round.

Puebla is often called "city of the angels" because, according to legend, a Dominican friar dreamed he saw two angels laying out the city. Be that as it may, the Spanish, ten years after the conquest, did decide to build a city midway on the Veracruz–Mexico City route, and the city was to become Puebla. Puebla is a city of straight streets, for the most part, because of the methodical plotting of avenues by the Spanish.

Famed for Tile. Puebla is a city of fine polychromatic, or multicolored, tiles which have been used extensively in its handsome churches and many other buildings. The famous tile is about the best that is made in Mexico, being fine work in a hard glaze and multicolored, in comparison with the single-color pottery of other areas. It is Puebla tile, most often in squares of bright yellow and dark blue, which provides the handsome tile colonial kitchens, the interesting tile fountains and benches, and the glistening yellow tile domes of many churches seen in Mexico. Naturally, one sees more of this tile work in Puebla than anywhere else.

Serapes. While people are often enthusiastic about one city or another in Mexico, Puebla is rarely their favorite city. At the same time, almost everyone agrees that it is a pleasant place and has some points of interest worth seeing. One of the things to do is to stop at the village of *Huejotzingo* (whay-hot-SIN-go), just beyond San Martín Texmelucan coming from Mexico City, to see what are probably Mexico's finest serapes, the heavy wool blankets used for robes or floor throws. Huejotzingo has them in profusion, in the brightest colors and at wildly varying prices. They are at stands directly along the road as you go through the little town. Most of them are made in the little village of Santa Ana.

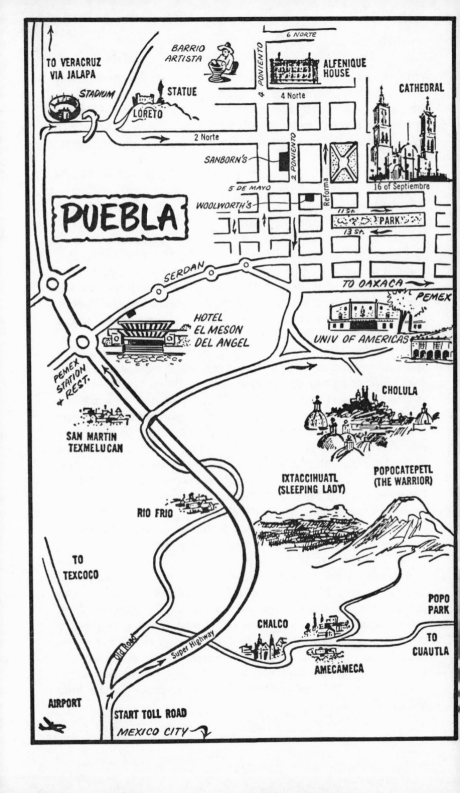

Cinco de Mayo. On May 5, 1862, Puebla was the scene of one of Mexico's most famous battles, when 2,000 Mexican soldiers succeeded in driving back 6,000 French troops who were instructed to place Maximilian on the throne of Mexico. Ten days later, the French returned and overcame the resistance. But the initial victory was widely heralded and many of the streets in Mexico are named "5 de Mayo" in honor of this event, and it is one of the great national holidays. Distinguishing himself in this battle was young Porfirio Díaz, later to become Mexico's great dictator.

A Church for Each Day. One of the most interesting sights to be seen in a trip to Puebla is the nearby village of Cholula, 5 miles before Puebla if you are driving from Mexico City. It was a pre-Hispanic holy city of the Tlaxcalans, who are said to have built here the largest pyramid in Mexico, which is possibly the largest in the world. Some say that it is 20,000 years old. Largely overgrown now and looking more like a good-sized hill, it is exceeded in interest by the many churches which have been built in Cholula (some say one for each day of the year, although a careful count reveals it is somewhat less but still an impressively large number).

University of the Americas. Adjoining the Cholula archeological zone, and only 8 miles from Puebla, is the handsome new campus of the prestigious University of the Americas. Built on a 164-acre tract of land, it has a score of new buildings all constructed in colonial design, including a library and learning resource center, a College of Arts and Sciences, Technological Institute, administration and classroom buildings, sports facilities seating 2,600 persons, sixteen residence halls, and a faculty village of sixty homes. The new campus was a gift of the Jenkins family, who made a fortune in Mexico from sugar and supermarkets (among various ventures) over several decades. The university, formerly Mexico City College, was founded by Henry L. Cain, then superintendent of the American School, and his principal, Paul Murray. Classes are taught in both English and Spanish, and credits are accepted by most American institutions. The university is coeducational, and offers regular year and summer classes. Tuition is $300; board and room, $225. The director is Dr. Macias Rendon. Address is Apartado Postal 507, Puebla, Puebla, México. Tel: 3-10-55.

University of Puebla, the state university for the area, is located in the city of Puebla and is much larger, at least in number of students (20,000), than University of the Americas. It has a new campus, Ciudad Universitaria, in the southeast outskirts of the city. It has a medical school and a law school, and offers degrees in business, engineering, pharmacology, and chemistry.

Puebla also has a teachers' college, conservatory of music, art school, and the Emiliano Zapata School of Agriculture.

How To Get There

Car or bus is the most usual means of transportation to Puebla, and this can be your own car, the usual turismo or limousine, or one of several bus lines. Driving time from Mexico City is two hours. The old road is curving and mountainous, rising to 10,000 feet at one point, but it is paved and has guard rails. A new superhighway, which branches off from the old road just beyond the Mexico City airport, is much faster (it saves thirty minutes driving time), and there is an 18-peso toll, but it bypasses the interesting little villages along the way, including Cholula. Buses operating from Mexico City to Puebla include Autotransportes Unidas, Fray Servando 350 (tel: 5-42-42-10); Estrella Roja, Fray Servando 266 (tel: 5-22-36-87); and ADO, Buenavista 9 (tel: 5-67-66-03). The development of new bus terminals may cause a change in departure points. Check by phone. Pullman bus or first-class travel is suggested.

Train or Plane. There is good equipment, but the train trip is time-consuming. The train goes on to Veracruz. You can get information at the main railroad stations in Mexico City or in Puebla. There is no good air service, as the distance is too short; the trip is quicker by car or bus.

Where To Stay

Puebla has one very good hotel, *El Mesón del Angel,* and some older ones that are charming in their way and comfortable. Of these, the *Hotel Lastra,* in a quiet area with gardens, is perhaps the best. Both of the hotels mentioned are on boulevards that lead out of the heart of the city.

Hotels and Trailer Parks in Puebla

El Mesón del Angel (*122 rooms*)   Moderately expensive
At Av. Hermanos Serdán 807, just off the first exit from the tollway from Mexico City as you reach Puebla. A new, modern three-story motor inn with luxury rooms each with its own balcony. Some have view of volcanoes. Gardens, heated pool, tennis. Has probably the best restaurant in Puebla. Also coffee shop. Reservations recommended. AE, DC. Tel: 42-49-50.

Hotel Lastra (*50 rooms*)   Moderate
On Calzada de los Fuertes, a boulevard joining the third exit on the Mexico City tollway as it arrives in Puebla. An older hotel about 1½ miles from the center of town. Still modern and comfortable. Heated pool. Dining room. Cocktails. Nice gardens. Same management as Mesón del Angel. AE, DC. P.O. Box 649. Tel: 2-46-30.

Gilfer Hotel (*98 rooms*)   Moderate
At 2 Oriente 11 in downtown area, has garage, luxury rooms, pool, bar, music in rooms, restaurant, nightclub. Modern. The best downtown hotel. Tel: 42-98-00.

Hotel Senorial (*72 rooms*)   Inexpensive
A new hotel four blocks north of the zócalo at Calle 4 No. 602. Rooms small but well furnished. Has TV, modest dining room. Tel: 42-49-30.

Hotel Royalty (*40 rooms*)   Inexpensive
Portal Hidalgo No. 8 on the zócalo; probably the second best of the downtown hotels. Rooms small. Has fair dining room, also street café under arches which is fun. Turkish and Russian baths. AE, DC. Tel: 2-47-40 and LD 28.

Pan-American Courts (*62 rooms*)   Inexpensive
Reforma 2114, on old highway entering city. Ordinary courts. With or without meals. Also a trailer park. Tel: 42-46-90.

Hotel San Miguel (*52 rooms*)   Inexpensive
At Avenida 3 Poniente 721, a fair hotel with comfortable rooms. Has dining room with good food. AE, DC. Tel: 42-48-60.

Cuatro Caminos Trailer Park (*10 spaces*) $3
At entrance to city, from expressway to Serdán, near Mesón del Angel. Has all hookups and small restaurant.

Hotel Spa Agua Azul

South of town on Calle 11 Sur. Hotel is not acceptable, but it has space with connections for ten trailers. Has good mineral pool.

WHERE TO EAT IN PUEBLA

Sanborn's   Moderate

At 2 Oriente No. 6, a full-fledged Sanborn's with good dining room, coffee shop, and soda fountain, plus the usual Sanborn shops for newspapers, pharmaceuticals, film, perfume, etc. Serves from breakfast till midnight with American food and Mexican dishes. One block over from plaza.

El Mesón del Angel   Expensive

In hotel of same name about 2 miles from center of town at Hermanos Serdán 807, which is boulevard to superhighway. This is the fanciest and probably best restaurant in Puebla. International cuisine, very lavish menu. Sandwiches for children. Cocktails. Manager: Sr. Rosas. Dining room open 7:30 A.M. till 11 P.M. Tel: 42-49-50.

El Merendero   Moderate

At Lastra Hotel 1½ miles from center of town on Calzada de los Fuertes, or ten minutes by taxi. Serves trout and bacon, charcoal-broiled steaks, good seafood and Mexican dishes. Tel: 42-46-30.

Royalty Restaurant-Café   Moderate

On main Reforma Street in hotel of same name opposite plaza. Open for service in either dining room or popular sidewalk café from 6:30 A.M. till 2 A.M. Interesting place to watch passersby. Serves full range of Mexican dishes plus sandwiches, steaks. AE, DC.

Woolworth's   Inexpensive

On 5 de Mayo a half block from the plaza and cathedral. Has a lunch counter that can be useful. Also a good shopping place.

WHAT TO DO AND SEE

First of all, congested traffic is prevalent in Puebla, and you may have trouble parking, or even driving, in the very center of town. There are several parking garages in the center, but they are often full. Tourists can sometimes park by the plaza, but your best bet is to park some distance from the center of town and walk the rest of the way.

Puebla Tile and Pottery. A walk, starting from the main plaza located off Reforma Street in the center of Puebla, with the cathedral to one side, will show you the interesting tile of Puebla on many buildings, benches in the park, fountains, and the sixty churches Puebla is said to have. Potters were brought to Puebla from Toledo by the Spanish shortly after they founded the city in 1531. The potters taught the natives how to make the traditional blue, white, and yellow Talavera pottery, and throughout the colonial period the Spaniards kept a firm hand on the local industry, insisting on strict adherence to the Talavera designs.

The techniques thus perpetuated gave the Puebla tile a reputation for quality, but the natives did not take well to copying other designs and began to incorporate their own colors and designs which pleased them. The results were much more successful and became known internationally as *Talavera de Puebla.*

This tile and pottery are still undoubtedly the best in Mexico. The craftmanship is not only in the tile you see in the buildings, but you can purchase tea sets, vases, jars of all sizes, and flowerpots. *Convent Santa Rosa,* Calle 3 Norte near Poniente 12, contains the famous Talavera-tile-covered kitchen. It is open to visitors.

Barrio del Artistas is an area of several blocks near the Hotel Senorial in the vicinity of the streets of 2 Oriente and 6 Norte (just take 2 Norte from alongside the cathedral north to 6 Norte and go right two blocks). You will find an entire area of shops with native crafts, onyx works, Talavera pottery, baskets, and serapes. Avenida 4 Oriente and Calle 8 Norte have whole streets of artists at work in shops and studios. Well worth visiting, and a fine place to shop.

The cathedral, located on the main plaza (Plaza de la Constitución, but more commonly called the zócalo), was started in 1550 and was not completed until over 100 years later, in 1665. It is almost as large as the cathedral in Mexico City. As you pass through the huge carved facade and great doors, you can see the main altar of gray Puebla onyx and the fine workmanship in the wood carvings. Paintings are by Indian artists, including Miguel Cabrera, José Ibarra, and Zandejas. It is possible to ascend to the towers and see a magnificent view of the surrounding countryside, including the famed volcanoes and the city of Puebla itself.

The Casa de Alfeñique or Sugarcake House is an easy walk from the cathedral plaza—down Reforma (or General Camacho Avenue as it is called farther along), which is the street on the opposite side of the plaza from the cathedral, to Calle 4 Norte and Av. 4.

The Casa de Alfeñique is said to have been built of stucco composed of the whites of eggs and sugar, while others say it looks as if it were made of rose water and whipped cream. It now houses a state museum, but it was built in the late 1700s as a guest house for Spanish viceroys. The museum has many articles relating to Puebla's interesting history.

Santo Domingo Church and Rosary Chapel can be reached, upon leaving Sugarcake House, by walking three blocks down Av. 4 Oriente back toward the center of town. It is on the corner of 5 de Mayo Street. Santo Domingo is an old Dominican monastery built of gray stone, but the Capilla del Rosario (Rosary Chapel) is probably the most beautiful individual chapel in all Mexico. One is met at the entrance by a dazzling sight: gold leaf on all sides, with intricate carvings and multicolored statues. The church is a seventeenth-century structure.

The Secret Convent of Santa Mónica may be found by going down 5 de Mayo Street, from either the zócalo or Santo Domingo, some six or seven blocks to the corner of Av. 18 Poniente, where you take a turn to the left and come almost immediately upon No. 103 and the hidden convent. The story is that this was built in 1606 by two prominent Pueblans who wanted an institution to serve as a well-chaperoned place for noble married ladies when their husbands were absent on trips to Europe or other parts of Mexico. This idea did not take well with the ladies, who disdained such protection and preferred to remain at home with their families or relatives. Consequently, it was left unused.

In 1609, the building was turned into a shelter for prostitutes who were to be reformed under force, governed by a rectress, but this plan seems to have fared no better, lacking cooperation from the new residents.

However, the next effort was somewhat more successful. A

college for young girls, with official approval of the Church in Rome, was founded on September 14, 1682. It was called Santa Mónica.

With the political troubles that befell Mexico, the advent of the revolution in 1810 and the Reform Laws of 1857 (which forbade convents), the nuns were expelled several times, but they continued to operate the convent in secret. They used secret entrances to the convent, thus giving it its present name, the Secret Convent of Santa Mónica. Finally, in 1934, the nuns were discovered there and the government formally closed the convent. It has been turned into a museum and is open to the public.

You may buy tickets at the entrance. It is possible to view the offices and cells of the mother superior, which have a rather forlorn collection of totally unrelated art on the walls. However, after passing through the cells of the nuns, you come to an interesting chapel. It contains the crown of thorns by which the nuns of many convents in Mexico's colonial period used to suffer voluntary penance. It also contains some rather good religious paintings. All in all, a long-lost scene from Mexico's history is revealed.

Lunch. We suggest lunching at the *Royalty Café* on the zócalo or driving to the *Mesón del Angel* out on Serdán Street for a fancier and more expensive lunch. By going to the Lastra Hotel, where there is *El Merendero* restaurant, you would drive out General Camacho Avenue from the zócalo and you would be in sight of Forts Loreto and Guadalupe. These two old forts were important defense points on the summit of two hills during Puebla's famous battle.

Cholula. The famed village of Cholula, 8 miles outside Puebla on the old road to Mexico City, has something close to a church for each day of the year. Some 300 churches in a town with not many more inhabitants can be seen from the Mexico City highway as you approach Puebla, or you can easily turn in on an alternate route through Cholula, which winds back out to the main highway again. Driving on Calle Hermanos Serdán toward town from the expressway en route to Oaxaca, you can see Cholula, and several roads offer opportunities to turn in.

While the vast number of churches with their bell towers

rising up from virtually every hilltop in the vicinity are certainly impressive, Cholula has more of a story to tell than this tale of sheer numerical achievement.

Long before the Spanish came, Cholula was the holy city of the Tlaxcalans, and 100,000 persons are estimated to have been living there when the Spanish arrived. In its center was the great pyramid which had been erected long before the Aztecs first came. According to legend, the great benevolent god Quetzalcoatl paused in Cholula on his way to the seacoast, and spent twenty years there teaching the Toltecs the great secrets of contentment and life.

To honor Quetzalcoatl, the Toltecs began the huge pyramid, which is the largest in Mexico and which rivals the great pyramids of Egypt in size. As centuries passed, layer after layer was added to the pyramid, more setbacks made, and a sacred fire was always kept burning at the summit. Images of other gods, such as the god of air, were made and kept on the scene. Some had plumelike flames coming from their heads, wore gold collars, and held scepters with jewels. At times as many as 6,000 human sacrifices a year were made in their honor.

The pyramid was soon surrounded by lesser temples and shrines, and many priests and holy men lived in adjoining structures. The site was held in veneration throughout Mexico. Thus it was when the party of Cortés arrived on its initial visit to Mexico. It was here that the treacherous plot to wipe out Cortés was arranged upon instruction of the Aztec king. Cortés and his party were made welcome at Cholula, after their hard climb from the sea, and were invited in most cordial terms to spend the night there, but the plot was to massacre them in the night as they slept. The Indian maiden Malinche, who was Cortés's mistress and interpreter, sensed the plot and warned him. Cortés alerted his men and reversed the proceeding by falling upon the Cholulans first, killing some 3,600, according to handed-down reports, and laying waste much of the holy city.

Subsequently as the Spaniards tore down the pagan temples, they decided to replace each one with a Christian church, and thus began the new tradition of Cholula—a church for nearly each day of the year.

Coming to Cholula today, you will first notice the many

churches as you approach, each set casually around the countryside, most often on a knoll, but above them all is an especially prominent church on the top of what is apparently a high hill. This church is called *Nuestra Señora de los Remedios,* and its huge dome can be seen for miles. It is covered with glazed yellow, white, and green tiles. The church has been radically rebuilt over the years and is no longer of great historical interest, but the view is worth the climb.

The great pyramid on which Los Remedios was built is said to be the largest pyramid in the world, and a $3-million excavation and restoration program started by the Mexican government will show the dramatic size of this great structure, as well as twenty other pre-Hispanic satellite structures including priests' dwellings and other religious buildings. Four smaller pyramids have also been uncovered. They are said to be of the same ancient period as the Pyramids of the Sun and Moon outside Mexico City.

A modern motel-type establishment, the Archaeological Villa-Cholula, is open near Cholula Pyramid and offers rooms and restaurant. Pool and tennis.

Many of the churches in Cholula can be visited, but while each is different architecturally, you will usually find them to be, in large measure, empty shells of the religious structures they were originally. Each church has a caretaker and is usually supported by some community church elsewhere in Mexico.

The University of the Americas, described on page 309, is just a mile and a half beyond the intersection where you entered Cholula. You can easily drive in and find yourself welcome. Visitors are asked to report to the Administration Building before touring.

African Safari. A wild-animal park called African Safari is located about fifteen minutes south of the city of Puebla. Here you can see, in a privately owned preserve, fenced-in but free-roaming elephants, camels, lions, zebras, monkeys, and wildebeests. The entire preserve is said to contain 2,500 animals and 500 birds, including ostriches. Captain Carlos Camacho, an animal lover, is owner.

NEARBY RESORTS

There are some very interesting, in fact exotic, resorts within a few hours' drive of Puebla, and the new toll road to Córdoba-Veracruz makes this an easy trip. It is 110 miles from Puebla to Orizaba (location of the highest peak in Mexico); the toll road costs 23 pesos.

Fortín de las Flores is beyond Orizaba on the tollway (Mexico 150D), and there is a Fortín exit and tollhouse where you leave the tollway, before you get to the town of Córdoba.

Hotel Ruiz Galindo in Fortín is famed for its gardenia-covered swimming pool and gardens with orchids. It is a big rambling structure, well-kept, with austere but comfortable rooms and good food. It has an office in Mexico City for reservations. Owner Ruiz Galindo heads one of the most famous families in Mexico with nearby coffee plantations and other industrial interests.

Posada Lomas, also in Fortín about a mile east of town on old 150, is a unique small hotel with twenty cottages set in a lush tropical garden with many orchids and camellias. It has a pool, and guests can use a nearby golf course by paying greens fees. Excellent food and a charming hostess, Sra. María Dolores Álvarez. Write for reservations or telephone 2-36-58. (Neither Ruiz Galindo nor Posada Lomas accepts credit cards.)

Orizaba and Córdoba. Orizaba, a city of 95,000, has a fairly good hotel, the *Trueba.* Córdoba, farther ahead, has a good commercial hotel, the *Hotel Palacio*, with dining room and coffee shop. These cities are in a coffee-growing, orange grove area. There is also a big brewery (Superior and Dos X) at Orizaba.

Tehuacán is another resort area reached by much the same road (you turn off the tollway sooner), and it has mineral springs from which is bottled much of the mineral water sold in Mexico. It is a very clean little village with pleasant gardens. The way to go is on tollroad 150D from Puebla toward Veracruz, but turning off at the Esperanza exit onto Highway 144 (later Highway 28) onto old Highway 150 junction right to Tehuacán. About 30 miles off tollway.

Hotel Spa Peñafiel has 150 rooms on nicely landscaped grounds, two pools fed from springs, tennis, golf, frontón, bowling, and riding (extra charge for last two). Dining room open only till 9:30 P.M. Reservations by mail, or telephone 2-01-90. Moderately expensive.

Hotel México with eighty very good rooms is similar but smaller. Dining room, cocktails. Built in Spanish style. Tel: 2-00-19. Moderately expensive.

It is possible to go south on Highway 125 to join with the good paved Oaxaca road at Huajuapán de León. See Chapter 19 on Oaxaca.

Tlaxcala was the capital of the powerful tribe which united with Cortés to overwhelm the Aztec empire. It is 34 miles north of Puebla on a side road. It is now a quaint and colorful Indian town, noted for woolens such as serapes. The village of Santa Ana, five minutes farther on, has the best serape buys of all.

Five tours of interesting adjoining areas where you can drive through a variety of villages have been put together in a brochure by the Puebla Government Tourist Office, at Reforma 702 just a few blocks from the zócalo. Each tour has a name such as *ruta de la flor, ruta de aguacate,* or *ruta del arte*. They run something less than 100 miles each, which makes for a day's trip on each one.

WHERE TO SHOP

The Puebla Government Tourist Office at Reforma 702 is most helpful. They have listings of hotels, shops, etc.

Onyx y Cerámica de Puebla, 18 Poniente 105, next to Santa Mónica Convent, sells hand-carved pieces of onyx.

La Trinidad, 20 Poniente 305, where the sisters Guevaras make some of the most authentic Talavera ware of Puebla.

Potteries Uriarte, 4 Poniente 911, where you can see Talavera pottery being made.

Casa Rugerio, 18 Poniente 107, specializes in Talavera pottery.

Puerto Vallarta, Mismaloya, and Yelapa

TALES OF OLD MEXICO

In the play Night of the Iguana, *Tennessee Williams describes the tropical town on Mexico's west coast that actually is Mismaloya, a little town south of Puerto Vallarta.*

Mismaloya until recently could only be reached by boat, a nice trip offered daily from Puerto Vallarta. The sets used for the movie are still there—marked EL SET. *The bungalows built for Richard Burton and Elizabeth Taylor, and Ava Gardner, Sue Lyon, and the rest of the cast, now make up a small hotel.*

The great green jungle grows right down to the edge of the sea, parted only by cliffs on which the rotting movie-set hotel stands. The palms hang out over a beach in a small cove, its white sand glistening under the soft lapping of the transparent green waves, with the running, pulsating lights and shadows created by the tropical sun.

Down the side of the cliff is one of those pathways, occasionally broken by branches set in the soil, along which Ava Gardner ran pell-mell to the beach and her brown-skinned beach boys, their maracas of tortoiseshell clicking out a tropical beat to which they both danced with their mistress.

Nothing in the South Pacific could be more romantic, nor more tropical. The Burtons have gone their separate ways, but both still return for visits.

PUERTO VALLARTA

THIS WAS ONCE a charming little fishing village, with cobble-stoned streets tumbling down the hillside to the waterfront. It didn't have very good hotels, and there was no road there, and only a grassy landing strip, but this made it quite charming and attractive to visitors.

Puerto Vallarta has grown to a community of 60,000 persons, but its cobblestoned streets are still there, running up and down the hills overlooking huge Bandera Bay and the Pacific Ocean. It is still a place to get away from it all, and there are beaches up and down the coast if you find the ones in town too crowded. Palm trees abound, and a soft balmy breeze is usually blowing.

Puerto Vallarta is connected by a good paved road to the main west coast highway at the city of Tepic. It has a fine modern airport where big jets from Los Angeles and Mexico City, among other places, can land, and it has a number of big luxury hotels and undoubtedly will get more.

The great Bahía de Banderas, a truly lovely bay bigger than the one at Acapulco and much cleaner, has some excellent beaches stuck in coves here and there, while the lush tropical foliage brings everything from royal palms to purple bougainvillea.

The little fishing village has now grown to a sizable town, and unfortunately this has meant that the good-natured natives are now lost among a host of newer arrivals who seem to bring the hustle, and bad manners, of some of the more sophisticated tourist centers.

Still, it is fun to walk along the *malecón*, or waterfront, watching the fishing boats or the lighters being loaded, to stop in the Oceano dining room, gathering place of the town, for a coffee, or later in the day at El Patio for a drink with Connie Gutiérrez.

There are many boats of all kinds for charter, and two make the trip down the coast each day for day visits to Yelapa and Mismaloya, where Richard Burton and Ava Gardner made the film *Night of the Iguana* while Elizabeth Taylor looked on. There is also now a road (Highway 200) to drive there.

Going to Puerto Vallarta

By Air. Both Mexicana and Aeromexico fly jet planes to Puerto Vallarta, and both connect with various points in the United States as well as having flights from Mexico City and Guadalajara to Puerto Vallarta. Their U.S. flights originate in Los Angeles, Chicago, San Antonio, Tucson, Houston, Miami, and New York.

They also fly from the Mexican cities of Tijuana, Mexicali, Nuevo Laredo, Ciudad Juárez, and Matamoros, all with connections, usually Guadalajara or Mazatlán, to Puerto Vallarta. Hughes Air West flies from many West Coast, New Mexico, and Arizona points to Puerto Vallarta.

By Road. It is usually at least three days from Nogales, Arizona, on the west coast route 15 to Tepic, where you pick up the new Highway 200, paved all the way and traveling through some lovely green hills, past lakes, and down to the palms and the tropical coast. It is roughly 100 miles from Tepic and an easy two-hour drive. The highway takes you directly into Puerto Vallarta. The Pacific Railroad can bring you to Tepic, but you will then have to take a bus to Puerto Vallarta. This also holds true if you take one of the west coast air-conditioned Guadalajara–Nogales buses. But it can be done. Transportes del Pacífico luxury air-conditioned express buses run from Nogales, Arizona, and Mexico City (Central de Autobúses del Norte, Cien Metros Street, Mexico City, tel: 5-78-92-58).

What To Do in Puerto Vallarta

Pools and Beaches. All of the big hotels and most of the smaller ones have lovely pools, and the one at the Holiday Inn is both beautiful and immense, with a floating bar. Beaches are available to all, and many hotels have beach locations where you can try the surf.

At the Camino Real a hostess arranges hilarious polo matches on burro back, using brooms for polo sticks. Great fun. Usually every Sunday. The Posada Vallarta also has "donkey polo."

For those staying where there is no beach, you can go to *Playa del Sol* or *Delicias Beach*, just outside town, a wonderful place to spend day after day. A small truck, converted to a bus, picks up passengers from the hotels hourly and takes them the mile or so out to the beach for a small fee. However, if you are willing to remove your shoes while crossing a minor stream along the beach, you can walk from your hotel in ten minutes. The spot where most tourists spend the day is in front of *Palapa Beach Restaurant* (note its canoe hoisted in the air as a landmark), where beach chairs, cold drinks, and a good lunch are available.

You may see native fishermen come by the beach carrying an entire tuna which they have barbecued over a charcoal fire. Eat a piece—it is excellent. Broiled oysters and lobsters are also available. More than that, schools of fish often come right into the beach area and can be seen jumping in the air. They are relatively small fish and completely harmless.

Picnics at *Los Tullis Beach*, lying to the other side of town north of the Rosita Hotel, can also be arranged for at your hotel, and this is fun, too. A taxi will drive you to Los Tullis.

Horseback Riding. Horses are available for riding (they are pretty tame steeds, but still fun), and you can make a trip with or without a guide up the mountains behind the town. This makes a good morning trip.

Sailing. You can rent a launch for a few dollars an hour and sail out to the three prominent rocks (*Los Arcos*) in the bay.

Fishing is excellent and the water is said to teem with sailfish, sea bass, bonito, and other game fish. A favorite fishing spot easily reached is three large rock islands called Los Arcos because the waves have worn holes through them. You can drop a line overboard on this short trip and possibly pick up a Spanish mackerel or an amberjack tuna.

Hunting is good at certain times of the year, and one can arrange to go by horseback into the forested hills where there are duck, wild turkey, deer, and jaguar. Both hunting and fishing require a local license, and it is best to get a permit in advance.

Sailing Trip to Mismaloya and Yelapa. One of the first things you should do in Puerto Vallarta is to allocate a day—or several days, if you wish—for a trip to the very isolated and quite enchanting jungle spots of Mismaloya and Yelapa.

The yacht *Sombrero* leaves at about 9 A.M. from the north side of the Hotel Playa del Oro, stops at the pier on Playa del Sol, and makes an all-day trip to Mismaloya and Yalapa. Mismaloya, where *Night of the Iguana* was filmed, is a lush spot of palms and waterfalls. It has a cantina and a hotel, and the remains of "El Set." Lunch at Yelapa, in a Polynesian setting, offers a variety of fresh seafoods.

Other Sailing Trips. A trimaran, the *Bora Bora*, departs from Playa del Sol before 10 A.M. en route to Colomitos Beach for a picnic lunch. You can fish en route, and a bar is available. A catamaran, the *Shamballa*, makes a trip to Quimixto leaving from Playa del Sol at about 9 A.M.

Skin diving and waterskiing can be arranged through your hotel. Puerto Vallarta is a fine place for both.

Cocktail time can mean either drifting down to the courtyard of your hotel or going to any of the cocktail lounges and bars in other hotels, or to the various restaurants along the malecón which usually have bars welcoming visitors. Some serve hors d'oeuvres of sautéed shrimp or other delicacies. You can sit in these places and watch the sun drop into the Pacific, a truly enchanting moment. *La Bota* is one such place.

The Holiday Inn, the Camino Real, and the Posada Vallarta usually have a *Noche Mexicana* with fireworks on one night a week, and this spectacle is both fun and entertaining. A Mexican buffet, open to the public, is served for a flat price.

Night Spots. The best night spot is *El Patio*, where everyone sits around informally, trying Connie Gutiérrez's planter's punch or, later in the evening, her *café filipino*, which is a steaming-hot blend of coffee and Kahlua (a Mexican chocolate liqueur). *City Dump* is a popular discotheque for late stayer-uppers (after 11:30 P.M.). At Vallarta 58. Tel: 2-07-19. *Leonardo's International Discotheque* at the Holiday Inn is spectacular with a large room filled with psychedelic lighting, glorious colors, high-fidelity music, and cameras projecting pictures on the walls. Reservations at 2-17-00.

RESTAURANTS IN PUERTO VALLARTA

La Bota   Moderately expensive
New popular restaurant which has one knowledgeable visitor remarking, "Serves the best steaks I have ever found in Mexico." Nice patio, rustic chairs at bar overlooking bay. On Malecón, main street, facing waterfront. Fixed-price dinner. Happy hour from 7 to 8 P.M. Tel: 2-05-40.

Carlos O'Brien's   Moderately expensive
A mad, fun place with great informality but good food and drink. Serves shrimp and other seafood, and specializes in barbecued spareribs. Open late. All cards.

La Fonda del Sol   Moderately expensive
One block from plaza at Morelos 54. Beautifully decorated bar-restaurant with sunken bar, hanging plants, candlelight, and usually a lone guitarist. Daily selections of fish, meat, chicken, shrimp, and

homemade soup and bread. Good service, excellent food, and relaxed, intimate atmosphere. All cards. Tel: 2-07-42.

Flamingo Moderate
A most recent addition with signs of great success. On Malecón, with large interesting menu and reasonable prices. Try the Barataria filet, jalapeño red snapper, rice fusil, baked crab, or ask Tony San Román or Alex Sánchez for a recommendation—you can't go wrong. Open till midnight. Tel: 2-08-77.

Garza Blanca Expensive
Four miles south of town on Highway 200, in hotel of same name, this wonderful dining room is said to have some of the best lobster in the world. Try their "lobster à la Garza Blanca." Hotel located by waterfall with beautiful view of sea. Restaurant open 7 A.M. to 10:15 P.M. AE, DC. Tel: 2-02-48.

El Patio Moderate
On the boulevard facing the bay up toward the Rosita Hotel, this is a charming spot built around an open patio. Has a Mexican-style kitchen, but features all kinds of food. Connie Gutiérrez makes you feel at home. Try her café filipino.

La Margarita Moderate
At Juárez 512, one block from Oceano Hotel. Has the best Mexican food in Puerto Vallarta, as well as a mariachi band and a relaxed, fun-filled atmosphere. Open for both lunch and supper. Ernesto Ramírez is owner with Connie Gutiérrez. Tel: 2-02-15.

Daiquiri Dick's Moderate
At Olas Altas 246, this was opened by a former San Francisco caterer and serves dishes from that city such as lobster bisque, seafood supreme, prime ribs, and crepes Suzette. Has terrace overlooking beach. Lunch and dinner. Tel: 2-05-66.

El Set Moderately expensive
On road south of town before Camino Real. An attractive restaurant on four terraces where drinks are served and you can watch the sunset. Grilled steaks and seafood. Open lunch and dinner. Tel: 2-11-83.

El Deli Inexpensive
At Insurgentes 203, this a sidewalk café-delicatessen with cold cuts, cheese, pickles, rolls, and pastry. Also offers takeout service and box lunches. Has cold beer. Open all day.

El Panorama   Expensive
Atop Hotel Siesta at Domínguez and Miramar, this is a posh place
with a fine view of the bay. Has choice food including lobster, frogs'
legs, langostino, shrimp, onion soup, and oysters. Entertainment,
dancing. Tel: 2-18-18.

Oceano Hotel Restaurant   Inexpensive
Good food, bar, serves breakfast. A full menu in the evening, and
a good place for a drink before dinner. Visitors tend to gather here.
Open to the public.

Los Arcos   Expensive
Very fancy dining room at Posada Vallarta, outside town. Menu is
very elaborate. Good hors d'oeuvres. El Pueblito, an outdoor
restaurant also here, is less formal. Tel: 2-12-82.

Chez Elena   Expensive
At Matamoros 172 in Los Cuatros Vientos. Fabulous food, but
reservations well ahead of time required. Dinner only. No cards.
Tel: 2-01-61.

La Iguana   Moderate
Highly unusual restaurant off main highway three blocks beyond
Río Cuale toward waterfront. Under thatched roof, guests seated at
rustic tables have choice of turtle steaks, Chinese dinners, steaks,
and Mexican plates. Music and dancing. Lunch and dinner in
winter season, dinner only in summer. Bar. Open till 1 A.M. All
cards. Tel: 2-01-05.

Posada Río Cuale dining room   Inexpensive
In small hotel of same name. Said to have some of the best food to
be found in Puerto Vallarta. Run by owner, it is a rustic dining
room overlooking sea. Good variety of Mexican dishes. Public
welcome, noon and night. AE.

HOTELS IN PUERTO VALLARTA
(reservations most advisable)

Posada Vallarta *(252 rooms)*   Expensive
Very large modern hotel with air-conditioned rooms, some overlooking beach and others handsome gardens, plus thirty-eight villas
with private beaches and private pools. Two dining rooms, three
bars with entertainment. Children's playground with two pools.
Tennis, water sports, horseback riding. AE, VISA. Call Utel in
United States, 5-33-64-40 in Mexico City, 2-14-59 in Puerto Vallarta.

Camino Real (*250 rooms*)   Expensive
A modern twelve-story hotel sitting on a delightful beach in a cove
1½ miles south of town on Highway 200. Almost all rooms have
fabulous view of sea. Large baths. Completely air-conditioned. Fine
beach club with palms and thatched-roof bar. Polo on burro back
for guests. Large pool, lounges for sunbathing. Waterskiing and
fishing available. Entertainment. Good dining room open 7 A.M.
till midnight. All cards. Operated by Western Hotels; has their
family plan. In United States, toll-free (800) 228-3000. Or write P.O.
Box 95, Puerto Vallarta, Jalisco, México. Tel: 2-00-02.

Holiday Inn Puerto Vallarta (*234 rooms*)   Moderately expensive
On airport road at excellent location overlooking beach, this ultramodern air-conditioned hotel is a fine place to stay. Has immense
swimming pool, a fine view of city, gourmet restaurant, coffee shop,
several bars including fabulous one at poolside, sauna, tennis,
fireworks, and discotheque. Main dining room open late. All cards.
Enrique Rangel, Innkeeper. Holiday Inn reservation network or
phone 2-17-00 in Puerto Vallarta.

Hotel Delfín (*90 rooms*)   Moderately expensive
Modern nine-story hotel right on beach at edge of town. Fully air-
conditioned, small pool, some balconies overlooking sea, open-air
dining room, rooftop nightclub, tennis courts. All cards. Tel: 2-18-
14.

Hotel Garza Blanca (*34 units*)   Expensive
Five miles south of town on Highway 200, this is directly over
water with some cliffside chalets and some cottages down on beach.
Has own secluded beach, and each chalet has own small pool. Very
handsome rooms, good management, exceptional dining room.
Tennis, scuba diving. AE, DC. P.O. Box 58. Tel: 2-10-83.

Tropicana Hotel (*100 rooms*)   Moderate
On Las Delicias Beach. Dining room, pool. Big rambling structure
with more tropical atmosphere than all the rest put together.
Bartender Ben Cruz mixes fine frozen daiquiris. All cards. P.O. Box
31.

Posada de la Selva (*52 bungalows*)   Inexpensive
A group of attractive bungalows in native style with dining room
and pool, and within sight of beach. No cards. P.O. Box 54.

Posada Río Cuale   Inexpensive
A fine small brick hotel, about two blocks from the beach, with
balconies overlooking the sea. Good restaurant, pool. Children
discouraged. Owner is Manuel Azurmendi. P.O. Box 146.

Océano Hotel (*46 rooms*) Moderate
In town, on street fronting bay. Older but good. Restaurant and bar very good and a popular meeting place. P.O. Box 45.

Hacienda del Lobo (*39 rooms*) Moderate
Near Posada Vallarta to north of town. An attractive two-story colonial-style hotel built around nice pool within walking distance of beach. Tennis courts. Fully air-conditioned. Bar, dining service. P.O. Box 276. Tel: 2-04-11.

Hotel Las Palmas (*64 rooms*) Moderately expensive
A five-story modern hotel about a mile out of town on La Gloria Beach next to Holiday Inn. Colonial-style rooms. Air-conditioned. Pool, restaurant. All cards. P.O. Box 55. Tel: 2-05-43.

Econhotel Pelicanos (*236 rooms*) Inexpensive
Next to Las Palmas on La Gloria Beach. Air-conditioned. Ice and soft drink machines, cafeteria-restaurant, bar, discotheque, pool. Filtered water. A good family hotel. Toll-free in United States: (800) 221-6509 or 854-3048.

Hotel Playa de Oro (*40 rooms*) Moderate
Air-conditioned modern three-story hotel north of town near the Posada. Beach, tennis, two pools, sports. Dining room and bar. AE, MC, VISA. P.O. Box 78. Tel: 2-03-48.

Bungalows Los Cuatros Vientos (*7 suites*) Moderate
Recommended. Has fine view of bay. Write: Elena Cortés, Matamoros 172.

Hotel Playa Bucerias (*45 rooms*) Moderately expensive
Hidden away in the jungle with its own isolated beach, this hotel can provide seclusion and tranquillity for those who want it. Each unit air-conditioned with its own private terrace. Heated pool, tennis, playground, riding. Restaurant. Sixteen miles north of town on Highway 200. All cards. P.O. Box 522.

Rosita Hotel (*74 rooms*) Inexpensive
In town, overlooking bay. Pleasant hotel with nice courtyard. Rooms very plain. New wing has more modern rooms overlooking sea. Tel: 2-10-33.

TRAILER PARKS IN PUERTO VALLARTA

Puerto Vallarta Trailer Park (*70 spaces*) $3
About ¼ mile off Highway 200, 1 mile north of town on way to

airport. Located in banana grove across from Playa Gloria. Shaded patios. Restrooms and showers. Connections. American management. Reservations necessary in winter season. P.O. Box 141, Puerto Vallarta, Jalisco, México.

Tacho's Trailer Park (*155 spaces*) $3
Three miles north of city on Highway 200, off road ½ mile on Pitallel Road. Pool. P.O. Box 315.

CAR RENTAL IN PUERTO VALLARTA

Transpocar S.A.
Rents Volkswagens. Mileage charge over 230 kilometers per day. Buy your own gas. Will deliver to hotels. Office at Juárez 26 in town (near Oceano Hotel). Tel: 2-04-52. Also has office at airport. Avis and Hertz also deliver rental cars to hotels.

MISMALOYA

I guess everyone yearns to get away to the "real tropics," and I suppose few make it. Everything turns out to have been cluttered by civilization. But Mismaloya and the even more remote Yelapa are two beauty spots that are still really wilderness—and as unspoiled as you can get. And they are indeed beautiful, having lovely white beaches over which palms hang in profusion.

It is possible to drive to Mismaloya on the new Highway 200, but the more fun way is to go by one of the several launches that make trips there each day. The yacht *Sombrero* leaves each morning about 9 A.M. from the Hotel Playa del Oro, stops at the pier on Playa del Sol, and makes an all-day round trip to Mismaloya and Yelapa with lunch along the way. Other boats also make the trip, and you can usually sign up at your hotel. Ticket price includes cold drinks on the voyage. Great fun!

The launches go out by Los Arcos, the small rock islands in which the waves have washed holes, and then head south. About an hour after you leave, you come to Mismaloya.

Mismaloya was built out of uninhabited jungle by John Huston for the filming of the picture *Night of the Iguana*, after the stage play by Tennessee Williams. It is an idyllic setting for a tropical picture.

Cliffs several hundred feet high come to the water, and between them are little coves with white sand beaches and lovely green water. Palm trees hang over the cliffs, and down over the water. You cannot see inland for the dense tropical growth.

You go ashore to find a small thatched-roof bar (yes, open in the morning) adjoining a restaurant which was used to feed the cast and the crew during the filming. Up the hill a bit are a number of solidly built bungalows, including the one where Richard Burton, who starred as the defrocked minister leading a cheap tour group that included Sue Lyon, lived with his wife-to-be, Elizabeth Taylor, who was only an onlooker. Ava Gardner played the keeper of the ramshackle tropical hotel which can still be seen if you have the energy to climb a few steps up the steep earth path above you. It is clearly marked EL SET.

Hotel Accommodations. The bungalows of the film company have been turned into a small hotel, the *Mismaloya*, and it is possible to stay here. You can make reservations by writing to Hotel Mismaloya, Mismaloya, Puerto Vallarta, Jalisco, México. *Lomas de Mismaloya* is a condominium development; you can get details there, or in Puerto Vallarta at Hidalgo 126, tel: 2-04-77.

YELAPA

Yelapa is another hour down the coast, and is even more remote from civilization than Mismaloya. Here the bay is more open and there is more of a view, though you don't have the immediacy of the jungle that you do at Mismaloya.

Small dugouts row out to unload you from the launch, and soon you ground on a fine sandy beach. A few steps away is a grass-roofed open-air restaurant, and behind it are some very primitive cabanas built on the hillside.

The restaurant, *Lagunita*, is surprisingly good. There is a menu and, as it now is noon, you find yourself willing to consider broiled fish or meat, or a ham sandwich, but you can also at times get turtle steak, oysters, or lobster. Cold beer is available, as are other drinks. The food all seems to be safe and the kitchen is quite respectable. The service is a bit lackadaisical, but it was the tropics you wanted, wasn't it?

An American has built this restaurant, and also the seventeen very unusual cabanas on the hillside. Though primitive, they are very attractive. And they do have hot water, indoor plumbing, and showers handsomely lined with shells from the seashore. In fact, you ought to have a look at them even if you don't stay there.

The name of the hotel is also *Lagunita*, and you can make a reservation, if you really yearn to get away from it all, by writing to Hotel Lagunita, 5 de Mayo No. 62, Puerto Vallarta, Jalisco, México. You will be well cared for, but no one can reach you, and when the sun goes down you had better be happy with swinging in a hammock, or curled up with your favorite entertainment. Manager is Ben Medina, a gracious gentleman enthusiastic about his hidden paradise.

22

San Miguel de Allende and Querétaro

TALES OF OLD MEXICO

The street sounds and cries of Mexico are more fascinating than those of Paris.

Remembering Roberto Gayol Street, where we lived for several years, I can still hear the shrill whistle of the night watchman, called the sereno, *since he was paid to keep things serene, as he made his rounds throughout the night. Each block had a sereno and each family paid him 10 pesos a month. It was said that if you didn't pay, you were sure to have a burglary.*

And in the morning there was the clanging of a bell as a man walked one block ahead of the garbage disposal truck. This was the big moment of the day for the maids, who would hasten to the corner with the family trash, and manage to spend a half hour exchanging gossip with each other.

In the late afternoon the organ grinders always came by. Children would hang out of windows and toss them copper coins.

Madame de la Barca, 100 years earlier in Mexico City, had told of peddlers in the street: the carbonero, *calling his price on charcoal; the grease man calling "lard,* manteca"; *or the button peddler, whose shrill voice soon got the maids out to look at bits of ribbons.*

But we loved best the "dulce man" who sold dulce de leche or caramelized milk. "Caramelos de espuma! Bocadillo de coco," he would cry.

And then as evening fell again, the lottery-ticket sellers, crying, "Last chance to win a fortune. Here is the winner."

SAN MIGUEL DE ALLENDE is a wonderful little colonial town, now largely given over to artists and tourists who are tempted to settle down and enjoy the quiet life and the balmy weather.

Still retaining the cobblestoned streets and old buildings of colonial days, San Miguel has first-class hotels and almost as many resident Americans as local citizens. It is a rather small town, but it boasts one of the country's best art schools, which gives special summer classes for schoolteachers from the United States.

Querétaro, nearby, is an important city in Mexico's history. It is a much larger city than San Miguel, but lacks the first-class hotel accommodations of its smaller neighbor. Our advice is to stay in San Miguel but to stop and see Querétaro and its historic buildings either coming to or going from San Miguel. Both places are only three hours from Mexico City by car, and even less on the new Central Superhighway. San Miguel is also a stop on the main railway from Mexico City to Laredo, Texas.

SAN MIGUEL DE ALLENDE

One of the group of missionaries and religious leaders who moved directly behind the Spanish conquistadors included a Franciscan friar, Juan de San Miguel, who carried out his work of converting and educating the Indians in the western state of Michoacán about 1531. Friar Juan moved from community to community, and eventually went from Querétaro, where the Spanish had established a fortified outpost, to the area immediately to the north.

Humble and barefooted, Friar Juan de San Miguel moved about, teaching the Indians how to use millstones, plant crops, and weave gloves and stockings. He arrived in the San Miguel vicinity about 1540, and decided to establish a village in the pleasant valley. He marked off the streets, distributed the land to the natives, and founded a church. He called the village San Miguel, after his own patron saint. The second part of its name, Allende, was to come two centuries later when a youth born in San Miguel, Ignacio Allende, became one of the principal forgers of Mexican independence in the frustrated uprising of 1810. The town honored him by adding his name to the already existing name of San Miguel.

The ruins of the original village can still be seen near the railroad station, somewhat apart from the present town. Today, San Miguel is a town of Spanish-style houses built close to the street, with grilled windows looking out on the passersby. It

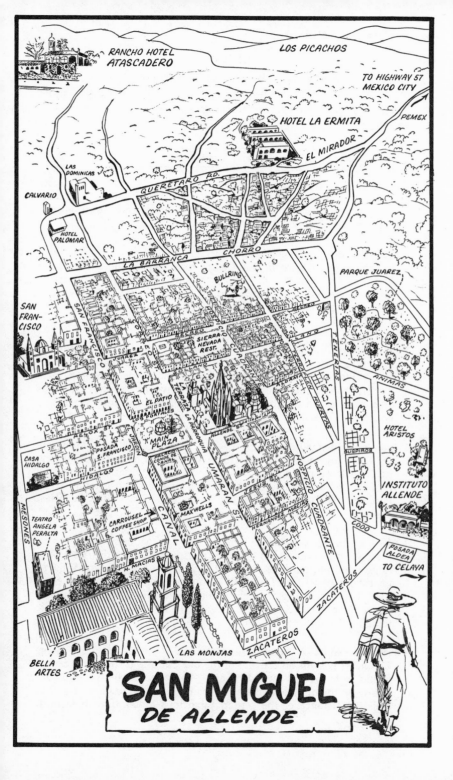

has a Gothic-style church, unique in Mexico, standing on the main plaza, which with its huge trees is one of the most charming spots in the Republic and one of the most photographed. The weather is usually perfect all year.

WHERE TO STAY IN SAN MIGUEL DE ALLENDE

Posada de San Francisco (*42 rooms*)   Moderate
Charming colonial hotel on the main plaza. Good dining room, bar, garage. Write P.O. Box 40, San Miguel de Allende, Guanajuato, México. Tel: 2-00-77.

Aristos Parador San Miguel (*60 rooms*)   Moderate
On the edge of town on the Celaya road, this is the old Instituto Hotel taken over by the Aristos chain. Luxuriantly landscaped grounds, heated pool, tennis. Dining room, cocktails. Reservations through the Aristos chain, Mexico City, or P.O. Box 85, San Miguel. Tel: 2-01-49.

Rancho-Hotel El Atascadero (*50 rooms*)   Moderate
One mile east of town up winding roadway from plaza, or enter from Querétaro highway. Well-run old hacienda managed by a Cornell hotel-school graduate, Alberto Maycotte del Río. Operates as a guest ranch with riding and pool. Pleasant dining room, bar. DC, MC, VISA. P.O. Box 103. Tel: 2-03-07.

Posada de Aldea (*60 rooms*)   Moderate
On Calle Ancha de San Antonio on outskirts of town. A brand-new hotel enclosed in a courtyard with rooms around patios. Owned by Posada de San Francisco. Rooms well decorated in colonial style. Pool, tennis, basketball. Dining room, bar. Convention facilities. Manager: Felipe Zauala Ramírez. P.O. Box 40. Tel: 2-10-22.

La Misión de los Angeles (*65 rooms*)   Moderately expensive
A striking new hotel, built in three stories with balconies, enclosing huge pool and gardens. A resort location in the pleasant Villa de los Frailes area 1 mile from San Miguel at kilometer 2 on the Celaya road. Lake adjoining, boat club, horseback riding, golf. Restaurant, coffee shop, bar. Tel: 2-10-26. In Mexico City: Insurgentes Sur 1783; tel: 5-34-92-18.

Posada La Ermita (*24 suites*)   Expensive
The hotel is built on the site of the old Cantinflás (Mexico's famed comic) home and is owned by him. A large colonial-style structure sitting on the hill where the main road goes out of town, it is within walking distance of the center. Luxurious suites have balconies,

fireplaces, color TV. Price includes three meals. Pool. All cards. Address: Calle Real 64. Tel: 2-07-77.

Villa Santa Mónica (*10 suites*)   Moderate
An eighteenth-century colonial home converted to a charming posada across from French Park at the edge of San Miguel in a rather run-down location. Rooms have private patios. Pool. Sauna, masseuse. Address: Baeza 22. Tel: 2-05-42.

Mansión del Bosque (*24 units*)   Moderate
Near the plaza, and close to Instituto de Allende, a mansion converted to rooms. Comfortable. For reservations, write to Ruth and George Hyba, P.O. Box 206. Tel: 2-02-77.

Hotel La Huerta (*16 units*)   Inexpensive
Four blocks north of plaza at Cerrado de Becera 9. Six units have kitchens. Parking. No pets. Dining room, bar. P.O. Box 190. Tel: 2-03-60.

Hotel Colonial (*25 rooms*)   Inexpensive
Small Mexican-style hotel, with fair rooms, near the plaza. Garage.

Motel La Siesta (*24 rooms*)   Inexpensive
Modern motel on the Celaya road. Pool, horses. Breakfast served in room. P.O. Box 72. Tel: 2-02-07.

KOA Campgrounds (*100 spaces*)
Just outside San Miguel off Highway 49 (through Villa de los Frailes subdivision). Free hot showers, pool, picnic tables by lake, laundry, groceries, tennis, golf nearby. Jaap and Sibylle Van Dijk, owners. Write Apartado 523, San Miguel.

WHERE TO EAT IN SAN MIGUEL DE ALLENDE

The best and most expensive place to dine in San Miguel is currently the *Casa de Sierra Nevada*, an elegant French-style restaurant in a mansion full of antiques with a small garden to one side. Owner and manager is Jorge Palomino y Canedo. The emphasis is on fine service and excellent cuisine including consommé, tournedos béarnaise, chicken parmesan or with curry, whitefish, and salads. Open evenings only, but on Sundays from 1 to 5 P.M. Closed Tuesdays. All cards. Reservations imperative at 2-04-15.

Bodega del Marqués, at Recreo 5, a hidden side street off San Francisco just two blocks from the plaza, is a very pleasant, small, friendly restaurant with good pepper steaks, Italian and Chinese cuisine. Open 1 P.M. to 1 A.M. Guitar music after 9 P.M. Owners are Enrique and Connie Torres. No credit cards. Tel: 2-14-81.

El Patio, just off the plaza on Correo Street, is probably the liveliest and most popular place in town. It is open for both lunch and dinner. Built around a courtyard with ancient fountains, it has a rustic atmosphere. Menu features red, green, or Swiss-style enchiladas, shrimp salad, good soups, and T-bone steaks. Chaotic but fun. Sunday buffet a specialty.

An adventure in dining as good as any you will find in this world can be had if you arrange to eat at the *Jacaranda Hostelería* at Aldama 53. Telephone 2-10-15 for reservations. Don Fenton, the owner, has a small hotel with exquisitely furnished and shining-clean rooms. A fixed menu is served from 7 to 10 P.M., featuring a different cuisine each night, such as Japanese, Chinese, or Russian dishes. Wine included for a reasonable price. Highly recommended. Do reserve in advance.

The *Carousel,* one-half block off the plaza across from Maxwell's well-known arts store, is a splendid soda fountain and coffee shop serving hamburgers, corned beef, and plate lunches as well as ice cream. Open 8 A.M. till midnight.

La Terraza, next to the church on the plaza, is a pleasant soda fountain and restaurant situated so its windows afford a view of those passing by in the plaza. Serves breakfast, fruit salads and fish plates for lunch, and malted milks and colas all the time. Inexpensive.

Bugambilia II is a block over on San Francisco just off the plaza, and it has a carry-out ice cream shop plus an inner courtyard with a wide menu including enchiladas, chili con carne, hot dogs, grilled chicken, beefsteak Tampico style, beer, and banana splits. Locals favor this place, and a chess game is always going on among the students.

The *Posada de San Francisco* on the main plaza welcomes the public to its dining room and has good food.

La Botica Drugstore bar is where everyone gathers to pass the time of day after picking up the local papers and magazines. At San Francisco 11 off the main plaza.

What To See and Do in San Miguel de Allende

San Miguel Parroquia Church, the outstanding building, is a pseudo-Gothic church standing on the main plaza overlooking the town square. Its tall tower houses three bells named "La Luz," "San Miguel," and "San Pedro." They were purchased with money and jewels contributed by local families. Outside in the corner is a statue of Friar Juan de San Miguel.

Although sophisticates sniff at the pseudo-Gothicism of the Parroquia—since it is merely the local Indians' concept of Gothic architecture as they saw it in illustrations and without any formal study—even granting that some of the work is crude, there are still those who say it is one of the most handsome churches in Mexico. Certainly it lends a note of charm and elegance to this town.

Replacing a primitive colonial church on the same site, La Parroquia was begun on October 8, 1880, from a design by Zeferino Gutiérrez, a native who loved his village and who devoted many years and at times his own money to help build this church as well as the Church of the Conception. Gutiérrez was a poor man of pure Indian blood, completely self-trained and with no technical knowledge of architecture. He often described his ideas to his workmen by drawing them in the sand with a stick.

Inside the Parroquia there is a polychrome image of Friar Juan at the main altar. A cherished relic, said to have been sent by Carlos IV of Spain, is a crucifix of Christ of the Conquest. There is a famed vaulted chapel at the back of the church, where a number of famous men, including the former president Anastasio Bustamente, are buried. Emperor Maximilian is said to have called this "a tomb fit for a king." Maximilian was later executed at nearby Querétaro, but did not receive burial at the Parroquia.

San Rafael Church, next to the Parroquia, has been largely rebuilt over the years; of the original structure, only its portal remains, with a stone medallion and a sculptured Christ. Zeferino Gutiérrez also built a chapel here at his own expense.

Walking about San Miguel

The Calle Real is the most important place to visit after you have seen the main plaza and the Parroquia. From this old cobblestoned street you rise above the town, in a short walk, and get a commanding view of the town and the countryside. Walk up Calle de San Francisco, in front of the Posada de San Francisco, a rather long three blocks, and turn right on the street sloping up the hill. This is the Calle Real, connecting with the road to Querétaro. Along the way, you can drop in at the Posada La Ermita, located on the Calle Real, for a drink.

A House and Garden Tour is given at noon each Sunday, and is a most interesting excursion. As the tour points out, Mexicans live behind walls, and this is a chance to look behind them. You meet at the Biblioteca Publica (Public Library) at Insurgentes 9, and are driven to four different homes, some new and some old but all distinguished by beautiful gardens and unusual architecture. You meet both Mexican and American residents. The tour is followed by refreshments at the library. Highly recommended.

San Francisco is a group of buildings which includes the Franciscan church and convent and the Church of the Third Order. They are all located on San Francisco Street, at the corner of Juárez, two blocks from the plaza. They are worth seeing. *Tercer Orden*, the Third Order, inaugurated in 1713, is a primitive Franciscan-style church with bare stone walls and simple portals. *San Francisco Church*, built by the wealthy families of San Miguel in the latter part of the eighteenth century, has a handsome bell tower. The convent is the oldest building of the group; it was built about 1606.

The San Felipe Neri Oratory, on Los Insurgentes Street two blocks from San Francisco, is interesting because it commemorates the joint privileges of a mulatto group that had a church, Eccehomo Chapel, which was used by the congregation of San Felipe Neri when it was first founded. The present building was built in 1712, and the legend over the doorway explains the joint privileges of the church. A number of religious oil paintings, credited to the painter Cabrera, may also be seen here.

The Convent and Church of the Conception are also worth seeing, principally for the two-story dome built with Corinthian pillars by Zeferino Gutiérrez.

The Casa del Mayorazgo de Canal, located at the corner of the

Plaza de Allende and Canal Street, is typical of some of the elaborate homes that were built by Spanish nobility during the colonial period. This is virtually a palace. Also, by the zócalo, one can see Allende's house, where the town's famous son lived.

A visit to Atotonilco Church, which is 8 miles from San Miguel on the road to Dolores, is well worth the trip. It is one of the artistic treasures of Mexico, as its walls inside are covered with frescoes, poems, and sculptures of great color and fantasy. A fine show of popular Mexican art. It is historically of note, as Hidalgo once visited here and created a national flag by presenting a banner of the Virgin of Guadalupe to the church.

The Instituto de Allende is a recognized educational institution long popular with schoolteachers and others from the United States. The school was founded in 1949. It has a professional faculty teaching arts, crafts, humanities, and intensive Spanish. It has an accredited undergraduate and graduate degree program as well as noncredit short courses. There are classes in painting, sculpture, ceramics, and photography. Students can live at the Aristos Hotel if they choose, but most find less expensive accommodations in nearby small hotels and boardinghouses.

To get to the Instituto de Allende, you must drive through an archway in a large wall on the left as you leave town toward Celaya, and proceed up a drive to the main building. Ample parking space is available. Reservations are advised at all hotels, including the Aristos at the Instituto, during the summer months. Teachers wishing to take courses should write well in advance, addressing all communications to the Director, Instituto de Allende, Box E, San Miguel de Allende, Guanajuato, México.

Centro Cultural Ignacio Ramírez. Perhaps an even finer, and certainly more extensive, art school can be found in San Miguel in a lovely old colonial convent just a short way from the center of town. This is the Centro Cultural Ignacio Ramírez at Hernández Macias 75, and is well worth a visit.

The 500 or more students here study not only drawing and painting, but textiles, ceramics, and metalwork, and have classes in dance and guitar. Lessons cost as little as $4 registration and $2 a month.

This school is often called "Bellas Artes" in San Miguel, as it is a branch of the renowned Instituto de Bellas Artes in Mexico City. You will find yourself welcomed here without admission charge. A famed Canadian watercolorist and his talented photographer wife, Leonard and Riva Brooks, have given enthusiastic support to this school.

The Academia Hispano Americana, located at Insurgentes 21, caters to groups of high school and college students who come to Mexico to learn Spanish. Under the direction of Carmen Masip de Hawkins, the founder, the school has a most successful intensive Spanish teaching method. Two hours of classes each day are followed by one hour of "guided conversation." Students are placed with families in San Miguel for a modest cost of living. Advanced courses are offered in Mexican history and Spanish literature. Write for a brochure to Director, Academia Hispano Americana, Insurgentes 21, San Miguel de Allende, Guanajuato, México. Tel: (465) 2-03-49.

The Escuela Ecuestre, a famed riding school, undoubtedly one of the best in the world, is located outside San Miguel near the Posada La Ermita. The school also operates its own well-appointed hotel, and has a landing strip for twin-engine planes. It can also arrange to put up its students at the Ermita.

Riders are trained by the best Mexican cavalry officers, using fine horses schooled in jumping and dressage. Large training fields, cross-country trails, and stadium obstacle courses are available. Daily course is usually for three hours. A heated swimming pool, putting course, frontón, and tennis are available. Write to Harold Black, Director, Escuela Ecuestre, Apartado 185, San Miguel de Allende, Guanajuato, México. Tel: 2-02-55.

Teatro Angela Peralta, on a side street just off the main plaza a few blocks, is an old opera and theater building which has been lovingly restored by the Cultural Association of San Miguel. This eighteenth-century gem, still used for local theatrical productions, is well worth a visit.

Taboada is a small, informal *balneario* (bathing place) with curative springs located 5 miles from San Miguel out the road to Hidalgo. There is a Hotel Balneario there with a dining room and such sports as swimming, horseback riding, table tennis, and volleyball. Daily excursions are offered for a flat price of $5 (less for children), including bus transportation, hot lunch, and a leisurely swim. There is a special Sunday buffet. Reservations can be made in San Miguel at Cuna de Allende 9, tel: 2-02-88. Buses depart from the reservations office at 7, 9, and 11 A.M., at noon, and at 1, 3, 5, and 7 P.M.

WHERE TO SHOP IN SAN MIGUEL DE ALLENDE

Casa Maxwell's, just off the main plaza (on San Francisco Street), has a fabulous collection of furniture, clothing, crafts, woven materials, and popular art. Outstanding designs and excellent work. Run by Bob and Lucha Maxwell, who ship to the United States. Tel: 2-02-47.

Casas Coloniales has an unusual combination of real estate, business, and popular arts and textiles. At Canal 36.

Casa Cohen, Reloj 18, has decorative tiles and solid brass pieces.

Artes de México, Aurora 49, ships all types of handicraft to the United States.

Armando García, on the plaza, has popular art and antiques.

Llamas Hermanos, Zacateros 7, has tinwork.

Galería San Miguel, Portal Allende 8, on the main plaza, sells paintings by local artists.

Beckmann, Pila Seca 8, has hand-wrought silver and local gem jewelry.

García Zavala, San Francisco 13, has fine embroidery and needlework.

Artes Populares de Tequis, Plaza Principal 14, has outstanding rugs and wall tapestries.

QUERÉTARO

Where San Miguel is a village, Querétaro is a city. Where San Miguel's part in Mexico's history was through its son, Querétaro is the place where historic events actually occurred. The history of Querétaro is interwoven continually with the larger history of the nation. Querétaro has had three especially interesting phases in its history.

Pre-Hispanic and Colonial Days. Before the Spaniards came, Querétaro was an outpost of the Aztecs, used as protection against the marauding tribes to the north. The word *Querétaro* is said to mean "rocky place" in the Chichimec tongue.

When Cortés conquered the Aztec capital, one of his local followers, Don Fernando de Tapia, undertook to establish trade with the Indian tribes in the Querétaro area, the Chichimecs and Otomis. He was named governor of the area after he persuaded them to submit to Spanish rule.

Don Fernando began at once to encourage agriculture and mining, and soon, with the aid of the colonists, he had a flourishing community and began to build a proper city and numerous churches. The story is told that one of his daughters wished to become a nun but was refused admission because she looked too Indian in appearance. Don Fernando thereupon built the Convent of Santa Clara and appointed his daughter Mother Superior.

In the early 1700s Querétaro began its golden age, and one of the leading citizens of this period, Marqués de la Villa del Villar del Águila, began work on the aqueduct which is still used for the city's water supply. Eduardo Tresguerras, one of Mexico's greatest architects, built the Church and Convent of Las Teresitas and the Fountain of Neptune. Ignacio Casas built the Church of Santa Rosa de Viterbo, an architectural landmark. The building which now houses the federal offices appears on the 20-peso bill currently used in Mexico.

The War of 1848. During the Mexican-American War in 1848, the federal government of Mexico was forced to withdraw to Querétaro. It was here that the famed *Treaty of Guadalupe-Hidalgo* was signed, which concerned the departure of the United States troops and ceded important sections, including all the territory from Texas to California and from the Rio Grande to Oregon, for the sum of $15 million.

Execution of Emperor Maximilian. Napoleon III succeeded in placing Archduke Maximilian of Austria and his wife, Carlota, on the Mexican throne in 1864. The United States at this time was involved with its own Civil War. The French troops kept Maximilian on the throne until 1867, when they withdrew from the country before the rebellious Mexicans.

Carlota fled to Europe to plead for help from various governments, but Maximilian stayed behind and was forced to abandon his palace in Mexico City and flee to Querétaro, where he was captured and tried before a military court sitting in the National Theater. He was then taken to the outskirts, on a little knoll called *Cerro de las Campañas* ("Hill of the Bells"), and was executed by a firing squad.

The last Emperor of Austria, Franz Josef, sent money to Mexico, which was used to build a small chapel on this site to the memory of the ill-fated Maximilian. This can be visited by riding out Madero Street to the outskirts of the city.

Querétaro in the Future. Querétaro, now a city of 200,000 inhabitants, is on the threshold of blossoming into one of Mexico's most important industrial centers. The recently completed Central Superhighway places it within two hours of Mexico City and on a direct route to important cities in the north such as San Luis Potosí and Saltillo.

New industries have already moved into the area and have constructed modern factories. They include Carnation Milk, Kellogg's Corn Flakes, Singer Sewing Machine, Ralston-Purina, and many others.

Local labor has been absorbed by these new industries, and there is no doubt that this will become a prosperous community. The city lies in a fertile agricultural valley.

GETTING TO QUERÉTARO

Traveling to Querétaro is very simple by bus, turismo, or car. From Mexico City, first-class buses are run by Autobúses Anahuac, Omnibus de México, Transportes Chihuahuenses, and Tres Estrellas de Oro. All buses depart from Central Terminal de Autobúses del Norte at Cien Metros, found by taking the trolley car from the Metro station at Insurgentes, or by taxi or small buses. Turismo limousines operated by Corsarios del Bajio, located at Buenavista 4, Mexico City, offer very good service. From San Miguel de Allende, the best thing to do is to hire a car and go over to Querétaro for the day, returning to San Miguel in the evening. There is also second-class bus service operating between the two points. If you are driving yourself, the main highway from Mexico City to El Paso goes directly by Querétaro. The drive from Mexico City takes about three hours. By air, Querétaro is serviced by Aéreo-Transportes, S.A.

Where To Stay in Querétaro and Nearby Tequisquiapan

Hacienda Jurica (*90 rooms*)   Moderately expensive
For sheer comfort and elegance, the best place to stay in Querétaro is 5 miles north of town off Highway 57. This two-story inn constructed around a 200-year-old hacienda has beautifully furnished large rooms. Air-conditioned. Thermal pool. Attractive dining room. All cards. P.O. Box 338, Querétaro, Querétaro, México. Tel: 2-10-81. In Mexico City, 5-48-43-30.

Gran Hotel (*69 rooms*)   Inexpensive
At Av. Madero 6 Oriente, south side of the main plaza. Old hotel which has been modernized, but still is only fair in facilities. Fair dining room.

Hotel Impala (*50 rooms*)   Inexpensive
At entrance to town just off Highway 57, at Juárez y Zaragoza, a modern five-story hotel with a rooftop dining room. Clean, but modest. Food good. Bancomatico, Carnet, VISA.

Azteca Motel and Trailer Park (*25 rooms, 50 spaces*)   Inexpensive
On Highway 57, 9 miles north of interchange with Highway 45. Mansion-type structure. Some units have kitchenettes. Restaurant and coffee shop open twenty-four hours. Complete dinners, cocktails. All connections for trailers. P.O. Box 224. Tel: 2-20-60.

Casa Blanca Motel (*54 units*)   Inexpensive
On Mexico 57 and 45, ½ mile west of town. Modern two-story motel. Dining room, cocktail lounge, heated swimming pool. Most cards. P.O. Box 194. Tel: 2-11-34.

El Barón Motel (*17 rooms*)   Inexpensive
One and one-half miles northwest of town on Mexico 57. Rooms with showers. Dining room, bar, pool. P.O. Box 165. Tel: 2-15-75.

Golf-Hotel La Mansión (*200 rooms*)   Moderately expensive
At kilometer 176 on Mexico 57 and 45 between Querétaro and San Juan del Río, this is a well-advertised old inn with landscaped gardens. Attractive comfortable rooms in remodeled sixteenth-century hacienda. Heated pool, par-three golf course, riding, tennis, playground (extra charges for some). Dining room open 7 A.M. till 10 P.M. Cocktails. Reservations at P.O. Box 16, San Juan del Río, Querétaro, México. Tel: San Juan (467) 2-01-20; Mexico City 5-66-43-66.

Posada Tequisquiapan   Moderate
This is 42 miles from Querétaro, off on a side road from the Mexico

City highway to San Juan del Río. First-class hotel with swimming pool. Old but comfortable. P.O. Box 16, Querétaro. Tel: (467) 2-01-02.

Hotel Río (*82 rooms*)   Moderately expensive
Also at Tequisquiapan, a newer hotel with fine gardens, two large thermal pools, and three private pools with some housekeeping cottages. Good food, family menu. Cocktails. Tel: Tequisquiapan 15.

El Relox (*45 rooms*)   Moderate
Also at Tequisquiapan, an older hotel with new two-story section. Has three large thermal pools. Seventeen other rooms have private pools. Well-landscaped grounds. Dining room with good food. Children under five half rate. DC.

WHERE TO EAT IN QUERÉTARO

Fonda del Refugio, on the Plaza Corregidora, is a very pleasant place to eat under the awning overlooking the little plaza just off the main plaza. Run by Antonio Sánchez Barrientos, the restaurant has excellent seafood soup, avocado and shrimp, spaghetti *al burro,* broiled kid, and very cold beer served with tortilla chips and hot sauce. Open 10 A.M. to 2 A.M. Music in the evening.

Restaurant San Antonio, at Corregidora 38, near the main square in Querétaro, is a popular local restaurant serving a wide variety of food, including some excellent Mexican dishes. Good service. Accepts all cards.

Hostería del Márquez, at Juárez Norte 104, serves heavier dishes in elegant surroundings. Favored by businessmen. All cards.

La Mariposa, on the corner opposite the main plaza, is a very good snack bar; a restaurant, under the same name, is at Angela Peralta 7. Good Mexican food. Reasonable.

Flor de Querétaro, a small restaurant on the main plaza, serves garlic soup.

WHAT TO DO AND SEE IN QUERÉTARO

Plaza Obregón, the main plaza (also called the zócalo), is a good starting point for touring the city. On one side of the zócalo is the Gran Hotel, and there are sidewalk vendors who sell opals and amethysts from the local mines. On Sundays a band concert is held here. Parking is difficult, but you can park on Calle Allende at Super Servicio Allende, or below the ground at Plaza Constitución. The narrow and crooked streets sometimes make it difficult to find your way about, but a question here and there will solve your problem.

San Francisco Church, also on the main plaza, dominates the entire area. The church dates back to 1545, making it one of the oldest churches in this part of Mexico. Apart from its huge size and its fine tile work, the church is undistinguished. However, it does contain some ancient carvings and a library of parchment books. Adjacent to it is an old monastery, now used as a museum for historical matter.

Plaza de la Independencia, up the street behind the Church of San Francisco a block or two, is a quiet spot surrounded by old colonial buildings. In the center of the plaza is a monument to the aqueduct builder, Marqués de la Villa del Villar del Águila. Water in the fountain is from the aqueduct. When Emperor Maximilian was surrounded in Querétaro by the troops of Juárez, in the closing days of the war against the French, he used to walk in this plaza. Upon learning this, the supporters of Juárez shelled the plaza, but succeeded only in destroying the statue to the marqués. Maximilian was captured in Querétaro and executed just outside town.

The Old Aqueduct can be seen as you are leaving Querétaro on the way to Mexico City. It was begun in 1726 and completed in 1735. You can see local women coming to the various fountains to fill their jugs with water. To build the aqueduct cost $131,000, a fortune at the time, and it is said that the Marqués del Villar contributed $88,000 from his own pocket. The aqueduct brings water from a 5-mile distance and still supplies two-thirds of the city's water. It is a mountain-skirting canal in the beginning, but later the water rises on seventy-two arches, at points 100 feet high.

Palacio del Gobierno del Estado, the State House, is on Madero Street, which runs off the main Plaza Obregón and is the way out to the new superhighway to San Miguel. The palacio is a red stone building bearing a plaque which states that the great Mexican leader and father of his country, Benito Juárez, was there on June 4, 1863, and again on July 5, 1867, when he defeated the French. The building is undistinguished except for this historical note.

Santa Clara Church is also on Madero Street. It was founded in 1633 and rebuilt in the eighteenth century by Tresguerras.

Cerro de las Campañas is farther out this same avenue at the outskirts of the city. It was here, on this so-called "Hill of the Bells," that Maximilian and his staff surrendered their swords and met death before a firing squad. The Expiatory Chapel was built on this slope by the Austrian government in commemoration of Maximilian's untimely end. The Empress Carlota had meanwhile fled to Europe to seek aid for her besieged husband, but failed in her effort. Upon learning of his death she went mad. She lived in Belgium until her death in 1927.

Shopping in Querétaro

Opals and amethysts are a good buy in Querétaro. It is best to purchase them from a reputable shop such as El Rubí, Madero 3 Poniente, just off the main plaza. Most of the opals are genuine, but the quality varies greatly and you will probably be buying the lowest quality if you buy on the street from a vendor. A jeweler can give you an idea of the quality he is selling. Other people say the jewelers charge outlandish prices and you can do better in the smaller shops.

Eugenio Ontiveras, owner of the biggest opal mine in the area (there are 140 opal mines nearby), has a house in town where he sells gems; also, you can visit his big operation and see opals being mined. Some are fire opals gleaming like live coals, but others are emerald in color with flashes of violet-blue and carmine. One was as big as an orange. His mine is called the Carbonera.

23

Taxco

TALES OF OLD MEXICO

One of the most regular, and most distinguished, visitors to Taxco was the late long-time editor of the Chicago Tribune, *Don Maxwell. Don always stayed at the Hacienda del Chorillo, an old colonial smelter rebuilt into a luxury hotel. Over the years he came to know most of the local people, and among them Margarita Figueroa.*

Margarita is a charmer, with brown eyes, dimpled features, and neatly braided hair in the Mexican fashion. She was once married to an American artist, and speaks good English with a slight accent.

Don Maxwell took to calling Margarita "cousin," and together with his wife, Marge, always urged her to visit them in Chicago. Finally, one year Margarita agreed to go.

When she changed planes in Dallas, she was seated next to a husky gentleman, George Halas, long-time owner and coach of the Chicago Bears professional football team. Halas was an old friend of Maxwell's. Halas, kindhearted but gruff, spoke to the quiet little Mexican woman absent-mindedly:

"Where are you going?" he inquired.

"To see my cousin in Chicago," she replied demurely.

"And what is the name of your cousin in Chicago?" Halas asked.

"Don Maxwell," Margarita replied.

Halas almost burst his seat belt in astonishment.

"Your cousin is Don Maxwell!"

Maxwell and Halas had been bosom friends for many years. Devotees of "Maxwellisms" still tell the story.

TAXCO IS undoubtedly the most picturesque village in Mexico. Clinging to the side of steep hills, its red tile roofs, dripping with purple bougainvillea, tumble up and down along the cobblestoned streets, and from their cascading midst rises the famed Santa Prisca Church, built by the mining king, José de la Borda.

Long forgotten after colonial times, when the silver mining gave out on any large commercial basis, Taxco was bypassed by the outer world and retained much of its primitive charm. Then one day in the 1930s a young professor from Tulane University, William Spratling, came upon this virtually abandoned old mining town and decided to live there while working on a book about Mexico.

Spratling found that the natives had lost practically all of their ancestors' ability to do fine work in silver. He hunted for ancient Aztec designs which they could reproduce in the workshops he set up, and he gave lessons. From this simple start, the art of silvercraft was revived in Taxco. Most of the master craftsmen there today started as pupils of Spratling, and the silver they turned out became famous. Now, in turn, they have taught many pupils. Spratling died a few years ago, but others continue to teach new protégés. Spratling's workshop, about 6 miles south of town, may still be visited, and an attractive museum in the center of town displays his pre-Hispanic art collection.

The old homes, the narrow streets, and the cobblestone pavement are now protected by a law enacted to preserve the village as a colonial monument. All the new hotels and shops that have been built must conform to the old style; consequently, the colonial appearance of Taxco has been retained.

Taxco is just over 100 miles south of Mexico City, a two-and-one-half-hour drive on a paved road; the last half hour is tortuous and steep—keep to your right! Many people drive to Taxco for lunch and back to Mexico City the same day. But to get the real flavor of the peace and quiet of this little town, it is best to stay a night or two.

Newly arrived visitors will be amazed at the steep streets, but they will soon find themselves climbing up and down them with ease. Coming down the cobblestone streets in the morning, with the bright sun shining on the myriad flowers hanging on most of the walls, one comes to the little plaza in the center of town. This is easily found, as the graceful towers of Santa Prisca rising on one side of the plaza can be seen from anywhere in the entire area.

The zócalo has huge old trees and benches set casually around the inner square. It is peaceful here in the morning to sit and watch the people passing by. Later in the morning you can

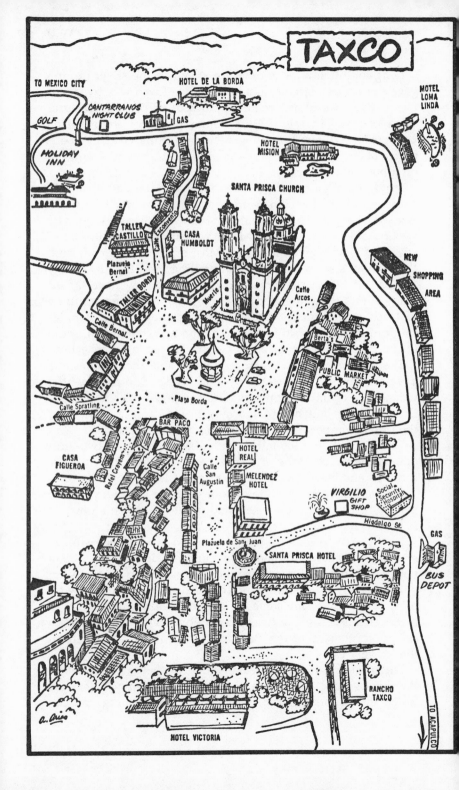

mount the stairs to *Paco's* bar, on a balcony overlooking the square, for a *limonada*, and enjoy a wonderful view. Then comes the morning paper, the mail, a glance into some of the myriad shops that line the streets, and a slow walk back to your hotel for the main event of the day—lunch. This peaceful existence has been known to attract visitors to permanent residence and perhaps to add a decade to their lives. Such is Taxco!

GOING THERE

Bus, turismo, or car is the means of transportation to Taxco. Estrella de Oro operates big Greyhound-type buses from Mexico City, with reserved seats on first-class, luxury express, and super luxury express. Their terminal is located at Calzada Tlalpan 2205 (tel: 5-49-85-20) in Mexico City, and buses leave from the Terminal de Autobúses del Sur, at the end of Metro line 2, every hour. Reservations must be made in advance. Or your hotel can arrange for a chauffeur-driven car.

By car, either your own or a rented one, it is possible to drive from Mexico City to Taxco in two and one-half hours, using the new superhighway to Cuernavaca, and off at a tollgate beyond the 100-kilometer mark, where the road to Taxco leaves the superhighway. Driving up into Taxco itself, at K-157, is puzzling because of the winding streets, and we therefore suggest that once under the arch at the entrance to Taxco, you stop and pick up a small boy who will guide you to your hotel.

Because some of the boys are not above bribery by the hotels, we suggest you pick any guide carefully and insist that he take you to the hotel of your choice. Pay no attention to his recommendation; use your own. Also, do not shop with guides, as they collect a 20-percent commission, which just means you pay higher prices.

HOTELS IN TAXCO

Holiday Inn (*159 rooms*)   Moderately expensive
Atop La Cantera mountain overlooking the town and its miles of surrounding mountains. Beautiful pool, nine holes of "golf in the sky," clay tennis courts, attractive bar and restaurant, special programs for children, bus service to town. (Entrance is a steep winding drive to your right just before entering Taxco from the

north.) All cards. Reservations: Holiday Inn, Taxco, Guerrero, México. Tel: 2-13-00.

Victoria Hotel (*77 rooms*)   Moderately expensive
Beautiful view overlooking town, terraced gardens, bar, two blocks from the plaza. Best hotel in the town center—usually excellent food. Have lunch on the lovely terrace. Operated by Dubin Hotels. Tel: 2-00-10.

Posada de la Misión (*100 rooms*)   Moderately expensive
Fair hotel, wonderful pool with Juan O'Gorman mural, fair food. On highway entering town. Music and dancing nightly. Now part of Nacional Hotelera chain. Tel: 2-00-63.

Hotel Hacienda del Solar (*12 rooms*)   Moderately expensive
On the southern outskirts of town, this 35-acre ranch has a heated swimming pool, tennis, and horseback riding at no extra charge; a nearby nine-hole golf course is available with reasonable greens fees. Outstanding La Ventana restaurant. Owners are Sam and Claire Polk. Reservations: Apartado 96. Tel: 2-03-23.

Hotel Rancho Taxco (*47 rooms*)   Moderately expensive
Next door to the Victoria, but smaller, first-class hotel with good food. Shares Victoria's dining facilities. Also operated by Dubin Hotels. Tel: 2-00-04.

Hotel de la Borda (*150 rooms*)   Moderately expensive
Big first-class hotel on outskirts of town. Fine view, pool, good food and service. Also a Dubin hotel. Tel: 2-00-25.

Hacienda San Francisco Cuadra (*28 rooms*)   Moderate
On dirt road off highway, 3 miles south of Taxco. Rustic, rather run-down ranch life, with riding horses and pool. Taxi ride to town. Write Apartado 37 for reservations.

La Cumbre Sonada (*9 rooms*)   Moderately expensive
An elaborate home with a number of guest suites. High above Taxco, it has a magnificent view and a fine small restaurant. Write Apartado 5 for reservations. Also by week and month. Tel: 2-08-56.

Santa Prisca Hotel (*26 rooms*)   Moderate
In town, small hotel but first-class. Good food. American management. At Cena Obscuras 1, one block from the plaza. P.O. Box 42. Tel: 2-00-80.

Los Arcos Hotel (*27 rooms*)   Inexpensive
Small hotel in town, one block from plaza at Juan Ruiz Alarcón 2.
Tel: 2-00-74.

Meléndez Hotel (*30 rooms*)   Inexpensive
Small hotel in town at Cuauhtemoc No. 4.

Hotel Aqua Escondida (*40 rooms*)   Inexpensive
Convenient, just off the square. Neat and clean.

Loma Linda Motel (*70 rooms*)   Inexpensive
At K-161 on highway just south of Taxco. Good rooms and bungalows, pool, restaurant, nightclub, view. Recommended. Tel: 2-
02-06.

Posada de los Castillo (*15 rooms*)   Moderately expensive
Small attractive inn off the plaza. Decorated in Mexican style and
hosted by Tony Castillo of the talented designing family. Juan Ruiz
Alarcón 7. Tel: 2-13-96.

Hacienda del Chorillo   Moderate
This charming old restored hacienda was *the* place to stay in Taxco
until its owner, L. A. Sullivan, retired as an innkeeper. Now long-
term rentals are available for the several attractive cottages on the
lovely grounds. Contact Mr. Sullivan at P.O. Box 24.

WHERE TO EAT IN TAXCO

La Ventana de Taxco   Expensive
Taxco's loveliest restaurant is in the Hotel Hacienda del Solar
opposite the Government Tourist Office on the highway just south
of town. Picture windows overlook the town in an attractively
appointed dining room. Try the fettuccine Alfredo, veal parmigiana,
or shrimp en brochette. Open from 1 to 4 P.M. and 7 to 10:30 P.M.
Carnet, MC, VISA. Tel: 2-05-87.

Victoria Hotel   Moderate
Lunch on the Victoria's terrace is still one of the very pleasant things
about a trip to Taxco. Sip a cold drink, admire the bougainvillea,
and enjoy. The food is fairly good. All cards. Tel: 2-00-10.

El Taxqueño Restaurant   Moderately expensive
In the Holiday Inn high above the town. The buffet table is
beautiful, the scenery is grand. All cards. Tel: 2-13-00.

La Cumbre Sonada   Moderately expensive
South of Taxco up a winding road above the town, this attractive
guest house offers excellent meals, with reservations only. Tel: 2-08-
56.

Sr. Costilla's   Inexpensive
Ribs and steaks. Informal dining on the square. Convenient.

Los Balcones   Inexpensive
If you like Mexican food, try the tacos or enchiladas here. Elvira's
mango pie is special. Just off the square near Casa Figueroa.

What To Do and See

Victoria Hotel. Upon arrival the obvious thing to do is recover
from your ride at your hotel, if you have made a reservation
ahead of time. If you haven't, we recommend heading for the
terrace of the Victoria Hotel, where you can lean back and begin
to enjoy the impressive view on all sides. You can be sure the
lunch will be pleasant.

The plaza, or zócalo, in front of Santa Prisca Church, is usually
the next order of business. It is best to leave your car parked
at the hotel and make your way down to the church on foot.
Low-heeled shoes are a must for women on the cobblestone
streets.

Around the plaza, the main building is Santa Prisca Church,
whose twin towers can be seen from all parts of Taxco. Casa
Borda, now housing a silver shop, is on one side of the zócalo,
while adjoining it is an attractive arcade filled with small shops
and boutiques, where it is fun to browse. On one wall is an old
colonial fountain with four spouts, which is said to have been
in use since 1741. On opposite corners are Paco's bar and Berta's
bar, both popular spots for a refreshing drink.

The plaza has some ancient Indian laurel trees, under whose
shade there are a number of benches; the nicest thing about
Taxco is to be able to sit down and watch the world go by.
Coca-Cola is sold in the corner *puesto*, and the daily English-
language newspaper from Mexico City arrives about noon.

Santa Prisca Church, with its tall towers, is said to be the finest
example of the ornate churrigueresque architecture in all of
Mexico, and this is saying a lot for the country that made

churrigueresque a household word. Over 200 years old, the church was built in 1759 by the fabulously wealthy mining king, José de la Borda, as a gesture of thanks for his good fortune. The famed phrase of his is "God gives to Borda, and Borda gives to God." The church is now lighted each night and makes a beautiful sight.

Santa Prisca Church is one of the handsomest in Mexico, and de la Borda is said to have supervised every detail of its construction. Certainly the lavish altar, with its gold-encrusted carvings, is a sight to see. You may enter at any time during the day. Donations are received in a small box inside. One of Mexico's greatest religious painters, Cabrera, is credited with paintings now worth a fortune. The architect was Diego Durán.

The Spratling Museum behind the church, essentially a new building with colonial exterior, is modest but interesting, and worth a visit. William Spratling left part of his extensive collection of pre-Hispanic art to the city of Taxco. The early carvings, figures, sculpture, bowls, and vases from the western coast of Mexico are beautifully displayed in a modern interior. The basement has a fascinating collection of photos and documents of old Taxco. The museum is open from 10 A.M. to 2 P.M. and from 3 to 6 P.M. Closed Mondays. There is a small admission fee.

Casa Figueroa, known in colonial days as the "House of Tears" according to its present owners, is just off the zócalo behind the old fountain at Guadalupe Street No. 2. Anyone in the plaza will point it out willingly. Although it has been turned into a commercial business charging admission and selling curios, it is still worth visiting. The owners, the Figueroa family, have retained all its colonial charm. Here is a splendid opportunity to see exactly what the home of a wealthy Mexican family was like in colonial days, replete with its tile kitchen and thronelike bath.

The story is that Casa Figueroa was built by Count Cadena, one of José de la Borda's friends, about the end of the seventeenth century, when he was able to utilize the labor of persons penalized to work by the courts. It was, in turn, the home of priests, a government mint, and the abode of a respected family until an elderly spinster was found murdered there. Then it became a warehouse with a cantina in the front. A local artist,

Fidel Figueroa, whose wife is a writer of note, bought the building in 1934 and began restoring it to its present admirable state. It contains a permanent art exhibit.

Casa Borda, also on the main plaza, is the low pink building with delicate frieze work, around the corner from the church. Borda built it for his home and offices in 1759. It is situated on the edge of a steep hill, so that the front is two stories high and the back is four stories. He stipulated that seven rooms were to be left in perpetuity for the use of the priests of Santa Prisca, and all owners since then have accepted this condition of ownership. It now houses one of the better silver shops in Taxco.

Casa de Verdugo de Aragones is another building on the plaza, distinguished by its arched balconies. The Verdugo family lived here in the time of Borda, and two of the Borda brothers courted two of the Verdugo daughters and later married them. The house was built in the latter part of the seventeenth century by Don Manuel Verdugo.

Paco's bar, with its balcony which overlooks the plaza, is a fine place in later afternoon to have a limonada and watch the same people you have been watching all morning from the park bench. There are frequent serenades by mariachis or lone guitarists, usually in the evening starting at five o'clock and carrying on from there indefinitely.

Casa Humboldt was built by a wealthy Mexican family, the Villanuevas, but takes its name from the scientist Alexander von Humboldt, who is said to have made it his home about 1803. It has a fine baronial hall, two lovely terraces, and an unusual decorated facade. Formerly a pension, it is now owned by the state and has an attractive display of area arts and crafts for sale. It can be found below Los Arcos Hotel on Pineda Street.

Silver workshops are practically everywhere, and at most of them the artisans are genuinely working on silver, not just putting up a front for the tourists. The easiest to reach are those of Castillo Talleres, down the cobblestone street just below the Borda silver shop on the main plaza. They will give you a guided tour. The very best places to visit now are about 6 miles out on the main highway south of Taxco. Rancho La Cascada is the Castillo brothers' out-of-town workshop, complete with waterfall and lovely gardens. Another ½ mile along the road you will find the workshops and studio of the late William Spratling, where craftsmen trained by the great silversmith still produce and sell Spratling-style silver. Taxco's Silver Fair at the beginning of December attracts an international gathering.

Colonial furniture is another flourishing industry in town. Many shops offering attractive designs may be found, and some will arrange for shipment. However, our expert says, beware of green wood.

The open markets of Taxco are a picturesque sight, tumbling up and down a series of stone steps off to one side of Santa Prisca, just beyond the Remo silver shop on one side of the plaza. There are numerous little shops open every day selling everything from huaraches to frijoles. On Sundays, many other vendors come and huge white cloths are spread as awnings over the street to shade the market from the sun. This makes for an exotic, bustling, noisy market scene worth visiting.

Dances in the evening can be either a variety you watch or the kind you dance yourself beside the beautiful heart-shaped pool at the Posada de la Misión. A popular spot is a nightclub called the Cantarranas, near the archway on the highway to the north. Located in a sixteenth-century hacienda, it offers a variety of Mexican folk acts. Action starts at 10:30 P.M. except Sundays. Rather expensive.

Cockfights and fiestas in the evening are strictly for tourists and are about as interesting as the peep show at a cheap carnival. Our advice is to save yourself considerable expense, as this is not only a waste of money but a waste of valuable time when you might be enjoying yourself elsewhere. At least you have been warned.

Religious fiestas, however, are bona fide celebrations and add to the excitement of Taxco during the year. Two are particularly popular. The possibility of getting reservations in Taxco during *Semana Santa* (the week preceding Easter Sunday) is remote unless you have planned well in advance. Activities include a variety of colorful religious festivals and processions. The *Christmas posadas*, from December 16 to 24, feature candlelight processions, piñatas, and elaborate fireworks.

Caves of Cacahuamilpa. For an out-of-town trip, the caves of Cacahuamilpa are well worth seeing. Known as Las Grutas, these huge underground caverns are about forty minutes north of Taxco on the Mexico City highway. Signs on the highway identify the road to Las Grutas. It's about a 5-mile drive into the caves.

The caverns, hollowed out beneath the mountains by two rivers, were discovered about 100 years ago and are still being explored. Chamber after chamber is filled with sculptured stalactites and stalagmites, including a huge concert hall that, it is said, can seat 1,000, and all effectively lighted as only Mexicans do it. Competent guides will accompany you, but although the walkway is wide and paved, don't attempt it unless you feel physically up to the almost two-hour walk.

The caves are open from 10 A.M. to 4 P.M. daily, and tours leave about every fifteen minutes. There is a modest entrance fee and a small fee for parking. Trips may be arranged through most hotels.

WHERE TO SHOP

Silver and Jewelry

Los Castillo, Plazuela de Bernal 10. One of the best. Same shop as in Mexico City. Castillo has workshops to visit here and at Rancho La Cascada at K-115 on the Acapulco highway.

Casa Borda, the pink house by Santa Prisca Church, has nice silver, rosewood, and other things.

Spratling, on the highway south of Taxco at K-117. Pieces here are done by protégés of the late famed designer.

Janna, S.A., at Fundiciónes 6, has elegant and expensive flatware, jewelry, and crystal. Internationally known, Janna did the original designs for Tiffany's silver flowers.

Antonio Pineda, near Santa Prisca Church, has had shows of his silver at the Waldorf in New York.

Uxmal, by the plaza, is excellent and pays no commission to guides, so you get a better deal in silver.

Virgilio, Miguel Hidalgo 24, is best for gold jewelry and rings.

Platería Real, a little shop next to the Hotel Real, off the plaza, has some nice jewelry at good prices.

Margaritas, on the corner of the plaza, has fine silver.

La Ventanita, on the square, is a shop with a good reputation.
Emma's, half a block from the square beside Santa Prisca
Church, is a family affair where everyone speaks English.
Margot, on the highway near the Posada de la Misión, has
beautiful inlay work.
Reveri, Bernal 3, offers nice modern flatware.

Clothing

Tachi, near the plaza, has unusual items, women's sportswear.
Estudios Taxco, just off the plaza on the path up to the Victoria,
has good shorts and blouses, as well as typical Mexican
costumes for children. A good spot for bargaining.
Teresa Original, off the square on Bernal, has very attractive
blouses.
Huaraches San Carlos, behind Santa Prisca Church, has fine
sandals for men and women.

Paintings

Carl Pappe, off the main plaza, sells bronzes and modern
sculpture.
Jaime Oates, whose shop is behind Remo's on the square, is
an internationally known Spanish artist.
Casa Domínguez, above the square on Calle Spratling, has
unusual Christmas cards and note paper.

Crafts

Casa Humboldt, on Pineda Street, is the state-owned arts and
crafts museum with a wide collection of attractive items for
sale.
The Arcade, at the corner of the plaza next to the Casa Borda,
is a maze of small shops and boutiques displaying a wide
range of Mexican talent. Note the shop featuring colorful
papier-mâché figures made by prison inmates. Another shop
sells lovely jewelry made from shells. The patio, with its

splashing fountain and grillwork benches, is a pleasant spot to rest your weary feet.

The Indian market, with its open stalls and the challenge of bargaining, is the place to visit on Sundays.

24

Mexico South:
Tehuantepec and Chiapas

TALES OF OLD MEXICO

The women of Tehuantepec are noted for their statuesque beauty, but few realize what perfect wives they make.

One person who does is Edgar Erikson, for he has been married for over half a century to a Tehuana. It all started after World War I, when the accounting firm for which Mr. Erikson worked in Chicago was given the job of auditing the books of a coffee plantation in southern Mexico.

After his arrival in Arriaga via the narrow-gauge railway, Erikson moved into the plantation house and spent several months reviewing the books. By then he had fallen in love with the tropical climate, the softly waving palms, and the Tehuanas.

He cabled the Chicago firm to send him his severance pay, used it to buy a plot of land with 100 coconut palms, and married the loveliest of the Tehuanas.

Between two of the palms he strung up a hammock, from which he watched his new wife pick 100 coconuts each day (each tree produces one coconut per day, year round) and take them to market for 30 centavos each, and bring him back the 30 pesos total. In those days this was worth almost $15 a day—more than enough to buy choice seafood and staples, aged rum, and a steady supply of good novels from the States.

He became one of the happiest men in the world.

WHENEVER A true lover of Mexico wants to do something different, we recommend, without hesitation, that the very southernmost part of Mexico is the place to go.

This is the area beginning with the narrow Isthmus of Tehuantepec, where Mexico slims to a waist only 200 miles across, and below, widens out to the wild and partially unexplored giant state of Chiapas, bordering on Guatemala. This is Mexico South!

The Pan-American Highway runs directly through this fabulous country, which lies a day's drive south of Oaxaca. It is possible to drive there in your own car, to take a bus which has improved its service but is still somewhat rigorous, or to fly to Ixtepec Airport in Tehuantepec, or to Tuxtla Gutiérrez, capital of the state of Chiapas.

A road only a few years old now goes from a turnoff south of Tuxtla on a most spectacular mountain trip to Pichicalco and connects with a road to Villahermosa and thence connections to Palenque and Mérida—all paved. This is probably the most scenic trip in Mexico. For details, see page 372.

Tuxtla Gutiérrez is the capital city of the state of Chiapas, the great coffee-growing area of Mexico, whose vast jungles contain literally thousands of unexplored ancient Mayan cities and ruins. Most famous are *Bonampak,* discovered in recent years; *Palenque,* whose towering stone buildings are now being restored; and *Yaxchilán,* where the strange race of the Lacandon Indians, speaking a language unlike any other, live.

The jewel of all Mexico South is the little city of *San Cristóbal de las Casas,* set high in the mountains two hours south of Tuxtla Gutiérrez. Its pleasant though cool weather, perfectly preserved colonial atmosphere, and Indians with their picturesque dress make it a fine vacation hideaway.

There are fine beaches along the Isthmus, and some of the hotels have good swimming pools. But, by and large, those journeying to Tehuantepec and Chiapas go there to see some of the most colorful people and country of the world, and to do this they have to accept what accommodations there are.

This can mean a variety of things. It usually means a clean room in a fairly good hotel, but most are *not* air-conditioned, and the weather can be very hot in the lower places. It can mean some pretty ordinary meals, but wholesome, safe food. Above all, it can mean an extraordinarily exciting vacation, and if you have the proper spirit, it can mean high adventure. But be warned: The accommodations are not now luxurious. In time, they may be.

It is only a four-hour drive from Oaxaca to *Tehuantepec,* and it is possible to make the trip there and back in one day. The alternative is to stay overnight in the one acceptable hotel, the Calli, which is small and modest but clean and air-conditioned.

Or you can push on that same day all the way to Tuxtla, where there are fairly good hotels. To see the Tehuanas, you really have to drive into Juchitán, the town adjoining Tehuantepec. The Colón restaurant in Juchitán, next to the Pemex station, is a good place to eat. Clean, with cold beer. And it is fun to go down to the Pacific at Salina Cruz and see the old port town, but don't plan to stay there.

Salina Cruz is a weather-beaten port on the Pacific 11 miles from Tehuantepec. It is largely blocked by huge sandbars but still a major port through continual dredging operations. It handles most of the oil going from the Gulf by pipeline to tankers in Salina Cruz harbor. The Mexican Navy also has a base here, and sailors can usually be seen in the small town.

The next night's stop should be in *Tuxtla Gutiérrez*, where there is the Hotel Bonampak, a big modern place with comfortable (though far from luxurious) rooms, a restaurant, and a pool. Your goal from here can then be *San Cristóbal*, two hours farther on, which has two small hotels, the better of which is the Hotel Español. From San Cristóbal you can journey to the Guatemalan border, visiting *Comitán* and some other interesting villages. The road is paved all the way.

GOING THERE

By Air. CMA flies to Oaxaca, on to Ixtepec (Tehuantepec's airport), and from there to Tuxtla Gutiérrez. There is no airport at San Cristóbal, but you can go on to Tapachula, the isolated city on Mexico's far southwest coast.

By Bus. The first-class buses of Autotransportes del Sureste Cristóbal Colón, located at Héroes Ferrocarriles No. 38 in Mexico City, have daily service, leaving from the Terminal Central de Autobúses del Sur, on Calzada Tlalpan, but make a seat reservation. Flecha Roja runs second-class buses over the same route. First-class buses have reclining seats, but we suggest carrying a few snacks and a thermos of water.

By Train. It is a strange trip, but entirely possible. A train leaves Mexico City's Buenavista Station daily for Puebla and Córdoba, usually carrying a Pullman, and you are either switched or change to a train going south to the Trans-Isthmus Railway, which brings you to Ixtepec Station, near Tehuantepec.

It is possible, in Ixtepec, to pick up the narrow-gauge, old-fashioned *Ferrocarril Pan-Americano*, which makes its way south to Arriaga, near Tuxtla Gutiérrez, and then down the Pacific coast to Tapachula. The narrow-gauge portion is a rough trip, only for railroad buffs. It is possible to enter Guatemala this way, but the better way by far is the Pan-American Highway through San Cristóbal and Comitán. From Ixtepec, you can also go back on the Trans-Isthmus to Coatzacoalcos on the Gulf coast and connect for Yucatán.

HOTELS IN MEXICO SOUTH

Tehuantepec

Hotel Calli (*30 rooms*)   Inexpensive
A mile north of town on main highway, this is a newer but modest hotel with small air-conditioned rooms, dining room open from 7 A.M. to 10 P.M., pool, nice garden landscaping, music. Some trailer spaces. Best hotel in area. AE, DC, VISA.

Hotel Tehuantepec (*50 rooms*)   Inexpensive
On the Pan-American Highway south of town. This passable hotel is run-down; fair rooms, some air-conditioned. Small pool, poor restaurant.

Tuxtla Gutiérrez

Hotel Bonampak (*105 rooms*)   Moderate
On highway west of town, the best in this part of Mexico. Located in luxuriant gardens. Older cottages fine, but new air-conditioned tower units are recommended. Pool, restaurant, bowling alleys, and tennis courts. Dining room and coffee shop open 6:30 A.M. till midnight. Cocktails and soda fountain. Tel: 2-02-01.

Gran Hotel Humberto (*112 rooms*)   Moderate
A modern commercial hotel in center of town with underground parking. All rooms air-conditioned. Noisy but lively restaurant and cabaret. All cards. Tel: 2-20-80.

San Cristóbal de las Casas

Hotel Español (*36 rooms*)   Inexpensive
Old colonial home remodeled, well-run. Good food at patio-style restaurant open till 11 P.M. Cocktails. AE, MC, VISA. Write P.O. Box

12, San Cristóbal de las Casas, Chiapas, México, for reservations. Tel: 25.

El Molino de la Alborada (*11 rooms*) Moderately expensive
Two miles out of San Cristóbal on a side road beyond the landing strip. A tourist ranch on hillside overlooking area. Large rooms in masonry cottages with fireplaces. Attractive and comfortable. Dining room, with cocktails, open only during meal hours. Good home cooking. Fishing, hunting, riding available, and tours to archeological zones. Operated by Wally and Fran Franklin, formerly of Michigan and South Dakota. Write P.O. Box 50 for reservations.

Tapachula

Loma Real Motor Hotel (*63 rooms*) Moderate
On hilltop on highway about 1 mile out of town, this is a modern structure operated by Western Hotels. Large attractive air-conditioned rooms. Pool. Dining room with entertainment and dancing; service 7 A.M. till 11 P.M. Hunting arranged. All cards. Tel: 14-40.

Hotel San Francisco (*38 rooms*) Inexpensive
In town at Central Hidalgo Sur 94. Small but good hotel with some air-conditioned rooms. Garage nearby. Tel: 14-54.

Kamico (*55 rooms*) Moderate
New two-story motor inn on Highway 200 at east entrance to town. Set in tropical grounds. Pool, good dining room, central air conditioning. Double rooms. Colonial decor.

Hotel Rochester (*23 rooms*) Inexpensive
A modern hotel near the plaza. Rooms air-conditioned. Coffee shop. All cards.

TEHUANTEPEC

The famed Isthmus of Tehuantepec is said to be the home of the most beautiful women in the world. This superlative usually leads to a certain amount of disillusionment for the traveler, but no one can fail to admire the grace and symmetry of these women. They are truly statuesque and handsome.

The women wear bright-colored jackets and skirts, Burmese or Oriental in style, and they completely overshadow the males, who are relatively insignificant in appearance. The women are not only taller and more animated than the men, but they successfully run the markets and many other businesses such as the banks. They set the tone of social life and also indulge in the salty stories and remarks which are more common to the men in other societies. At the same time, modern life has meant that men have become government officials and the principal land owners in the area, although who can deny that they probably report in turn to their wives?

Costume. The daily costume of the Tehuanas is rich and elaborate, usually gold embroidery on red cloth, but it is virtually sackcloth compared with their dress for special occasions and fiestas.

The gala dresses for special occasions are made of satin and velvet in the form of skirts and sleeveless blouses, with starched ruffles of finely pleated white lace extending for 7 or 8 inches about the bottom of the skirt. A magnificent headpiece, the *huipil*, a great bonnet of white lace, is worn much like the headdress of the American Indians.

The huipil headdress is really a small lace garment about the size of a baby's dress; in fact it has two small sleeves which dangle unused. The story goes that centuries ago a shipload of cargo was wrecked on the coast and natives found a box of fine lace baby dresses. Not understanding their use, they adopted them for headdresses.

The headdress is worn in two different ways. One, for ordinary use, is with the ruffled collar of the little dress used as a frame for the face, with the rest draped about like a cape. The other, for more festive wear, is with the skirt of the baby dress used as a headdress like a bonnet.

For those who are interested, these costumes are on sale. Prices vary widely with the quality of the garment and the handwork. Stores in Mexico City also carry them.

Gold Coin Necklaces. No Tehuana costume is complete without a necklace containing some gold coins. Originally these coins were given to ladies by their admirers, often outsiders who came in to help with the railroad project, and they have been handed down from mother to daughter. Inasmuch as these coins now sell for up to $100 each, most Tehuanas have been forced to sell theirs and substitute gold-washed silver coins, which, fortunately, have the very same government design.

Climate. Tehuantepec is in the full tropics, and the climate is unvaryingly hot. The rivers are full of curious tropical fish, and the dark-green jungles are spotted with beautiful yellow and black orioles and parrot-beaked birds.

Beaches at Salina Cruz and Ventosa. Tehuantepec town is only fifteen minutes from Salina Cruz, a port on the Pacific, and here there are fine beaches for swimming, except when the wind is blowing hard. Then, the sand flying through the air can be a stinging blast. Just south of Salina Cruz is another beach area, beautifully wild and isolated, called Ventosa. Make local inquiry. It is a short drive over a dirt road. Salina Cruz is the western terminus of the Trans-Isthmus Railroad and of a pipeline carrying oil from the Gulf of Mexico fields to be loaded on tankers in the Pacific.

The town of Tehuantepec is a dusty community of old houses around courtyards, and the sand drifts in over the cobblestone streets. There is a city hall and a little plaza with some shops. The only two-story home of note is a tile house built by the famous Dona Juana C. Romero, whom the expert on the area, Miguel Covarrubias, says was a peasant girl who grew wealthy when her friend, the great dictator Porfirio Díaz, made the railroad track pass her house. She is still considered the patron saint of Tehuantepec.

Juchitán (pronounced hoot-chee-TAN) is really the place to see the women of the Isthmus. It is a sister town (population 30,000) only 17 miles farther south on the Pan-American Highway. The town has by far the best market. A taxi will drive you there, or you can go in your own car easily. Those going from Tehuantepec to Juchitán should carry their tourist cards, as, at this writing, there is a government immigration checkpoint along the road at this spot.

While the people look so much like the Tehuanas that you will not be able to tell them apart, they refer to themselves as Juchitecos, and a history of the area shows that the two towns are usually on opposite sides in most political struggles and quarrel over such other little things as the length of skirts, nature of ruffles, and so forth.

The markets are best seen in the early morning, and the first arrivals come to set up their stands when it is still dark. Sunrise finds vendors from all parts of the area bearing their merchandise on their heads. They come in with huge piles of *totopos*, large corn puffs wrapped in a white cloth, with great baskets of fruit and flowers, and others set up stands of coconuts, loaves of brown sugar, or pottery and even furniture. The women glide by with matchless grace. There is a steady hum of chatter as they bargain with each other, and this goes on until noon when they all pack up and go home for lunch, to return in the late afternoon.

Jaguar Hill. The name *Tehuantepec* comes from the Nahuatl word meaning "Jaguar Hill," which refers to the principal hill around which Tehuantepec is built. A path up a brush-cluttered way can be found, and one can climb to the top of the hill, which is surmounted by a small white chapel. According to legend, fierce jaguars lived on the hill until natives appealed to a Huave sorcerer who caused a gigantic turtle to come from the sea and drive them away. The sorcerer then turned this turtle into the present hill. The hill, if you puff your way up, dominates the entire area and gives you a fine view. You can see Juchitán off to the east, and the great lagoon of Tehuantepec, along the Pacific, to the west.

In both towns more people speak pure Zapotec than they do Spanish, and the Indian tongue is heard throughout the market. Of course, the Juchitecos criticize the Tehuana accent in speaking Zapotec.

La Zandunga. Both towns possess a lively sense of music and dance. The traditional songs, "La Zandunga" of the Tehuanas and "La Llorona" of the Juchitecos, are heard constantly. Nowhere in Mexico do the people have such an intense social activity as in Tehuantepec, and their festivals are held weekly. They not only have lavish traditional fiestas, but they also like the modern dance in its snuggling-up version. Each neighborhood has its own patron saint and has a celebration on one particular day each year, when a day-long festival is culminated with the *tirada de fruta*. At this time, pretty girls climb to the roof of the largest nearby building and throw fruit down to the crowd; this is nice with mangos and bananas but tough when you get hit with a pineapple.

Life and Love on the Isthmus. According to the leading authority on the Tehuanas, the late Miguel Covarrubias, who wrote the classic account of this culture, the Tehuanas, while they have won social and economic independence, are still romantic and passionate, and they will often submit to natural unions rather than lose their lovers. At the same time, they are not promiscuous, and one girl found walking alone on the road at night said she had no fears of being attacked, as there were enough rocks along the road to take care of any unwanted advances.

Marriage. Courtship includes the usual romantic serenading, fleeting glances around the plaza or market, and Saturday-night dancing, but the wedding ceremony is relatively formal. It is still the custom of the older people that a young man should send a delegation of three persons to ask the *mother*, not the father, for the hand of the girl. The marriage is performed at the girl's home, usually by a judge, and a band then strikes up a gay tune. Two speechmakers make speeches, the girl answers the speech of the boy. Each speech lasts three hours, dwelling on love, life, and married behavior; then the entire party adjourns for a fiesta and lunch.

They dance until late afternoon, when the newlyweds withdraw indoors. The guests go home and relatives all sit about outside shouting encouragement to the young people inside. In former days, a blood-stained handkerchief was thrown out to show that the young lady was a virgin. This permitted all the female relatives to wear a red flower in their hair the next day to show that all had gone well.

Funerals are another occasion where the special characteristics of the Tehuanas appear. The Zapotecs usually face death without fear, concluding that it is inevitable and part of one's fate. According to Covarrubias, the people talk about death as the most natural thing in the world.

However, at funerals, the women are given to wild screaming, and an unearthly distraught appearance is considered respectful to the dead. Watching a funeral procession pass, you will hear the wails of the women following the coffin, which is usually carried on the shoulders of the men. It is the custom of those attending the funeral to drop a few coins as alms at the home of the bereaved family. Flowers are heaped on the mound of the grave for nine days; at the end of this time, the mound is spread even and mourning ends.

Thus from birth, accomplished in a sitting position among

the Tehuanas, to death, an unusual social pattern has been developed which interests not only anthropologists but all who visit this isthmus land.

TUXTLA GUTIÉRREZ

As we have said before, the place to stay in Tuxtla Gutiérrez is the Hotel Bonampak. It is large, well equipped, has a fine pool, is reasonably comfortable, and there is no other hotel with similar facilities. CMA lands its planes in Tuxtla daily at a new mountaintop airport 20 miles north of town.

Tuxtla is an old Spanish-type city, long isolated from the rest of Mexico. It is the capital of the state of Chiapas and the headquarters for the coffee business in the area, although Tapachula has more of a coffee market. But Tuxtla is a bustling business center and prosperous in appearance all the same.

There is a state museum, a park with a zoo attached where one can see some of the wild animals that roam the forests in this area, such as jaguars, anteaters, and deer. There is also the state capitol and the Palace of Fine Arts. A new University of Chiapas has been built on the highway just north of the city, and there is a very handsome and very large tourism building on the main street just beyond the Bonampak. Stop in for information.

Mountain Trip to Yucatán Peninsula

A new, completely paved road from a junction just south of Tuxtla Gutiérrez to the mountain town of Pichicalco and thence to Villahermosa, in Tabasco state, connects with the regular paved highways to Palenque, Campeche, Mérida, the ruins of Chichén-Itzá and Uxmal, Chetumal, and the fabulous new Caribbean resort center of Cancún. You can then return via the Gulf coast and Veracruz if you wish.

The Pichicalco section goes through some of the most spectacular mountain scenery in Mexico, if not the world, which is well worth the trip all by itself. The dips and curves are all well protected. There are not too many gasoline stations but enough with lead-free gas to get you by if you use them as you see them. There are some small restaurants, but a box lunch is helpful.

TALES OF OLD MEXICO

When we used to go to San Cristóbal de las Casas, it was always a must to stop at the Hotel Español, and then go over to call on Franz Blom.

Franz, a spare, kindly man with a mane of white hair, had been a professor of anthropology at Tulane University and a noted scholar when he retired to Las Casas in a formal sense. Actually, he continued important studies of the Lacandon Indians until he died a few years ago.

Franz and his wife, Gertrude Doby, a noted German photographer, lived in a typical Mexican town house with rooms around a large patio. It was their custom to hold Sunday-afternoon soirees, and welcome almost everyone who wanted to join them.

One time when I went there, there was a Lacandon Indian with two sons. I have forgotten his real name, even if I knew how to spell it, which I am sure the man himself didn't, but I recall they named him Bor, and he wore a white sheet.

Bor had never heard of money, law, the United States, or even the country in which he lived, Mexico, until Franz rescued him from the deep jungle.

Bor, who was living happily with four wives in the jungle finding food with his bow and arrow for the nomadic household, was hit by tragedy when four chicleros, a rough crowd of white itinerant gatherers of sap of the tropical Chicozapote tree, came upon Bor and proceeded to steal all four wives, leaving Bor dumbstruck, downcast, and alone with two boys.

Franz brought Bor back to their home in Las Casas, an incredible sight in itself to Bor, and let him live as a part of the Blom household while he restored Bor's spirits and reinstilled a desire to live. By the time I arrived, Bor was quite happy, even outgoing, and we had some fine conversations in sign language.

He and his boys had discovered "candy," and it had added a new dimension to their pleasures. I think Bor was spoiled for jungle life, but he undoubtedly became the first Lacandon guide. Actually, the trip through the jungle to see the Bonampak ruins, discovered by an American, Charles Frey, who lost his life on the trip in 1947, was hazardous and required a day on horseback from the nearest small-plane landing strip at El Cedro. But Bor would know the way well.

SAN CRISTÓBAL DE LAS CASAS

Some two hours beyond Tuxtla Gutiérrez, by paved road on the Pan-American Highway, is the charming mountain village of San Cristóbal de las Casas. Where Tuxtla is hot and tropical, San

Cristóbal is high and temperate and has very pleasant weather. It is necessary to drive there or go by bus.

The village, which seems to have been sleeping ever since it was founded almost 400 years ago, consists of squat houses and cobblestone streets filled with visiting Chamula and Zinacatecan Indians. The latter wear the flat hats with ribbons (put on to attract feminine admirers). If women in your party are moved to buy such hats, prevail upon them not to wear them in town. The local males view this with considerable displeasure.

San Cristóbal has some modest but exceedingly accommodating hotels which many visitors find so pleasant and inexpensive that they have stayed here for months. The Hotel Español is really an overgrown pension built around a charming courtyard where coffee is served in the morning. Meals are served until 11 P.M. and are good. A fine American-operated dude ranch, El Molina de la Alborada, is just out of town with comfortable rooms and good home cooking including cinnamon rolls, country ham, and hot chocolate. They offer horse backpack trips. See hotel listings on pages 366–367.

Flat Hats and Ribbons. In the streets one sees gnomelike Chamula Indians hurrying along. Their colleagues, the Zinacatecans, whose men are said to have the most beautiful legs in the world, stride along in short shorts, wearing flat hats bedecked with ribbons. The Chamulas carry goats' horns (in which they keep salt) at their waists.

These Indians live in the forests around San Cristóbal and visit the town to participate in the markets. Practically all produce is carried on their backs, and they are very much like the mountain people of Guatemala to the south in that each tribe wears exactly the same dress.

Markets. There are two markets in San Cristóbal. One, just off the central plaza on Calle Real de Guadalupe, sells handicrafts, while eight blocks north of the plaza, beyond the Church of Santo Domingo, is the real native market selling produce and all manner of things largely for the inhabitants themselves. It is open every week but not on Sunday. However, nearby San Juan Chamula has a Sunday market (see next page).

Colonial Buildings. In San Cristóbal, one can wander about seeing the old colonial churches and buildings. The city was founded in 1524 when one of Cortés's captains, Luis Marín, entered the valley and found the Chamulas had set up a fortified point here, and resisted mightily. Eventually they withdrew, and a city of San Cristóbal was started. Later its full name was given to it to honor a famed bishop of the area, Bartolome de las Casas, who was a vigorous defender of the Indians.

The cathedral on the main plaza is not particularly noteworthy for its architecture, but it is worth going inside to see the gold-encrusted pulpit and the elaborate *retablos*. Santo Domingo on the outskirts of town also has some interesting retablos as well as a baroque entrance.

Nearby Villages. There are two nearby villages worth visiting. One is Zinacantán, a small group of community buildings with one street, which is the community center of the Zinacatecan Indians.

The other village, on the other side of the mountain ridge, in another little valley, is the community center of the Chamulas, and their village is also a cluster of huts with a big austere whitewashed temple in the center. It is only a 7-mile drive done in a half hour, as the road is not the best, but you pass through orchard country and then see the village with its black or gray pirate-style turban-clad residents. Those with flat Chinese-coolie-looking beribboned hats are visitors from Zinacantán. The Chamulas' famed *Sunday market* features hand-woven material.

Both of these Indian peoples are shy, as tourists have only come of recent years, and it is difficult to approach them.

The Rancho Nuevo Caves, about 4 miles south of San Cristóbal just west of the Pan-American Highway, are worth visiting. Since they are largely unexplored, it is possible to enter them only in the dry season.

Lakes of Montebello. These incredibly beautiful lakes are a half-day trip over a new well-paved road. This is a chain of scenic lakes set in forest and mountains; they reflect the handsome sunsets of the area. In this area lived the long-lost tribe of Lacandon Indians. There are only rustic accommodations consisting of Posada Bosque Bello with three rooms for nine persons at 40 pesos each at this writing, so perhaps you must plan to return unless you have camping equipment. Still well worth the trip to one of the most beautiful areas of Mexico.

From Comitán, there are three round-trip buses to Montebello a day. Fare is 20 pesos, and buses leave from the Comitán–Montebello bus station.

Beyond San Cristóbal, it is possible to drive on to Comitán, another smaller village, and then finally to the Guatemalan border at El Ocotal. There are no accommodations in this place at this writing, though there undoubtedly will be as traffic goes through on the Pan-American Highway section.

Comitán is 34 miles south of San Cristóbal on the Pan-American Highway, and 52 miles from the Guatemalan border. From here you can take a bus to the Montebello lakes. There are two very modest provincial hotels in Comitán, the Hotel Internacional and the Hotel Delfín, but neither is recommended at this writing.

Guatemala. It is possible to go into Guatemala on the Pan-American Highway over a paved highway to the first large Guatemalan city of *Huehuetenango*, which has a good hotel and dining room, Hotel Zaculeu. A tourist card is necessary to enter Guatemala; proof of U.S. citizenship (passport or birth certificate) is required to obtain a tourist card. And of course you will have to surrender your Mexican tourist card upon exit, and secure a new one upon return unless you have one for multiple entries. Both countries issue cards at the border.

Tapachula. Another Mexican city of note on the Guatemalan border is Tapachula, center of the coffee and hide industry. Located on the Pacific, it also has a highway into Guatemala. See the hotel listings on page 367.

25

The Gulf:
Veracruz, Villahermosa, the Palenque Ruins, and Campeche

TALES OF OLD MEXICO

One of the most dramatic trips in Mexico has always been the route between Mexico City and Veracruz. It was on this route that Cortés led his conquistadores when they founded Veracruz and then set out on the painful march up the steep mountains through hordes of attacking Indians.

It was this route, several hundred years later, by then a cobblestoned carriage road, on which the Emperor-to-be and his Empress, Maximilian and Carlota, arrived—he to eventually die before a firing squad, she to return down the road to a madhouse in Belgium.

Up this ancient road came the troops of General Winfield Scott, with his two lieutenants, Robert E. Lee and U. S. Grant, after their amphibious landing in Veracruz in the war of 1848. And the French troops of Napoleon III proudly marched up this route only to lose a pitched battle at Puebla with Mexicans under the command of Porfirio Díaz, one of Mexico's highly commemorated victories.

The Veracruz train ride of later years was spectacular, the steep decline being something like dropping from Denver, Colorado, to sea level in a few hours. The roadbed passed immediately before the snow-capped peak of Orizaba, and then through tropical flowers.

Nowadays there is a superhighway, and the bus ride is still more than a small thrill.

THE GULF coast of Mexico is historic, scenic, and possessed of many places worth visiting. A trip down through Puebla, with perhaps an overnight stop in Fortín de las Flores with its gardenia-covered pools, thence to Veracruz, and south by car, bus, or train along the great sweeping coastline, with its beaches, famed shrimp grounds, and ancient ruins, is easily done and absolutely fascinating if you have the time.

A new seaside highway north from Veracruz is scenic and will take you to the ruins at Tajín, Papantla, and the vanilla country, and finally to Tampico, another seaport.

The trip south now is entirely paved all the way to the famed ruins of Palenque, among the largest and in my view the most interesting in Mexico, as they are part of the great Mayan empire extending all the way into Guatemala, while the same road continues on to Mérida in Yucatán. It is paved all the way and very easy to drive. If you take the coastal route, there will be some ferries, but you will see some of the finest beaches in the world.

VERACRUZ

Veracruz is the Republic's principal port and its oldest colonial city. Its quays moor ships from many nations. Its fortified port was built originally by the Spanish and has since seen bitter shots exchanged with French, Spanish, and American forces.

It is a charming city of old Spanish-style buildings, with balconies and iron grilles, cobblestone streets, palm trees, and sidewalk cafés set under arched patios along the street.

The climate is tropical, except for occasional storms (called *nortes*), which are usually confined to the fall months and can be virtual hurricanes. The beaches are not quite as good as those on the Pacific coast, as the land slopes down to a low coastal plain, rather than breaking sharply to the white sands as it does at Acapulco. The Gulf does, however, have wide beaches, and the swimming can be fine.

Good Fishing. The fishing and seafood are as good as the Pacific coast offers, as the Gulf has many types of fish not available elsewhere, such as sabalo. One of the great pleasures of Veracruz, almost worth the trip alone, is to sit at a sidewalk café and have shrimp in limitless heaps served minutes-fresh from the ocean. They are eaten as hors d'oeuvres as you sip an ice-cold brew. The veracruzanos are famous for their fish recipes, such as *pescado veracruzano* and *sopa de mariscos* or *sopa de pesca*.

Despite all this, it is important to note that Veracruz is a large city of 250,000 persons and a big commercial center. It is not

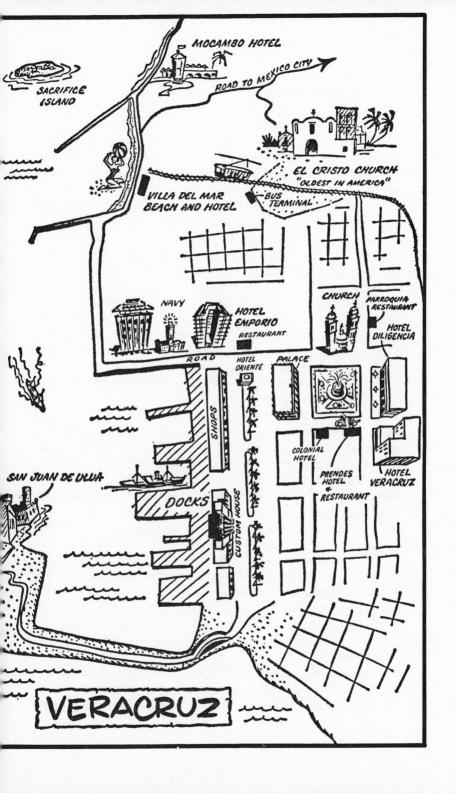

just a tourist town, and this is reflected in the fact that the hotels are comfortable but by no means luxurious, and that very often little attention is paid to the tourist.

Via Fortín de las Flores. Usually an added reason for going to Veracruz is to take the trip down from Mexico City to see Puebla, and then an overnight stop at Fortín de las Flores. Return can be by an alternate route through Jalapa, which is a seven-hour drive back to Mexico City.

Fortín is noted for its lush flowers and orchards; orchids and gardenias and a profusion of other flowers are in abundance. The *Hotel Ruiz Galindo*, with its pool daily covered with fresh gardenias, is a well-kept clean hotel but on somewhat austere lines. The 154 rooms are moderate to expensive. Reservations can be made in Mexico City at Reforma 90 (tel: 5-46-89-29), or by mail to the hotel name and town. The hotel accepts no credit cards. A more cozy place is *Posada Loma*, east of the town of Fortín on the Córdoba road. It has twenty cottage-style units set in interesting gardens full of orchids, camellias, and gardenias. There is a fine dining room with a striking view of Mount Orizaba. Telephone María Dolores Álvarez at Fortín 3-06-58. Rates are moderate. No credit cards.

Tehuacán. Another interesting spot on the Puebla–Veracruz road is the Tehuacán mineral springs area with two big hotels. Turning off the superhighway 55 miles beyond Puebla at Esperanza junction tollhouse, you go 30 miles on a paved side road to the famed *Hotel Spa Peñafiel*. There are 151 rooms at moderate rates for a double room with meals. Facilities include a large pool, tennis, and golf. Telephone 2-01-90. *Hotel México* has eighty rooms similarly priced. Both are old, rambling hotels, but still first-class. A fine place to rest.

Orizaba Volcano. It is a seven-hour drive from Mexico City to Veracruz, and the highway drops several thousand feet in the space of a half hour with some very spectacular scenery. A good part of the time the almost perfect cone-shaped volcano of Orizaba, the highest in Mexico, towers alongside the road; its snow-covered peak can be seen through palm trees and orchid plants.

Other Spots of Interest. In the general vicinity of Veracruz, meaning within a day's drive, are such other interesting spots as *Tecolutla*, a beach resort to the north; *Papantla*, a mountain village worth visiting in May or June when the spectacular flying Indian dancers descend from the rope-entwined flagpole; *Cempoala*, an archeological zone of pyramids near Veracruz; or, to the south, *Puerto Alvarado*, a sea town, near which is Alemán Dam, one of the largest dams in Mexico. Other interesting places are *San Andrés Tuxtla*, and *Lake Catemaco* with its fine primitive fishing.

La Bamba. As for us, we like to go down to Veracruz, sit at a sidewalk table on the main plaza, Plaza de Armas, often called "the Diligencias," and have a cool beer and some shrimp, leaving only to take a brief ride around town on the wonderful little open-air trolleys, perhaps down to the beach and back. Bring your tropical clothes.

Veracruz is noted for its lively dancing, especially the wonderful *bamba;* its flashing-eyed señoritas and red-kerchiefed, white-clad *chamacos* (boys) can dance up a storm. You should be able to see them in some of the hotels or nightclubs listed on pages 383–385.

HISTORY OF VERACRUZ

Veracruz is the place where the Spaniards originally landed in Mexico. It was first seen in 1518 by Juan de Grijalva, sailing from Cuba under directions to explore for the Spanish governor of that island. Grijalva sailed along the coast of Yucatán until he came to the site of the fort in the bay, then an island, which he named San Juan de Ulua.

The governor of Cuba then ordered a second expedition fitted out for a more extensive trip, and it was commanded by Hernando Cortés, who was to become the conqueror of all Mexico. Cortés arrived on Good Friday, April 21, 1519, at the site of the present town and named it *la Villa Rica de la Vera Cruz*, "the Rich City of the True Cross." Such it has remained until this day.

The Landing. Cortés's ship sat off the shore the first day, but the next day the men landed and immediately started building some palm huts and declared themselves, in the name of the saints, possessors of the entire continent.

Cortés marched shortly thereafter to the Indian town of Cempoala, and through intrigue and a show of force, brought the first Indian group under his command as his so-called allies.

With his successful march upon the rest of Mexico, heavy sea traffic developed to Veracruz. A port was built, surrounded by a sea wall, and such wealth was moved out that at one time pirates actually attacked the town itself, sacking even the cathedral. They are said to have carried off gold and silver worth 4 million pesos or roughly that much in dollars (then the equivalent).

One author has written: "The very name Veracruz is interwoven with all the fighting and bloodshed of the great days of the Spanish Main. Through her streets the bearded and bepistoled buccaneer in all his awful glory once swept, plundering, burning and ravishing. If the old walls could speak, they could relate such stories of sack and fire, of such devilish cruelty and desperate combats, the like of which even dims the murderous renown of Morgan's sack of Panama."

War of Independence. With Mexico's War of Independence (1810–1821) the Spanish were driven out; but before the Spanish Navy finally sailed out of Veracruz harbor, they shelled the town so heavily that it was laid practically flat.

In 1833, the French Navy bombarded the town and landed troops. On March 27, 1847, during the Mexican-American War, General Winfield Scott's troops captured Veracruz and landed under fire, going on to capture Mexico City. The effects of this destructive bombardment are still seen in the scars on Fort Ulua.

The French landed again in 1861 and were driven out, as were Emperor Maximilian's forces in 1867. All this time, the great and wealthy had passed back and forth through Veracruz on their periodic visits to Europe. One last touch of violence was the appearance of United States warships in 1914 when United States Marines again took over the town for several weeks.

GOING TO VERACRUZ

By Air. CMA flies from Mexico City in just over an hour and a half. Good airport at Veracruz.

By Bus. There is good first-class and Pullman service from Mexico City on ADO lines, which go either via Fortín and Córdoba, or by Jalapa, with both passing through Puebla. ADO is located at Buenavista 9, Mexico City, although buses now leave from Terminal Central de Autobúses del Sur, Calzada Tlalpan. Travel time is about eight hours. Fare is about $4 to Veracruz, or $12 all the way to Mérida (a twenty-nine-hour trip).

By Car. You can drive to Veracruz, via Puebla, in about seven hours from Mexico City. It is a mountainous drive, but the road is paved, safe, and interesting. You have a choice of route via Córdoba or Jalapa. We suggest going by one and returning by the other. To Puebla you can go by the superhighway toll road which now extends all the way to Córdoba, practically to Veracruz. Jalapa, on the other road, which is the standard two-lane paved highway, is a charming city of gardens and flowers with the University of Veracruz and a symphony orchestra. It has a fine new Museum of Anthropology. A modern hotel is María Victoria, 120 rooms, good dining room; accepts most cards. Hotel Salamone is older but still acceptable.

By Train. It is entirely possible to go to Veracruz by train, and, in fact, it makes for an interesting trip. Ferrocarriles Nacionales de México has a fascinating trip which winds through some spectacular scenery, dropping down from the mountains to the coast. There is a ticket office at Bolívar Street, Mexico City, or in the main railroad station in Mexico City, Buenavista.

WHERE TO STAY IN VERACRUZ

Hotel Veracruz (*148 rooms*)   Moderate
This is the biggest and one of the newer hotels in town. On main plaza. Air-conditioned, coffee shop, Turkish baths. A bit noisy. Rooms austere, but those overlooking plaza have fine view. Night-club and roof garden share fine view. Run by Diligencias management. All cards. Tel: 2-00-80.

Colonial Hotel (*185 rooms*)   Moderate
An inconspicuous hotel also on zócalo, but perhaps the best hotel downtown both in service and rooms. Has new air-conditioned section which costs more but is well worth it. Attractive lobby, pleasant management, cafeteria and restaurant. Indoor pool, drive-in parking. All cards except AE. Tel: 2-01-93.

Hotel Mocambo (*95 rooms*)   Moderate
Five miles out of town on one of the favorite beaches. Big,

handsome, and badly run, but is still the best place to stay if swimming is your pleasure. Has two pools, beach, and ordinary restaurant. Recently new management has tried to improve it. AE, DC. Tel: 3-15-00.

Emporio Hotel (*120 rooms*)   Moderate
Near waterfront. New hotel, some air-conditioned rooms, pool. Rooftop restaurant-bar with good view of harbor. All cards. Tel: 2-00-20.

Diligencias Hotel (*100 rooms*)   Inexpensive
A historic old hotel not very well maintained. Choice location on main plaza and one of best restaurants in town. Service has deteriorated badly in hotel. Tel: 2-01-80.

Costa Verde Hotel (*43 rooms*)   Moderate
Modern three-story hotel with balconies overlooking water and Sacrifice Island. Air-conditioned. Restaurant. Thirty spaces for trailers with all hookups, showers. DC, VISA.

Villa del Mar (*60 rooms*)   Inexpensive
On the waterfront, closer to downtown than other beach hotels. Guests use public beach across road. Rooms neat, attractive but modest. Some air-conditioned, some have view of sea. Informal but pleasant dining room. Takes trailers under palms in garden with all connections. AE.

Hotel Ruiz Milán (*50 rooms*)   Inexpensive
On Paseo del Malecón, facing the sea, near downtown. A fair five-story hotel with some air-conditioned rooms. Pool. Restaurant. Most cards. Tel: 2-01-87.

Prendes Hotel (*35 rooms*)   Inexpensive
Small hotel near center of town. Fair rooms. Good restaurant.

Hotel Oriente (*80 rooms*)   Inexpensive
A rather ordinary hotel on Customs House Square by waterfront. Restaurant. Some air conditioning. Carnet, VISA.

Parador Los Arcos Trailer Park (*44 spaces*) $3
A mile south of Hotel Mocambo on Route 150 and 180. Across from beach and has use of Mocambo public beach area. All hookups. Showers, toilets.

Restaurants in Veracruz

Prendes   Moderate
On main plaza in town. Has both sidewalk café and an indoor air-conditioned section. Waiters in black ties and tables with linen cloths. Serves fine carne tampiqueña (steak with vegetables), shrimp cocktail, many fish dishes, and such things as spaghetti bolognesa. Nice in the evenings when the plaza is lighted and often music is playing. DC. Open till 1 A.M.

Parroquia   Moderate
On the other side of the plaza, by the Parroquia Church. Short-order-type restaurant, but good food with fillet of sole, carne tampiqueña, and, of course, shrimp. Open 6 A.M. till 1 A.M.

Gran Café de la Parroquia   Bargain
On the Malecón (waterfront) near the Emporio Hotel. A modern block-long building functioning as sort of a super-seafood restaurant. Very popular with local people, and jammed on nights of serenatas (band concerts). Fernando Fernando is owner and manager of both Parroquias. Parroquia soup is less than $1, fillet of sole, huachinango, very fresh shrimp, hot dogs, hamburgers, and ice cream as well as cold beer. Open evenings only, 6 P.M. to 1 A.M.

Los Cedros Malecón   Expensive
Probably the best and certainly the fanciest restaurant in Veracruz. Handsomely appointed, with a most elaborate menu featuring broiled oysters, seafood hors d'oeuvres, steaks, and Lebanese foods as well as many salads. Cocktails and dancing. Open from 1 P.M. till 1 A.M. DC, VISA. Maître d' is Fernando Soto Tapia. Go out Malecón toward Mocambo, near engineering school.

La Mansión   Moderate
A swinging place with organ music and dancing on Friday and Saturday nights. One block off Malecón near Villa del Mar at General Figueroa 417. Serves fresh seafood such as crab claws and shrimp in shell, as well as paella valenciana. Tito Santos Llinas is manager. All cards. Tel: 2-56-57.

Las Brisas   Moderate
In the Costa Verde Hotel on Boca del Río section of the boulevard circling the harbor, about five minutes from the center of town by taxi. Marvelous seafood soup, fresh shrimp cocktail, crab soup, stuffed seafood, róbalo (sea bass) veracruzano, shrimp in garlic, stuffed crab, steak and French fries. Open noon and evening.

What To Do and See in Veracruz

The main plaza, called Plaza de Armas, has hotels on two sides, the Diligencias and the Colonial, and each has arched pavilions along both sides and a sidewalk café. On the third side of the plaza is the *Parroquia Church.* The plaza is one of the principal sights in Veracruz—just to sit at a sidewalk café and order a refreshment and watch the interesting crowd going by, with people of many races and ancestry represented in the throng. You can also lunch here.

The zócalo has been beautifully landscaped with fountains and gardens, and at night the surrounding buildings are all floodlit while the center fountain turns into a galaxy of lights of all colors, dancing and changing. On Thursday and Sunday evenings, the *State Band* gives concerts here. On other nights there are always marimbas playing. You can dine under the arches while watching.

The oldest church on the continent is down the street. Walk down Independencia Street, the street in front of the Diligencias Hotel, to the right some six blocks to see *La Parroquia de Santo Cristo del Buen Viaje* ("Church of Christ of the Good Voyage") at the Plaza Gutiérrez Zamora.

Open-air trolleys go by the Plaza Gutiérrez Zamora, and you can step aboard and ride back down Hernan Cortés Street, seeing the markets and the old grillwork upon the houses, and eventually wind up back at the Plaza de Armas.

The trolleys also run between the center of town and the Villa del Mar and the beach, so you can make this interesting but short trip also. Veracruz isn't too large a town, so you won't get lost. If you do, hail a taxi and be rescued.

The Fortress of San Juan de Ulua is the sight most tourists in Veracruz see, and it is interesting enough, though a bit murky and damp. A taxi will take you there in five or ten minutes, or you can drive in your own car by heading for the Customs House (*Aduana*) on the waterfront two blocks from the main plaza, and then crossing over a bridge beyond the Customs House to a causeway which leads past the docks, and finally out to the fortress, which juts out into the bay.

Begun only a few years after Cortés's arrival, this old fort has served many masters. The fact that it has stood up through centuries of hurricanes and storms, and various heavy gun duels, shows the massive structure it is.

It has been used as a prison more than as a fort, and it was the habit to chain prisoners to the walls, although rising tides washed over them to their waists. These dungeons were incredibly filthy, and much of this atmosphere is still evident. The guides are only too pleased to describe some of the torture in detail. Most interesting to note are the old iron doors brought from Spain, and the various sections of the fort, one of which held the great patriot Benito Juárez at one time.

Plaza Carranza. A drive north along the waterfront is fun, starting with the Plaza Carranza, where the handsome modern lighthouse structure is located. It looks more like a modernistic office building than a lighthouse. You can then drive along the waterfront boulevard, with its occasional detours, all the way out to the Hotel Mocambo, some 5 miles distant, and beyond it to another interesting place, the Boca del Río.

Boca del Río and Mandinga. Boca del Río is a cluster of fishing shacks and a bar or two at the mouth of the Río Atoyac. It is worth visiting to see the fishermen and perhaps to enjoy some of the river fishing yourself, which is entirely different from deep-sea fishing. A sandbar keeps the sharks from entering. Farther along about 3 miles is yet another fishing village, Mandinga, where you can see shrimp being caught, and cooked for you right from the water in little seaside restaurants. There are boat rides on a lagoon.

Nightclubs. Most of the hotels have some entertainment, although I must confess they are not strong on nightclubs. The Hotel Veracruz has a nightclub open Saturdays and Sundays. Here, or at the other larger hotels, you will very likely see the Jarochos, as the people of Veracruz are called, dancing the fine state dance, la bamba, which is very colorful. They knot a rope with their feet while dancing. When there is a dance on the terrace of the Hotel Mocambo, with its great promenades seemingly curving right out into the tropical moonlit night, this, too, can be fun. In fact, a jukebox there makes this possible almost any night—orchestra or no.

Excursion to Isla de los Sacrificios. This island, sitting just off the harbor along the waterfront, was discovered by Juan de Grijalva on his first trip in 1518, before Cortés, and he found grisly evidence of human sacrifice carried out there. A boat leaves from the main wharf to take visitors to the island, but actually there is little to see. It is just a boat trip.

POINTS NORTH OF VERACRUZ

Cempoala. About 56 miles out on the main highway to Jalapa, one turns off at Puente Nacional onto a dirt road which leads to the archeological zone of Cempoala. These are the ruins of pyramids built by the *Totonacs*. Some 30,000 Indians lived here when Cortés arrived, and they joined with him to fight the hated Aztecs. There are two minor pyramids and a conical-shaped building. Nothing very great when compared with the huge cities of Chichén-Itzá and Monte Albán, but interesting nonetheless.

Nautla, Tecolutla, and Papantla. One of the nicest resort and bathing areas on the Gulf of Mexico lies about 150 miles to the north of Veracruz. This is the area of Nautla, Tecolutla (which has some weather-beaten but entirely acceptable rustic hotels), and Papantla, where the "Dance of the Voladores" is held for twelve days in late May or early June. Performed by the Totonac Indians in a traditional appeal to the god of rain, the ritual involves a circular descent by ropes from a 90-foot pole. Each of four men twirling by his feet from the pole must circle the pole thirteen times on his way down, to represent the four seasons each with thirteen weeks. It is spectacular and well worth seeing.

Highway 180 runs both north and south of Veracruz and in either case is spectacular driving. Going north, you will be right on the seashore for many miles; the writer thought it was one of the loveliest drives in Mexico.

To reach the seaside resorts from Veracruz, you go out toward the Hotel Mocambo, confusingly south of town, then take a sharp right back at the Pemex station on Highways 150/180 headed for Jalapa. It is 41 miles from Veracruz on this road to *Puente Nacional* (notable for its big resort hotel, Hotel Spa Puente Nacional). Here at the junction with 180 you turn north to Nautla, Tecolutla, and Papantla.

The two hotels in Tecolutla are the *Hotel Balneario Tecolutla,* which is old but comfortable, and the *Hotel Marsol*, which is newer but equally worn, and is also located on the beach. Along the road a better place to stay is the seaside *Motel del Palmar*, about 12 miles south of Tecolutla.

In Papantla, there is the *Hotel Tajín*, small but clean, and it has a fair restaurant, the *Restaurant Tajín*. Papantla is the center of the vanilla industry, and is a relatively prosperous area. Vanilla comes from an orchid plant, with a creamy-white bloom, which is indigenous to the area and was growing wild until the Indians learned to cultivate it for flavoring for chocolate. They hand-fertilize each flower, then later collect the string beans and dry them for sale to extractors. Plants have been sent over the years to the Far East, and to Madagascar, which is now the principal grower of vanilla. But it is still the main source of income for many families in the Papantla area. Samples of vanilla are for sale here in various shops, and at the little town of Gutiérrez Zamora just beyond Tecolutla, you can visit the Gaya vanilla factory, where vanilla extract is made and sold.

El Tajín, an important archeological zone, is only an hour or so from Papantla. Best route is via Poza Rica, one of the country's major oil towns, nearby. In the fifth or sixth century, El Tajín was the huge sacred city of the Totonacs, and one of its ancient buildings is seven stories high, containing 366 nichelike windows. From them it gets its name, *Pyramid of the Niches.*

These are spectacular ruins, indeed, of a very interesting nature and well worth the some 7 miles on a side road and the 12 miles on the continuation to Poza Rica. Tajín is part of a 2,400-acre archeological reservation, and many more ruins may be found.

Poza Rica and Tuxpan. From Poza Rica, the big oil center, you can drive on to Tuxpan, where the *Motel Los Mangos* on the river is fairly good; it has a satisfactory dining room and a pool.

TAMPICO

Tampico lies 100 miles north of Tuxpan, and just before it is the only ferry still left on this new paved route. Tampico is a big port, but, more important for visitors, it has some fine restaurants and several good hotels.

WHERE TO STAY IN TAMPICO

Posada de Tampico (*130 rooms*)   Moderately expensive
A well-landscaped three-story hotel on a hillside 3½ miles north
of the city, on Highways 80 and 180 near the new airport. Air-
conditioned, wall-to-wall carpeting. Tennis, putting green, sauna,
pool. Coffee shop, bar. P.O. Box C-71, Tampico, Tamaulipas, México.
Tel: Tampico 3-30-50 or Mexico City 5-33-51-19.

Camino Real Hotel (*101 rooms*)   Moderately expensive
A modern, well-run typical Camino Real with low, rambling rooms
grouped around pool and garden patios. On Highways 80 and 180
just north of town. Good shops in area. Good restaurant and bar.
Music. All cards. Tel: 3-11-01.

Inglaterra Hotel (*126 rooms*)   Moderate
At Díaz Mirón 110 downtown on main plaza, a seven-story building
with elevator. Basement parking. Air-conditioned rooms. Ice machines. Tel: 2-56-78.

Howard Johnson's Motor Lodge (*250 rooms*)   Moderate
Opposite the main plaza, at Calle Salvador Díaz and Olmos. A
typical Howard Johnson's installation.

Motel San Antonio (*75 rooms*)   Inexpensive
Air-conditioned two-story motel on Highways 80 and 180 between
Camino Real and Holiday Inn. Pool. Newer section fair. MC only.

WHERE TO EAT IN TAMPICO

Corona Restaurant   Moderate
A busy and good restaurant a block from the Camino Real Hotel on
main highway. Air-conditioned. Open late. Good service and
excellent food such as charcoal-grilled meats, all kinds of seafood,
and a specialty of the house, shrimp and spinach omelet. Bar.

Del Mar   Inexpensive
A real seafood restaurant in town on Libertad Plaza at 309 South
Aduana. Air-conditioned. Open 7 A.M. till 2 A.M.

Kentucky Fried Chicken   Inexpensive
On Highways 80 and 180 north of Camino Real Hotel. You can
either eat there or take out.

SOUTH FROM VERACRUZ TOWARD YUCATÁN

By Car. There is now a good, largely paved road stretching some 700 miles south from Veracruz along the Gulf all the way to Mérida, capital of Yucatán. You can drive your own car on this stretch to Yucatán, keeping in mind that there are a number of ferry points, or you can go as far as Acayucán, and then cross over on the Trans-Isthmusian Highway to the Pacific, getting to Tehuantepec in one day's driving. The drive to Yucatán would require a minimum of three days with overnight stops at Coatzacoalcos, Villahermosa, and possibly Campeche.

There are now two paved routes from Villahermosa to Mérida. The old one runs along the Gulf shore with the necessary ferries and the spectacular scenery. A new all-paved inland route goes from Villahermosa past the Palenque ruins and across inland country to join the older road again at Champotón on the Gulf about 40 miles before Campeche. It is naturally faster. The auto traveler can take the shoreline route and the ferries going one way, seeing the lovely beaches of Isla del Carmen, and then return by the faster inland route.

By Bus. There is daily first-class bus service between Veracruz and Mérida, Yucatán, and the buses of the ADO lines, reservations usually required, take twenty hours from Veracruz at a fare of roughly $10. You have a choice of inland or coastal route. The difficulty with disembarking for stays at Coatzacoalcos for a rest—or at Villahermosa, where it would be unthinkable to go without having a look at its fine museum and taking a side trip to the fabulous Palenque ruins—is that continuing reservations on the bus must be made after you stop there. You can usually get them, but not always for precisely the bus you wish.

You can get your tickets in Veracruz at the bus terminal at Calles Doblado and Prim, just slightly out of the main downtown area. It is a modest terminal, with a lot of noise and confusion. Buses leave at 5 P.M. and 9 P.M. This means you go through Coatzacoalcos in the dark morning hours, but see Villahermosa by daylight. There are numerous ferries where you disembark and reload. Snack or restaurant facilities have little more than soft drinks, so bring sandwiches, water or coffee in a thermos, and perhaps a candy bar or two, and a warm sweater, as it gets cold toward morning.

The scenery is fascinating, the big windows of the Greyhound-type buses presenting an endless view of tropical foliage, villages with grass huts, and miles of sandy white beaches. One big ferry, at Ciudad del Carmen, is an oceangoing ship, and as you usually reach it at noon the next day, it is pleasant to find a good restaurant aboard for lunch. At the other end of Isla del Carmen, a further hour-long lunch stop is made at Aguada, where there is an excellent country restaurant.

By Train. You can get the *tren directo* (Ferrocarriles Nacional), which leaves Buenavista Station in Mexico City in the morning on Sundays, Tuesdays, and Thursdays, stopping at 7:30 P.M. in Veracruz, and arriving at seven the next morning in Coatzacoalcos. It has sleeping accommodations. At Coatzacoalcos you pick up the Sureste railway, a different line, which has sleeping cars leaving at 7 A.M. on Mondays, Wednesdays, and Fridays.

The *Sureste Ferrocarril*, starting at Coatzacoalcos, runs several types of diesel-powered mixed freight or passenger services, so it is important to go first-class, and on the tren directo. A dining car is usually carried, but it is still wise to take some snacks. The roadbed is very rough, but the scenery is even more fascinating than that on the bus trip. If you disembark at Teapa, you can get a bus into Villahermosa, and this is a stop we recommend. If you disembark at Palenque Station, you can take a taxi to the village of Palenque or to the ruins directly, but the train usually arrives in the early morning or late evening and the hour is not convenient. Planes fly to Palenque from Villahermosa, which is a better plan. At Campeche, a larger town with good hotels, you change from the Sureste to the Yucatecan railroad to continue to Mérida.

BETWEEN VERACRUZ AND VILLAHERMOSA

Puerto Alvarado. About 50 miles south of Veracruz, you come to the wide estuary of the great Papaloapan River, which upstream is the site of Mexico's TVA-type project, with its great dam, power installations, and huge lake.

Lake Catemaco. Another 85 miles brings you to *San Andrés*

Tuxtla, a small town said to be the site of the first textile mill in the Americas. Beyond it there is an area of moundlike hills which the Indians compare to the breasts of a fertile woman. At a distance of just over 2 miles, one comes to the shores of Lake Catemaco, said to abound in trout, perch, and a species called pepesca. Nearby are three beautiful waterfalls, while the village has a mineral-water plant.

A fair hotel at Lake Catemaco is the *Berthangel*, although the food leaves something to be desired. Coffee shop open till 10 P.M. Tel: 3-00-89.

Coatzacoalcos. At the mouth of the Coatzacoalcos River, this town is the old Puerto México, at the Gulf end of the Trans-Isthmusian Railway, and a very busy port nowadays as it loads sulfur, petroleum, and tropical fruit. It is a few kilometers off the main road near Minatitlán (the refinery town). It is near a fine sandy beach for ocean swimming.

You will not find Coatzacoalcos any place to spend a vacation; it is too bustling and too hot, but it is a desirable break in your trip.

The *Hotel El Presidente* with 100 rooms is by far the best hotel in the area. It is several miles north of town on the Minatitlán–Veracruz highway off the west side of the road several hundred yards and obscured by a gasoline station. A modern two-story structure, it is built on the banks of a river. Has pool, restaurant, and fine air-conditioned rooms. Reserve through El Presidente chain.

Another excellent hotel is the *Hotel Valgrande*, completely air-conditioned with sixty-two rooms. A good restaurant open 7 A.M. till midnight serves a wide choice of dishes from spaghetti and pork chops to local sea bass and mole poblano at very reasonable prices. Takes most credit cards. *Hotel Margón* is smaller and fair. *Lamarroy* is older and has confused service, although it does also have an air-conditioned restaurant and a Hertz office.

Beyond Coatzacoalcos, you cross the huge river and then head through a land of grass huts, low tropical brush with many strange birds, and finally into heavier jungle and many banana trees as you approach Villahermosa, some 170 miles from Coatzacoalcos.

VILLAHERMOSA

Located on the shores of the broad tropical river, the huge Grijalva, Villahermosa, which is the capital of Tabasco state and getting to be a crowded bustling shopping center of over 100,000 population, is still a jumble of weather-worn buildings and narrow one-way streets.

Along the bank of the Grijalva runs a riverside boulevard covered with swaying palms, beneath which are nice walks lit by lamp posts which play music to content the lovers strolling along its way.

All manner of craft are moving up and down the river. At one time most of the retired Mississippi steamers were sent here, but even these have succumbed to the hot tropics, and the larger boats now are especially built for carrying passengers and goods from the interior to the port at *Frontera*. It is a fascinating traffic and helps to pass pleasant time on the boulevard.

The two principal sights in Villahermosa, apart from the Grijalva, are the famed museum (right on the plaza, with a field annex outside the town near the *Lagoon of Illusions*) and the ancient stone city of *Palenque*—predating Christian history. These are described in the sections following the hotel and restaurant listings.

Hotels in Villahermosa

Aristos Villahermosa (*265 rooms*)   Moderately expensive
On Av. Grijalva, which is the main highway going through town, at the famous flower clock circle. Near the park and the Lago de Illusiones, this is an easily reached location although not immediately downtown. A modern white stucco building of three stories, with a red tile roof. Each room has a balcony overlooking landscaped grounds. Restaurant, cocktail lounge, pool, tennis. All cards. Tel: (905) 5-33-05-60 (Mexico City).

El Presidente Villahermosa (*120 rooms*)   Moderately expensive
Also near Lago de Illusiones and the park, this modern hotel has terraces overlooking the river and rooms around a courtyard with garden landscaping. All rooms air-conditioned. Two restaurants, swimming pool, sight-seeing arranged. All cards. In United States

call toll-free (800) 421-0722. Or reserve through El Presidente chain in Mexico.

Hotel Manzúr (*116 rooms*)   Moderate
In heart of city at Madero 422 near main plaza, this is a completely rebuilt hotel with all rooms air-conditioned and new decor. Dining room on second floor noted for good food. Buffet Sundays 1–4 P.M. Write: Hotel Manzúr, Villahermosa, Tabasco, México. Tel: 2-24-99.

Hotel Maya Tabasco (*140 rooms*)   Moderate
On highway bypass from north to south, this fairly new hotel is easily reached but not near other conveniences. Coffee shop, pool, somewhat desultory management. All cards. Tel: 2-11-11.

Hotel Olmeca (*64 rooms*)   Moderate
On nice arcade walkway downtown near Manzúr, this is a new hotel with air-conditioned rooms, reasonable dining room, and bar. AE, MC, VISA. Tel: 2-00-22.

Hotel María Dolores (*80 rooms*)   Inexpensive
Two blocks from Plaza de Armas, at Calle Aldama and Reforma, this is a new but modest hotel with some air conditioning. Dining rooms open 7 A.M. to 3 A.M. Bar. Tel: 2-22-11.

San Rafael Hotel (*25 rooms*)   Inexpensive
We said this was a scene from an old Humphrey Bogart movie, and here is the place to prove it. It is a run-down tropical hotel with a lot of charm. Looks out on the river. Rooms bare but passable. Some halfhearted air conditioning.

RESTAURANTS IN VILLAHERMOSA

Restaurante Reina   Moderate
A modern restaurant with good food and coffee bar. Located at Madero 414 three blocks north of Plaza de Armas, and almost under Hotel Manzúr with entrance on back street. Elaborate menu with all kinds of egg and steak dishes, chicken every style, Mexican dishes, many sandwiches including hot dogs and hamburgers, ice cream, and a full-scale bar selection. Tel: 19-21.

El Mural   Expensive
A good air-conditioned restaurant on Independencia near the Governor's Palace, and near the museum. Spanish decor and international food. Open evenings only, with entertainment. Open late.

Visit to the Museo de Tabasco

This is the second best museum in Mexico, after the Museum of Anthropology in Mexico City, and, accordingly, the second best museum of this type in the world, in our opinion. It is located on the southeast corner of the main plaza in Villahermosa, in a massive old building which once was a prison. However, don't let this thought discourage you. It is most attractive inside, and air-conditioned as well. An outdoor adjunct to the downtown museum is located several miles away (see below).

The museum is the lifework of a leading citizen of Villahermosa, Carlos Pellicier. He has spent a lifetime collecting and installing the fine pieces of pre-Hispanic sculpture which are unmatched in any other museum. The scores of exhibits vary from a female torso beautifully bejeweled to multicolored vases from the ruins of Bonampak—still not reached by any but archeologists. Figures of fertility, joy, and love can be found in immense profusion.

The Great Hall has one of the colossal heads from La Venta, while ten other halls are filled with exhibits from the Mayan period, the Totonac culture, and reproductions of the famed Bonampak murals.

La Venta. One of the most heralded archeological finds in all the world was La Venta, a deep jungle area where immense stone heads were found scattered among the trees, half buried in swampland. Some measured more than 9 feet in diameter and weighed over 16 tons. All were notable for their Negroid features, and the helmets, not unlike modern-day football helmets, that they wore.

Parque Museo de la Venta. This outdoor museum, a little over 2 miles from the center of town on the airport road, near the Lagoon of Illusions, is a successful effort to re-create this remote jungle scene by hauling the original ancient carvings to this site, and reimbedding them in the same type of swampland in which they were found, among brilliantly colored jungle foliage. The effect is striking.

There is a large wooden gate at its entrance with the lettering "La Ventosa Parque," and admission is 10 pesos. It takes about half an hour to wander about this rather confused and untidy park, but it has its charm, too. There are no signs, but merely some red footprints in cement patches thrown down in the swamp, over which you can walk. An occasional number alone marks the exhibits, of which we might point out the following:

A 30-ton carved altar with monkey motif, followed by a carving of a monkey ascending to heaven. A basalt jaguar. A gigantic fish with carvings. A bearded face peering from an altar decorated with owls. A monument to mothers, holding children, with other faces. A nude figure of a woman, perhaps the best piece in the exhibit, with a serpent necklace, reclining before a jaguar carving representing the sun.

Exhibit 8 is one of the colossal heads mentioned above, this one weighing over 20 tons. A similar head was brought to New York City and exhibited at the 1965 World's Fair, and another is in the Museum of Anthropology in Mexico City.

Exhibit 17 is a 19-ton stone carving of a bearded man; its straight-nosed rawboned face is notable for Caucasian features. Exhibit 19 is a reconstructed royal tomb, and exhibit 25 is the largest of the huge stone heads, this one of an old man.

A small, rather homemade zoo with alligators, monkeys, and butterflies has recently been added. The outdoor museum is open from 9 A.M. to 6 P.M. Walking shoes or rubbers in rainy weather are recommended, and insect repellent is necessary at all times.

A booklet in English describing both the downtown museum and the park museum is sold at a counter at each place and is well worth buying to get the details on the signts you are seeing. It is written by Carlos Pellicier, who created the museums, and sold as an official publication of the National Institute of Anthropology.

TALES OF OLD MEXICO

There are many changes in travel through Mexico. I often recall visiting the Palenque ruins and the long-isolated southeast of Mexico on the very first train to ever run there. That was in 1952, and it came after twenty-five years of railroad building through wild jungle, across broad tropical rivers, and miles of scrubby savannah.

We traveled on the presidential train, called then el tren olivos, *and it had several cars for the press and the foreign correspondents, and also an* auxiliary train which carried boxcars of ice to run our air conditioning, such as it was in those days, and to keep the good Mexican beer, in an adjoining boxcar, cool as needed.

At each stop, and we would pause at least briefly at each little village, the mayor would present a welcome to the President of the Republic, and usually we would disembark to see some native dances and try the local refreshments. It took us three weeks to go from Mexico City until we arrived in Campeche, adjoining the state of Yucatán. Our visit to Palenque, then deep in the jungle and inaccessible by road or plane, was on a four-wheel-drive truck brought along on a flatcar.

Twenty years later I went back to Palenque under very different conditions. We were touring Mexico this time by Winnebago, a self-propelled motor home some 24 feet long, which we had driven down the west coast, then across the central mountains, up to 10,000 feet in height, and then down to the tropics of the Yucatán via the narrow Isthmus of Tehuantepec (where the Pacific and Gulf are only three hours apart).

The Winnebago had a gigantic W on the side, and our friends, who were often seeing such a vehicle for the first time in this part of the world, readily believed it carried my initial. What the Indians of the remote jungle thought, we will never really know. Many had hardly seen an automobile, let alone this strange home on wheels with air conditioning, running water, toilet and shower, gas kitchen, and electric refrigerator. A strange meeting of the new and the old as we came to the ruins of Palenque.

We parked in the street outside the small Hotel Palenque, and it happened to be a fiesta night. The muddy street was thronged with local residents who had tramped miles through the surrounding jungle to reach the only municipal center they knew, the small puebla of Palenque. Homemade carnival booths were all about, and the local aguardiente, a fiery raw rum, made things the noisier if not the merrier.

Palenque is from the middle Mayan period and at least 1,000 years old. But its stone temples are better preserved than most of the ancient stone cities, and its tall stone temples, often seven stories high, are as dramatically located as anything I have ever seen from Angor Wat to Machu Picchu.

The waterfalls, the luxuriant green foliage, the clear air, the actual colors of the many murals, and the imposing rows of graven stelae, plus the temples with running water, and even what is considered man's first indoor sanitary facilities, make this a fascinating visit.

You can do it in any car now, by paved highway with good service stations along the way, but bringing our own home in the form of a Winnebago lent additional wonder to the whole scene. I am sure my family will never forget this trip.

Nor I the earlier one on the tren olivos.

Visit to Palenque

Palenque is a group of ancient stone buildings, about 90 miles from Villahermosa over a new paved road leading into the deep jungle not too far from the Guatemalan border. The world-famous Palenque ruins, perhaps the most dramatic sight you will see in all of Mexico, were for long considered difficult to reach, but now you can easily drive there in your own car or take a first-class bus from Villahermosa.

Buses leave Villahermosa from Lino Merino 14 at 8 A.M. and return at 5 P.M. The ADO line runs buses directly from Mexico City to Palenque leaving the capital at 4 P.M. and arriving in Palenque at 8 A.M. the next day. There are also buses to Mérida and Tuxtla Gutiérrez. A Bonanza aircraft flies from the Villahermosa airport to a landing strip in Palenque (its control tower has a thatched roof!).

Where To Stay in Palenque

The small town of Palenque is about 7 miles from the ruins themselves, which are cordoned off as part of a national archeological zone. In the town, a primitive place, on a muddy street is the *Hotel Palenque*, which has twenty rooms. It is a two-story structure built about a garden, and it does boast air conditioning and private baths. But at best it is a second-rate hotel and service is practically nonexistent. A ground-floor restaurant has a few wooden tables and can manage to come up with steak and French fries, and beer or Coca-Cola, but little else. Service is very, very slow.

The best place to stay at this writing is a modern and quite charming group of cabanas on the road to the ruins about 2½ miles from the ruins. This is the *Hotel Chan-Kah*, operated by Roberto Romano and his wife. They have fourteen cottages in a group around a central open-air dining room. All cottages have air conditioning, good showers, comfortable beds, and charming decor. The place is immaculately clean. Rooms can be had with or without meals, and prices are moderate. Their restaurant observes meal hours, and the public is welcome. Serves steaks, tacos, and enchiladas until 9 P.M. Also breakfast and lunch. A UNESCO movie on Palenque is shown most nights. Make reservations by writing Apartado 26, Palenque, Chiapas, México, or by telegram. There are no telephones.

La Cañada is a nearby motor court with rather austere rooms. Next door is a trailer park with thirty spaces with hookups.

THE RUINS

The entrance to the ruins is a well-kept park area with shady trees where you can park your car or have a picnic lunch. Good guides will meet you there, one of whom, Francisco "Pancho" Amezcua, we found extremely knowledgeable about the ruins. Admission is 10 pesos. Guides charge about $7.50 for a four-hour tour.

These large temples and edifices, often rising to seven stories or more, are believed to have been built in the middle Mayan period of the fifth to eighth centuries. They were overgrown completely by thick jungle, but now have been cleared sufficiently so that you can see a good part of the main group, although many more are still lost in the green jungle.

The seven-story main ruin, jutting steeply up from the heavy forest, the pristine stone breaking from the heavy green foliage, is a sight no visitor forgets. It has the mystery, the awe-inspiring silence of a race forgotten.

It was first discovered by Spaniards following after Cortés, probably a Captain Antonio del Río. Archives in Spain have reports to the throne telling of this discovery. Charles IV was later to send a special expedition to explore it.

In 1840 an American explorer, John Lloyd Stephens, with an English gentleman and accomplished artist, Frederick Catherwood, reached the scene. Stephens wrote a two-volume book, illustrated with fine engravings by Catherwood, which first gave the world an idea of the beauty of Palenque.

Covering an area of perhaps 5 or 6 miles square, Palenque is centered on a plaza on which is the principal structure, the Palace. The Temple of Inscriptions, built atop the highest pyramid, contained numerous tablets with hieroglyphs still not completely understood, but apparently describing events of those times. One tablet fixes the construction date at 692 A.D. Other buildings are the Temple of the Sun, the Temple of the

Cross, and the Law Courts. A tomb was discovered in the main pyramid, down a secret passageway, wherein was buried a noble surrounded by attendants and jewels.

Work on restoration is going on continuously. Many of the elaborate murals, in vivid color, have been revealed, while a score of buildings can now be visited and more are being uncovered. Passageways through some of the buildings permit you to see interior paintings and carvings. Chambers where the priests lived are easily seen, including devices believed to have been used for water supply and sanitation.

Beyond the ruins, a plunging waterfall gives indication of the heavy rainfall that keeps the forest green and constantly menacing to the ruins. Another waterfall, at kilometer marker 58, Cascada de Agua Azul, runs in a churning cascade for 6 kilometers along the road.

ON TO FRONTERA AND ISLA DEL CARMEN

We think one of the prettiest bus rides (or by car if you have one or can rent one) is the five- or six-hour trip from Villahermosa to Isla del Carmen. True, it involves two or three ferry crossings, one practically a sea voyage on open water, but the road is paved and the scenery worth it.

The ADO bus line runs first-class equipment from Villahermosa to Isla del Carmen and on to Campeche and Mérida, Yucatán, from where you can pick up planes back to Mexico City or over to Miami and New Orleans. ADO can be crowded, so make a reservation, or try a second-class bus if you don't mind bouncing around a bit. Most buses travel the new inland route, so be sure you are on the coastal route through Isla del Carmen. CMA does fly to Isla del Carmen, but you miss the seaside scenery. CMA flies to Ciudad del Carmen twice a day, and you can arrive there from either Mexico City or Mérida. There is a local CMA office in the center of town, and nearby a few modest restaurants with good seafood. Private planes can of course land here also.

Frontera is a weather-beaten tropical town located 44 miles from Villahermosa and just beyond the junction of the huge Grijalva and Usumacinta rivers where they pour into the Gulf of Mexico. It is the area's principal port, as oceangoing ships transfer cargo here to river steamers which go up the network of waterways to serve the entire state of Tabasco. Just before Frontera you pass Miramar Beach, a turnoff on a sandy road, which is undeveloped but good for swimming. Frontera is the other side of the river, so you cross on a ferry before seeing the town. This ferry can be slow, and waits of an hour are possible. One small restaurant at the bus stop in Frontera serves passable beans and coffee, but little else.

Isla del Carmen. The point of this whole trip is to see the miles of dazzling white beaches and rows of stately palms, which begin to appear after a 59-mile trip from Frontera to Zacatal, where you embark upon the huge ferry, *City of Carmen*, which has an interesting snack bar with good shrimp cocktails.

After crossing a stretch of open water on the ferry, you disembark right in the port of Ciudad del Carmen, which is on the island proper. The Isla del Carmen is 24 miles long, with the huge Laguna de Terminos on one side, and the open Gulf on the other.

Originally known as the Isle of Tris, the island and the huge bay behind it were first discovered by the pilot of the original Spanish expedition, Antonio de Alminos, who came from Cuba and thought he had discovered the end of the Yucatán peninsula, so he called it *Laguna de Terminos*. In 1588 pirates led by an Englishman named McGregor established a headquarters from which to strike at the Spanish galleons by then carrying fabulous cargoes of gold back to Spain. Many ships were sunk and some gold is still believed to lie beneath the water. For the next 160 years various pirates held the island until driven out by troops sent by the governor of Yucatán in 1717. Spanish forces had placed the island under the protection of Our Lady of Carmen, where it got its permanent name.

Ciudad del Carmen was long a pirates' lair in the days of Billy the Kid and Henry Morgan, but today it is the richest shrimp area in the world, as well as having a wide variety of seafood, including huge prawns. There are numerous villas and beach houses along the oceanfront as well as opportunities for sports fishing by chartering a boat at the waterfront.

Hotels. About a mile east of the plaza, on the main highway, there is a new motel, *Lino's Motel*, which is the best place to stay. Lino's is a two-story building with a tropical garden, and ten of the twenty rooms are air-conditioned. Dining room, cocktail lounge, pool. There is also space for seven trailers with connections. There is also a *Hotel Lli-re* in town on Calle 29 with a restaurant open from 7 A.M. till midnight. Tel: 2-05-88.

Beach Area. There is a fine public beach at the outskirts of town on the ocean side, and it is possible to drive your car there and park right on the beach. It is the center of social life for the younger set of the city, and it has a dance pavilion and a few open-air bars. Farther out of town along the 24-mile shoreline are other even prettier beaches usually open to the public but without lifeguards or any facilities. The main highway skirts these beaches. Stores in town sell all kinds of supplies for fishermen and picnickers.

Isla Aguada, which is at the other end of the 24-mile-long island, is perhaps the better fishing place for sports fishermen (Ciudad del Carmen is too commercial). Here are many places catering to sportsmen, with all lodging, meals, boats, and tackle. *El Tarpón Tropical* fishing camp at Isla Aguada is closed from September 1 to January, a period when there are frequent storms. A little house with a screened porch just by the ferry crossing has one of the best restaurants in the area, serving Mexican food. Unfortunately, it has no name.

CAMPECHE

About 100 miles from Isla Aguada, after some of the most scenic beachside driving you will ever see in the world, you come to the second largest city in the Yucatán peninsula, Campeche.

Campeche is the capital of the state of Campeche, and a fairly modern city of over 85,000 population. The name comes from the Mayan words *kim* and *pech*, meaning "tick of the serpent." Built in 1540, it still has heavy stone walls erected as fortifications against repeated pirate raids in the seventeenth and eighteenth centuries. It is a major fishing port, and also produces tortoise-shell combs and Panama hats, woven in caves with underground lakes, with which all Yucatán is blessed, where the humidity is exactly right.

The *Museo de las Armas*, about two blocks from the Hotel Baluarte, is built in part of the old seawall structure, and contains some of the muskets and cannons used to beat off such pirates as Diego the Mulatto and the Dutchman Laurent de Graff (who later invaded and burned a good part of the town in 1672). Another museum, the *Archeological Museum*, located in the Soledad battlement at 8th Street and 57th, has some Mayan artifacts, but the most interesting section is the Jaina room, showing burial ceremonies carried out on the island of Jaina in the Gulf. It has several halls with exhibits from cultural periods and in its garden some Mayan stelae. It is open from 9 A.M. to 12 noon, and from 6 P.M. to 9 P.M. Entrance is 10 pesos.

The *Cathedral of Campeche*, located on the plaza with the typical two tall bell towers, was ordered built by Don Francisco de Montejoy-León on the day he founded the city of Campeche, October 4, 1540. It was ready for use five years later.

While the old plaza and the famed embattlements still exist throughout this area, the city has gone far to create a more modern appearance through a seaside boulevard with gardens and parks, and two ultramodern buildings facing the Hotel Baluarte just off the center of town on a promontory jutting out to the sea. These are the new Government Building, housing the tourism department among other things, and alongside the new Congress Building for the state senate. Modern fountains are located here also.

A new bus depot has been built in the San Pedro Fortress section, and nearby a huge new modern public market and a water monument called the Electric Industry Fountain. On the outskirts of the city are some huge sports parks and a campus for the University of the Southeast.

Along the waterfront can be seen large shipbuilding facilities (to build fishing boats) and huge wharfs with facilities for freezing the catches of shrimp and fish for shipment to the United States and elsewhere. A modern Coca-Cola plant along the boulevard will provide campers with supplies of fresh purified water.

WHERE TO STAY IN CAMPECHE

El Presidente Campeche (*92 rooms*)   Moderate
  The newest hotel in this seaport city is on the waterfront entering by the Malecón drive. Built in colonial style, it has air-conditioned rooms, restaurant, swimming pool, fine view of boat-filled bay. All cards. Reservations through El Presidente chain (toll-free in United States: (800) 421-0722).

Hotel Baluarte (*78 rooms*)   Moderate
This hotel sits out on a promontory jutting into the Gulf, just off the
center of town and facing the Congress Building and its fountains
and parks. The name means "Fortress Hotel." Some of its rooms are
air-conditioned. Almost all have balconies overlooking the sea or
town. It has a good-sized pool overlooking the water, a terrace with
tables, a bar, steam bath, and a fair dining room. Major cards. Tel:
6-39-11.

Hotel López (*35 rooms*)   Inexpensive
A very modest but acceptable hotel in the center of town on Calle
12. An older three-story building with pretty garden. Air conditioning extra. No pool. Restaurant. No garage. DC.

Campeche Trailer Park (*20 spaces*) $2
Rather out of the way but with its own charm. Located in suburb
of Samula, reached by turning up the hill at the corner of the Coca-
Cola plant on the main boulevard coming into Campeche from
Veracruz. About 1½ miles up the hill following signs, you will find
an American couple who have their home with parking spaces
among their fruit trees. All connections, showers, but you are right
among the local neighborhood.

Hotel Siho Playa (*36 rooms*)   Moderately expensive
About 30 miles outside Campeche on the road to Champotón. This
is an old ruin, overlooking the sea, which has been converted to
a colonial mansion for guests. It is a first-class hotel, entirely air-
conditioned with private baths, run by a Mayan family related to
the governor. All sports, fishing and beach. An interesting place for
a rest. AE, DC. Write Apartado Postal 275, Campeche, Campeche,
México.

RESTAURANTS IN CAMPECHE

Baluarte Restaurante   Moderately expensive
In hotel of same name on waterfront in center of town. The
restaurant is nothing fancy, and the service sort of lackadaisical,
but the seafood is good. They feature pompano cooked in many
ways, and of course it is fresh from the sea. Also seafood soup,
shrimp cocktails, steaks, roast pork, and some Mexican dishes.
Adjoining bar, El Olones, is air-conditioned and has music. Informal. Most cards. Open 7 A.M. to 11 P.M. Tel: 6-39-11.

Miramar Restaurant   Inexpensive
In a small corner building facing the Baluarte. It is busy with the
local trade, but if you can stand the hustle and bustle and rather
rude service, you can get some good seafood here. Best at noon.

26

Yucatán:
Mérida, Chichén-Itzá, Uxmal, and Chetumal

When the drought came to the cornfields of Yucatán, as in many years it did, the corn withered on the stalk, the deer faded away, and the parched earth caused fear in the Mayan people. To appease the gods, they would bring offerings to the great cenote, *the underground lake at the edge of the holy city of Chichén-Itzá.*

When still no rain came, they would prepare the maximum offering, a human sacrifice, usually chosen from the most beautiful of the maidens who lived in a virginal state in the holy nunnery.

The chosen maiden, who sometimes would volunteer "to go and plead with the gods," or who at other times would be forcibly selected, was fed the most exquisite of foods, including a soporific, usually tea brewed from the white sapote leaf or from the "heavenly blue morning glory," known as the manto de la virgen, *whose flinty black seeds have been found to contain a hallucinogenic drug, eleliuqui.*

Before dawn, the drugged maiden was painted blue, her hair was adorned with flowers, and she was dressed in an embroidered white gown, a jade necklace around her neck. She was led barefoot from the nunnery past the House of Dark Writings, whose stone carvings can still be seen, past the high priest's grave, and down the sacred way 325 yards to the edge of the huge cenote, alamandra vines cluttering its limestone edge. It was 180 feet across the open cenote, and down its steep sides 80 feet was the slimy green lake containing a never varying 30 feet of murky water.

On a stone pedestal at the cenote's edge, the priests, wearing glorious feather headdresses in many colors, bare-chested but bejeweled and with copal incense burners pouring out a blue haze, uttered incantations to the gods, words for the maiden to bring to the feared rain god, Chac. As the high priest, Ahkin, watched, two batabs would seize the forlorn maiden and throw her high into the cenote—even though her frantic shrieks broke the silence.

Authorities studying bone fragments point out that some males also were apparently sacrificed.

THE YUCATÁN PENINSULA, jutting practically northward between the Gulf of Mexico and the Caribbean Sea, was for many years cut off from all easy access to the rest of the Mexican republic by an impenetrable band of swamps, rivers, and jungle. The people have almost regarded themselves as an independent nation. They call themselves Yucatecos.

Descended from the ancient Mayas, many of them are still full-blooded Mayan, and the Mayan language is spoken as a living language—with most people speaking both Spanish and Mayan. Some of the older generation speak only Mayan.

A rail line connecting the peninsula with the rest of the Republic was put into operation in 1952, after twenty-five years of construction work. A modern highway now runs the 700 miles from Veracruz to Coatzacoalcos, then inland to Villahermosa, and then along the Gulf coast to Isla del Carmen, Campeche (see Chapter 25), and finally on to Mérida. This seacoast route involves several small ferries, and one large one across the Lagoon of Terminus to Isla del Carmen.

A new, much faster, inland route now runs from Villahermosa past the ruins of Palenque to Escárcega and rejoins the other road at Champotón just before Campeche. It is entirely paved, too, and avoids all ferries. This paved road now goes on to Mérida and Cancún, then along the Quintano Roo coast past Playa Carmen and the Cozumel ferry, on to Tulum and eventually Chetumal, adjoining Belize. You can return on an even newer road past some fabulous newly discovered ruins at Kohunliche and Xpuhil back to the junction at Escárcega near Palenque and Villahermosa.

The principal city in Yucatán is Mérida, capital of the state of Yucatán. Another important city in this area is Campeche, in the state of the same name. A third state, the largest and wildest, consisting of unexplored mahogany jungles, is Quintana Roo. Mérida has a port on the Caribbean, Progreso, which is not too far from Cuba.

The great attractions in Yucatán are, of course, the two ancient

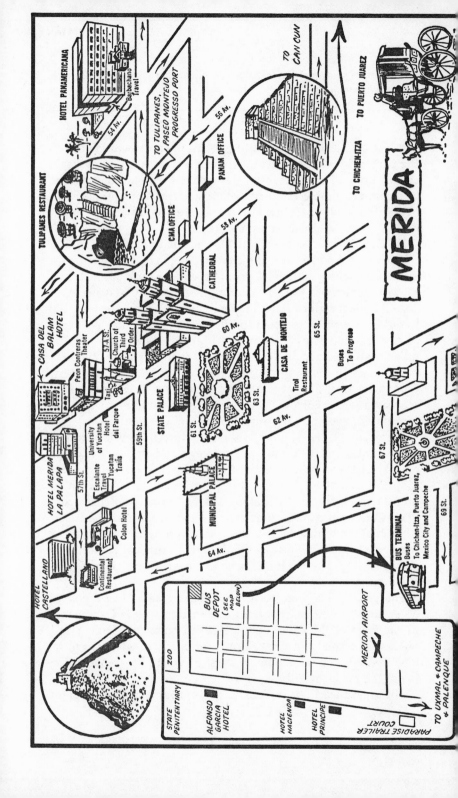

cities of the famed pre-Hispanic civilization of the Mayas, Chichén-Itzá and Uxmal. These are the largest ruins to be restored in all of Mexico, and are internationally celebrated archeological areas. Each has several dozen elaborate structures which can be seen pretty much as the Mayas built them over 1,000 years ago.

Chichén-Itzá (chee-CHEN-eat-ZA) is 75 miles east of Mérida on a paved road. Tours are conducted daily. Uxmal is to the west of Mérida on the road to Campeche. You can visit Uxmal in a day and then return to Mérida. The ruins are described in detail on pages 423–431. A history of the Mayas is given on pages 431–435.

Yucatán is a hot, flat land, blessed part of the time with cooling breezes from the Gulf. Its principal occupation over the years has been the growth of *henequén*, or sisal, which is made into hemp rope and binding twine. The spiny henequén bush grows well in the climate of Yucatán, and for years it made many families wealthy, until the advent of competing fibers from the Philippines and India plus the discontinuance of the old-fashioned binder on American wheat farms (which now use combine harvesters, thus eliminating the need for binding twine).

The entire area is remarkable for its maze of underground rivers and underground lakes, called cenotes, which account for the tens of thousands of windmills in the area, pumping up water practically everywhere. Unfortunately, the water is often brackish or contaminated. The underground lakes are occasionally turned into garden areas, and there is even a nightclub in Mérida to which visitors descend by a stairway for dancing and dining by an underground lake.

MÉRIDA

This is a hot tropical town, but one that has much charm and perhaps is much cleaner than most Mexican provincial cities. It has narrow streets and low buildings, but a good deal of iron grillwork, handsome carved-stone entrances, and interesting little parks.

It is the capital of the state of Yucatán, and has over 250,000 population. Long isolated from the rest of Mexico, it has for centuries preserved its own peculiar culture. Even today some forty families descended from Spanish ruling classes still dominate the society of the town.

As the henequén industry has faltered, the economy of the area has suffered considerably. There is still some henequén grown, some chicle gathered, some hardwood brought in and dyes made, but poverty abounds and only the tourist industry has provided any recent growth.

Mérida is known as the "white city," as its residents not only keep their streets clean and their gardens neat, but are inclined to wear white clothing such as the white Yucateco jackets. The famed baths of the town still operate, and a fine example can be seen at the Hotel Colón, whose steam baths and pools are open to the public.

The faces around the town are obviously Mayan, with the broad features, the curved nose, and the slanting forehead, but mixed among them now are many Lebanese, who dominate the clothing market and run many of the restaurants.

Mérida's streets are crowded as people bustle about their business. On many street corners can be seen the old carriages and horses still used to tour the town. But everyone has time to stop for a morning coffee and chat with their neighbors.

Mérida was founded in 1542 by Don Francisco Montejo, who represented the Spanish crown, and who chose the site of the ancient Mayan city of Tiho. Tiho had its own temples, and one atop a pyramid, the Temple of H-chun-Caan, was torn apart to form the present plaza, and some of the stones were used in buildings seen there. The Casa Montejo, on the side of the present plaza, is the original Montejo family home.

Making the Trip

By Air. It is entirely possible to include Yucatán as a part of your trip to Mexico, and in fact an air ticket from New York, say, to Mexico City, can be routed back through Mérida at no extra cost. Planes (CMA) leave Mexico City each morning at 10:10 with a stop an hour and a half later in Mérida. A side trip over to Cozumel by plane is possible. Leaving Mérida, you have a choice of Pan-American planes to Miami or to New

Orleans, leaving each day on alternate days. Aeromexico and Lufthansa also serve Mérida. Bonanza Airlines runs a round-trip service to Villahermosa, Palenque, Cozumel, and Tulum.

By Train. You can make a three-day trip to Mérida on a Pullman starting in Mexico City or Veracruz (Ferrocarriles Nacional) and changing the next morning to the Sureste line in Coatzacoalcos (see Chapter 25 for details). Cost is low for the seventy-hour trip including Pullman.

By Bus. The ADO bus line in Mexico City runs first-class buses with reserved seats leaving at 10 A.M. and 1 P.M. for a fare of only $15 or $20 all the way to Mérida. It takes twenty hours nonstop, and we recommend stops at Veracruz, Coatzacoalcos, and Villahermosa. Be sure you have continuing reservations. The office of ADO is at Buenavista 9, Mexico City (tel: 5-66-00-55).

By Car. The new road, national route 180, is in excellent condition and you can drive it without worry. You will have three ferry points (see Chapter 25 for details) unless you take the new inland route, which is less scenic but does pass by Palenque.

What To See and Do in Mérida

The plaza is the heart of the city, and is notable for the interestingly sculptured trees and shrubs, as well as the love-seat-like *confidenciales,* whose S-shaped concrete seats let young couples speak in confidence without displaying unseemly proximity.

The streets of Mérida are numbered, and the plaza is bounded by 61 and 63 streets, and by 60 and 62 avenues. All even-numbered streets run north and south, odd-numbered east and west. If you don't feel like hunting out the plaza, hail a taxi and say, "Cathedral."

The cathedral, on one side of the main plaza, is a handsome building, its twin white towers rising majestically above the plaza's laurel trees brought from India by the British. Begun in 1561, by architect Pedro de Aulestia, the cathedral was completed in 1598 by Juan Miguel de Aguero.

Above the main entranceway is the coat of arms of royal Spain, while the side doors have statues of St. Peter and St. Paul.

Inside the church is a bronze statue of the Savior, which was given to the church by the famed Mexican dictator, Porfirio Díaz, when during his long term as president of the country he visited Mérida. Díaz dedicated the statute in honor of Bishop Crescencia Carrillo y Ancona, whom he favored for concluding a boundary dispute with England over Belize territory. Nearby is a painting of the first Spanish governor, Montejo, receiving the Mayan King Tu-Tul-Xiu. The pre-Hispanic city of Tiho can be seen as it looked before it was destroyed to build Mérida. Aside from being the largest church building in Yucatán, the cathedral is not distinguished. It is dedicated to San Ildefonso, and often called by that name.

The Montejo House, located on an adjoining side, was built, amazingly for a building still used as a private dwelling, in 1549, at which time it occupied the entire side of the plaza. From the street, one can note the impressive entrance with its elaborate plateresque decoration, and its heavy steel-nobbed doors. The side carving, interestingly enough, shows a Spanish conqueror with his foot on a Mayan Indian's head. Above, the facade shows Adelantado Montejo in the center, at his right his wife, Dona Beatriz, and on the left his daughter, Catalina.

The house is still owned by descendants of the original Montejo family, now the Arriguenaga family through marriage, and it can be visited from 10 A.M. till noon, and again from 4 till 6 P.M. for a fee of 10 pesos. It is well worth the visit, as the interior is decorated in ornate French-provincial style with fine furnishings brought from France in the late nineteenth century. A garden in back is also open to visitors.

The Municipal Building is across the plaza from the cathedral and is attractive for its arched colonnade along the street, and its pointed spiral tower with a clock. It does have some interesting plaques, including one honoring a visit of revolutionary President Francisco I. Madero.

Palacio del Gobierno. The fourth side of the plaza is occupied by the Palacio del Gobierno, or State House, which is worth visiting for a series of paintings by Pacheco giving the history of Yucatán. The governor's office is on the second floor.

A walk down 60th Street, to your left as you face the cathedral, will bring you at the next corner to a tiny tree-shaded plaza with a statue of a general (much too small for its huge pedestal).

The general is a Yucatecan patriot, Manuel Cepeda Peraza. This little park, *Parque Cepeda*, has a magazine and novelty shop on one side. At this corner you will always find one of the horses and carriages waiting to drive you.

The *Café Exprés* is just across the street from this park, and here you will find the Mérida business community having coffee and vigorously discussing town affairs.

Also by the park, the *Church of the Tercer Orden* rises at the adjoining corner, while alongside is the *Biblioteca Cepeda*. The Tercer Orden is very fashionable and noted for its society weddings. It is also called Iglesia de Jesús.

In the next block along 60th Street, at the corner of 57th Street, you will find a huge yellow building, the Peón Contreras Theater. The *Teatro Peón Contreras* was built for stage and opera in the epic days of Mérida, but now shows movies. Across the street is the *University of Yucatán Law School*.

Hotel Mérida La Palapa. At the corner of 57 and 60, you come to the Hotel Mérida La Palapa, long the landmark of the city. Even if you are not staying there, you will find you are welcome at its dining room or bar, which opens off a courtyard. Across the street is the handsome *Hotel Casa del Balam*, styled in Spanish colonial decor, but having the most modern equipment and a pool. Their bar and dining room are open if you wish to drop in.

Located in the Hotel Balam is the *Mérida Travel Service*, No. 488, 60th Street. Its manager, Ricardo Gutiérrez, has been particularly helpful in arranging bus trips and accommodations not usually part of expensive package deals.

Hotel and Baños Colón. Turning back toward the main plaza on 62nd Street, at No. 483, you come to the Hotel and Baños Colón, a wonderful institution. It has undoubtedly the most lavish steam baths in the world. Some have their own private pools. One large pool has a mirrored ceiling so you can watch yourself swim. Trips to the regular tourist sites as well as unusual trips to hidden villages can be made through Pedro Gullotti, a Swiss manager at the Colón, who also arranges tours. He also has a travel bureau, and across the street at No. 482 is the well-known office of *Yucatán Trails*, which is run by Felipe Escalante.

At the next corner you come again to Calle 59, and by turning left you can walk down 59th, again to the little plaza and the waiting surreys.

Montejo Boulevard, with its parks and stately mansions, is worth seeing. This is a good place for your surrey to take you, although a cab can do it as well. The trip will take you down North 60th Street beyond 47th Street, where you will enter Montejo Boulevard.

This handsome avenue was opened in 1902 and was soon lined with the homes of the wealthy families. One of the first mansions you will pass is the Palace of General Canton, as it is called, and it now houses the Museum of Archeology. All in all, the boulevard is a miniature Champs Elysées. Although only eight blocks long, it has scores of distinguished mansions.

The Museum of Archeology of Yucatán, on Montejo Boulevard, is located in the *Palacio Canton,* a large stone structure originally built as a governor's home but hardly ever occupied, as the governors have preferred their own homes. The museum is open from 9 A.M. to 7 P.M. Monday through Saturday, and Sunday from 9 A.M. to 2 P.M. Admission is 10 pesos on weekdays, free on Sundays. The exhibits, while not too different from those you may have seen elsewhere of pre-Hispanic artifacts recovered from the many ancient ruins, are neatly arranged by periods, and several are unique to this museum. They are housed in the basement of the Canton mansion.

The exhibits start with the pre-classic Mamon period dated about 600 B.C., consisting of primitive tools and vases, then progress to real Mayan stelae with carved hieroglyphs dated from 300 A.D. onward. Deformed skulls attest to the Mayan penchant for slanting the forehead even more by use of curious implements.

The Monument to Mexico stands at the entrance to *Park of the Americas,* which adjoins Montejo Boulevard. The monument, dedicated in 1955, was carved by the sculptor Romulo Rozo. With thirty-one columns in its 143-foot length, it tells the history of Mexico from Mayans to present day. For the park, trees were brought from all the Americas.

Menéndez Library, facing the park, was erected a few years ago by the sons of Carlos Menéndez, publisher of Mérida's leading newspapers. It has probably the most complete bibliography on Yucatán in the world, including a rare edition of the diary and itinerary of Juan Díaz on the Grijalva expedition, published in Venice in 1535, and a collection of daily newspapers of early years, including the *Gaceta de Mérida*, 1823–25. It is open from 9 A.M. to noon, and again at 5 P.M. for several hours for scholars.

The Parque Zoológico, or zoo, is at the end of 59th Street, and it is excellent. Children especially enjoy the many deer and the amusement park. The zoo includes lions, wolves, parrots, llamas, monkeys, jaguars, and a wide variety of tropical birds.

The public market can be found easily not too far from the center of town by asking or by taking a taxi. It is called, in Spanish, *el mercado*. It is now housed in a modern building and for a public market is quite clean and orderly. Tourists will find linenlike hemp sandals, guayabera jackets for men, sisal hammocks, hemp bags, tortoiseshell combs, and real linen trousers for men (a specialty in Mérida). Local housewives buy pheasant, venison, and tropical fruit, not to mention the usual poultry and fish. You can smell the latter.

WHERE TO STAY IN MÉRIDA

El Castellano (*170 rooms*)   Moderately expensive
   At Calle 57 No. 513, this is the largest and newest hotel in Mérida. Operated by Nacional Hotelera, this tall building in the center of town offers large, fully air-conditioned rooms in colonial decor. Two restaurants featuring Mayan and continental cuisine, discotheque, bar, shops, and swimming pool. Conveniently located. All cards. Reserve through toll-free (800) 421-0722 or, in Mexico City, tel: 5-21-40-48.

Hotel Panamericana (*110 rooms*)   Moderate
   This is a first-class hotel but has ordinary rooms. An eight-story modern hotel building sits behind a handsome old mansion through which you enter. Fully air-conditioned, pool with restaurant beside it, music at the bar. Operated by Barbachano family. All cards. Tel: 1-79-60.

Hotel Mérida La Palapa (*110 rooms*)   Moderate
   This older hotel has a ten-story tower of modern air-conditioned rooms located behind the facade of a low colonial building. Its once distinguished dining room no longer is that, but it still is good. Pool. Operated by La Palapa hotel chain. All cards. Tel: 1-75-00.

Hotel Casa del Balam (*55 rooms*) Moderately expensive
A very handsome and modern hotel with Spanish colonial decor.
Entirely air-conditioned. Quiet, charming patio and pool. Good
restaurant and bar. Centrally located in town on 57 Street across
from Hotel Mérida. Two roof terraces provide spectacular view of
city. Operated by Carmen Barbachano. All cards. P.O. Box 407,
Mérida, Yucatán, México. Tel: 1-92-12.

Hotel Paseo de Montejo (*94 rooms*) Moderately expensive
A new modern hotel built on the famed Paseo Montejo in Mérida,
after which the hotel takes its name. While somewhat out of the
downtown district, it is quiet and offers complete services, including
an air-conditioned coffee shop and dining room open till 11 P.M.,
bar, entertainment and dancing nightly except Sunday. Pool, steam
baths. Rooms air-conditioned, some with TV and radio or balconies.
P.O. Box 961. Tel: 1-16-41.

Principe Maya (*52 rooms*) Inexpensive to moderate
A new modern hotel on road to nearby airport. Attractive air-
conditioned rooms around courtyard. Pool. Coffee shop. Part of
Sureste Hotels international chain. All cards. Write P.O. Box 314.
Tel: 1-09-19.

Hotel Colón (*60 rooms*) Inexpensive
This is a modest hotel, but to many it is the favorite. All rooms air-
conditioned, and immaculately clean. Has lovely pool, and the
famed Turkish baths, very elaborate, are here. Operated by Pedro
Gullotti, a Swiss hotelman. Also good economical travel service.
Tel: 1-79-80.

María del Carmen (*94 rooms*) Inexpensive to moderate
A five-story hotel at west edge of business district. Some rooms air-
conditioned. Good restaurant which usually has venison on menu.
Pool, bar, shops. Major cards. Tel: 1-75-26.

Autel 59 (*29 rooms*) Inexpensive
A modern motel conveniently located in town at Calle 59 No. 546,
six blocks from center of town. Very nice modern rooms, all air-
conditioned. Restaurant and bar, TV, interior parking. All cards.
Tel: 1-91-75.

Hacienda Inn (*70 rooms*) Moderate
On the airport road. A modern hotel in mission style around a very
large pool. Mexican decor. Attractive bar by pool with entertainment
at night, dancing. El Campanario restaurant serves Yucatecan food.
P.O. Box 14. Tel: 1-16-80.

San Luis (*40 rooms*)   Inexpensive
A modest two-story hotel on west side of business district with
some air-conditioned rooms, free parking, pool, coffee shop. Member Azteca group. Tel: 1-75-80.

Hotel Cayre (*100 rooms*)   Inexpensive to moderate
At Calle 7 No. 543 in town close to bus depot. Air-conditioned.
Built around patio and gardens. Filtered pool. Restaurant. Tel: 1-16-
52.

Hotel García (*36 rooms*)   Inexpensive
A very clean, modern two-story motel-type hotel outside Mérida on
road to Mexico City. Rooms small but air-conditioned. Pool in
tropical garden. Clean coffee shop. Tel: 1-64-96.

Gran Hotel (*28 rooms*)   Inexpensive
An older hotel with nondescript rooms, but located right on the
interesting Plaza Cepeda, which is really the heart of town. Good
in its way, and has the good Patio Español restaurant on its ground
floor, serving Italian food. Pleasant.

Hotel Montejo Palace (*90 rooms*)   Expensive
Operated in conjunction with the Paseo de Montejo, this is a similar
hotel on the famed Paseo. Shares many of its facilities with its sister
hotel. Tel: 1-16-41.

Mayan Trailer Park (*85 spaces*) $4
A very attractive trailer park near entrance to airport on highway
to Campeche just outside city of Mérida. Set in lovely trees and
lawns. Baths with hot and cold water. Pool. Well run. P.O. Box 13.
Tel: 1-90-70.

WHERE TO EAT IN MÉRIDA

Continental Restaurant   Moderate
In a handsome colonial mansion right in the center of town at the
corner of Calle 64 and Calle 57 (two blocks from the Hotel Mérida),
this is probably the best restaurant in Mérida. Run by Alberto
Salum, who will personally attend you. Features *camarones moje de
ajo*, a heaping platter of tasty shrimp scampi cooked in garlic butter,
or *arrollados de repollo*, cabbage stuffed with meat and rice. Personnel
speak English. Good bar. Open 11 A.M. to midnight. Tel: 1-22-98.

Real Montejo   Moderately expensive
This is the best place for Yucatán food, as it specializes in regional
dishes, but also serves international cuisine. Has a Hawaiian

lounge-bar, dancing and floor shows. At Calle 60 No. 332, which is the old road to Progreso. Tel: 1-27-93.

El Levant   Moderately expensive
At distinguished Hotel Paseo de Montejo on street of same name. Serves both local and international cuisine. Music. Also has Café Les Parapluies serving twenty-four hours and nightclub La Conquista. Tel: 1-90-33.

Balam dining room   Moderate
In Hotel Casa del Balam on Calle 57. Serves good food in modest-sized but immaculately clean dining room. Some very interesting dishes, but also such familiar fare as ham and eggs. Open 7 A.M. till 10:30 P.M.

Hotel Mérida La Palapa dining room   Moderate
Open to the public until 9 P.M. It is clean, attractive, and offers some Mexican dishes as well as a wide selection of American favorites such as tuna-fish salad, club sandwiches, cheeseburgers, and pork chops. Also steak tampiqueña, giant shrimp any style, and chicken Oriental stew. Convenient.

Restaurant Cantamayec   Moderate
A typical Yucateco restaurant at Calle 59 No. 630, toward the zoo. Specializes in *poc-chuc*, fried beef or pork accompanied by small dishes of frijoles, tomato sauce, hot peppers, fried onions, tortillas, and a special sauce called *chile kut*. Also *queso relleno*, which is cheese stuffed with ground meat and served in a bland cream sauce, or *papadzules*, tacos with boiled eggs. Cheerful service. Cold beer.

Los Almendros   Moderate
At Calle 59 and Calle 50, this is another Yucatán restaurant serving poc-chuc as well as char-broiled steaks and other meats. Not too far from Hotel Panamericana.

Going Out at Night in Mérida

Folklórico Dances
The Hotel Mérida La Palapa presents a typical local dance with costumes and music of the region each Friday night at 8:30 P.M. The price is in the neighborhood of $10 and includes a dinner. Tel: 1-75-00 for reservations. Check the night, as it can change.

Faisan y Venado   Moderate
A nightclub at Calle 59 and Calle 82, it serves the pheasant and venison after which it is named. The floor show is a sporadic thing,

on the bizarre side. It is performed every half hour if enough people are there. Consists of some garish Mexican folk dances, and includes the sacrificial theme with someone plucking a bloody heart out. Oh well, it's fun for some. Families welcome. Tel: 1-99-55.

La Conquista bar
At Hotel Paseo de Montejo. There is usually a show in area overlooking pool with music by a trio. Minimum of about $5. Tel: 1-90-33.

Aloha bar
At Hotel Montejo Palace. Usually offers two bands, and two shows nightly. Cover charge of about $5. Tel: 1-16-41.

La Discotheque
A popular spot for the younger set. Loud music. Next to Hotel Paseo de Montejo.

Los Tulipanes
A long-famed location beside one of the underground lakes, or cenotes, this outdoor restaurant and nightclub has been a disappointment to many tourists. Cover charge varies and gets expensive.

TRIPS TO THE RUINS

CHICHÉN-ITZÁ, UXMAL, KABAH, DZIBCHALTUN, AND PALENQUE

There is endless discussion over the best way to visit the ruins, but essentially your pocketbook will determine your plan.

By all-expense guided tour with stops at the luxury hotels that have been built at the principal ruins, you undoubtedly can be most comfortable. *Barbachano Travel Service* owns the only really good hotels at the ruins, and they offer four-day trips to Chichén-Itzá and Uxmal as well as trips to Palenque, Sayil, Kabah, and some of the newer discoveries. The usual way is to go in a limousine with others, though they can also provide private cars. Stops can also be made at the Lagoon of Xel-Ha (tropical fish) and the seaside ruins of Tulum. Trips can be either first-class or deluxe, which means staying in the best hotels (recommended)—that is, the fine Mayaland meals versus the lesser Hacienda Chichén.

Barbachano has offices in Mérida in the Hotel Panamericana

(tel: 1-76-40), Mexico City (5-66-46-44), or toll-free in the United States (with instant confirmation) at (800) 327-2254 in the eastern and western United States, and (800) 323-3180 in the Midwest. *Mérida Travel Service* in the Hotel Casa del Balam in Mérida, P.O. Box 407 (tel: 1-92-12), offers similar and somewhat less expensive service. Both offer licensed guides to go with you.

By day trip from your own hotel in Mérida, both Barbachano and *Yucatán Trails* (482 62nd Street, Mérida) as well as the *Colón Travel Service* (483 62nd Street) and the Mérida Travel Service (Balam Hotel) offer limousines accommodating four persons which leave in the morning for Chichén-Itzá or Uxmal, furnish guide service and lunch, and return in the afternoon. Cost is about $12 per person except for Barbachano, which charges $16. Barbachano offers the best lunch at its own hotels; the others send a picnic or stop at a new restaurant at Chichén which is passable.

By private taxi, which you can find on 60th Street near the Mérida Hotel by the little Parque de La Madre, you can hire your own car and driver, set your own hours, take up to four persons, buy a good handbook at the ruins, pay 10 pesos per person admission, and wander around, perhaps picking up a guide if you wish. Actually, this works pretty well. Of course, you will want to look over your car and driver pretty well before you sign up for an all-day trip (make sure he will send a specific car you have seen, and not substitute one).

By bus, you can indeed get to Chichén-Itzá about as promptly as you can via other modes of transportation, and see just as much, and it only costs 11 pesos (about $1). The problem is that the only bus leaves at 8:30 A.M. (check time) from the terminal at the corner of 69th Street and 68th. It returns in the afternoon (please make sure you have the correct departure time). Meanwhile you can pay your 10 pesos to enter the ruins, use your guidebook, go over to the Pirámide Inn restaurant within walking distance of Chichén-Itzá on the main highway, or carry a lunch. Mérida Travel Service also offers a bus trip leaving at 8 A.M. for Chichén at about the same price.

Renting a car is entirely possible, with Hertz, Avis, and others at both the airport and leading hotels, while Budget Rent is at the airport and at 62nd and 69th streets. National and Rent-a-Volkswagen have offices in Mérida, too. Hopefully our street map (or one you can pick up that is more explicit) will get you out of town, which takes a bit of dodging about. Driving time to Chichén-Itzá is two hours.

Traveling to Palenque. We discussed Palenque, one of the most interesting but one of the most difficult to visit of the archeological zones, in Chapter 25, along with Villahermosa, the nearest city. Barbachano can arrange for you to fly from Mérida, change to a Cessna in Villahermosa, or take a bus (ADO) to Villahermosa and transfer to Palenque, if they do not go direct. You can drive to Palenque, too, on a very good road which turns off at a junction east of Villahermosa. Also, Bonanza Airlines at the airport will put you on a round-trip flight to Cancún, Cozumel, Tulum, and Palenque for something over $50. The *Hotel Chan-Kah* right at the ruins is the best place to stay. Modern cabanas, restaurant, bar.

HOTELS AND RESTAURANTS AT THE RUINS

Chichén-Itzá

Hotel Mayaland (*60 rooms*)   Expensive
This is a fine luxury hotel located adjoining the archeological site. Excellent food and rooms. Pool. Tropical gardens. Air-conditioned bar. Operated by Barbachano. Representatives are William Wolfe in Boston, New York, Philadelphia, and Toronto; S. W. Lincoln in Chicago; and George R. Smith on West Coast. Or Barbachano Travel, Panamericana Hotel, Mérida, Yucatán, México. Lunch available for about $5.

Hotel Hacienda Chichén (*14 cottages*)   Expensive
This is run by Carmen Barbachano and consists of the old Carnegie Institute headquarters, which have been nicely redone into comfortable hotel rooms. The main building is a seventeenth-century structure once lived in by the famed Eric Thompson, the greatest of the authorities on Chichén-Itzá and the Mayas. It has a pool with filtered water. Favored by bird-watchers, among others. Has some trailer parking. Reserve through Mérida Travel, Hotel Balam, P.O. Box 407. Tel: 1-19-12.

Hotel Chichén-Itzá La Palapa (*50 rooms*)   Expensive
On main highway at edge of town of Piste about 2 miles from Chichén-Itzá ruins. Two-story motel-type hotel, completely air-conditioned. Only fair service. Pool. Serves lunch to public consisting of fixed menu at $5. Bar.

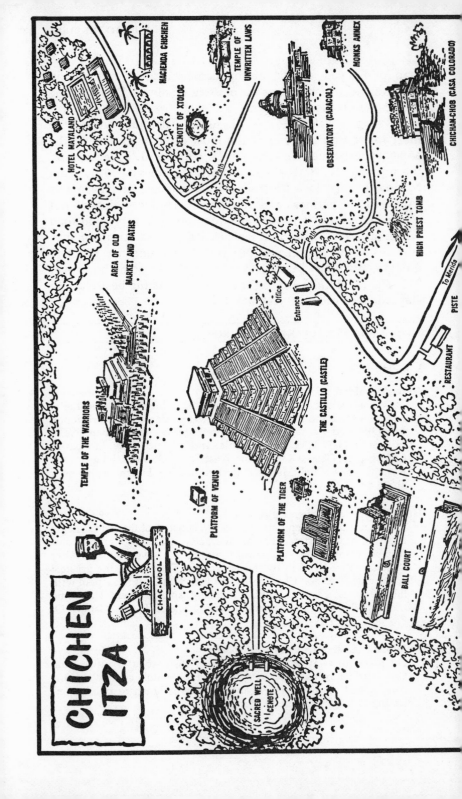

Pirámide Inn Motel (*47 rooms, 60 spaces*) Moderate
On main highway in village of Piste, 1¼ miles from Chichén-Itzá ruins. Modern motel with pool. All rooms air-conditioned. Restaurant serves a full meal or sandwiches (public welcome). Trailer park has all hookups, showers. Owners: Ernesto Perez and Joe Ellicker. AE. P.O. Box 433, Mérida. Tel: Piste 5.

Cunanchen Restaurant Moderate
For those who don't eat at the Mayaland dining room, a new small restaurant has been opened right on the road in the adjoining village of Piste. They serve a fixed menu usually with soup, a choice of pork or chicken, and including beer (hopefully iced) and the world's worst coffee. The food is pretty good, restaurant attractive. Also has ten rooms for rent.

Uxmal

Hacienda Uxmal (*80 rooms*) Expensive
Another fine hotel operated by Carmen Barbachano. Pool. Good dining room. Attractive landscaping. Serves fine luncheon to public for about $5. All cards.

La Palapa Uxmal (*49 rooms*) Moderately expensive
About 3 miles from Uxmal ruins, but with distant view of them from attractive terrace and restaurant. Pool and bar. All air-conditioned. Restaurant serves public. All cards. Office in Mérida.

DESCRIPTION OF THE MAYAN RUINS

Chichén-Itzá

It takes about two hours to travel by road from Mérida to the Chichén-Itzá ruins 75 miles east. One passes through the little Mayan towns of Tahmek, Kantunil, Libre Unión, Yokdzonot, and, just before Chichén-Itzá, the little village of Piste, which has a restaurant, the Cunanchen, which is equipped for tourists. The drive is through henequén fields, and along the way you begin to see the oval thatched huts which are the typical home of the Mayas, and have been for centuries.

The great pyramid of the Castillo looms ahead as you get to Piste, and you see the first of the stone buildings of this immense archeological zone. It was not a city, but a religious center, with the temples and public buildings in the center and the homes of many thousands, no longer in evidence, scattered about for miles.

Entrance. There is a small headquarters building of the Instituto Nacional de Antropología y Historia at the entrance, and you pay an entrance fee of 10 pesos and park your car here or dismount from your bus. If you have a guide, he will show you what is called "New Chichén," which is the area you are in, first, and then, probably after lunch, the "Old Chichén," which is actually across the road and of the same period.

The headquarters building usually has a small booklet on sale which is called the "official guide," and it is useful to have one, and a good remembrance to take away. If you don't have a guide, the book will permit you to get about by yourself, or you may link up with some group with a guide if you are fortunate. While there is no set pattern for viewing the many structures, open from 6 A.M. to 6 P.M., you must be guided by hours for three structures to which you must gain admittance. These are:

Temple of the Warriors. Open 10 to 11 A.M. and 2 to 3 P.M.

Temple of the Jaguars. Open 11 to 12 A.M. and 3 to 4 P.M.

El Castillo (interior). Open 12 to 1 P.M. and 4 to 5 P.M.

You can wander about all of the others, and even see the exteriors of the above, as you wish. The reason for the restricted hours is to permit the small permanent staff to supervise the visits.

Chichén-Itzá comes from the Mayan words *chi* and *chen*, which mean "mouth of the well," and from *Itzá*, which is the name of a wandering tribe that selected this place to live. The well is the sacred cenote, which is a huge open-mouthed underground lake 325 yards down a special path from the Castillo pyramid. Into this cenote were thrown the human sacrifices described at the beginning of this chapter. A second cenote, on the other side of the main road, was used for water for consumption by the populace.

Chichén-Itzá was founded about 435 A.D., according to an account from the books of the Mayas, and was occupied in different epochs until 1204 A.D. The most important period was the Classic Maya period, when such buildings as the House of the Phalli and the Temple of Three Lintels were constructed. They conform with other Mayan cities of the same period.

In 1882, a twenty-two-year-old engineering student at Harvard was appointed U.S. consul for Yucatán by President Chester Arthur. Encouraged by the Peabody Museum at Harvard, he spent years searching the wilderness of the area and came to focus his attention upon the cenote at Chichén-Itzá. He was moved to buy a 30,000-acre hacienda, including the Chichén ruins and the cenote, and he dredged up thousands of artifacts including skeletons of eight females, thirteen males, and twenty-one children, according to Dr. Frank Saul of the University of Toledo. The hacienda owner, E. H. Thompson, also found hundreds of pieces of jade, gold, and opal jewelry and adornments, all of which he quietly shipped back to the Peabody Museum. Some 600 of these jade pieces were returned to the Mexican government by a grandson of Thompson accompanied by the president of Harvard, Derek Bok, in 1976. They will be displayed in a museum, probably in Mérida. Mexico has long since prohibited the exportation of relics and artifacts, but it was not illegal when Thompson did so before 1909.

El Castillo. This is the building nearest to the entrance, and by far the most imposing. It is a huge pyramid with steps (there are ninety-one, and the hardy can climb them) leading to the top. Actually, one pyramid has been superimposed over another, probably a Toltec imposed over an earlier Maya-period pyramid.

An entrance at one side enables visitors to climb an interior stairway (steep, narrow, and damp) to view the famed "red jaguar" with jade encrustations as well as the god Chac-mool. This is well worth doing, but not for any person with claustrophobia.

The Ball Court. Just north of the Castillo is a huge rectangular area between two walled structures, on each of which is a vertical stone ring. Opposing teams, using only knees and buttocks, tried to get a rubber ball about the size of a softball through these rings. Nobles watched from a special stand on one side. It is said that the loser forfeited his life, and the winner took his possessions, including his wife.

The Temple of the Warriors. This structure is notable for its "thousand columns," which no longer support any roof although they undoubtedly did at one time. Behind the columns is a pyramid, decorated with sculptured panels. There are two large rooms you can enter. From the top of the temple you can get a fine view of the old market patio, with another set of columns.

Other buildings to be seen in this section, called "New Chichén," are the Temple of the Jaguars, the Wall of Skulls, the Venus Platform, the Platform of the Tigers and Eagles, and the Steam Bath.

Old Chichén. By leaving from the entrance where you came in, then going down the road a few hundred feet, you come to the entrance to another large area of Chichén-Itzá with other very interesting structures. A walk down a shady pathway will take you past them. They are:

Well of Xtoloc. This is the other cenote, and this one was used to supply a great part of the water needed for the residents. A small temple sits on the edge of the well.

Grave of the High Priest. This is only partially restored, but it is possible to see the remains of a stairway with snakelike decorations on the balustrades. A stairway inside leads down to a cavern. It was apparently used by the Toltecs as a burial place for nobles.

The Red House. Called the *Casa Colorado*, this is a temple built on a platform with a strip of red running the length of the portico. It has three doorways in a good state of preservation, adorned with three masks of the rain god, Chac. It is apparently from the Classic Maya period, predating the Toltec era.

The Caracol. This is a circular tower atop a great platform of stone. It is called "the snail," in literal translation, referring to the circular stairway. It is believed by experts that it served as an observatory, and that openings in the wall of the round tower pointed to cardinal positions on the compass, and could be used for astronomical studies.

Other points to see in this area are the Nunnery, where some feel the virgins were kept, although this point is far from settled; the Church, with its impressive carvings; and the temple of obscure writing, called Akab-Dzib.

Farther along is the old Hacienda of Chichén, and beyond it is an area properly called "Old Chichén" with the House of the Phalli, the Temple of Lintels, and many other mounds not as yet uncovered or studied. The name is a misnomer, as the area seems to be no different from "New Chichén" in its range of periods.

Uxmal

The trip to Uxmal is on a different road from the one to Chichén-Itzá. To reach Uxmal, you head west (toward Campeche) a distance of 61 miles, which takes about an hour in a motorcar. Regular buses run to Uxmal, or it is possible to join a tour group or to go by private car or limousine (see pages 419–421).

While it is easy enough to make this trip in one day, you will find there is only one hotel which has a dining room and also operates a cafeteria nearby. This is the Hacienda Uxmal, owned by the Barbachano family. They charge $20 per person for the day trip, including lunch in their dining room, which is excellent.

The name "Uxmal" is said to be a variation of the Mayan word *oxmal*, or "thrice built," and since its first recorded dates, in the seventh century, it apparently did pass through this many stages. But most of the buildings at Uxmal were erected during the Classic Maya period. The area is one of the most important archeological zones and well worth your visit. In addition, you can easily go on to Kabah during the same day if you wish.

The site at Uxmal covers an area about ½ mile long and almost that wide. Some few buildings lie outside this general area. The site is adjacent to the highway. An admission fee of 10 pesos is charged here. A good booklet is sold in English, and the site is open from 6 A.M. to 6 P.M. every day. The main buildings are the following:

Pyramid of the Magician. The entire structure, actually five different buildings each erected over the other in varying stages, stands over 100 feet high, which is equivalent to a ten-story building. A very steep stairway leads up one side of the pyramid to the temple atop. Those who are hardy enough can climb it and will find a worthwhile view of all the surrounding countryside.

The temple at the top, which has been built over previous temples which were filled in to create the present pyramid, has a row of rooms, with a facade decorated with entwined serpents. A legend tells how a dwarf overcame the king by having this large temple built overnight, giving it the name it holds, but this fantasy seems hardly adequate for the impressive structure.

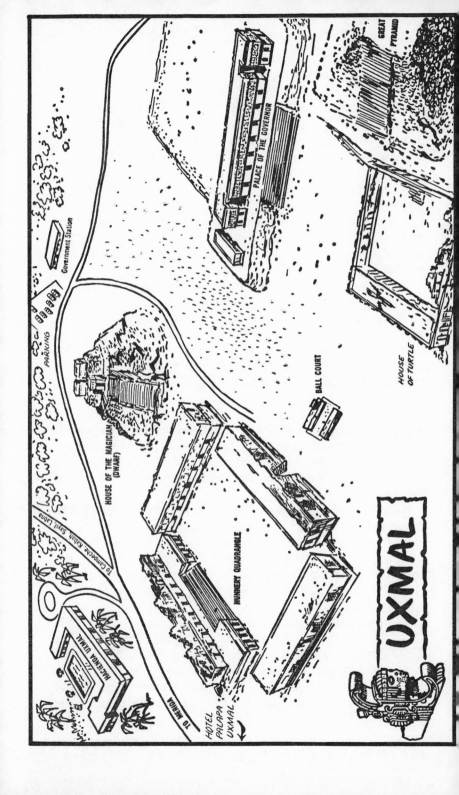

The city was abandoned before the first written records, and little else is known.

The Nunnery. This is a very impressive group of large buildings around a courtyard. It is not known if this was indeed a nunnery or whether it served as quarters for priests, but the large number of separate chambers would indicate some such use. The great quadrangle does resemble a cloister. Much has been restored, and one can see the incredibly detailed work. The corbeled arch of the Mayans, who lacked the true arch in their engineering skills, can be seen in various places. Many masks of the rain god, Chac, are displayed.

The Palace of the Governor. This consists of a great central building on a broad terrace, with a small stairway on the western side. On each side are two lateral buildings connected by high arches, said to be perhaps the highest such arches ever erected by the Mayas. A handsome frieze runs along the structure. The motif on the frieze is again the rain god, Chac. The entire structure is said to be one of the greatest of the Mayan period, notable both for its design and its execution. The fitting of the stonework is most precise.

The Great Pyramid, which appeared only as a dirt mound to visitors ever since the discovery of Uxmal, standing to the southwest of the Palace of the Governor, is being uncovered now. Beneath the rubble-covered mass show nine triangular sections resembling church dovecotes and considered important by archeologists. Steps up the Great Pyramid will give visitors a new view of Uxmal.

Other sites to see at Uxmal are the Ball Court, which is a rather obscure ruin between the Nunnery and the Governor's Palace, and by no means equal to that at Chichén-Itzá, and the House of the Turtles. A group of buildings as yet unrestored is called the Cemetery. They are west of the Ball Court. Also one can see the Platform of the Stelae, the Chimez Temple, House of the Old Woman, and the Temple of the Phalli (which has some rather obscure phallic symbols which are actually more in evidence in other buildings).

OTHER ARCHEOLOGICAL ZONES

Kabah is a smaller archeological zone about 10 miles farther on from Uxmal. The Codz-Pop structure, roughly a coiled building, is the principal building of interest. Traces of an ancient road between the two cities can be found.

Sayil and Labná can be reached, through rather a rough trip best done by jeep, by turning off 18 miles south of Uxmal at Chac, going in 3 miles to Sayil and 10 miles to Labná. While the zone is undoubtedly archeologically important, little restoration has yet been carried out, although some of the larger buildings are easily visible and very impressive. One at Sayil, the Palace, is three stories high.

Dzibchaltun, north of Mérida a short way, is just now being cleared by archeologists, and only one building, the Temple of the Seven Dolls, was of a size and state to be interesting to the casual tourist. However, it is said to be a most important zone, the area of ruins covering 1¼ miles, and it dates back to pre-Classical Mayan times. There is a large cenote in the center.

Tulum. The only Mayan temple built overlooking the sea is at Tulum, about 80 miles south of Cancún on a paved highway. A trip to Tulum can be combined with lunch at the coastal resort of Akumal and a visit to the natural aquarium of Xel-Ha along the way. Tulum is not the largest archeological zone, but it does have an interesting group of stone ruins, and some evidences of wall paintings. There is a parking lot, and soft drinks for sale, but not much else. Admission is 10 pesos.

Coba. At the Tulum intersection with the highway, a road in the opposite direction goes some 30 miles inland to what may turn out to be the largest archeological zone ever discovered in Mexico. Work is just getting under way to uncover and restore these ruins, and the extent of them is unknown at this writing.

Kohunliche is 59 kilometers beyond Chetumal on the road returning to Villahermosa via Escárcega (from where you can also return to Mérida). Kohunliche is notable for its ancient stone masks and faces which are more like the ruins of Guatemala than those found in most of Mexico. A small sign marks the turnoff, which is a road that takes you several kilometers to a rest center from where you must hike into the ruins. But it's well worth the trip, as they may be the most unusual in the area.

Becan, a major Mayan temple lost for sixty years since it was first sighted by a Peabody Museum group, is 69 kilometers beyond Chetumal. Becan, or Río Bec as it is known for its location, was built by the ancient Mayans about 800 A.D. "Temple B" is a large structure 55 feet high and 85 feet long with splendid carved stonework and containing six rooms on the ground floor with towers on each end. Moss has been removed to reveal mural drawings of a nature not seen previously in Mayan art. Stone trellises and other embellishments are evident. Becan's Temple B is said to rank with the Temple of the Sun at Palenque and the Governor's Palace at Uxmal in archeological importance. Its architecture is now known as "the Río Bec style."

After the Peabody group from Harvard found this ruin in 1912, others later failed to relocate it until a television documentary team found it, with the help of local chicle gatherers familiar with the jungle, in 1973. Even then it was mostly by luck. Now it has been taken over by the government and is slowly being uncovered from the dense jungle growth that made it invisible even to those almost on the spot.

EXCURSION TO PUERTO PROGRESO

Puerto Progreso, the shipping center for the entire peninsula, is only 22 miles from Mérida by paved road, and you can easily run down to see the docks and ships, as well as to visit a pleasant swimming beach nearby. Yucatán Trails in Mérida will take you to the Dzibchaltun ruins and on to Progreso all in the same day.

HISTORY OF THE MAYAS

While Europe still languished in the Dark Ages, a great Mayan culture flourished through a wide area of Central America that now embraces Yucatán, Belize, Guatemala, and the northern part of Honduras.

At their greatest period, from A.D. 296 to about A.D. 800, the Mayans did not number more than 3 million persons, according to the best authorities. But they built great stone cities, usually religious centers, numbering in the thousands.

These elaborate hand-carved stone structures—often buildings two, three, and even eight stories high, perched on pyramids many times that high in places—are one of the marvels of mankind. Their stones are neatly jointed, their bas-relief carvings elaborate, and often they contain stelae or panels recording events of the time.

Between the eighth and tenth centuries, there began a mysterious decline of the Mayan civilization that is still unexplained. The Mayans moved from their elaborate temples in the higher rain-forest areas to the hot and parched land near the sea. Finally, they seem to have even abandoned those latter-day cities such as Chichén-Itzá, Mayapán, and Uxmal.

About the year A.D. 1000, a movement of Mayan-speaking Toltec tribes, and later Toltec tribes from central Mexico, arrived, and there was a merging of the cultures, a rehabitation of some of the cities such as Chichén-Itzá, and an imposition of the Toltec culture. The god of the Toltecs, a plumed serpent figure called Quetzalcoatl, became also the god of the Maya, the great Kukulcán. This merging of deities is of uncertain date, as most of the Mayan structures have stone figures of Kukulcán.

One of the wandering tribes was the Itzá, and upon coming to the great cenote at the present Chichén-Itzá, the Itzá made it their new capital. They built a new religious center, and formed with other tribes the great Mayapán league.

The walled city of Mayapán, capital of Yucatán from 987 to 1441 A.D., was built. It was enclosed by a wall 5½ miles in circumference, over 12 feet high, and 9 feet wide, and more than 3,500 buildings were placed within the walls. The League of Mayapán endured for nearly 500 years until 1194, when it was sacked and destroyed in a civil war before the arrival of the Spanish.

The ancient Mayans were a soil community who lived on cultivated corn. The average Mayan was about 5 feet tall, had a round head (they loved to flatten the head by binding a board to slant the forehead of an infant), and had dark eyes with the epicanthic fold that gave an Oriental appearance. They considered it an honor to be cross-eyed, and mothers often kept baubles dangling before children's eyes to cause this crossed vision. Women, according to Spaniards who saw them bathing, had lighter skins than the men, and had a bluish mark at the base of the spine, called the "Mongolian spot," as it is distinctive to the females descended from races of early Asia and America.

The men seemed able to grow all the maize they needed during about two months of the year, and apparently were assigned to temple building or the allied crafts during the balance of the year. Prisoners were captured in intertribal warfare to help with the immense labor involved in cutting and moving great pieces of stone. As Yucatán is almost solid limestone, over which there is a thin layer of earth, stone could be had easily.

Monogamy was the custom, with parents selecting the couples. The women married young, wore a shapeless dress which was an original version of today's popular "shift," bore seven to ten children, had large breasts—reputedly as a result of leaving the bosom free while grinding corn for tortillas—and were very chaste in most cases. However, adultery was frequent enough to promulgate certain rules; for instance, discovery of the guilty in flagrante delicto would cause the erring wife to be evicted from the household and the guilty male to be held to the ground while the injured husband was free to stone him to death.

The Mayan house in ancient times, much as it is today, was an oval-shaped thatched hut with a beaten floor on which mats were placed for eating and sleeping. At other times hammocks were used, with those at rest lying crosswise. The houses were grouped in belt patterns beyond the religious center in which were the temples, the priests' homes, and immediately beyond, the homes of the nobles, then the skilled workers, and finally the *yalba uinicob*, or peasants.

The great Mayan calendar was in its beginning based on the menstrual cycle. However, as perfected, the Mayan calendar had eighteen twenty-day months, which came to 360 days, leaving five special days, called *uayeb*. The Mayans recorded the movement and positions of planets, phases of the moon, and eclipses of the sun, and were able to project predictions of these occurrences 90 million years into the past, according to some experts, and to predict eclipses that were to occur. (Occasionally they were baffled when some failed to be visible although modern astronomers have established those predicted did occur but were only seen in northern Europe, or other areas.) They also had holy calendars based on 260 days. They calculated time as beginning in the Mayan era 48 Cumhu, which was equivalent to our year 3111 B.C., and this enables us to translate all their multitude of dates.

The Mayan society was organized in city-states, led by a chief lord known as the *halach uinic*, which means the "true man." While having only one wife, he was allowed any number of concubines. The right to rule was passed along by heredity to the eldest son. As each city-state had its own chieftain, there were many of them. He usually had some understanding with the surrounding chieftains, and met in councils.

The Mayan chieftain had councillors, the *Batabob*, who controlled administration and collected taxes, and their orders were carried out by a lesser group, the *batab*. Education was restricted to the upper class, although crafts were taught to lower classes.

This worked very well, as can be seen from the sensible pattern of the Mayan cities, and the orderliness of daily life, with time and plans to build the great centers. This brought about, too, the great skills in carving and sculpture, painting and weaving.

Religion was in the hands of the Mayan high priests, called *ahkin*, and under them were the cure doctors. They believed the world had been destroyed four times and that they were living in its fifth creation. The rain god, Chac, was a quadruple god in nature. Yum Kaax was the corn god, and there were other gods for war, death, and women.

The priests' main duty was to withdraw for consultation with the gods, and to choose auspicious days on which to start important events. And, of course, to call for the sacrifices when necessary to appease the gods.

The Mayans never learned to use the wheel, either for transportation or for such uses as a potter's wheel, nor did they ever learn to build the true arch, with its keystone. Instead they had the corbeled arch, which was a narrowing of an arched area until a flat stone could be placed across the opening.

We have spoken of the astonishingly accurate Mayan calendar, but they also had a knowledge of such intangibles as zero, and were able to do calculations involving large numbers. Their great architectural skill can be seen in the buildings and cities described. In addition, they were expert weavers, dyers, made rope, baskets, and mats of considerable complexity, and elaborate pottery and jewelry which is still being recovered and can be seen in many museums both in Mexico and in other countries.

They had great festivals, and played the music that they composed on instruments. They had great ball games, some in the immense ball courts such as you can see at Chichén-Itzá.

When death came, the nobles were buried in great ceremonies, and tombs of high priests and nobles are still being discovered. One important one at Palenque was only found in 1952. Such was the civilization that existed before William the Conqueror came to England, before the Crusaders moved across Europe, before Charlemagne was crowned, and before Genghis Khan conquered China. And also before Cuzco was built in Peru, or Tenochtitlán, the Aztec capital, was even started in Mexico.

And, of course, when the great Maya civilization fell about the year A.D. 900, it was some 500 years before Columbus was to discover America.

Juan Grijalva, sailing from Cuba, saw Yucatán in 1518. Hernando Cortés, landing on the shores of Yucatán en route to found Veracruz, came in the year 1519. By then the great days were only legend. But the stone cities remain, and you can see them.

CHETUMAL

The long-isolated town of Chetumal, a free port, sits on the large bay separating it from Belize, which can be reached by the international bridge. It is a dusty gray and worn little town although it has the state capitol, right on the waterfront, of Quintana Roo. There is a war monument and benches for resting along the Malecón, or waterfront drive. Here also are several seafood restaurants. Statues of national heroes are located along the main street, Av. Héroes.

It is hard to find the gasoline stations, and there are only one or two hidden away on obscure corners. It is equally difficult to find the shops, although there are many bargains to be had in this duty-free port.

Where To Eat and Stay in Chetumal

El Presidente Chetumal (*80 rooms*)   Moderate
In center of town, on Av. Héroes, at last Chetumal has a fine modern hotel. It is a low, flat, white building set in trees and gardens but with a very narrow entrance drive and difficult parking. But inside is a good air-conditioned bar and restaurant, and comfortable air-conditioned rooms. Pool. Operated by Nacional Hotelera. All cards. Reservations through toll-free (800) 421-0722.

Hotel Continental Caribe (*24 units*)   Inexpensive
Eight blocks north of government palace, on Av. Héroes 171. A modest hotel with shower baths, refrigeration. Pool, some TV. Tel: 4-41.

El Dorado (*23 rooms*)   Inexpensive
Three blocks from the government palace, this is a modest but acceptable establishment with some air-conditioned rooms. Bar but no restaurant.

El Caribe Restaurant   Moderate
Facing bay, near Hotel Bahía, has open-air service but good seafood, and bar.

Imperial Restaurant   Moderate
Two blocks from waterfront near hotel, Jacaranda is a fine small restaurant with sparkling-clean appearance.

27

Central Mexico:
Tula, Pachuca, León, Aguascalientes, San Luis Potosí, Zacatecas, and Durango

NORTH OF Mexico City, but still on the broad plateau, one finds a number of colonial cities, usually built originally because they were mining centers. There is much agriculture, often with the help of irrigation.

These cities played a large role in Mexico's struggle for liberty. We have talked of Querétaro and Hidalgo, where the cry of liberty first rang out, in Chapter 22. But there are other important communities. All can be reached by starting out on the Querétaro superhighway and going north. The road eventually becomes the central main highway to Saltillo and the border.

TULA

About 55 miles north of Mexico City is the famed archeological zone of Tula. It is about 10 miles off the Querétaro superhighway (57D) beyond the town of Tepeji del Río.

Tollán (Tula) was established about 900 A.D., and was destroyed 200 years later. The ruins, where excavations started in the early 1940s, are still being uncovered. Centerpiece of the ancient city is a large pyramid-temple built in five tiers, topped by colossal 15-foot-high statues of warriors which, along with elaborately carved pillars, some of which still stand, upheld the huge temple roof. The stone warriors appear to be wearing helmets and carry strange boxes at their chests—as do modern astronauts. No one can explain this. To one side of the pyramid is a 130-foot wall, 7 feet high, decorated with the serpent carvings found in much Mexican architecture. Excavations have revealed the remnants of palaces, temples, colonnades, and a ball court, as well as a cluster of dwellings. Of special interest are a reclining figure of Chac-mool and a number of decorated benches. Somewhat to the north, a round pyramid built to honor Quetzalcoatl presumably dates from the later period. There is also a small museum at the site.

In the town there is a Spanish church structure built in the embattlement style of the early colonial period. One can also visit the church of Tepozotlán en route to Tula by turning off the Querétaro highway just before the first tollgate. The church, built in the 1750s on the site of a 400-year-old Jesuit mission, is an outstanding example of churrigueresque art—a dazzling display of rococo religious carvings covering walls and ceilings with gold and brilliant colorings. The former convent is now a museum with an impressive display of religious artifacts and armor; underneath the museum are the restored colonial kitchens. The church is set in well-kept gardens where a restaurant, the Hostería, offers a pleasant stop for lunch.

PACHUCA

By taking Highway 85D north from Mexico City, the road to Monterrey, one can visit the old mining town of Pachuca. It is the capital of the state of Hidalgo and has a population of over 90,000. It is still one of the greatest silver-producing centers in the world, and about 15 percent of the world's supply comes from here.

It has a government tourist office below the clock tower in the main plaza, and there you can arrange to visit one of the silver mines. The Casa Colorado, built by the Count of Santa María de Regla, is one of many interesting colonial buildings in the center of town. The Church of San Francisco was built in 1596.

A famous resort hotel, the *Hacienda de San Miguel Regla*, which has a golf course and a swimming pool, is located 21 miles from Pachuca on the Real del Monte road. Reservations are recommended.

LEÓN

Located in the state of Guanajuato, León is the shoe-manufacturing center of Mexico. It is a large city of nearly half a million population. It is not a tourist center, but is a convenient place to stop, as it is on the main highway north to El Paso from Mexico City.

A largely commercial city, it does have parks dotted about. Its history dates back to 1656, and its cathedral was built in 1746. The leather factories turn out mass-produced inexpensive shoeware for most of the country, but they also do fine leather work such as boots and saddles.

The *Hotel León*, just off the main plaza, is a well-run, pleasant hotel with a good dining room, open until 11 P.M. Drive-in registration. A good motel is the *Real de Minas*, at the east entrance to the Boulevard López Mateos (Highway 45), which has a heated pool, sauna, cocktails and entertainment, and a dining room open until 10:30 P.M. The *Motel Estancia* on Highway 45 is only 1 mile from the center of town, with pool, coffee shop, restaurant, and a bar.

AGUASCALIENTES

Also on Highway 45, going toward El Paso, one comes to the capital of the state of Aguascalientes, noted, as its name indicates, for its many hot springs, colonial buildings, and parks. The city is said to sit over pre-Hispanic tunnels, almost catacombs, which were evidently dug by early Indian tribes. They are not open to the public, but occasional air shafts indicate they are there.

Aguascalientes was founded about 1575 by the Spanish as a station on the royal road over which silver and gold bullion were carried. The city is modern in many ways and has a number of plazas and churches as well as the state capitol building. It now has a population of over 250,000.

There are two older but dignified hotels in town on the main square. The *Hotel Francia* (tel: 5-60-80) is the more distinguished. The *Hotel Paris* is also on the main plaza. Both have pleasant dining rooms open until 10:30 and 11 P.M., respectively.

SAN LUIS POTOSÍ

This is a modern city in appearance, with some 350,000 inhabitants. However, its actual founding dates back to 1589 when

Franciscan missionaries entered the area and found that extremely rich gold mines were being operated in the nearby San Pedro Hills.

San Luis Potosí is a handsome city, clean and neat, and possessed of considerable charm with its flagstone streets, fountains in the plazas, and iron Spanish lanterns adorning all public buildings. On its famed Avenida Carranza are many attractive mansions. One particularly handsome home has been converted into a Casa de la Cultura, housing one of the country's finest art schools. There is also a Fine Arts Institute, and a Mexican–North-American Cultural Institute teaching English and Spanish.

The best restaurant is *La Virreina*, on Av. Carranza, which is also Highway 80. La Virreina is an elegant dining facility in an old mansion with continental and regional dishes. Cocktails, parking lot. Accepts most cards. Has a children's menu. Open 1 P.M. until 11 P.M. *La Lonja*, in town opposite the Colonial Hotel, is a long-respected restaurant.

The *Panorama Hotel* is a modern ten-story downtown hotel with attractive comfortable rooms and good service. Heated pool, free parking, good restaurant. The *Cactus Motel*, on the outskirts of town on Highway 57 just south of Juárez Circle, is a large modern establishment with heated pool, playground, and dining room. Also trailer spaces. The *Sands Motel*, the *Santa Fe*, and the *Tuna Courts* are all on Route 57 and also good.

ZACATECAS

An ancient mining town, its streets and homes tumbled together in the hollow of the mountains, Zacatecas is quite charming with its arched aqueducts and its boulevards and plazas. It was founded in 1548 by four Spanish viceroyal delegates, and for nearly 300 years it poured out over a billion dollars' worth of silver. Some mines are still being worked, but largely Zacatecas' day has passed.

This colonial wealth provided the town with some important architectural accomplishments, including the cathedral on the plaza, Our Lady of Assumption, and the Church of Santo Domingo, a block from the plaza. The Calderón Theater is another product of these lavish times.

Behind the town lies Bufa mountain. On the summit of Bufa

there is a small chapel, La Capilla de los Remedios, and also a good place to view the city below.

La Quemada or Chicomoztoc ruins are about 30 miles from Zacatecas on a side road branching off Highway 45, just north of the city. This was once a fortified city built by the Nahua tribes as they migrated from the Gulf of California area toward what was to be Mexico City. Some 400 years before the Spanish arrived, they built this stronghold, dwelling there until they branched out in six separate tribes when they reached Tula and overcame the Toltecs. Visitors will see the remains of temples, towers, and streets resting on terraced levels much like the stone cities of the south of Mexico.

The best hotel in Zacatecas is the new *Hotel Aristos Zacatecas*, a modern three-story sprawling structure atop a slight hill on the road coming from the north as it enters the city at a roundabout. With 120 rooms (all air-conditioned), a restaurant with pretty good food (open to the public and accepting all cards), heated swimming pool, sauna, barber shop and beauty salon, and a nightclub with dancing, it is a good place to stop. Tel: 2-17-88.

Other possibilities are the *Motel del Bosque*, also on a hill overlooking the city (1 mile off Highways 45 and 54, 1½ miles west of the city), and the modest *Zacatecas Courts* at López Velarde 602.

The *Aristos dining room* is open long hours and is a pleasant place with a menu featuring steaks, tacos, frijoles, and tortilla soup. Prices moderate. *Las Pampas*, an Argentine restaurant at the highway entrance to the town from the north, López Mateos 123, has fancier cuts of meat which they charcoal broil as well as chicken. Small but attractive. Tel: 2-13-08.

There is a daily tourist trip at 11 A.M. and 4 P.M. to visit the Convent of Guadalupe, the Chapel of Napoles, and lunch at the Restaurant Minas del Edén, a restaurant some 4,000 feet inside a famed mine near the Hotel Aristos. Tickets can be purchased at the hotel desk, or you can go directly to Minas del Edén, paying 2 pesos to enter (food served from 2 P.M. to 10 P.M.).

DURANGO

About 300 miles north of Zacatecas on the road to El Paso, Texas, and only 318 miles over a paved but very mountainous road to the coast at Mazatlán, this is a mining town of some 177,000 people. It is not of much interest to tourists, although it has comfortable places to stop. It is a major railroad junction, with a spectacular connection to Mazatlán. Occasionally a movie company will come here to use the superb scenery and smog-free air.

The newest hotel in Durango is *El Presidente*, a Spanish-mission-type structure with ninety-eight rooms (all air-conditioned) facing the Ramos River. It has a coffee shop and a fine dining room, and a pool. It is next to a shopping center with a supermarket, pharmacy, dry cleaner, and other stores. Reservations can be made through the El Presidente chain. Fair hotels downtown are the *Casablanca*, the *Posada San Jorge*, and the *Reforma*, all accepting most credit cards. The best motel at this writing is the *Campo México Courts*, 1½ miles from the junction of 40 and 45, which has fifty units, air-conditioned restaurant, and playground (tel: 1-55-60). The *Posada Durán* is a highly recommended colonial inn with eighteen rooms, located in the center of town two blocks from the main plaza and facing the east side of the main cathedral. Good food in a charming dining room, garage nearby, accepts AE and VISA (tel: 1-24-12).

There are two good rock shops, selling agates and other stones, Durango Rock and Gift Shop (at 134 Madero, near the Durán Inn) and the American Agates (across from the Hotel San Luis).

A tourist information office is in the state capitol building behind the Hotel Casablanca.

There are several interesting sights in Durango. The Chupaderos permanent movie set for western pictures is where many U.S. westerns have been filmed as well as Mexican pictures. It is 8½ miles out of the city on the highway to Parral.

A mountain of iron can be seen from the hilltop church of Señora de los Remedios. The immense Cerro de Mercado is estimated to contain as much as 50 million tons of almost pure iron ore. It is said to be embedded in the earth as far down as it is high. It provides raw material for the steel mills of Monterrey.

Other minerals mined in this area include copper, mercury, gold, lead, silver, and manganese. A railroad runs to Mazatlán to permit the loading of minerals for ships in the Pacific.

A drive to Guadalupe Victoria Dam, four hours away along a meandering stream, or to El Águila Dam, makes a pleasant excursion. The central building of the state university is a colonial building erected by the Jesuits in 1590, and it is still in use. The Sanctuary of Guadalupe, built in 1772, contains remains of patriots who fought with Mexican revolutionary leader Miguel Hidalgo. Durango is also the home state of the famed Pancho Villa.

Around the area are still some great ranches raising cattle, though they are not as large, nor are as many individually owned, as at one time. Exhibits of prizewinning cattle are still held here, however.

28

North Central Mexico Plains:
Chihuahua, Torreón, Gómez Palacio, and Lerdo

In busy Santo Domingo Plaza, scene of the Inquisition court and once home of Malinche, Saturday morning is busy as worried young girls pour out love letters to men hunched over old-fashioned battered Oliver typewriters. These are the famed escribanos, *or writers, and the young ladies either can't write or can't write well enough to compose their own letters. Peasants with messages to far-away relatives, or people with simple transactions in business, also wait in line for the service of the letter-writers, who use very flowery language.*

Of all the trades in Mexico, they have one of the most fascinating. But there are others.

Have you seen the boys on bicycles magically balancing a huge basket, 6 feet in diameter, filled with hot rolls they are delivering through heavy traffic? Or the bakers themselves who make these unmatched bolillos, *as the rolls are called? There are several kinds: The bolillo itself is a dinner roll and has a ridge on top; the* telera *is used for sandwiches, or* tortas; *the* colchón *has a quilted appearance. There are also sweet rolls such as* rosca, *or "ring";* sugar-covered *bizcochos; and roll-shaped* regas de manteca. *All are delicious.*

Or the glassblowers to be seen on Carretones Street in Mexico City or Independencia in Guadalajara, where hot glass literally bubbles as small boys dip in pipes and then rush to the master blowers, who magically turn them into goblets or bowls or lanterns of myriad shapes, colors, and translucencies.

Or the balloon salesman in the park with his incredible collection of bright colors, balloons within balloons, balloons tied like animals, balloons with faces, or stars, or names.

All of this adds to the delight of Mexico.

THE GREAT PLAINS of northern Mexico are really much like their northern neighbor, Texas: far-reaching cattle lands where much of the beef of Mexico is raised, as well as vast farm acreage in some areas. The plains do not have the irrigation of the adjacent western state of Sonora, where much more wheat and cotton land exists, but some parts such as La Laguna near Torreón and Gómez Palacio have marvelously rich land and adequate water supplies. Here vast fields of cotton are grown.

The mines of the area have been among the richest of all Mexico, and La Nevada mine had silver so pure that it required practically no refining. The Santa Eulalia mines at Aquiles Serdán were among the most productive in all Mexico. Many of the mines are still working.

The great canyons crossing the Sierra Mountains, an extension of the Rockies, are so vast that one of them, the famed Copper Canyon, is said to be bigger than the Grand Canyon in the United States. All in all, there are twenty major canyons in Chihuahua state, and one of the most spectacular railroad trips in the world, with good modern equipment, is from Chihuahua to Topolobampo on the Pacific. Well worth a vacation trip in itself as it traverses the rim of the immense Copper Canyon.

You can board a train in El Paso and come to Chihuahua, and there pick up the Canyon train, or you can simply make reservations at the office of the Mexican Railways, Calle 3A 206, or perhaps more easily from Rojo and Casavantes Travel Agency at 1000C Bolívar Street, Chihuahua (tel: 2-60-30 or 2-88-89). Be sure to insist upon self-contained diesel Fiat-built trains, as they make the trip in twelve hours compared with twenty-four on older Pullmans. See Chapter 14 for more information on this most scenic train trip, with stops at Creel, the halfway point, and then at the outlook point, El Divisadora, some 28 miles away, where you can see four of the immense canyons at once. There are hotel accommodations there. This area also is home for the Tarahumara Indians. It is possible to reboard the train the next day for return to Chihuahua, or on to Los Mochis on the Pacific Coast Highway, or the port of Topolobampo and then return to Chihuahua.

There are station wagons waiting at Creel (population 3,000) to take visitors to two recommended hotels: Hotel Nuevo is near the station, and Copper Canyon Lodge is an adobe and log structure a forty-five-minute ride over an all-weather road passing by Arareko Lake and where trout fishing is good.

A side trip off the road from El Paso, Texas, to Chihuahua, capital of the state of Chihuahua, can take you to Casas Grandes, an archeological zone where the ruins of an ancient pre-Toltec village sit on a ridge. The builders are still unknown, but the construction is much like the Indian pueblos of Arizona and New Mexico. Some parts with ball courts indicate that later races such as the Toltecs may have existed here.

The shy Tarahumara Indians, relics of the Stone Age of some 30,000 years ago, are semi-nomadic and often live in caves. They can be seen living in the Barranca de Urique, which has a 4,000-foot plunging wall. It looks like a barren and lifeless chasm to visitors, but it is home to the Tarahumaras. Water has always been a problem in this area, and the Tarahumaras have ceremonial rain dances.

The railway plan was conceived by an American, Albert K. Owen, and completed in 1961 with incredible engineering skill. It includes thirty-nine bridges, eighty-six tunnels, and some of the most difficult of roadbeds, but its welded steel rails make for smooth traveling.

CHIHUAHUA CITY

Chihuahua is a fairly modern city of some 300,000 inhabitants, with an interesting mixture of Spanish colonial and more modern homes, some pretty boulevards, some fairly good hotels, and some sights worth seeing. Tarahumara Indians are occasionally seen on the streets. The city also has the University of Chihuahua.

It is, however, best known for two things. It is the source of the tiny, practically hairless dogs, weighing 2 pounds and sometimes less, called *perros chihuahuenos*, or "Chihuahua dogs," which are much like Chinese sleeve dogs. Anyone purchasing one must be very careful to get the genuine breed, and not a mongrel which will grow to ordinary size.

The other pride of Chihuahua is that it was for long the home of Pancho Villa, and the home has now been turned into a museum with such memorabilia as the bullet-riddled car in which he was driving when he was killed. The thirty-room home was given to the state by his widow, Luz Corral de Villa. There is also a monument to Villa and another to the División del Norte, the great fighting band which he used to conquer much of Mexico during the hectic days of the 1910 Revolution and the practically continuous skirmishes that followed the death of the martyr president, Francisco Madero.

The monument can be found by going out the Av. Universidad, which also leads to the state university campus and the home of the governor. The home of Pancho Villa, now a museum, can be found in the southern part of the city at Calle 10 No. 3014, which is near the intersection of Av. Ocampo and 20 de Noviembre.

On the central plaza, one can find the twin-towered cathedral. Three blocks away is the federal building which houses the cell where Father Hidalgo, who uttered the cry for independence which led to the break with Spain, was jailed by the Spanish authorities. The cell is a relic of an old Jesuit church, and has been left intact within the federal building. A plaque on the state capitol across the street marks the site of the execution of Hidalgo in 1811. A new state museum is also housed in a turn-of-the-century mansion.

HOTELS AND MOTELS IN CHIHUAHUA

El Presidente Chihuahua (125 *rooms*) Moderate
A tall multistory hotel at Libertad 9 in the downtown area. New, all air-conditioned. Three restaurants, grill, bar, discotheque, pool, sauna. Coffee shop open until midnight. All cards. Tel: 2-68-83.

El Capitán Motel (22 *units*) Inexpensive
Two miles north of town on Highway 45, at Tecnológico 2300. Pleasant, air-cooled. Showers. MC, VISA. P.O. Box 146, Chihuahua, Chihuahua, México. Tel: 3-08-24.

El Dorado Hotel (66 *units*) Inexpensive
One-half mile northwest of plaza at Julian Cabrillo and 14th Street. Some rooms air-conditioned. Dining room open until 11 P.M. Cocktails. Tel: 2-57-70.

Hotel Fermont (84 *rooms*) Moderate
A modern seventeen-story hotel on north side of main plaza, this is probably the best place to stay in Chihuahua. Air-conditioned, children under ten free, rollaways, parking nearby, indoor pool,

cocktails, steam bath. Dining room and coffee shop open until midnight. All major cards. Tel: 2-68-83.

Posada Tierra Blanca (*71 rooms*)   Moderate
A modern two-story motel four blocks north of main plaza behind the Fermont, at corner of Independencia and Niños Héroes. Pool. Dining room with garden terrace. TV. Ask for new section. Major cards. Reservations at 2-00-00 or in El Paso, Texas, at 772-4231.

Motel Mirador (*41 units*)   Inexpensive
On Highway 45 on north side near Villa monument. Two-story motel with wall-to-wall carpeting, enclosed free parking, pool. Restaurant open 6 A.M. till midnight. AE, VISA. Tel: 2-68-83.

Terminal Motel (*53 rooms*)   Inexpensive
Fairly new two-story motel in northwest part of town near river and bus depot. Some rooms carpeted. Coffee shop.

Victoria Hotel and Motel (*128 rooms*)   Inexpensive
An attractive older hotel in colonial style with a new motel behind (motel open only in summer). On east side at Juárez and Colón and next to Calesa restaurant. Air-conditioned. Pretty gardens, pool. AE, DC.

RESTAURANTS IN CHIHUAHUA

La Calesa Restaurant   Moderate
The city's best steak house and highly recommended. Notable for carriage outside (which gives it its name). On east side of town at Juárez and Colón across from Victoria Hotel. Reasonable prices for local steaks. Serves Calesa special plate with avocados, refried beans, and steak. Major cards.

Futurama Restaurant   Moderate
A colonial-style restaurant 1 mile north on Highway 45 at Universidad and División del Norte near Pancho Villa monument. Air-conditioned. Serves steaks and seafood. Major cards. Tel: 3-15-55.

Los Parados Restaurant   Moderate
Next door to the famed Chihuahua Brewery, at 3331 Juárez Street, this old restaurant serves ice-cold beer from the brewery along with a special Alexander porterhouse or Kansas City sirloin. Rough and ready, but they let you pick out your own steak.

Colonel Sanders Kentucky Fried Chicken   Inexpensive
Just like in the United States, this establishment at Carranza just

north of the bridge coming into town serves chicken, potatoes, gravy, and all the rest.

México y España

A Spanish-type restaurant near Posada Tierra Blanca off Carranza on Niños Héroes, near downtown. Serves paella, lobster thermidor, shish kebab, and steaks. Run-down look is deceptive. Major cards. Open morning till midnight.

TORREÓN, GÓMEZ PALACIO, AND LERDO

These are the triplet cities of the La Laguna agricultural area where lakes and heavy irrigation have produced fertile fields of wheat, cotton, and vineyards as well as vegetables. Torreón is the capital of the state of Coahuila, while nearby Gómez Palacio and Lerdo are in the state of Durango. And the area also borders on the state of Chihuahua.

All are relatively new towns, and do not have a great deal to offer tourists. But they are important to the economy of Mexico, as they not only rank high in agricultural production, but also in smelting.

HOTELS AND MOTELS IN TORREÓN

Hotel Palacio Real (*120 rooms*)   Moderate
On main plaza at Morelos 1280. A modern hotel, completely air-conditioned, with TV. Dining room and sidewalk coffee shop open 7 A.M. till midnight. All cards. P.O. Box 436, Torreón, Coahuila, México. Tel: 2-64-22.

Motel and Hotel Paraiso del Desierto (*105 units*)   Moderate
A mile and one-quarter north of city on Highway 30 at Blvd. Independencia and Calle Jiménez. A fine new motel and hotel. Air-conditioned, heated pool and wading pool, garage. Dining room and coffee shop open 7 A.M. till midnight. Cocktails, nightclub. Major cards. P.O. Box 728. Tel: 6-11-22.

Hotel del Paseo (*80 rooms*)   Moderate
A modern hotel six blocks from the main plaza. Air-conditioned, steam bath, cocktails. Dining room open 7 A.M. till 11 P.M. Tel: 2-41-60.

Hotel Río Nazas (*157 rooms*)   Moderate
Five blocks from plaza in town. Air-conditioned, free garage, dining room and coffee shop open 7 A.M. till 11 P.M., cocktail lounge. Tel: 2-61-71.

Motel Diana (*20 rooms*)   Inexpensive
Two miles from plaza between Revolución and Juárez on Diagonal Torreón. Pool, restaurant, bar.

Hotel Calvete (*80 rooms*)   Moderate
Opposite federal building at Av. Juárez and Corona, this is older but well-kept hotel. Air-conditioned, garage, dining room and cocktails. Tel: 2-51-02.

Hotel Elvira (*120 rooms*)   Moderate
Commercial hotel on main plaza. Roof garden, dining room, coffee shop (open till 11:30 P.M.), and bar. Tel: 2-64-22.

RESTAURANTS IN TORREÓN

Restaurant Apolo Palacio   Inexpensive
On west side of main plaza. Air-conditioned. Bar. Open from 6 A.M. until 2 A.M. Both American and Mexican food and soda fountain.

Restaurant de Doña Julia   Inexpensive
One block from Hotel Río Nazas, on Av. Matamoros. Specializes in Spanish cooking.

29

Price Guide to Hotels in Mexico

We have used a general classification, or price guide, throughout the previous chapters, and here we will relate these designations to actual dollar figures insofar as we can. The readers must realize that prices are constantly changing and we can give only an approximation. This may be helpful, but you cannot hold a hotel to the prices we give. However, prices are fixed by the government, and a price table showing your actual room number and rate should be posted (usually in the closet of the room).

Here are our price ratings converted to dollars:

Throughout Mexico Generally

Our Rating	Dollar Range	Double Room (two people)
Very expensive, European plan	$50 and up	All prices for
Expensive, European plan	$40–$50	standard
Moderately expensive, European plan	$30–$40	double room without meals
Moderate, European plan	$20–$30	
Inexpensive, European plan	Less than $20	Usually only
Bargain, European plan	Less than $10	European plan available

In Acapulco and Cancún

Very expensive, European plan	$60–$116	Standard double
Very expensive, modified American plan (two meals included)	$80–$138	
Expensive, European plan	$50–$80	
Expensive, American plan	$60–$80	
Moderately expensive, European plan	$35–$50	

Moderately expensive, American plan	$40–$60
Moderate, European plan	$30–$35
Moderate, American plan	$40–$50
Inexpensive, European plan	$20
Inexpensive, American plan	$25–$30
Bargain, European plan	$19 or less

We will now list actual hotels and the prices as we can best estimate them at this writing. The hotels are listed to conform with our chapters in the book. Some of the hotels listed in the chapters are not included here, because price information was not available at press time. Some of the newest hotels are included in this listing although not described in the corresponding chapter. Remember, prices can rise and we cannot predict the future.

ACAPULCO (Chapter 7)

Hotel	Double Room, Summer*		Double Room, Winter†	
Acapulco Princess	$30–$70	EP	$90–$120	AP
Fiesta Tortuga	$24–$36	EP	$40–$60	MAP
Acapulco Torreblanca	$25	EP	$40–$60	MAP
Las Brisas	$52–$64	CP	$88–$116	CP
Condesa del Mar	$40–$45	EP	$60–$90	MAP
Americana/El Presidente	$30–$40	EP	$55–$85	MAP
Hotel Pierre Marqués	$30–$60	EP	$80–$110	MAP
Elcano	$25	EP	$50	EP
Ritz	$30	EP	$50	EP
Casablanca	$20		$30	EP
Holiday Inn	$30–$45	EP	$40–$50	EP
Plaza International Hyatt Regency	$35	EP	$87	MAP
Caleta	$30	EP	$40	EP
Boca Chica	$30	EP	$50	EP
Acapulco Malibu	$60	MAP	$80	MAP
Maris	$30–$50	EP	$50–$60	EP

* May 1 to December 15
† December 15 to April 30
    EP—European plan (no meals)
    CP—Continental plan (with breakfast)
  MAP—Modified American plan (breakfast and dinner)
    AP—American plan (three meals)

Hotel	Double Room, Summer		Double Room, Winter	
Club de Pesca	$25–$35	EP	$35–$45	EP
El Mirador	$15–$20	EP	$20–$35	EP
Paraiso/Marriott	$28–$36	EP	$68–$74	MAP
Costera	$20–$32	EP	$40–$60	MAP
Posada del Sol	$25	EP	$32	EP
Ritz Auto Hotel	$22	EP	$55	EP
Impala	$18	EP	$22	EP
Motel LaJolla	$14	EP	$16	EP
Motel Bali-Haí	$24	EP	$36	EP
Pozo del Rey	$25–$32	EP	$45	MAP
El Tropicano	$18	EP	$25	EP
El Cid	$20	EP	$30	EP
Las Hamacas	$28	EP	$42	EP
El Matador	$24–$36	EP	$36–$42	EP
Belmar	$19	AP	$23	AP
Lindavista	$18	AP	$24	AP
San Antonio	$18	AP	$24	AP
Motel Caribe	$10	EP	$14	EP
Sao Paulo	$20	EP	$24	EP
Los Pericos	$12	EP	$14	EP
Sands	$22	EP	$32	EP
Puerto Arturo	$10	EP	$12	EP
Leighton	$10	EP	$14	EP
Pacífico	$15	AP	$15	AP
Villa	$16	EP	$20	EP
Continental	$38	EP	$52	EP
			$68	MAP
La Palapa	$30	EP	$55	EP
			$75	MAP
Romano Palace	$24	EP	$36	EP
Villa Vera Racquet Club	$26	EP	$38	EP

Restaurant Prices in Acapulco

Very expensive	$15–$25 per person
Expensive	$10–$15
Moderately expensive	$7–$10
Moderate	$4–$6
Inexpensive	$2–$3
Bargain	Under $2

BAJA CALIFORNIA (Chapter 8)

City	Hotel	Price Range	Double Room
Tijuana	Palacio Azteca	$20–$32	EP
	Royal Inn	$20–$30	EP

City	Hotel	Price Range	Double Room
	Country Club Motel	$15–$25	EP
	El Conquistador	$27–$35	EP
	La Sierra Motel	$10–$12	EP
Rosarita	Rosarita Beach Hotel	$17–$24	EP
	DeAnza	$10–$14	EP
	Rene's Motel	$12–$14	EP
Enseñada	Ramada Motor Inn	$26–$32	EP
	San Nicolas Hotel	$22–$30	EP
	Hotel La Pinta Presidente	$18–$20	EP
	Travelodge	$20–$22	EP
	Cortez Motel	$14–$16	EP
	Bahia Resort Hotel	$18–$20	EP
	Santa Maria Motel	$14–$16	EP
	El Cid	$24–$28	EP
	Villa Marina	$14–$16	EP
	Estero Beach Resort Hotel	$20–$32	EP
	Villa Carioca	$10–$14	EP
Enseñada Area	Mike's Sky Ranch	$34	AP
	Meling Ranch	$40	AP
San Felipe	Augie's Riviera	$14–$18	EP
	Villa del Mar	$16–$20	EP
	El Cortez	$14–$16	EP
San Quintín	El Presidente	$21–$24	EP
	El Molino Viejo	$15	EP
Santa Ines	El Presidente Catavina	$21	EP
Guerrero Negro	El Presidente Paralelo 28	$21	EP
	Dunas Motel	$10	EP
Santa Rosalia	Hotel El Morro	$10	EP
San Ignacio	El Presidente	$21	EP
Mulegé	Hotel Mulegé	$21	EP
	Hotel Las Casitas	$28	AP
Loreto	Flying Sportsman Lodge	$40–$60	AP
	Hotel El Presidente	$21	EP
	Serenidad Mulegé	$20	EP
	Hotel Terrazas	$10	EP
	Hotel Oasis	$30	AP
La Paz	El Presidente	$36	EP
	La Posada	$26	EP
	Hotel Los Arcos	$26	EP
	Hotel Calafia	$18	EP
	Hotel Perla	$16	EP
	Econohotel	$17	EP
Cabo San Lucas	Hotel Cabo San Lucas	$60–$110	AP
	Hotel Finisterra	$60–$100	AP
	Camino Real	$72–$80	AP
	Las Cruces Palmilla	$76	AP

City	Hotel	Price Range	Double Room
	Palmas de Cortes	$32	AP
	Rancho Buena Vista	$50–$60	AP
	Hacienda	$60–$80	AP
	Hyatt Cabo San Lucas	NA	
	Hotel Solmar	$50	MAP
		$32	EP

CANCÚN (Chapter 9)

City	Hotel	Summer	Winter	Plan
Cancún	Aristos Cancún	$38	$52	EP
		$60	$68	MAP
	Bajorquez	$54	$64	MAP
	Camino Real	$52–$58	$66–$70	EP
	(add $20 per person for AP)			
	Cancún Caribe	$38	$80–$138	EP
	(add $15 per person for MAP)			
	El Presidente	$64	$80–$138	MAP
	(EP in summer $40)			
	Garza Blanca	$60	$80–$90	EP
	Maya Caribe	$40	$60	EP
	Hotel Parador	$24	$24	EP
	Playa Blanca	$25	$63	EP
	Plaza Caribe	$17	$17	EP
	Villas Tacul (four persons in villa)	$160–$200	$160–$200	EP
	Club Mediterranée (approximately $195 to $250 per person per week booked ahead of time)			
Isla Mujeres	Posada del Mar	$48	$48	MAP
	Zazil-Ha	$24	$24	CP
	Rocas del Caribe	$12	$12	EP
	Hotel Rocamar	$12	$12	EP

COZUMEL (Chapter 9)

	Double Room, Summer		Double Room, Winter	
El Presidente	$34	EP	$62	EP
Hotel Sol Caribe	$39	EP	$45	EP
Mayan Plaza	$66	MAP	$86	MAP
Cozumel Caribe	$46–$68	MAP	$68	MAP
Cabanas del Caribe	$50	MAP	$60	MAP
Hotel Mara	$22–$40	EP	$40–$50	EP

Hotel	*Double Room, Summer*		*Double Room, Winter*	
Hotel Cantarell	$23–$35	EP	$40–$50	EP
Caribe Islander	$18	EP	$24	EP
Playa Azul	$40	MAP	$54	MAP
El Cozumeleno	$34	EP	$48	EP

CHETUMAL (Chapter 9)

El Presidente	$24	EP	$24	EP

CUERNAVACA (Chapter 10)

Arocena Holiday	$16–$24	EP	$16–$24	EP
Hacienda Cocoyoc	$24–$32	EP	$24–$32	EP
Posada de Tepozteco	$20–$24	AP	$20–$24	AP
Casa de Piedra	$14–$22	EP	$14–$22	EP
Los Canarios	$10	EP	$10	EP
Casino de la Selva	$16–$24	EP	$16–$24	EP
Posada Jacaranda	$18–$52	EP	$18–$52	EP
La Posada Arcadia	$18	EP	$18	EP
Las Mananitas	$32	EP	$32	EP
Las Quintas	$18–$24	EP	$18–$24	EP
Casa Arocena	$16	CP	$16	CP
Hotel Vista Hermosa	$38–$46	AP	$38–$46	AP
Hotel Posada Borda	$10	EP	$10	EP
Hotel Paraiso Bungalows	$64 (for eight persons)			
Posada San Angelo	$20–$25	EP	$20–$25	EP

GUADALAJARA (Chapter 11)

Hotel	*Price Range*	*Double Room*
El Tapatio	$38–$42	EP
Guadalajara Sheraton	$30	EP
Camino Real	$24–$30	EP
Hotel Plaza del Sol	$22–$30	EP
Hotel Fenix	$18–$26	EP
Hotel del Parque	$10–$14	EP
Hotel de Mendoza	$22–$28	EP
Holiday Inn	$26–$32	EP
Hotel Morales	$12	EP
Hotel Genova	$16–$18	EP
Hotel Frances	$5	EP

Hotel	Price Range	Double Room
American Motel	$10	EP
Motel de las Americas	$14–$16	EP
Motel La Estancia	$12–$20	EP
Motel Malibu	$12	EP
Tropicana	$10	EP
Motel Suites Caribe	$12–$15	EP
Motel Chapalita	$8–$10	EP

GUANAJUATO (Chapter 12)

Castillo de Santa Cecilia	$16	EP
	$34	AP
Hotel Real de Minas	$25–$30	EP
Parador San Javier	$20–$24	EP
Hotel San Diego	$12–$16	EP
Motel Guanajuato	$12	EP
Hotel Valenciana	$16–$18	EP

IXTAPA/ZIHUATANEJO (Chapter 13)

	Double Room, Summer		Double Room, Winter	
Hotel Aristos Ixtapa	$36	EP	$52	EP
El Presidente Las Palmas	$34	EP	$52–$80	EP
Hotel Catalina Zihuatanejo	$35–$53	MAP	same	
Hotel Sotovento Zihuatanejo	$37–$49	MAP	same	
Hotel Irma Zihuatanejo	$25	MAP	$40	MAP
Posada Caracol Zihuatanejo	$15	EP	$22	EP
Famitel Ixtapa	$20–$30	EP	$22–$32	EP
Bungalows Pacifico	$12	EP	$12	EP
Holiday Inn	$34	EP	$52	EP

MAZATLÁN (Chapter 14)

Camino Real Mazatlán	$32–$36	EP	same	
Oceano Palace	$18–$22	EP	$22–$28	EP
La Palapa	$24–$32	EP	$32–$36	EP
Hotel Playa Mazatlán	$20–$26		same	
Hotel de Cima	$15 up		same	
Playa del Rey	$21–$24	EP	same	

Hotel	Double Room, Summer		Double Room, Winter	
Don El Guia	$21–$28		same	
Azteca Inn	$13	EP	same	
Holiday Inn	$25–$27	EP	$30–$40	EP
Cantamar Motel	$15	EP	same	
El Cid Hotel	$26	EP	same	
La Siesta	$12	EP	same	
Motel Aqua Marina	$14–$18	EP	same	
Sands Hotel	$10	EP	same	
Belmar Hotel	$16–$18	EP	same	
Hotel Las Brisas	$12	EP	same	
Posada de Don Pelayo	$15	EP	same	
Hacienda Mazatlán	$28	EP	same	
Posada Colonial	$10	EP	same	

MANZANILLO (Chapter 15)

Hotel				
Hotel Las Hadas	$43–$53	EP	$70–$80	MAP
Playa de Santiago	$20–$25	EP	same	
Hotel la Posada	$12	EP	same	
Casa Blanca Alamar	$20	EP	same	

MEXICO CITY (Chapter 16)

	Price Range	
El Presidente	$28–$40	Only European plan
El Presidente Chapultepec	$39–$50	in Mexico City
Fiesta Palace	$42–$50	
Camino Real	$34–$43	
Maria Isabel Sheraton	$28–$40	
Continental	$30–$36	
Del Paseo	$30–$35	
Bamer	$20–$28	
Reforma	$20–$65	
Del Prado	$30–$40	
Hotel Aristos	$29–$38	
Hotel Bristol	$18–$22	
Hotel Casa Blanca	$25	
Hotel del Angel	$15–$20	
Hotel El Ejecutivo	$15–$20	
Hotel Metropol	$9–$14	
Holiday Inn Zona Rosa	$30–$35	
Holiday Inn Airport	$30	
Hotel Sevilla	$10–$14	
Alameda Hotel	$25–$30	

Hotel	Price Range	Double Room
Plaza Vista Hermosa	$18–$24	
Premier Hotel	$12–$16	
Monte Cassino	$16–$24	
Gran Hotel Ciudad de México	$22–$32	
De Cortés Hotel	$15–$25	
Maria Cristina	$12–$24	
Majestic Hotel	$15	
Geneve Hotel	$15–$30	
Francis Hotel	$12–$18	
Guadalupe Hotel	$11	
Purua Hidalgo	$14–$18	
Regis Hotel	$14–$28	
Emporio Hotel	$12–$18	
Luma Hotel	$20–$24	
Meurice Hotel	$14–$18	
Alffer Century Hotel	$30	
Ritz Hotel	$19–$22	
Montejo Hotel	$12–$30	
Hotel Oxford	$8–$10	
El Diplomatico	$20–$25	
Polanco Hotel	$8–$11	
Plaza Florencia	$30–$36	
Dawn Motor Hotel	$14–$18	

MONTERREY (Chapter 17)

Hotel	Price Range	Double Room
Ramada Inn Monterrey	$20–$24	EP
Gran Hotel Ancira	$26–$30	EP
Monterrey Holiday Inn	$32	EP
Anfa Motor Inn	$18–$20	EP
El Paso Autel	$16–$22	EP
Ambassador Hotel	$32–$35	EP
Hotel Rio	$14–$22	EP
Jolet Hotel	$14–$18	EP
Hotel Yamallel	$10–$12	EP
Alamo Courts	$10–$14	EP
Royal Courts	$11–$13	EP
Motel Chipinque	$15–$25	EP
Hotel Monterrey	$24	EP

SALTILLO (Chapter 17)

Hotel	Price Range	Double Room
Arizpe Sainz Hotel	$18–$20	EP
Bermea	$10	

Hotel	Price Range	Double Room
Camino Real	$21–$28	EP
Rodeway Inn Los Magueyes	$28	EP

MORELIA (Chapter 18)

Virrey de Mendoza	$18–$22	EP
Hostal de las Camelinas	$16	EP
Hotel Alameda	$19–$24	EP
Hotel de la Soledad	$19–$24	EP
Hotel Presidente	$16	EP
Suites Normandie	$30	EP
Villa Montana	$44–$72	AP
Villa San Jose	$38–$44	AP

PÁTZCUARO (Chapter 18)

Posada de Don Vasco	$20–$28	EP
Meson del Cortijo	$16–$24	EP
Motel San Carlos	$12–$14	EP
Posada de la Basilica	$14–$18	EP
Hotel Escuedos	$10	EP

OAXACA (Chapter 19)

El Presidente Convento de Santa Catalina	$36–$42	EP
Victoria	$28–$36	EP
Mision de Los Angeles	$19	EP
Casa Colonial	$12–$14	EP
Calesa Real	$16–$18	EP
Marqués del Valle	$16–$18	EP
Monte Albán	$15–$17	EP
Margarita Motel	$16	EP
Hotel Senorial	$13–$18	EP

PUEBLA (Chapter 20)

El Meson del Angel	$24	EP
Hotel Lastra	$16–$18	EP
Gilfer	$18–$20	EP
Hotel Senorial	$12–$14	EP

PUERTO VALLARTA (Chapter 21)

Hotel	Price Range	Double Room
Posada Vallarta	$32–$38	EP
Camino Real	$39	EP
Holiday Inn Puerto Vallarta	$42 winter	EP
	$30 summer	
Hotel Garza Blanca (bungalows)	$50–$60	EP
Tropicana Hotel	$16–$18	EP
Oceano Hotel	$16–$18	EP
Hacienda del Lobo	$15–$17	EP
Econhotel Pelicanos	$18	EP
Hotel Las Palmas	$30	EP
Hotel Playa Los Arcos	$13	EP
Hotel Playa de Oro	$32	CP
Hotel Eloisa	$16–$28	EP-MAP

SAN MIGUEL DE ALLENDE (Chapter 22)

Posada de San Francisco	$40	MAP
Aristos Parador	$14–$18	EP
Rancho-Hotel El Atascadero	$24–$32	EP-AP
Posada de Aldea	$26–$32	MAP
La Mision de Los Angeles	$20	EP
Posada la Ermita	$28	EP
Mansion del Bosque	$22–$28	MAP
Hotel Colonial	$10	EP

TAXCO (Chapter 23)

Holiday Inn	$32	EP
Victoria Hotel	$38	AP
Posada de la Mision	$18	EP
Hacienda del Solar	$32	CP
Rancho Taxco	$38	AP
Hotel de la Borda	$42	AP
La Cumbre Sonada	$41	AP
Santa Prisca	$24–$28	MAP
Agua Escondida	$6	EP

TEHUANTEPEC (Chapter 24)

Hotel Calli	$7	EP
Hotel Tehuantepec	$7	EP

TUXTLA GUTIÉRREZ (Chapter 24)

Hotel	Price Range	Double Room
Hotel Bonampak	$12–$18	EP
Gran Hotel Humberto	$15	EP

TAPACHULA (Chapter 24)

Loma Real Motor Hotel	$26–$28	EP
Hotel San Francisco	$12	EP

VERACRUZ (Chapter 25)

Hotel Veracruz	$24	EP
Colonial Hotel	$10–$12	EP
Hotel Mocambo	$20–$24	EP
Emporio Hotel	$18	EP
Diligencias Hotel	$19	EP
Costa Verde	$10	EP

COATZACOALCOS (Chapter 25)

Hotel El Presidente	$24	EP
Valgrande	$16	EP
Lammaroy	$20	EP

PALENQUE (Chapter 25)

Hotel Chan-Kah	$30	AP

VILLAHERMOSA (Chapter 25)

Aristos Villahermosa	$28	EP
El Presidente Villahermosa	$25	EP
Hotel Manzur	$18	EP
Hotel Maya Tabasco	$18	EP
Hotel Olmeca	$14	EP

CAMPECHE (Chapter 25)

Hotel	Price Range	Double Room
El Presidente	$28–$32	EP
Hotel Baluarte	$20	EP
Hotel Siho Playa	$32–$38	AP

MÉRIDA (Chapter 26)

El Castellano	$44	EP
Hotel Panamericana	$18–$24	EP
Hotel Mérida La Palapa	$19–$25	EP
Hotel Casa del Balam	$23–$27	EP
Hotel Paseo de Montejo	$19	EP
Hotel Montejo Palace	$21	EP
Principe Maya	$18	EP
Hotel Colón	$14	EP
María del Carmen	$18	EP
Autel 59	$21	EP
San Luis	$8	EP
Hotel Cayre	$10–$21	EP
Gran Hotel	$8	EP
Hacienda Inn	$19	EP

CHICHÉN-ITZÁ (Chapter 26)

Hotel Mayaland	$58	AP
Hacienda Chichén	$38	AP
Hotel Chichén-Itzá La Palapa	$42	MAP
Pirámide Inn Motel	$18	EP

UXMAL (Chapter 26)

Hacienda Uxmal	$50	AP
La Palapa Uxmal	$36	MAP

CHETUMAL (Chapter 26)

El Presidente Chetumal	$19–$24	EP

LEÓN (Chapter 27)

Hotel	Price Range	Double Room
Hotel León	$18–$20	EP
Real de Minas	$28–$36	EP

AGUASCALIENTES (Chapter 27)

Hotel Paris	$12–$14	EP
Hotel Francia	$12–$18	EP

SAN LUIS POTOSÍ (Chapter 27)

Cactus Motel	$20	EP
Sands Motel	$16–$18	EP
Tuna Courts	$8–$10	EP

DURANGO (Chapter 27)

El Presidente	$21	EP
Posada San Jorge	$10	EP

ZACATECAS (Chapter 27)

Aristos Zacatecas	$14	EP
Motel del Bosque	$10–$14	EP

CHIHUAHUA CITY (Chapter 28)

El Presidente Hotel	$22	EP
Hotel Fermont	$14–$18	EP
Posada Tierra Blanca	$14–$16	EP
El Capitán Motel	$10	EP
El Dorado Hotel	$7–$8	EP
Motel Mirador	$12	EP

TORREÓN (Chapter 28)

Hotel	Price Range	Double Room
Hotel Palacio Real	$20–$28	EP
Hotel del Paseo	$8–$10	EP
Hotel Rio Nazas	$12–$16	EP
Motel and Hotel Paraiso del Desierta	$18–$24	EP

Index

John Wilhelm has spent a lifetime traveling in most parts of the world, and gaining an understanding of foreign countries. And insight on how to enjoy life away from home.

He lived in Mexico for six years as a foreign correspondent, and visited Mexico numerous times both before and since that residence. While there, he traveled to most regions of Mexico, often with the party accompanying the president of Mexico on visits to inaugurate various developments such as new railroads, or even new towns.

The Wilhelm family (wife Margaret Maslin, Richard, Lawrence, Charles, and Martha) entertained many visitors during their residence in Mexico (one son was born there). It was in an effort to provide frank, factual, and helpful information for these visitors that John Wilhelm wrote his first guide to Mexico (a guide to Mexico City now in its seventeenth edition with sales of over a quarter of a million copies). The *Guide to All Mexico* followed in 1959 and has been revised frequently since that time. The extensive travel for the current edition and much of the revision was done by Lawrence, who is with Viking Press, and Charles, who is with *The New York Times*

John Wilhelm is now dean of the College of Communication at Ohio University and a professor of journalism. But he still visits Mexico several times a year. Ohio University has a permanent Study Abroad program at the University of Veracruz in Jalapa, Mexico.

Wilhelm was a foreign correspondent for eleven years, covering World War II and the reconstruction period in Europe for the *Chicago Sun* and Reuters, and then was bureau chief for McGraw-Hill World News in Buenos Aires and Mexico City. He later was director of McGraw-Hill World News and has been president of the Foreign Correspondents' Club of Mexico and the Overseas Press Club in New York. The Wilhelms currently live in Athens, Ohio, when not in Mexico.